2022–2023

Children's Liturgy of the Word

A Weekly Resource

Kristen Hempstead McGann

Scripture Backgrounds by

Mary A. Ehle, PhD
Peg Ekerdt
Marielle Frigge, OSB
Jean Marie Hiesberger
Biagio Mazza
Mary M. McGlone, CSJ
Abbot Gregory J. Polan, OSB
Denise Simeone
George Smiga
Paul Turner

Season Backgrounds by

Mary A. Ehle, PhD

LTP

LITURGY
TRAINING
PUBLICATIONS

Nihil Obstat
Rev. Mr. Daniel G. Welter, JD
Chancellor
Archdiocese of Chicago
October 20, 2021

Imprimatur
Most Rev. Robert G. Casey
Vicar General
Archdiocese of Chicago
October 20, 2021

The *Nihil Obstat* and *Imprimatur* are declarations that the material is free from doctrinal or moral error, and thus is granted permission to publish in accordance with c. 827. No legal responsibility is assumed by the grant of this permission. No implication is contained herein that those who have granted the *Nihil Obstat* and *Imprimatur* agree with the content, opinions, or statements expressed.

LTP acknowledges the numerous authors who have contributed to past editions of *Children's Liturgy of the Word* and *Sourcebook for Sundays, Seasons, and Weekdays* for providing additional prayers, dismissal texts, and liturgical music suggestions in this edition. LTP is especially grateful to Paul H. Colloton, OSFS, Mary Frances Fleischaker, OP, J. Philip Horrigan, Corinna Laughlin, Jill Maria Murdy, Danielle A. Noe, and Stephen S. Wilbricht, CSC, for writing this edition's prayers of the faithful and to John Marquez for writing this edition's dismissal text.

The sessions for the Solemnity of All Saints; Solemnity of Mary, the Holy Mother of God; Fourth Sunday of Easter; and Twelfth Sunday in Ordinary Time were written by Ann Dickinson Degenhard.

The session for the Solemnity of the Assumption of the Blessed Virgin Mary was written by Mary DuQuaine.

The session for the Solemnity of the Immaculate Conception of Mary was written by Maureen Kelly.

Excerpts from the English translation of *Christifideles Laici* © 1988; *Compendium of Social Doctrine of the Church* © 2006; *Deus caritas est* © 2005; *Documento Conclusivo de Aparecida* © 2007; *Ecclesia de Eucharistia* © 2003; *Ecclesia in America* © 1999; *Evangelii gaudium* © 2013; *Evangelii nuntiandi* © 1975; *Justitia in mundo* © 1971; *Marialis cultus* © 1974; *Mulieris dignitatem* © 1988; *Pacem in terris* © 1963; *Princeps pastorum* © 1959; *Redemptoris missio* © 1990; *Sollicitudo rei socialis* © 1987; *Spe salvi* © 2007 reprinted with the kind permission of Libreria Editrice Vaticana.

Excerpts from the English translation of the *Catechism of the Catholic Church* for use in the United States of America © 1994, United States Catholic Conference, Inc. —Libreria Editrice Vaticana. English translation of the *Catechism of the Catholic Church: Modifications from the Editio Typica* © 1997, United States Catholic Conference, Inc. —Libreria Editrice Vaticana. Used with permission.

Excerpts from *U.S. Catholic Catechism for Adults* © 2006 United States Conference of Catholic Bishops, Washington, DC. Used with permission. No part of this work may be reproduced or transmitted in any form without permission in writing from the copyright holder.

Excerpts from documents of the Second Vatican Council are from *Vatican Council II: Constitutions, Decrees, Declarations—The Basic Sixteen Documents*, edited by Austin Flannery, OP, © 1996. Used with permission of Liturgical Press, Collegeville, Minnesota.

CHILDREN'S LITURGY OF THE WORD 2022–2023: A WEEKLY RESOURCE © 2022 Archdiocese of Chicago: Liturgy Training Publications, 3949 South Racine Avenue, Chicago, IL 60609; 800-933-1800; fax: 800-933-7094; email: orders@ltp.org. website: www.LTP.org. All rights reserved.

This book was edited by Michaela I. Tudela. Michael A. Dodd was the production editor, Anna Manhart was the cover designer, Juan Alberto Castillo was the interior designer, and Kari Nicholls was the production artist.

Cover art by Martin Erspamer, OSB. Interior season line art by Martin Erspamer, OSB. Icons by Juan Alberto Castillo.

Printed in the United States of America

ISBN: 978-1-61671-652-3

CLW23

Contents

Introduction

Welcome

Welcome to *Children's Liturgy of the Word 2022–2023*! The Liturgy Guides in this resource will enable you to lead the Liturgy of the Word with children in a prayerful way that allows each child to deepen and explore his or her relationship with God. While you participate in the journey through the lectionary readings of the liturgical year with hopes for the children you work with, you will find yourself touched and changed by your involvement in the process. We hope that the materials in this resource will provide you with spiritual nourishment and practical guidance as you begin your journey as a minister of the Word with children.

What Is the Liturgy of the Word with Children?

The celebration of the Mass is at the heart of the Catholic faith. Many parishes follow the practice of a separate Liturgy of the Word with children as suggested in the *Directory for Masses with Children* (DMC). The primary purpose of dismissing children is to provide them with a focused environment where they are more likely to become conscious, active listeners and responders to God's Word. The intention of the Liturgy of the Word with children is not to babysit or provide entertainment for children. The celebration of the Liturgy of the Word with children is a liturgical experience that opens young people to hear and respond to God's Word in ways that enable them to be nurtured and challenged by its power, and to experience the grace of ongoing conversion to the vision and values of the Word of God.

The Liturgy of the Word with children tends to be most effective for children who are about five to nine years of age. The *Directory for Masses with Children* states that it is for children who have "not yet entered the period of preadolescence" (DMC, 6), and the "Introduction" to the *Lectionary for Masses with Children* (LMC) tells us that it is for "children of elementary grades" (LMC, 15). Children of this age can listen attentively to Scripture and respond to questions about what happens in the readings. They can also learn simple responses to the readings or prayers.

About This Resource

Children's Liturgy of the Word includes Scripture Backgrounds, Liturgy Guides, music suggestions, prayers, and a Homily/Reflection for each Sunday and Holyday of Obligation of the year. All of the materials in this resource closely follow the directives given in the *Directory for Masses with Children*, the *Lectionary for Mass*, and the *Lectionary for Masses with Children*. The following components of Children's Liturgy of the Word will help you to prayerfully and effectively celebrate the Liturgy of the Word with children.

Season Backgrounds: A Season Background is provided at the beginning of each seasonal section to help you set the context for the celebration of the Word with children during a specific time of the liturgical year. The Season Background describes the Church's understanding of each period of liturgical time, offers an overview of the lectionary readings associated with that time, and gives helpful suggestions for the liturgical environment.

Scripture Backgrounds: You will find a Scripture Background page at the beginning of each session. Written by experts in Scripture, liturgy, theology, and catechesis, these pages provide commentary on all three readings and the responsorial psalm, as well as connections to Church teaching and tradition.

Preparation: Directly following the Scripture Background, you will find information necessary to lead the session as well as a practical list of things that you need to have or prepare to lead the Liturgy of the Word. It also provides you with specific objectives and reflection questions that evaluate your practice and reflect on your experience.

Liturgy Guide: These two pages are your "script" for the celebration of the Liturgy of the Word. The Liturgy Guide provides you with a walkthrough of each of the elements of the celebration, including the procession, centering, readings, Homily/Reflection, Profession of Faith, and Prayer of the Faithful. Familiarize yourself with this material ahead of time each week, so that you can lead the children in prayer confidently and seamlessly.

This resource is divided into seven seasonal sections:

Ordinary Time during Fall, 2022: Twenty-Second Sunday in Ordinary Time (August 28, 2022) through the Solemnity of Our Lord Jesus Christ, King of the Universe (November 20, 2022).

Advent, 2022: First Sunday of Advent (November 27, 2022) through the Fourth Sunday of Advent (December 18, 2022).

Christmas Time, 2022–2023: Solemnity of the Nativity of the Lord (December 25, 2022) through the Solemnity of the Epiphany of the Lord (January 8, 2023).

Ordinary Time during Winter, 2023: Second Sunday in Ordinary Time (January 15, 2023) through the Seventh Sunday in Ordinary Time (February 19, 2023).

Lent, 2023: First Sunday of Lent (February 26, 2023) through Palm Sunday of the Passion of the Lord (April 2, 2023).

Easter Time, 2023: Easter Sunday of the Resurrection of the Lord (April 9, 2023) through Pentecost Sunday (May 28, 2023).

Ordinary Time during Summer, 2023: Solemnity of the Most Holy Trinity (June 4, 2023) through the Twenty-First Sunday in Ordinary Time (August 25, 2023).

The Prayer Leader's Role

What Is a Prayer Leader? This resource consciously refers to those who lead the Liturgy of the Word with children as prayer leaders, and not teachers or facilitators. The prayer leader's goal is not to teach religion; it is to lead prayer. The prayer leader reflects on the Word in a homiletic style rather than a didactic one. The prayer leader is not focused so much on conveying knowledge of Scripture to the children as he or she is on being a servant or channel of God's Word, accompanying the children on their faith journey, and listening to them as they share their own experiences of God's presence in their lives.

Especially during the homily or reflection, the prayer leader takes on an attitude of affirmation and wonder at the children's responses. We believe that the Holy Spirit is active in the liturgical moments when children share their experience of God. When the children are sharing their experience of the Word in their lives, the "rightness" of the children's answers should not be the prayer leader's first concern.

Preparing the Liturgy of the Word with Children

As you work to establish good practices for the celebration of the Liturgy of the Word with children within your parish, it can be easy to obsess over the details or "rules." As a result, you might forget that a truly effective prayer leader is a person of deep faith and personal spirituality. Children are easily engaged in a spirit of worship. If the leader is a genuine person of faith and prayer who loves children, children will respond readily and wholeheartedly in a spirit of worship. If not, they will sense when the order and details of the Liturgy of the Word overtake the proclamation of the Good News and praise of God as most important, and will begin to point out "mistakes" in the celebration. Children intuitively know and respond to faithful, prayerful leaders.

In light of this, you can prepare to celebrate the Liturgy of the Word with children by engaging yourself in regular personal prayer. During the week, take time in prayer with the Scripture readings that you will be proclaiming on Sunday. Be mindful of the themes of the readings as you go through your daily life, keeping your eyes open for ways in which they are illuminated or illustrated by your experiences and encounters. This will make your own experience of your ministry more meaningful and will also make you a better prayer leader as you celebrate the Word with children. Liturgy Training Publications offers a more robust Sunday prayer resource called *At Home with the Word®* and *Daily Prayer* that includes all of the readings and more materials for reflection. Both are available at www.LTP.org.

Before you begin the Liturgy of the Word, take time to offer yourself to God as an instrument that he will use to facilitate the growth of the children's relationship with him. Even if you only have a few minutes (or seconds!) before beginning the Liturgy of the Word, use that time to take a deep breath, center yourself in God's presence, and offer yourself and your ministry over to him.

Interacting with the Children

Many adults find it challenging to lead a prayerful experience with children. Some may bore or confuse the children with abstract concepts or too much talking. Others might become overwhelmed by the children's energy and will allow the Liturgy of the Word to devolve into playtime, or will allow an atmosphere of stern discipline to override the prayerful mood. Maintaining a peaceful, accepting spirit of prayer while holding onto the children's attention can be a difficult skill to master.

Try to refer to the children by name, and tell them what they may call you. As you get to know them, try to remember to recognize significant details of their lives, such as birthdays, the deaths of relatives, or the births of new siblings. You might choose to recognize these milestones in the Prayer of the Faithful.

Communicating with confidence and good body language can help you to capture and hold the children's attention immediately. Stand erect and use expansive hand

and arm gestures. Be aware of your facial expressions. Avoid any feelings of self-consciousness as you sing or pray with the children. The children will sense your discomfort and will respond accordingly. Instead, project yourself confidently and joyfully and the children will follow suit.

During the homily or reflection, you can interact with the children by asking them questions. It is best to avoid questions that can be answered with a simple yes or no in favor of more evocative questions, such as the ones written in this resource. Listen to the children's responses with the goal of affirming and celebrating their experiences of God in their lives, rather than worrying about correct answers. You might occasionally need to clarify a child's response, but you should avoid correcting or negating them.

If you ask a question or invite the children to bring forth prayers but are met with silence, then welcome and respect it. It is not necessary to fill all of the time with talking or singing. Silence is prayer. You might pause after the Scripture readings or allow silent time during the homily or reflection when the children do not immediately respond to a question. It is fine for them to think or just to be with the question and listen to the Holy Spirit working within them.

Involving Assistants

To help you maintain a prayerful atmosphere, you will want to have a number of assistants appropriate to the number of children participating in the Liturgy of the Word. Assistants can help you process with the children to and from the main assembly and can watch for and quietly help any children who are acting out or having trouble sitting still. You will want to assign an assistant or two to care for children who need to use the restroom or who do not want to remain apart from their families and need to return to the main assembly before the conclusion of the Liturgy of the Word. You will also want to assign an assistant to watch the progress of the Liturgy of the Word in the main assembly to be sure that you return at the appropriate time.

Those who participate in the Liturgy of the Word with children need to have some basic training in and awareness of their liturgical roles. The same care should be given to their preparation as is given to those who serve as liturgical ministers in the main assembly. It is important for those who serve as liturgical ministers in the celebration of the Word with children to be aware of and comfortable with the fact that they are involved in a full liturgical experience, and not a catechetical session, a time for play, or a child care.

When recruiting assistants, music ministers, or any other adults to participate in any aspect of the Liturgy of the Word for children, be sure to check with your parish or diocese to find out about the conditions under which they may work with children. It may be necessary for them to undergo training or background screening. As an adult who has been given the tremendous honor of caring for the spiritual development of children, you are responsible for ensuring that they can develop their relationship with God in a safe and nurturing environment.

Celebrating the Liturgy of the Word with Children

Liturgical Environment

To help the children carry the deep reverence that they feel for the sacred space of the church into their space for the Liturgy of the Word, careful attention must be given to liturgical environment. The space should be arranged and decorated as a liturgical space, not a classroom or play space.

Try to decorate the space so that it feels continuous with the liturgical environment of the space where the main assembly is worshiping. The prayer table, lectern cloths, and banners should show colors appropriate to the liturgical time. You may also use symbols to reinforce different times of the liturgical year. For example, you may use an Advent wreath during Advent.

If you are using a classroom, rearrange the chairs and move desks out of the way. Remember to consider the space in relation to the movement associated with the celebration so that you and the children can participate in the procession and the proclamation of the Word with ease and grace. Put away any toys or games, and do your best to temporarily remove or cover any distracting posters or displays. Create a space where the lectionary, candle, and any other liturgical symbols are prominent and easily seen.

The additional information on liturgical environment in the Season Backgrounds will be useful as you prepare to celebrate the Liturgy of the Word with children during the different times of the liturgical year.

Dismissing the Children

The celebration of the Liturgy of the Word with children begins with the dismissal of the children from the main assembly. The children should first gather with the main assembly to celebrate the Introductory Rites. Between the conclusion of the Opening Prayer and the beginning of the first reading, the priest celebrant should formally send the children and those leading the Liturgy of the Word with children to their separate space. This resource provides words of dismissal for each Sunday and holyday of obligation that may be used by the priest celebrant. You will want to confer with the priest celebrant to find out whether he would like to have the words provided for him or use his own words to dismiss the children. If the priest celebrant would like to have the words provided for him, be sure to prepare a copy of the words ahead of time and make sure that it is in the proper place before the Mass begins.

You will need to establish procedures for a quick and quiet procession from the church into the space where you celebrate the Liturgy of the Word with children. Pay special attention to the procession from the main assembly into your space, helping the children to see it as a sacred, ritual act that seamlessly transitions them from one part of the Mass to another.

As you are leading the Liturgy of the Word with children, you will want to keep an eye on how things are progressing in the main assembly. Assign an assistant to coordinate the timing of the Liturgy of the Word with children with that of the main assembly. By the time the main assembly is reciting the creed, the children should be reciting the creed, too. The children should return to sit with their families after the Liturgy of the Word is finished, but before the Liturgy of the Eucharist begins. When you return the children to the main assembly, be sure to watch for those who are having trouble finding their families.

Centering

As the children enter their own space, take a few moments to lead a prayer and a song to orient the children to the new space and refocus their attention. You will want to make this transition feel as seamless as possible. The children should feel as though the procession to their space and beginning of the Liturgy of the Word is part of the experience that began when they came into the church, and not as though one thing has ended and another thing is beginning. The essential goal of this brief moment is to enable the children to listen to the Word of God that is about to be proclaimed.

Lectionary Readings

In conjunction with the pastor or liturgist, you will need to choose the lectionary readings that will be proclaimed during the celebration of the Liturgy of the Word with children. According to the *Directory for Masses with Children*, with the consent of the pastor, the prayer leader discerns which readings are best suited for the group as long as the Gospel reading is always proclaimed. You will need to decide how many readings you will do, which readings are best, and how many verses you will proclaim, keeping in mind that the proclamation of the Gospel is always necessary.

The Liturgy Guides and Scripture Backgrounds in this resource use the standard lectionary readings. When there is an option for a shorter form of the reading, both options are given. For the Liturgy of the Word with children, some parishes prefer to use the *Lectionary for Masses with Children*. These readings are, at times, different from those in the lectionary used in the main assembly. On those occasions, you may want to use a study edition of the Catholic Bible for background on the Scripture readings. On other occasions, you might notice that the readings from the *Lectionary for Masses with Children* differ only by a verse or two, or are a shortened form of the reading in the lectionary used in the main assembly.

The table that follows this Introduction contains the Scripture citations from the *Lectionary for Mass* and *Lectionary for Masses with Children* for each Sunday and holyday of obligation, along with their associated themes. It lists options for longer and shorter forms of readings from the standard lectionary as well as citations of readings from the *Lectionary for Masses with Children*. This table will help you plan which readings you will proclaim each week. The numbers in parentheses are the lectionary numbers that identify the appropriate readings. For holydays of obligation, the readings come from the weekday lectionaries.

Homily/Reflection

Each Liturgy Guide contains the words of a homily or reflection. Only the ordained can give a homily. A lay leader of prayer may provide an explanation of the reading. Because this resource may be used by both ordained and lay leaders of prayer, the terms *homily* and *reflection* are both used to describe the preaching or breaking open of the Scripture readings that occurs during children's Liturgy of the Word. The reflections in this resource are intended to help the children bring the Word into their hearts and actions. They are written to facilitate conversation with the children, rather than to instruct them.

As a prayer leader, you will want to rehearse the words of the homily or reflection ahead of time, so that you are able to look away from the book to engage the children better. Use the scripts provided but make what you will say in your homily or reflection your own. Adapt or supplement the words of the homily or reflection to make them more closely related to your community. Sometimes the scripts include a sample personal story to be told to engage the children. Personalize the provided story as needed.

Another characteristic of good homiletics is the ability to understand the assembly and relate your words to their lived experience. When you do this with children, you help them bring what they hear at church into their daily lives. A good homily will inspire the children to respond with sentiments of praise, joy, hope, and gratitude.

Prayer

Basic religion texts often define prayer as the raising of one's mind and heart to God. Prayer can take many shapes and forms. It may be private or public, spoken or silent. It is multifaceted. The celebration of the Liturgy of the Word with children is a public, liturgical prayer. Liturgical prayer is ritual prayer, and children are born ritual makers. They readily communicate and understand others through ritual and gesture. From realizing that the outstretched arms of a caregiver means "come to me," to imitating the lives and roles of adults through play and ritual expression, children are naturals at ritual action. Liturgical prayer provides a way for them to sense the mystery of God. When led well, liturgical prayer awakens and stimulates the child's natural capacity to encounter God's presence and experience God's transcendence.

Each Liturgy Guide calls for a centering prayer, the recitation of the creed, and the Prayer of the faithful. The words of the centering prayer and intercessions for the prayer of the faithful are provided. You will need to decide whether the children will recite the Apostles' Creed or the Nicene Creed. Since some children may not yet have learned the words of the creed by heart, it can be helpful to display them. You might display these words using a poster or a projector.

During the prayer of the faithful, you may want to write petitions on behalf of the children or help them to speak some of their own. You may wish to offer one as an example so that they have a framework from which to speak by saying: "For . . . let us pray to the Lord." If your group frequently has new children, you may find that the children are shy about offering intentions. If you have a relatively consistent group of children who have been coming for a while, they may be so enthusiastic that their petitions become too numerous for the allotted time. In these instances, you might intervene with a petition for all of the unspoken prayers in the children's hearts.

Music

Music and song play an important role in good liturgical celebration. Music evokes a sense of the transcendent deep within both children and adults. Liturgical music forms, shapes, and gives voice to what we believe. It echoes God's Word and actions in our lives, and is a specific form of prayer. The importance of music in the celebration of the Liturgy of the Word with children cannot be understated. Children naturally learn and create community through song. Unlike many of the adults in our parishes who feel uncomfortable singing in front of others, children are eager and nonjudgmental participants in song.

Many adult leaders of the Liturgy of the Word with children find music to be an especially challenging component of the celebration of the Word. Those who are not musically trained can feel insecure when selecting or performing music. When selecting music, involve your parish music minister if possible. Just as you look at the readings that will be proclaimed in the main assembly and then consider how they can be best presented to children, you should look at the music that will be sung in the main assembly and consider how you can best make it accessible and engaging for children. It is best if the music used in your celebration of the Word mirrors the music that is used in the main assembly. This gives the children the chance to learn the songs that the rest of the parish community is singing and prepares them for a fuller participation in the Mass.

If you prefer not to select music that mirrors what is being used in the main assembly, music suggestions are given in the Liturgy Guide for each Sunday and holyday of obligation. These suggestions are musically, liturgically, and pastorally sound. They are available from the major liturgical music publishers whose resources are most widely used in parishes today: Oregon Catholic Press and GIA.

Live music led by trained music ministers is ideal. Although it is not always possible to have a parish musician or song leader available for the celebration of the Liturgy of the Word with children, it is worthwhile to consult your parish liturgist or music director about this option. He or she may be able to suggest someone who would be willing to be the music minister. If there is no option for live accompaniment or a trained cantor to lead your group, do your best to facilitate an atmosphere of joyful song on your own. You might bring in simple musical instruments such as chimes or bells that the children can use as you sing. If the children are too young to learn entire songs, you might sing with them by using the "call and response" method, singing one line to them and then inviting them to sing it back to you. Or, if you have one available, you can use a recording as accompaniment. You might also play recordings of instrumental music as the children process into their space. Listening quietly to instrumental music can be a prayerful and centering experience for children.

About the Author

Kristen Hempstead McGann began her ministerial work in youth ministry and leadership development, serving the Archdioceses of New York and Chicago. She is certified through the National Association of the Catechesis of the Good Shepherd and serves as a formation leader and catechist. Kristen holds an MDIV from the University of Notre Dame.

Doctrinal Connections Key

The following is a list of documents that are referenced in the Connections to Church Teaching and Tradition section on the Scripture Background pages. Full texts of the following documents can be found in LTP's four-volume Liturgy Document series, in *Vatican Council II: Constitutions, Decrees, Declarations—The Basic Sixteen Documents* (translated by Austin Flannery, OP, and published by Liturgical Press), on the Vatican website (www.vatican.va), on the United States Conference of Catholic Bishops website (www.usccb.org), or in other websites by typing the English or Latin title into a search engine.

AA	Second Vatican Council, *Apostolicam actuositatem*
AG	Second Vatican Council, *Ad gentes divinitus*
Aparecida	Fifth General Conference of Latin Bishops (CELAM), *Documento Conclusivo de Aparecida*
CCC	Interdicasterial Commission for the Catechism of the Catholic Church, *Catechism of the Catholic Church*
CD	Pope Paul VI, *Christus Dominus*
CL	Pope John Paul II, *Christifideles laici*
CSDC	Pontifical Council for Justice and Peace, *Compendium of the Social Doctrine of the Church*
DCE	Pope Benedict XVI, *Deus caritas est*
EE	Pope John Paul II, *Ecclesia de Eucharistia*
EG	Pope Francis, *Evangelii gaudium*
EIA	Pope John Paul II, *Ecclesia in America*
EN	Pope Paul VI, *Evangelii nuntiandi*
GS	Second Vatican Council, *Gaudium et spes*
JM	Synod of Bishops *Justitia in mundo*
LG	Second Vatican Council, *Lumen gentium*
MC	Pope Paul VI, *Marialis cultus*
MD	Pope John Paul II, *Mulieris dignitatem*
NDC	United States Conference of Catholic Bishops, *National Directory for Catechesis*
PP	Pope John XXIII, *Princeps pastorum*
PT	Pope John XXIII, *Pacem in terris*
RMI	Pope John Paul II, *Redemptoris missio*
SRS	Pope John Paul II, *Sollicitudo rei socialis*
SS	Pope Benedict XVI, *Spe salvi*

Ordinary Time during Fall 2022

Sunday/Holyday of Obligation	Date	Theme	Lectionary for Mass	Lectionary for Masses with Children
Twenty-Second Sunday in Ordinary Time	August 28, 2022	God Provides	Sirach 3:17–18, 20, 28–29; Psalm 68:4–5, 6–7, 10–11 (see 11b); Hebrews 12:18–19, 22–24a; Luke 14:1, 7–14 (126)	Sirach 3:17–18, 20; Psalm 68:3–4acdef, 5–6abcd, 9–10 (see 11b); Luke 14:1, 7–14 (121C)
Twenty-Third Sunday in Ordinary Time	September 4, 2022	Send Us Your Spirit	Wisdom 9:13–18b; Psalm 90:3–4, 5–6, 12–13, 14, 17 (1); Philemon 9–10, 12–17; Luke 14:25–33 (129)	Wisdom 9:16c–18; Psalm 90:12–13, 14abc and 17; Luke 14:25–27 (124C)
Twenty-Fourth Sunday in Ordinary Time	September 11, 2022	Christ Jesus Came into the World to Save Sinners	Exodus 32:7–11, 13–14; Psalm 51:3–4, 12–13, 17, 19; (Luke 15:18); 1 Timothy 1:12–17; Luke 15:1–32 or 15:1–10 (132)	1 Timothy 1:12–15b; Psalm 111:1–2, 3–4, 7–8; Luke 15:11–32 (127C)
Twenty-Fifth Sunday in Ordinary Time	September 18, 2022	Right Relationship	Amos 8:4–7; Psalm 113:1–2, 4–6, 7–8; 1 Timothy 2:1–8; Luke 16:1–13 or 16:10–13 (135)	Romans 12:9–12; Psalm 25:4–5ab, 5cd–6; Luke 16:10–13 (130C)
Twenty-Sixth Sunday in Ordinary Time	September 25, 2022	Woe to the Complacent!	Amos 6:1a, 4–7; Psalm 146:7, 8–9, 9–10 (1b); 1 Timothy 6:11–16; Luke 16:19–31 (138)	1 Timothy 6:11b–12a; Psalm 25:4–5abc, 6 and 7cd; Luke 16:19–31 (133C)
Twenty-Seventh Sunday in Ordinary Time	October 2, 2022	God Hears and Responds	Habakkuk 1:2–3, 2:2–4; Psalm 95:1–2, 6–7, 8–9 (8); 2 Timothy 1:6–8, 13–14; Luke 17:5–10 (141)	Habakkuk 1:2–3, 2:2–4; Psalm 95:1–2, 6–7abcd, 7e–9; 2 Timothy 1:6–8; Luke 17:5–10 (136C)
Twenty-Eighth Sunday in Ordinary Time	October 9, 2022	God Offers Salvation to All	2 Kings 5:14–17; Psalm 98:1, 2–3, 3–4 (see 2b); 2 Timothy 2:8–13; Luke 17:11–19 (144)	2 Kings 5:14–17; Psalm 98:1, 2–3ab, 3cd–4; 2 Timothy 2:11–13; Luke 17:11–19 (139C)
Twenty-Ninth Sunday in Ordinary Time	October 16, 2022	Prayer Opens Us to God	Exodus 17:8–13; Psalm 121:1–2, 3–4, 5–6, 7–8 (see 2); 2 Timothy 3:14—4:2; Luke 18:1–8 (147)	2 Timothy 4:1–2; Psalm 96:1–2a, 2b–3, 4–5; Luke 18:1–8 (142C)
Thirtieth Sunday in Ordinary Time	October 23, 2022	The Lord Hears the Cry of the Poor	Sirach 35:12–14, 16–18; Psalm 34:2–3, 17–18, 19, 23 (7a); 2 Timothy 4:6–8, 16–18; Luke 18:9–14 (150)	Sirach 35:12b–14, 16–17; Psalm 34:1–2, 17–18; 2 Timothy 4:6–8; Luke 18:9–14 (145C)
Thirty-First Sunday in Ordinary Time	October 30, 2022	The Lord Is Gracious and Merciful	Wisdom 11:22—12:2; Psalm 145:1–2, 8–9, 10–11, 13, 14 (see 1); 2 Thessalonians 1:11—2:2; Luke 19:1–10 (153)	Wisdom 11:22—12:1; Psalm 145:1–2, 8–9, 13cd–14; 2 Thessalonians 1:11–12; Luke 19:1–10 (148C)
Solemnity of All Saints	November 1, 2022	Longing to See God's Face	Revelation 7:2–4, 9–14; Psalm 24:1–2, 3–4, 5–6 (see 6); 1 John 3:1–3; Matthew 5:1–12a (667)	Revelation 7:9–10; Psalm 24:1–2, 3–4, 5–6; Matthew 5:1–12ab (402C)
Thirty-Second Sunday in Ordinary Time	November 6, 2022	God Gives Us the Strength We Need	2 Maccabees 7:1–2, 9–14; Psalm 17:1, 5–6, 8, 15; 2 Thessalonians 2:16—3:5; Luke 20:27–38 or 20:27, 34–38 (156)	2 Maccabees 7:1–2, 9–14; Psalm 17:1, 5–6, 8 and 15; 2 Thessalonians 2:16—3:5; Luke 20:27–38 (151C)
Thirty-Third Sunday in Ordinary Time	November 13, 2022	Various Challenges in a Lifetime	Malachi 3:19–20a; Psalm 98:5–6, 7–8, 9 (see 9); 2 Thessalonians 3:7–12; Luke 21:5–19 (159)	Malachi 3:19–20; Psalm 98:5–6, 7–8, 9; 2 Thessalonians 3:7–12; Luke 21:5–19 (154C)
Solemnity of Our Lord Jesus Christ, King of the Universe	November 20, 2022	Today You Will Be with Me	2 Samuel 5:1–3; Psalm 122:1–2, 3–4, 4–5; Colossians 1:12–20; Luke 23:35–43 (162)	2 Samuel 5:1–3; Psalm 47:1–2, 7–8; Colossians 1:15–18; Luke 23:35–43 (157C)

Advent, Christmas Time, and Ordinary Time during Winter, 2022–2023

Sunday/Holyday of Obligation	Date	Theme	Lectionary	Lectionary for Masses with Children
First Sunday of Advent	November 27, 2022	Awaken!	Isaiah 2:1–5; Psalm 122:1–2, 3–4, 4–5, 6–7, 8–9; Romans 13:11–14; Matthew 24:37–44 (1)	Isaiah 2:1–5; Psalm 122:1–2, 8–9; Romans 13:11–13a; Matthew 24:37–44 (1A)
Second Sunday of Advent	December 4, 2022	Justice Shall Flourish	Isaiah 11:1–10; Psalm 72:1–2, 7–8, 12–13, 17 (see 7); Romans 15:4–9; Matthew 3:1–12 (4)	Isaiah 11:1–4a, 5–6, 9b; Psalm 72:1 and 8, 17; Romans 15:4–6; Matthew 3:1–9, 11 (4A)
Solemnity of the Immaculate Conception of Mary	December 8, 2022	Mary's Response to God's Will	Genesis 3:9–15, 20; Psalm 98:1, 2–3, 3–4 (1a); Ephesians 1:3–6, 11–12; Luke 1:26–38 (689B)	Genesis 3:9 –15, 20; Psalm 98:1, 2–3, 3–4 (1a); Luke 1:26–38 (429B)
Third Sunday of Advent	December 11, 2022	The Lord Comes to Save	Isaiah 35:1–6a, 10; Psalm 146:6–7, 8–9, 9–10 (see Isaiah 35:4); James 5:7–10; Matthew 11:2–11 (7)	Isaiah 35:1–2, 5–6ab, 10; Psalm 146:6d–7ab, 7c–8abc, 10; James 5:7–10; Matthew 11:2–11 (7A)
Fourth Sunday of Advent	December 18, 2022	Promise Is Given Birth	Isaiah 7:10–14; Psalm 24:1–2, 3–4, 5–6 (7c and 10b); Romans 1:1–7; Matthew 1:18–24 (10)	Romans 1:2–4; Psalm 24:1–2, 3–4abc; Matthew 1:18–24 (10A)
Solemnity of the Nativity of the Lord (Mass during the Night)	December 25, 2022	There Is Nothing to Fear, God Is with Us	Isaiah 9:1–6; Psalm 96:1–2, 2–3, 11–12, 13 (Luke 2:11); Titus 2:11–14; Luke 2:1–14 (14A)	Isaiah 9:2–4, 6–7; Psalm 96:1–2a, 2b–3; 11–12a; Titus 3:4–6; Luke 2:1–14 (13A)
Solemnity of Mary, the Holy Mother of God	January 1, 2023	Mary, Blessed of God	Numbers 6:22–27; Psalm 67:2–3, 5, 6, 8 (2a); Galatians 4:4–7; Luke 2:16–21 (18)	Numbers 6:22–27; Psalm 67:1–2, 5 and 7; Luke 2:16-21 (15A)
Solemnity of the Epiphany of the Lord	January 8, 2023	Light in Darkness	Isaiah 60:1–6; Psalm 72:1–2, 7–8, 10–11, 12–13 (see 11); Ephesians 3:2–3a, 5–6; Matthew 2:1–12 (20)	Isaiah 60:1–6; Psalm 72:1, 2, 10abc, 10de–11; Matthew 2:1–12 (16A)
Second Sunday in Ordinary Time	January 15, 2023	You Are My Servant	Isaiah 49:3, 5–6; Psalm 40:2, 4, 7–8, 8–9, 10 (8a, 9a); 1 Corinthians 1:1–3; John 1:29–34 (64)	Isaiah 49:3, 5–6; Psalm 40:1 and 3ab, 8 and 11; John 1:29–34 (59A)
Third Sunday in Ordinary Time	January 22, 2023	The Kingdom of Heaven Is at Hand	Isaiah 8:23—9:3; Psalm 27:1, 4, 13–14; 1 Corinthians 1:10–13, 17; Matthew 4:12–23 or 4:12–17 (67)	Isaiah 9:2–4; Psalm 27:1, 4abc; 1 Corinthians 1:10–13, 17; Matthew 4:17–23 (62A)
Fourth Sunday in Ordinary Time	January 29, 2023	Blessed Be	Zephaniah 2:3, 3:12–13; Psalm 146:6–7, 8–9, 9–10 (Matthew 5:3); 1 Corinthians 1:26–31; Matthew 5:1–12a (70)	Deuteronomy 18:18–19; Psalm 95:1–2, 6–7 (8); Mark 1:21–28 (66B)
Fifth Sunday in Ordinary Time	February 5, 2023	Taste and See	Isaiah 58:7–10; Psalm 112:4–5, 6–7, 8–9 (4a); 1 Corinthians 2:1–5; Matthew 5:13–16 (73)	Isaiah 58:7–10; Psalm 112:4–5, 8ab and 9; 1 Corinthians 2:1–5; Matthew 5:13–16 (68A)
Sixth Sunday in Ordinary Time	February 12, 2023	Fulfillment of the Law	Sirach 15:15–20; Psalm 119:1–2, 4–5, 17–18, 33–34 (1b); 1 Corinthians 2:6–10; Matthew 5:17–37 or 5:20–22a, 27–28, 33–34a, 37 (76)	Sirach 15:15–20; Psalm 119:1–2, 4–5, 33–34; 1 Corinthians 2:6–10; Matthew 5:23–24 (71A)
Seventh Sunday in Ordinary Time	February 19, 2023	Imitate God's Holiness	Leviticus 19:1–2, 17–18; Psalm 103:1–2, 3–4, 8, 10, 12–13 (8a); 1 Corinthians 3:16–23; Matthew 5:38–48 (79)	Leviticus 19:1–2, 17–18; Psalm 103:1–2, 3 and 13; 1 Corinthians 3:18–20; Matthew 5:38–48 (74A)

Lent and Easter Time, 2023

Sunday/Holyday of Obligation	Date	Theme	Lectionary	Lectionary for Masses with Children
First Sunday of Lent	February 26, 2023	Create in Me a Clean Heart	Genesis 2:7–9, 3:1–7; Psalm 51:3–4, 5–6, 12–13, 17 (see 3a); Romans 5:12–19 or 5:12, 17–19; Matthew 4:1–11 (22)	Genesis 2:7–9, 3:1–7; Psalm 51:1, 10, 12, 15; Matthew 4:1–11 (18A)
Second Sunday of Lent	March 8, 2023	Listen to Him	Genesis 12:1–4a; Psalm 33:4–5, 18–19, 20, 22 (22); 2 Timothy 1:8b–10; Matthew 17:1–9 (25)	Genesis 12:1–4a; Psalm 33:4–5, 20 and 22; Matthew 17:1–9 (21A)
Third Sunday of Lent	March 12, 2023	Christ the Living Water	Exodus 17:3–7; Psalm 95:1–2, 6–7, 8–9 (8); Romans 5:1–2, 5–8; John 4:5–42 or 4:5–15, 19b–26, 39a, 40–42 (28)	Exodus 17:3–7; Psalm 95:1–2, 7e–9c; John 4:5–15, 19b–26, 39a, 40–42 (24A)
Fourth Sunday of Lent	March 19, 2023	Christ the True Light	1 Samuel 16:1b, 6–7, 10–13a; Psalm 23:1–3a, 3b–4, 5, 6 (1); Ephesians 5:8–14; John 9:1–41 or 9:1, 6–9, 13–17, 34–38 (31)	1 Samuel 16:1b, 6–7, 10–13a; Psalm 23:1–3a, 3b–4, 5b–6c; Ephesians 5:1–2, 8–10; John 9:1, 6–12, 35–38 (27A)
Fifth Sunday of Lent	March 26, 2023	Christ the Resurrection and the Life	Ezekiel 37:12–14; Psalm 130:1–2, 3–4, 5–6, 7–8 (7); Romans 8:8–11; John 11:1–45 or 11:3–7, 17, 20–27, 33b–45 (34)	Ezekiel 37:12–14; Psalm 130:1–2, 5 and 7bcd; John 11:3–7, 17, 20–27, 31–45 (30A)
Palm Sunday of the Passion of the Lord	April 2, 2023	Jesus the Son of David	Matthew 21:1–11; Isaiah 50:4–7; Psalm 22:8–9, 17–18, 19–20, 23–24 (2a); Philippians 2:6–11; Matthew 26:14—27:66 or 27:11–54 (37)	Matthew 21:1–11; Isaiah 50:6–7; Psalm 22:7–8, 16c–17a and 18, 19 and 22; Matthew 27:11–54 (33A)
Easter Sunday of the Resurrection of the Lord	April 9, 2023	Celebrate with Joy	Acts 10:34a, 37–43; Psalm 118:1–2, 16–17, 22–23 (24); Colossians 3:1–4 or 1 Corinthians 5:6b–8; Sequence: Victimae Paschali Laudes; John 20:1–9 or Matthew 28:1–10 (42)	Acts 10:34a, 37–43; Psalm 118:1–2, 15c–16ab and 17, 22–23; Colossians 3:1–4; John 20:1–9 (36A)
Second Sunday of Easter / Sunday of Divine Mercy	April 16, 2023	Christ Our Strength and Courage	Acts 2:42–47; Psalm 118:2–4, 13–15, 22–24 (1); 1 Peter 1:3–9; John 20:19–31 (43)	Acts 2:42–47; Psalm 118:2–4, 22–24; 1 Peter 1:3–4; John 20:19–29 (37A)
Third Sunday of Easter	April 23, 2023	Recognized in Bread Broken	Acts 2:14, 22–33; Psalm 16:1–2, 5, 7–8, 9–10, 11 (11a); 1 Peter 1:17–21; Luke 24:13–35 (46)	Acts 2:14, 22–24; Psalm 18:1–2, 46 and 50ab; Luke 24:13–35 (40A)
Fourth Sunday of Easter	April 30, 2023	The Voice of the Shepherd	Acts 2:14a, 36–41; Psalm 23:1–3a, 3b–4, 5, 6 (1); 1 Peter 2:20b–25; John 10:1–10 (49)	Acts 2:14a, 36–41; Psalm 23:1–3a, 3b–4, 6; John 10:1–10 (43A)
Fifth Sunday of Easter	May 7, 2023	Jesus Is the Way, the Truth, and the Life	Acts 6:1–7; Psalm 33:1–2, 4–5, 18–19 (22); 1 Peter 2:4–9; John 14:1–12 (52)	Acts 6:1–7a; Psalm 145:10–11, 15–16, 17–18; John 14:1–12 (46A)
Sixth Sunday of Easter	May 14, 2023	The Presence of God	Acts 8:5–8, 14–17; Psalm 66:1–3, 4–5, 6–7, 16, 20 (1); 1 Peter 3:15–18; John 14:15–21 (55)	Acts 8:5–8, 14–17; Psalm 66:1–3ab, 4–5, 16 and 20; John 14:15–21 (49A)
Solemnity of the Ascension of the Lord	May 18 / May 21, 2023	Taken into Heaven	Acts 1:1–11; Psalm 47:2–3, 6–7, 8–9 (6); Ephesians 1:17–23; Matthew 28:16–20 (58)	Acts 1:8–11; Psalm 47:1–2, 5–6, 7–8; Ephesians 1:17–21; Matthew 28:16–20 (52A)
Seventh Sunday of Easter	May 21, 2023	They Devoted Themselves to Prayer	Acts 1:12–14; Psalm 27:1, 4, 7–8 (13); 1 Peter 4:13–16; John 17:1–11a (59)	Acts 1:12–14; Psalm 27:1, 4abc, 7–8; 1 Peter 4:13–16; John 17:6–9 (55A)
Solemnity of Pentecost (Day)	May 28, 2023	Renewed by the Spirit	Acts 2:1–11; Psalm 104:1, 24, 29–30, 31, 34 (see 30); 1 Corinthians 12:3b–7, 12–13; Sequence: Veni, Sancte Spiritus; John 20:19–23 (63)	Acts 2:1–11; Psalm 104:1abc and 24, 30–31; 1 Corinthians 12:4–7, 12–13; John 20:19–23 (58A)

Ordinary Time during Summer, 2023

Sunday/Holyday of Obligation	Date	Theme	Lectionary	Lectionary for Masses with Children
Solemnity of the Most Holy Trinity	June 4, 2023	The Mystery of the Triune God	Exodus 34:4b–6, 8–9; Daniel 3:52, 53, 54, 55, 56 (52b); 2 Corinthians 13:11–13; John 3:16–18 (164)	Exodus 34:4b–6, 8–9; Daniel 3:52, 53 and 56; 2 Corinthians 13:11–13; John 3:16–17 (158A)
Solemnity of the Most Holy Body and Blood of Christ (Corpus Christi)	June 11, 2023	Our Living Bread	Deuteronomy 8:2–3, 14b–16a; Psalm 147:12–13, 14–15, 19–20 (12); 1 Corinthians 10:16–17; Sequence: Lauda Sion; John 6:51–58 (167)	Deuteronomy 8:2–3, 14b–16a; Psalm 147:12 and 14, 19–20; 1 Corinthians 10:16–17; John 6:51–58 (161A)
Eleventh Sunday in Ordinary Time	June 18, 2023	A Holy Nation	Exodus 19:2–6a; Psalm 100:1–2, 3, 5 (3c); Romans 5:6–11; Matthew 9:36—10:8	Exodus 19:1–6a; Psalm 100:1–2, 3, 5 (3c); Romans 5:6–11; Matthew 9:36—10:8 (86)
Twelfth Sunday in Ordinary Time	June 25, 2023	Do Not Be Afraid	Jeremiah 20:10–13; Psalm 69:8–10, 14, 17, 33–35 (14c); Romans 5:12–15; Matthew 10:26–33 (94)	Jeremiah 20:10–12a, 13; Psalm 69:13, 16, 29b–30a (14c); Matthew 10:26–31 (89A)
Thirteenth Sunday in Ordinary Time	July 2, 2023	Give without Expectation	2 Kings 4:8–11, 14–16a; Psalm 89:2–3, 16–17, 18–19; Romans 6:3–4, 8–9; Matthew 10:37–42 (97)	2 Kings 4:8–11, 14–16a; Psalm 89:1–2, 15–16; Romans 6:3–4, 8–9; Matthew 10:40–42 (92)
Fourteenth Sunday in Ordinary Time	July 9, 2023	Jesus Reveals the Mysteries of God's Kingdom	Zechariah 9:9–10; Psalm 145:1–2, 8–9, 10–11, 13–14; Romans 8:9, 11–13; Matthew 11:25–30 (100)	Zechariah 9:9–10; Psalm 145:1–2, 8–9, 13cd–14; Romans 8:9, 11; Matthew 11:25–30 (95)
Fifteenth Sunday in Ordinary Time	July 16, 2023	Fertile Ground for God's Word	Isaiah 55:10–11; Psalm 65:10, 11, 12–13, 14 (Luke 8:8); Romans 8:18–23; Matthew 13:1–23 (103)	Isaiah 55:10–11; Psalm 65:9, 11–12, 13 (Luke 8:8); Romans 8:14–18; Matthew 13:1–9 (98)
Sixteenth Sunday in Ordinary Time	July 23, 2023	The Lord Is Our Strength	Wisdom 12:13, 16–19; Psalm 86:5–6, 9–10, 15–16 (5a); Romans 8:26–27; Matthew 13:24–43 or Matthew 13:24–30 (106)	Wisdom 12:13, 16–19; Psalm 86:5–6, 9–10, 15–16de (5a); Romans 8:26–27; Matthew 13:24–30 (101)
Seventeenth Sunday in Ordinary Time	July 30, 2023	An Understanding Heart	1 Kings 3:5, 7–12; Psalm 119:57, 72, 76–77, 127–128, 129–130 (97a); Romans 8:28–30; Matthew 13:44–52 or Matthew 13:44–46 (109)	1 Kings 3:5, 7–12; Psalm 119:57 and 72, 127–128, (97a); Romans 8:28–30; Matthew 13:44–46 (104)
Feast of the Transfiguration of the Lord	August 6, 2023	Power Made Known	Daniel 7:9–10, 13–14; Psalm 97:1–2, 5–6, 9 (1a, 9a); 2 Peter 1:16–19; Matthew 17:1–9 (614)	2 Peter 1:16–19; Psalm 97:1–2, 5–6, 9; Matthew 17:1–9 (344)
Nineteenth Sunday in Ordinary Time	August 13, 2023	"Take Courage, It Is I"	1 Kings 19:9a, 11–13a; Psalm 85:9, 10, 11–12, 13–14 (8); Romans 9:1–5; Matthew 14:22–33 (115)	1 Kings 19:9a, 11–13a; Psalm 85:8abc and 9, 10–11, 12–13 (8); Matthew 14:22–33 (110)
Solemnity of the Assumption of the Blessed Virgin Mary	August 15, 2023	Rejoice in the Lord	Revelation 11:19a; 12:1–6a, 10ab; Psalm 45:10, 11, 12, 16 (10bc); 1 Corinthians 15:20–27; Luke 1:39–56	Isaiah 9:2–3a, 6–7a or Zechariah 2:14–15; Psalm 113:1–2, 3–4, 5–6, 7–8; Acts 1:12–13a, 14 or Ephesians 1:3–6; Luke 1:39–56 (352)
Twentieth Sunday in Ordinary Time	August 20, 2023	God's Mercy is for All Peoples	Isaiah 56:1, 6–7; Psalm 67:2–3, 5, 6, 8 (4); Romans 11:13–15, 29–32; Matthew 15:21–28 (118)	Isaiah 56:1, 6–7; Psalm 67:1–2, 4, 5, and 7 (4); Matthew 15:21–28 (113)
Twenty-First Sunday in Ordinary Time	August 27, 2023	"Who Do You Say That I Am?"	Isaiah 22:19–23; Psalm 138:1–2, 2–3, 6, 8 (8bc); Romans 11:33–36; Matthew 16:13–20 (121)	Romans 11:33–36; Psalm 138:1–2a, 2bc and 3, 6 and 8cde (8bc); Matthew 16:13–20 (116)

Season Background for Ordinary Time during Fall

Understanding Ordinary Time during Fall

As September begins, the lengthiest period of Ordinary Time continues. The shorter of the two periods of Ordinary Time occurred between the end of Christmas Time and the beginning of Lent. The Sunday liturgies of this second and lengthier period of Ordinary Time began with the celebration of the Solemnity of the Most Holy Trinity. On these Sundays, the Gospel according to Luke has been our guide. We have heard our initial call to be disciples of Christ. Recognizing that we are called by the Holy Spirit, we have listened to Jesus teach us, among other things, about how to respond to the needs of our neighbor and how to pray.

On the Twenty-Second Sunday in Ordinary Time, where *Children's Liturgy of the Word 2022–2023* begins, we continue our journey in Luke. As the Solemnity of Our Lord Jesus Christ, King of the Universe, grows closer, we ponder the coming end of the liturgical year and the meaning of the end-times. We do all of this in the context of the changing seasons of the natural world. As the leaves change color and then fall to the ground, we reflect on how we, too, have changed throughout the course of the past year.

The season of Ordinary Time is not named this because it is "ordinary" in any sense of the word. Rather, "Ordinary Time" comes from the fact that the Sundays of this season are counted. The ordinal numbers of these Sundays mark the progression of weeks through the season. Because of its length, the season can seem routine and ordinary to some people. For Christians, however, no time is ordinary. Every day is extraordinary because every day God acts in our lives. God sustains us. God the Father is creating us anew as his people in his Son through the Holy Spirit. Nothing is ordinary about people of faith who gather each Sunday as members of the Body of Christ, the Church.

Sunday is the original feast day. In the first several hundred years following the death and Resurrection of the Lord, it was the only feast day for the Church. From the time of the New Testament, we know it as the Lord's Day. In the busyness that autumn can bring, our Sunday gathering for liturgy gives us an opportunity to keep our eyes fixed on the presence of God and our ears attuned to his life-giving Word so that we are able to go forth into our world and lead others to faith in him. This is not an ordinary mission. We have the opportunity to do extraordinary things.

Liturgical Environment

The liturgical color of green continues to be used during this period of Ordinary Time during fall. In contrast to the autumn colors of brown, orange, red, and yellow that are around those of us in northern geographical locations, the color green reminds us of new growth and new life.

Ordinary Time during fall is a time to celebrate our own growth in Christ and our daily call to discipleship.

As a leader of the Liturgy of the Word with children, you will want to follow the direction of your pastor or liturgist in creating a liturgical environment in your space. Consistency between the space where the main assembly meets and your space is important. Remember, real and authentic materials should never be replaced with artificial ones when preparing the environment for liturgy. For example, in Ordinary Time during fall, use actual leaves in the environment, not plastic ones.

Overview of the Readings

First Readings   On each Sunday in Ordinary Time, the first reading is from the Old Testament and is related to the reading from the Gospel proclaimed on that Sunday. The first readings for this fourteen-week period of Ordinary Time come from a variety of books of the Old Testament, some of which may be unfamiliar to some people. The first readings include selections from the Torah or Pentateuch (Exodus), the Deuteronomist History (2 Samuel and 2 Kings), the later historical books (2 Maccabees), the Wisdom books (Wisdom and Sirach), and the Minor Prophets (Amos, Habakkuk, and Malachi). The first readings at this time of year are most often from the Minor Prophets in the three-year Lectionary cycle of readings. The poetic readings from Wisdom and Sirach are interspersed with readings from the Pentateuch, historical books, and Minor Prophets, which provide examples from Israel's history about how the people were stubborn and the prophets called them to change. As a whole, the first readings encourage us to repentance and stress the Lord's own mercy and justice, which will bring healing even in the face of a lack of repentance by his people.

Responsorial Psalms   Between the Twenty-Second Sunday in Ordinary Time and the Solemnity of Our Lord Jesus Christ, King of the Universe, a variety of responsorial psalms will be sung. Taken from the beginning, middle, and end of the Psalter, these psalms call us to praise the Lord, for he provides us with refuge and comfort. Twice during this period of Ordinary Time, the refrain for the responsorial psalm reminds us that the Lord lifts up the poor and hears their cry (Psalms 113 and 34, Twenty-Fifth Sunday in Ordinary Time and Thirtieth Sunday in Ordinary Time, respectively). As the end of the liturgical year approaches and we draw closer to the Solemnity of Our Lord Jesus Christ the King, the refrains declare the Lord's glory and speak of his reign of justice.

Second Readings   The second readings, as always, are from the New Testament. For these weeks in Ordinary Time, they are primarily from the pastoral letters of 1 and 2 Timothy. On the Twenty-Second Sunday in Ordinary Time, we hear a passage from Hebrews contrasting the previous covenants God made with the people. The second reading for the Twenty-Third Sunday in Ordinary Time is the Sunday Lectionary's only selection from Philemon, a very short letter on the institution of slavery that was acceptable in Paul's time and the spirit of equality in Christ, which characterized the Christian community. On the three Sundays prior to the Solemnity of Our Lord Jesus Christ, King of the Universe, the second reading comes from 2 Thessalonians. In this letter, Paul writes to the Christian community at Thessalonica about remaining faithful to the Gospel despite the deceptive teachings they are hearing about the Parousia from false teachers. The final second reading for Year C of the Lectionary cycle of readings comes from Colossians, which is a fitting conclusion to the liturgical year. It incorporates one of the early Christian liturgical hymns of praise and gratitude to Jesus Christ, redeemer of the human race and head of the Church, Savior and King.

Gospel Readings   The passages from the Gospel according to Luke include the beloved parable of the prodigal son and the narrative of the sole leper who returns to thank Jesus for being healed. Our journey through the final third of Ordinary Time begins with Jesus teaching his disciples to leave home and carry their own cross as they follow him. Our faith, like that of the Apostles, is increased when we follow Jesus' instruction to pray always, an instruction we hear on the Twenty-Ninth Sunday in Ordinary Time. Our constant prayer will be a sign of our faith when the Son of Man returns. On the Thirtieth Sunday, Jesus further emphasizes his teaching on prayer, showing his followers that they are to pray, not like the Pharisee, but in an ironic twist, like the tax collector, who prayed with humility. The Gospel readings of the final four Sundays of Ordinary Time begin with the proclamation of the beloved narrative of Zacchaeus, a sinner given new life in Christ. This theme continues on the Thirty-Second Sunday in Ordinary Time, as Jesus teaches that the God of life will carry those who persevere in faith through the trials that will mark the end-times. Those who believe in the resurrection of the dead, as the Gospel for the Thirty-Third Sunday tells us, will experience life with God. On the Solemnity of Our Lord Jesus Christ, King of the Universe, we are poignantly reminded that Christ's Kingdom is characterized by forgiveness. In his Paradise, he will remember those whom the world would forget. The message for those of us who have accepted the call to follow him, which has been heard and celebrated throughout the past liturgical year, is clear: Christ will remember us because of our faith in him as the Savior who reigns eternally.

August 28, 2022
Twenty-Second Sunday in Ordinary Time
God Provides

Scripture Background

Connections to Church Teaching and Tradition

* "To become a child in relation to God is the condition for entering the kingdom.[1] For this, we must humble ourselves and become little" (CCC, 526).

* "We have been made sharers in the divinity of Christ who humbled himself to share our humanity"[2] (CCC, 526).

* "The benevolence and mercy that inspire God's actions and provide the key for understanding them become so very much closer to man that they take on the traits of the man Jesus, the Word made flesh. . . . Jesus, in other words, is the tangible and definitive manifestation of how God acts towards men and women" (CSDC, 28).

* "Discussions on religious matters should be marked by clarity of expression as well as by humility and courtesy, so that truth may be combined with charity, and understanding with love" (CD, 13).

Sirach 3:17–18, 20, 28–29 Sirach, a wisdom book written in the early part of the second century BC, is literature that typically uses the form of proverbs to instruct and exhort young and old alike on what is important on our faith journey through life. This passage focuses on humility as a virtue that is to be cultivated, and one that others appreciate more than generosity in giving. This is especially true for those in high places of wealth or power, for in humility they find favor with God. Sirach also advises that one become aware of one's limitations and not seek or search beyond one's capabilities, so as not to be frustrated or disillusioned. Wisdom is acquired by attentiveness to the wise, and learning from experience encapsulated in proverbs. Finally, Sirach advises that just as water quenches fire, so almsgiving —that is, concern for others in need—atones for both personal and communal sin. Humility, coupled with attentiveness to the needs of others, activates the wisdom orientation necessary for right relationship with God and others.

Psalm 68:4–5, 6–7, 10–11 (see 11b) The psalmist images God as the powerful caretaker of the people, who showers bountiful rain upon the land, restoring it to fertility so that it can provide for the needy. God's power is made manifest in attentiveness to the needs of the just, who rejoice and exult in the Lord's goodness toward all, especially the poor. God is proclaimed as the "father of orphans and the defender of widows" (68:6a). God's loving power provides "a home for the forsaken" (68:7a) and "leads forth prisoners to prosperity" (68:7b). God's ways are unlike the machinations of other gods or unlike the categories that most humans operate from. Power and might are to be used not for one's benefit but are to be placed at the service of others, most especially the needy and the forsaken. This is what makes Israel's God so different from all the other powers and authorities. For this reason, the psalmist calls upon all the people to "rejoice and exult" (68:4b) and to sing and "chant praise" (58:5a) before God, as we exercise the same attitude toward others that God exercises toward us.

Hebrews 12:18–19, 22–24a This passage from Hebrews contrasts the previous covenants God made with the people, centered most especially on the covenant made with Moses on Mount Sinai, and the final covenant that God has made with the people, accomplished through Jesus' "sprinkled blood that speaks more eloquently than that of Abel" (12:24). This final covenant will enable all to approach Mount Zion, the heavenly Jerusalem, in which all will rejoice and celebrate in full, intimate relationship with God, something not fully possible in the previous covenants made with the people. This final and complete covenantal gathering will include all the followers of Jesus, as well as all the just who have gone before us. Together, we will be united with God and Jesus in loving relationship for all time.

Luke 14:1, 7–14 Meal scenes play a prominent role in Luke's account of the Gospel. Luke has Jesus use such rich occasions to teach the values of the reign of God that he consistently proclaims. This Sabbath meal at the home of "one of the leading Pharisees" (14:1) provides Jesus with the opportunity to highlight God's ways of thinking and acting in contrast to our own. Jesus' parable admonishes those who seek to be exalted and honored at the expense of others. Instead of exalting themselves, they should seek the lowest place in case someone more important comes, and they would be shamed into taking a lower place. From God's perspective, it is those who humble themselves that are exalted. This reversal of human ways of acting applies to all, especially those who consistently strive for honor, power, and prestige.

---

1. Cf. Matthew 18:3–4.
2. *Liturgy of the Hours*, Antiphon I for Evening Prayer for January 1.

Such meals were also used to build up connections and prestige by inviting the most honored and respected people of society, with the expectation that they would invite and honor you in return. Such prestige pandering was done by carefully avoiding any association with those considered shameful—namely, the poor, the homeless, and the stranger. Jesus proclaims that such are not God's ways. God looks favorably on those who invite others who cannot return the favor. In this manner, concern for others supersedes concern for one's prestige and honor. God's reign does not operate according to our social categories but on prevailing concern for the poor and disenfranchised. These will be rewarded by God at the "resurrection of the righteous" (14:14) for this is how God models what it means to be a member of God's reign.

 # Preparation

In today's Gospel, we hear Jesus' instructions regarding proper behavior at a feast. Luke provides the insight that these are parables, and they tell us about something beyond their immediate meaning; they tell us about the kingdom of God. As guests of the feast of the Lord, we too are invited to the great banquet of the kingdom of God. Our actions and choices should reflect our status as guests and should be marked by humility.

Lectionary for Mass #126C

Sirach 3:17–18, 20, 28–29

Psalm 68:4–5, 6–7, 10–11 (see 11b)

Hebrews 12:18–19, 22–24a

Luke 14:1, 7–14 (126)

Objectives

- To consider together Jesus' use of parables to invite pondering the surprising qualities of the kingdom of God.

- To introduce the word *humble* as a characteristic the God desires in us and its meaning as being rooted in our proper posture before the Divine Self.

Preparation and Materials

- Read the Season Background, the lectionary readings, and the Scripture Background.

- Bookmark the appropriate readings (see page xiv) in the lectionary, children's lectionary, or Bible. Place the book in a convenient location for the leader.

- Write the words of dismissal on a card for the priest celebrant.

- Prepare the words of the song the children will sing as they gather in the space for the Liturgy of the Word.

- Select volunteers (older children or adults) to proclaim the readings.

- Display the responsorial psalm refrain lyrics.

- Display the Apostles' or Nicene Creed.

- Prepare intercessions for the Prayer of the Faithful adapted for the needs of the Church, world, oppressed or marginalized, and local community.

Prayer Leader Reflection Questions

>> **How do you exhibit humility? How do you reach out to serve those who appear unimportant or on the fringes of our community?**

>> **How does your life reflect your identity as a guest at the great feast of the kingdom of God?**

Procession

Following the Collect of the Mass, the priest celebrant picks up the lectionary and invites those who would like to participate in the Liturgy of the Word with children to come forward and gather in the center aisle. The people who will lead the children out and facilitate the Liturgy of the Word also come forward at this time. Holding the lectionary so that all can see, the priest celebrant sends the children forth using his own words or the following:

Priest: **Dear children, God uses the seasons to teach us many things, and in fall, God teaches us about letting go. As the trees lose their leaves and the world prepares for winter sleep, we too can focus on what we need to change and what we need to let go of in our lives. Go now with your prayer leader(s) to listen for what God might be asking of you. May peace be with all of you.**

The leader processes out holding the lectionary, and the children follow behind. The parish music minister may have selected a song of dismissal for the assembly to sing while the children leave. A good option is "The Word of God: Children's Dismissal" by M. D. Ridge and Timothy R. Smith (WLP/GIA).

Centering

Continue to sing the song of dismissal that the assembly sang as you left the church. Or sing the refrain from "Lead Me, Lord" (Becker), or "We Are the Light of the World" (Greif), or have instrumental music playing as the children gather in the space for the Liturgy of the Word.

Place the lectionary on the ambo or lectern. Light the candle placed by the ambo or lectern, and then lead the following prayer:

**Mighty God,
all good things come from you.
Allow our hearts to be open to your Word
so that we may serve you completely.
Through Christ our Lord.**

Children: **Amen.**

First Reading

Sirach 3:17–18, 20, 28–29

Responsorial Psalm

Psalm 68:4–5, 6–7, 10–11 (see 11b) *Sing the same musical setting that is used in your parish's celebration of the liturgy.*

Second Reading

Hebrews 12:18–19, 22–24a

Gospel Acclamation

Sing the Gospel Acclamation used in your parish's celebration of the liturgy.

Gospel Reading

Luke 14:1, 7–14

Homily/Reflection

Do you know what Jesus' favorite thing to talk about was? It was the kingdom of God. Jesus explained what the kingdom of God was through parables. A parable is a story with more than one meaning. Parables cover things of this world: things that you and I know about, that we can see and touch and smell, like a seed, or a loaf of bread, or a coin. They also tell us much more—about things we cannot see with our eyes or touch with our hands or smell with our noses, but things that we know are still very real. Parables help us to understand better those things that we can only understand with our hearts and our souls.

Today, we hear Jesus tell us two parables about feasts. Jesus was at a feast when he told these parables and so the people who first heard these words would be thinking very clearly about the first meaning of the parables, the things of this world. They would have seen the people gathered around the table. They would have smelled the carefully prepared food. They might have paid attention to who else was there, where they sat, how they were dressed. In these parables, Jesus gave instructions about how to act at a feast.

» Were you surprised by what Jesus said?

He told the guests not to presume to sit in the special chairs for the most honored guests. If a guest turned out to be the most honored guest, he would be invited sit on that seat. He told the guests not to act more important than anyone else. Jesus also had surprising words for the host, who is the one holding the party or feast. Jesus told the host not to invite people who could repay him, but those who couldn't. The best guests would be the ones who would most appreciate the host's generosity.

Jesus said, "Everyone who exalts himself will be humbled, but the one who humbles himself will be exalted." We heard these words from the first reading too: "Humble yourself the more, the greater you are and you will find favor with God." To humble ourselves means to make ourselves small before one who is great.

>> **Who is the one who is greatest of all?** *(our Father in heaven)*

>> **What can this tell us about the kingdom of God? What is a another meaning for these words of Jesus?**

Perhaps this word, *humble*, might give us a clue. We know that God is greatest in this world and in the kingdom of God. Those who are least important in this world are most important in the kingdom of God. Perhaps the kingdom of God is not only for those who seem important, but for all of us, and especially for those of us who don't seem important in this world. Perhaps, as guests invited to this great feast of the kingdom of God, we must act like the guests and the hosts of Jesus' parables, humbling ourselves before every person and most especially before God.

Profession of Faith

Following the homily or reflection, the prayer leader invites everyone to stand to profess our faith. Together, sing or recite the Apostles' or Nicene Creed. Refer the children to the words of the prayer that you have displayed.

Prayer of the Faithful

Leader: **Our Father provides every good thing and he hears our every prayer. Please respond, "Lord, hear our prayer."**

For the Church, that we might always be humble before God who is great, we pray to the Lord: *Lord, hear our prayer.*

For government leaders, that, guided by the wisdom of our great God, they may use their influence to care for those in need, we pray to the Lord: *Lord, hear our prayer.*

For the hungry, that they might be fed, and that we may be mindful of the reverent use and sharing of God's gifts, we pray to the Lord: *Lord, hear our prayer.*

For teachers and students, that in the coming school year they may progress in knowing, loving, and serving God and neighbor with humility, we pray to the Lord: *Lord, hear our prayer.*

Invite other intercessions from the children, or add intercessions based on the current needs of the Church, the world, the oppressed or marginalized, and the local community. Conclude each of the children's petitions with **"we pray to the Lord"** and invite the response **"Lord, hear our prayer."**

For those who have died, that they may enjoy the heavenly feast of the kingdom of God, we pray to the Lord: *Lord, hear our prayer.*

**Mighty God, Giver of all good things,
we praise you for allowing us to draw close to you.
Thank you for hearing our prayers,
and feeding us with your Word.
Through Christ our Lord.**

Children: **Amen.**

Quietly return with the children to the main assembly. Be mindful of children having difficulty finding their families.

September 4, 2022
Twenty-Third Sunday in Ordinary Time
Send Us Your Spirit

 ## Scripture Background

Wisdom 9:13–18b   Some commentators call the prayer that is excerpted in this reading the high point of the Book of Wisdom. The whole of chapter 9 is King Solomon's prayer begging for wisdom. In the early part of the prayer, we find the affirmation that wisdom, portrayed as a feminine figure, was present with God at creation and is an attendant at God's throne. Prior to the selection we hear today, Solomon spoke of his responsibilities and his inability to complete his mission on his own. The prayer is full of modesty and hope. We hear words of striking humility as the King calls human efforts timid and unsure, recognizing that the body is little more than a weak shelter. The mind, too, he says, has difficulty learning about its own surroundings, much less things of heaven. Hope comes because all things are possible if God sends wisdom to aid us in our frailty.

Psalm 90:3–4, 5–6, 12–13, 14, 17 (1)   The mood of the verses we sing today echoes the development of Solomon's prayer. In the beginning, we concentrate on the fragility of humanity, especially in the face of God's power. Our sojourn on earth seems almost tragically fleeting, especially when we contemplate the God who created time itself. With the third strophe, the tone of lament changes to hope. God can, indeed, teach us to number our days aright. With grace, the heart of everyone who seeks is capable of wisdom. Finally, using the limited time that we have, the Holy Spirit can lead us to know God's kindness and our work can have true meaning.

Philemon 9–10, 12–17   This letter is addressed to an individual, Philemon, the head of a house church in Colossae. The letter revolves around the fate of another individual, Onesimus, a slave who ran away from Philemon and became a convert and friend to Paul. The entire letter is only twenty-five verses long, 335 words in the original Greek. The point of the letter is to encourage Philemon to accept Onesimus as a brother in Christ. Although Paul insists that he could order Philemon to do what is right, he claims to prefer that he do it freely. Nevertheless, Philemon's freedom to act seems to have been more fiction than fact as Paul reminds him of how much Philemon owes him. There are not-so-subtle comparisons made between Paul, a prisoner, and the slave Onesimus. Another element conditioning Philemon's freedom could have been Paul's request for a guest room. Paul would be checking up on Philemon's decision. The letter reveals Paul's tenderness and his theology of the Church as a community with no distinctions, as he said to the Galatians, "There is neither Jew nor Greek, there is neither slave nor free person, there is not male and female; for you are all one in Christ Jesus" (3:28). The fact that the letter survived for posterity offers testimony that Philemon did do the right thing: otherwise sharing the letter would have been too embarrassing.

Luke 14:25–33   As Luke tells us that great crowds were accompanying Jesus, the implication seems to be that while all journeyed to Jerusalem, the crowds were not necessarily his followers. Jesus turns to them and utters some of the strongest, most confusing Words in Scripture: only those who hate family and even their own life can be counted as disciples.

We cannot interpret this from the context of our own culture in which we understand love and hate primarily as emotions. In Jesus' day, they were understood as the attitudes from which all action springs. To love someone meant to be loyal, to do the right thing for them, and to give them preference. Thus, in line with the message of other readings from Luke, to "hate" father and mother meant to choose the community of disciples and the poor as one's primary family

1. Luke 17:33.

rather than hold to ties of blood and place of origin. In talking about the cross, Luke again, as he did in 9:23, uses vocabulary that indicates that the disciple's cross is not a singular event, but a way of life. If we follow the crucified, we will share his cross.

Luke finishes this section indicating that discipleship is a costly matter. People should know what they are getting into before they accept the responsibility. Like the tower, it will be more expensive than we might think. It will demand that we renounce everything that prevents us from following wholeheartedly. It will not be possible without the grace of God's Spirit, but that is the one thing we are promised (see 11:13).

 # Preparation

In today's Gospel reading, Jesus offers many images about discipleship, with a special emphasis on the cost of following him. The image of building a tower may have particular resonance for children. To sustain a life of discipleship, it is necessary to have a strong foundation and enough resources to nurture the ongoing work of following Jesus throughout one's life.

Lectionary for Mass #129C

Wisdom 9:13–18b

Psalm 90:3–4, 5–6, 12–13, 14, 17 (1)

Philemon 9–10, 12–17

Luke 14:25–33

Objectives

- To invite consideration of the necessity of perseverance in the life of discipleship.
- To identify specific means of grace as aids to the life of discipleship.

Preparation and Materials

- Read the Season Background, the lectionary readings, and the Scripture Background.
- Bookmark the appropriate readings (see page xiv) in the lectionary, children's lectionary, or Bible. Place the book in a convenient location for the leader.
- Write the words of dismissal on a card for the priest celebrant.
- Prepare the words of the song the children will sing as they gather in the space for the Liturgy of the Word.
- Select volunteers (older children or adults) to proclaim the readings.
- Display the responsorial psalm refrain lyrics.
- Display the Apostles' or Nicene Creed.
- Prepare intercessions for the Prayer of the Faithful adapted for the needs of the Church, world, oppressed or marginalized, and local community.

Prayer Leader Reflection Questions

≫ **What crosses do you bear? How does God's grace help you to bear them?**

≫ **Do you have the resources needed to sustain your own life of discipleship? Look to your parish leadership for guidance.**

Procession

Following the Collect of the Mass, the priest celebrant picks up the lectionary and invites those who would like to participate in the Liturgy of the Word with children to come forward and gather in the center aisle. The people who will lead the children out and facilitate the Liturgy of the Word also come forward at this time. Holding the lectionary so that all can see, the priest celebrant sends the children forth using his own words or the following:

Priest: **Dear children, God uses the seasons to teach us many things, and in fall, God teaches us about letting go. As the trees lose their leaves and the world prepares for winter sleep, we too can focus on what we need to change and what we need to let go of in our lives. Go now with your prayer leader(s) to listen for what God might be asking of you. May peace be with all of you.**

The leader processes out holding the lectionary, and the children follow behind. The parish music minister may have selected a song of dismissal for the assembly to sing while the children leave. A good option is "The Word of God: Children's Dismissal" by M. D. Ridge and Timothy R. Smith (WLP/GIA).

Centering

Continue to sing the song of dismissal that the assembly sang as you left the church. Or sing the refrain from "I Heard the Voice of Jesus Say" (KINGSFOLD), or "I Say 'Yes,' My Lord / "Digo 'Sí,' Señor" (Peña) or have instrumental music playing as the children gather in the space for the Liturgy of the Word.

Place the lectionary on the ambo or lectern. Light the candle placed by the ambo or lectern, and then lead the following prayer:

**O God,
you give us what we need to be close to you.
Allow our hearts to be open to your Word
so that we may serve you completely.
Through Christ our Lord.**

Children: **Amen.**

First Reading

Wisdom 9:13–18b

Responsorial Psalm

Psalm 90:3–4, 5–6, 12–13, 14, 17 (1) *Sing the same musical setting that is used in your parish's celebration of the liturgy.*

Second Reading

Philemon 9–10, 12–17

Gospel Acclamation

Sing the Gospel Acclamation used in your parish's celebration of the liturgy.

Gospel Reading

Luke 14:25–33

Homily/Reflection

» **Have you ever built a block tower?**
[Allow the children a minute to talk about their experience of using building blocks.]

Many of us have played with building blocks. We learned that having more blocks on the bottom as we stack the blocks causes the tower to be sturdier. The bottom, or foundation, has to be strong so the whole tower doesn't fall down.

In Jesus' time, a farmer builds a tower high enough so that he can have a wide view of his fields. This tower would need to be very high—much higher than you or I could build with our blocks! Building a tower like this would require many bricks, and the builder would want to make sure the foundation was well made. But what if the builder used all the bricks for the foundation? Would the tower serve its purpose? Would a farmer be able to see his all his farmlands? No!

Jesus reminded his listeners what a builder would need to do first. A builder would have a plan for how to build the tower with all the bricks he would need. He would be sure at the beginning that he had all the materials he would need to get to the end of the project. When Jesus talked about building a tower, he was not only giving advice about construction, but he was also talking about discipleship. A disciple is someone who follows a teacher. Jesus was helping his listeners to understand what it meant to follow him.

Jesus' words can tell us something about what it means to follow him, too. Just as it would take work to build a tower, it takes work to follow Jesus. We have to put effort into how we live our lives as Jesus would want. Not all the decisions we make are easy and sometimes it might even cost us something to be good disciples. There is an important difference between the builder Jesus talked about and the disciples of Jesus, though. The supplies we need to follow Jesus are things we can get more of. What we need most to keep building our tower, to keep following Jesus, is grace. We need God's special help.

>> **How can we get more of what we need to keep being Jesus' disciples?**

We can spend time with other people who love Jesus and who can show us how to live as a disciple. We can serve people in need. We can read the Bible, learning more and more about Jesus' own life to make our own lives more like his. We can pray to God anytime and know that God is listening. We can receive grace in the sacraments, most especially in the Eucharist.

Building our towers take our whole lives. We are always working toward following Jesus more closely. Just as the farmer who builds a tower might climb to the top to see his whole field, we hope and pray that what we will see is the face of God at the end of our lives when we have finally finished our towers. We trust in God's grace to help us to do that.

Profession of Faith

Following the homily or reflection, the prayer leader invites everyone to stand to profess our faith. Together, sing or recite the Apostles' or Nicene Creed. Refer the children to the words of the prayer that you have displayed.

Prayer of the Faithful

Leader: **Grateful for our faith, we now bring our prayers to God. Please respond, "Lord, send us your Spirit."**

For the leaders of our Church, that they may serve her with wisdom and the Spirit's counsel, we pray: *Lord, send us your Spirit.*

For local, national, and world leaders, that they may be guided on the path of peace, we pray: *Lord, send us your Spirit.*

For those suffering from the effects of war, violence, and terror, and those who bear the cross of illness, we pray: *Lord, send us your Spirit.*

For farmers, builders, and all who work in agriculture and construction, that the work of their hands may be a benefit and blessing for all, we pray: *Lord, send us your Spirit.*

Invite other intercessions from the children, or add intercessions based on the current needs of the Church, the world, the oppressed or marginalized, and the local community. Conclude each of the children's petitions with **"we pray"** and invite the response **"Lord, send us your Spirit."**

For all who have died, that they may see God's face, we pray: *Lord, send us your Spirit.*

O God, our Father,
who has adopted us as daughters and sons,
grant us the grace to follow you faithfully.
Accept the prayers of your children.
We ask this through Jesus Christ, your Son,
who live and reign in the unity of the Holy Spirit,
God, for ever and ever.

Children: **Amen.**

Quietly return with the children to the main assembly. Be mindful of children having difficulty finding their families.

September 11, 2022
Twenty-Fourth Sunday in Ordinary Time

Christ Jesus Came into the World to Save Sinners

 ## Scripture Background

Connections to Church Teaching and Tradition

* "Christ's call to conversion continues to resound in the lives of Christians. . . . [C]onversion is not just a human work. It is the movement of a 'contrite heart' drawn and moved by grace to respond to the merciful love of God [1]" (CCC, 1428).

* "Yet my encounter with God awakens my conscience in such a way that it no longer aims at self-justification, and is no longer a mere reflection of me . . . but it becomes a capacity for listening to the Good itself" (SS, 33).

* "God's passionate love for . . . humanity is at the same time a forgiving love. It is so great that it turns God against himself, his love against his justice . . . so great is God's love for man that by becoming man he follows him even into death, and so reconciles justice and love" (DCE, 10).

* "Holy Communion separates us from sin. . . . The Eucharist cannot unite us to Christ without at the same time cleansing us from past sins and preserving us from future sins" (CCC, 1393).

Exodus 32:7–11, 13–14 This conversation between Moses and God happened at the end of the forty days that Moses spent on the mountain talking with God. The beginning of chapter 32 tells us that the people had prevailed upon Aaron to fashion an idol for them and to offer sacrifice and make a feast. God, of course, is aware of their infidelity and thus speaks to Moses. Notably, addressing Moses, the Lord calls the people "your people" whom "you" brought out of Egypt (32:7). From the divine viewpoint, they have ceased to be a people of God. They are so depraved that they should be destroyed, leaving Moses as the progenitor of a new covenant people. Moses will have nothing of it. He will not accept the idea that these are not God's people and, like Abraham pleading for the people of Sodom, Moses dares to argue with his Lord. He recalls all that God has done for the people from the time of Abraham to that very day. In the verse that today's reading skips, he even says that the destruction of the people would be evidence to the Egyptians that God had never cared for this people or had made a mistake in starting the Exodus. With that successful prayer, Moses proved himself a father to his own people while God's unrelenting faithfulness and mercy was revealed.

Psalm 51:3–4, 12–13, 17, 19 (Luke 15:18) The title of this psalm indicates that it was David's prayer after being confronted by Nathan over his sin with Bathsheba and subsequent killing of Uriah. It is the classic prayer of confession and each line is worthy of meditation. With words repeated in every Eucharist, it recognizes that only with the grace of God can we have a clean heart. The final line reminds us of the most important sacrifice we can offer: a heart contrite and humbled.

1 Timothy 1:12–17 Timothy was a third-generation Christian whose grandmother, Lois, and mother, Eunice, were among the people converted by Paul. He was also probably Paul's most cherished companion in mission and ministry. Paul wrote the letter so that Timothy would "know how to behave in the household of God, which is the church of the living God" (3:15). The passage we hear today contains the core of Paul's teaching: "Christ Jesus came into the world to save sinners" (1:15). Throughout his correspondence, Paul will insist that it is faith in Jesus, not obedience to the law, which brings salvation. He gives profound witness to his own appreciation of that as he goes on to say that the enormity of his sin allowed for the immensity of Christ's patience to be revealed.

Luke 15:1–32 or 15:1–10 The Gospel writers did not divide their work into chapter and verse. That was done much later by scholars who wanted to create a common system of reference for use among the faithful. Therefore, it is often helpful to look at how a text fits into its context. In the case of today's Gospel, Luke is making a strong point by following Jesus' teaching about useless salt and the warning that "whoever has ears to hear ought to hear" (14:35) with the statement that it was tax collectors and sinners who were drawing near to listen to Jesus.

There are some details to Jesus' examples that might escape our notice. Jesus was addressing himself to the Pharisees, educated men who developed expertise in interpreting the Law. When Jesus addressed them as if they were lowly—and usually not law-abiding—shepherds, he was doing the equivalent of addressing physicians by saying, "which of you while driving your garbage truck . . ." Then, because he has used a masculine image he adds a feminine one in typical Lucan fashion. Each of the three parables contrasts the lost and found. In the case of the coin, it was probably worth about a day's wage—no great fortune, but still significant to the

1. Psalm 51:17; cf. John 6:44; 12:32; 1 John 4:10.

woman who lit her lamp, carefully swept her dirt floor, and then called in her friends to rejoice with her.

The parable of the lost son, perhaps the best known and loved of Jesus' parables, is the most pointed in response to the Pharisees. With all its details, including the revulsion they would feel at the thought of tending pigs and sharing their meal, the ultimate point is that the one who asks, who looks for grace and forgiveness, will receive it. The ones who righteously reject the sinner without admitting their own failings have excluded themselves from the feast.

 # Preparation

The full text of today's Gospel includes three parables that follow the same pattern. Something or someone who is beloved is lost. The one who loves the beloved seeks the return of the beloved with unending resolve. The one who loves and the beloved are reunited and the joy of the one who loves is so great that it must be shared not only with the beloved but with the whole community. These parables speak to our need to return to God when we have strayed, but even more, they speak of the depth of God's love for us even when we are lost and the abundant joy of God that is poured out to be shared when we return.

Lectionary for Mass #132C

Exodus 32:7–11, 13–14

Psalm 51:3–4, 12–13, 17, 19 (Luke 12:18)

1 Timothy 1:12–17

Luke 15:1–32 or 15:1–10

Objectives

- To announce that God's searching for the lost is inexhaustible.

- To consider together the joy in being found that is shared by the Finder and the one found.

Preparation and Materials

- Read the Season Background, the lectionary readings, and the Scripture Background.

- Bookmark the appropriate readings (see page xiv) in the lectionary, children's lectionary, or Bible. Place the book in a convenient location for the leader.

- Write the words of dismissal on a card for the priest celebrant.

- Prepare the words of the song the children will sing as they gather in the space for the Liturgy of the Word.

- Select volunteers (older children or adults) to proclaim the readings.

- Display the responsorial psalm refrain lyrics.

- Display the Apostles' or Nicene Creed.

- Prepare intercessions for the Prayer of the Faithful adapted for the needs of the Church, world, oppressed or marginalized, and local community.

- Look for a print of the Shepherd fresco from the Catacombs of St. Priscilla or the Shepherd statue from the Catacomb of St. Domitilla to display.

Prayer Leader Reflection Questions

» **Do you trust that God's love is inexhaustible and that nothing we do can make God stop loving us? How is this trust visible in your own life?**

» **When have you experienced forgiveness from God or others? Who might be waiting for your forgiveness?**

As you seek forgiveness of your own sins, consider receiving the sacrament of reconciliation soon.

Procession

Following the Collect of the Mass, the priest celebrant picks up the lectionary and invites those who would like to participate in the Liturgy of the Word with children to come forward and gather in the center aisle. The people who will lead the children out and facilitate the Liturgy of the Word also come forward at this time. Holding the lectionary so that all can see, the priest celebrant sends the children forth using his own words or the following:

> *Priest*: **Dear children, God uses the seasons to teach us many things, and in fall, God teaches us about letting go. As the trees lose their leaves and the world prepares for winter sleep, we too can focus on what we need to change and what we need to let go of in our lives. Go now with your prayer leader(s) to listen for what God might be asking of you. May peace be with all of you.**

The leader processes out holding the lectionary, and the children follow behind. The parish music minister may have selected a song of dismissal for the assembly to sing while the children leave. A good option is "The Word of God: Children's Dismissal" by M. D. Ridge and Timothy R. Smith (WLP/GIA).

Centering

Continue to sing the song of dismissal that the assembly sang as you left the church. Or sing the refrain from "Loving and Forgiving" (Soper), or the refrain from "Grant to Us, O Lord" (Deiss), or have instrumental music playing as the children gather in the space for the Liturgy of the Word.

Place the lectionary on the ambo or lectern. Light the candle placed by the ambo or lectern, and then lead the following prayer:

> **O God of mercy,**
> **you are seeker of the lost.**
> **We want to follow you always and to be close to you.**
> **Allow our hearts to be open to your Word**
> **so that we may serve you completely.**
> **Through Christ our Lord.**

> *Children:* **Amen.**

First Reading

Exodus 32:7–11, 13–14

Responsorial Psalm

Psalm 51:3–4, 12–13, 17, 19; (Luke 15:18) *Sing the same musical setting that is used in your parish's celebration of the liturgy.*

Second Reading

1 Timothy 1:12–17

Gospel Acclamation

Sing the Gospel Acclamation used in your parish's celebration of the liturgy.

Gospel Reading

Luke 15:1–32 or 15:1–10

Homily/Reflection

» **Have you ever been lost?**

Sometimes we might get separated by accident from someone we love who cares for us. Sometimes we might wander away, even though we know we shouldn't, and then we realize we don't know how to get back on our own. No matter how it happens, it can be frightening, and we don't always know what to do.

Today, we hear a parable about a shepherd and a lost sheep. *[Point to your display of the Shepherd and sheep if you have it.]* A shepherd is someone who takes care of sheep. Sheep eat grass and eventually they may eat all the grass in one place. A shepherd leads sheep to new grass areas so that they always have something to eat. Sheep have big fluffy bodies and tiny little legs. It is important for them to have a place to drink water where the water is fresh but not moving too quickly. If a sheep tried to drink water in a fast-moving river, its feet might be swept out from under it, and it would be very hard for the sheep to get back up again because of its heavy wet wool and its small legs. So the shepherd finds safe places for them to drink.

» **Do you get the sense that sheep need lots of care and that shepherds have a huge responsibility?**

» **What else do you think shepherds do to take care of the sheep?**

In the Gospel, Jesus described a shepherd with a flock of one hundred sheep. But the shepherd notices when one sheep is missing. He must know his sheep very well to be able to recognize that one among so many is gone! He goes looking for the one lost sheep. He does not stop looking until he finds it. When he finds the sheep, he does some things that might surprise us. He takes the sheep on his shoulders. The sheep doesn't return on its own power but on the power of the shepherd. The shepherd's joy is so great at finding this beloved sheep that he invites his friends and neighbors to celebrate with him.

Sometimes we get lost. Sometimes we wander away from God. We don't follow the good path that Jesus our Good Shepherd has shown us. When we realize we have made choices that have separated us from the God who loves us, how can we act like the sheep who was found? The sheep in the Gospel didn't really do much at all, did it? It simply trusted the shepherd would find it. When we realize we need to be reunited with God, we can trust that God will never stop looking for us. Nothing we do can keep God from searching until he finds us. God will be the one to carry us back and there will be great joy when we are reunited with him.

Profession of Faith

Following the homily or reflection, the prayer leader invites everyone to stand to profess our faith. Together, sing or recite the Apostles' or Nicene Creed. Refer the children to the words of the prayer that you have displayed.

Prayer of the Faithful

Leader: **Grateful for our faith, we now bring our prayers to God. Please respond, "Lord, in your mercy, hear us."**

That the leaders of the Church may have the strength to follow the example of the Good Shepherd who knows and loves the sheep so well and seeks the lost, we pray: *Lord, in your mercy, hear us.*

That God's Spirit may open opportunities for dialogue in places of violence, bring an end to injustice, and help all to respect the value and dignity of each person, we pray: *Lord, in your mercy, hear us.*

That those who feel lost and alone may know the joy of God's welcoming embrace, we pray: *Lord, in your mercy, hear us.*

That we may open our own hearts to be quick to forgive and ready to seek reconciliation, we pray: *Lord, in your mercy, hear us.*

Invite other intercessions from the children, or add intercessions based on the current needs of the Church, the world, the oppressed or marginalized, and the local community. Conclude each of the children's petitions with **"we pray"** and invite the response **"Lord, in your mercy, hear us."**

That all who have died may enjoy forever the heavenly sheepfold of the Lord, we pray: *Lord, in your mercy, hear us.*

O God,
your love for us is bigger than what we can imagine.
Forgive us when we stray away from your love.
Lead us to the joy of your embrace.
Fulfill now, Lord, our needs and prayers according to your will.
We ask this in the name of Jesus Christ, your Son,
Who live and reign in the unity of the Holy Spirit,
God, for ever and ever.

Children: **Amen.**

Quietly return with the children to the main assembly. Be mindful of children having difficulty finding their families.

September 18, 2022
Twenty-Fifth Sunday in Ordinary Time
Right Relationship

 ## Scripture Background

Connections to Church Teaching and Tradition

- God's love and forgiveness is for all people.

- One of the implications of faith in one God is "knowing the unity and true dignity of all men: Everyone is made in the image and likeness of God[1]" (CCC, 225).

- God's fourth commandment also enjoins us to honor all who for our good have received authority in society from God. It clarifies the duties of those who exercise authority as well as those who benefit from it (CCC, 2234).

Amos 8:4–7 It was a time not unlike our own. For the "haves" of Israel, the eighth century BC was a time of great prosperity. Business was good. The market was booming. Profits were growing. In fact, the only thing holding the "haves" of Israel back was government regulations mandating Sabbath time and religious holidays for workers.

For the "have-nots," however, times were not so good, for underneath the booming economy of eighth-century Israel was an increasingly poorer lower class. Thousands were suffering from the unfair business practices and the bottom-line thinking that were making the "haves" so successful. Many were being forced out of their homes. Some even had to sell themselves into slavery just to keep food on the table.

Amos gives his people a reality check in no uncertain terms. Such an oppressive system, he says, cannot continue. God will not tolerate this continual buying and selling or this continual cheating of the poor. Make no mistake about it, Amos says, the judgment of God is coming and will overturn the whole oppressive system.

How are we as people of faith to respond to such a situation? Amos doesn't say in these verses, but elsewhere he is quite clear. He denounces religious communities that collude with the system just as surely as he denounces the system itself. Our calling, he says, is to be faithful to the God of peace and justice. We are first and foremost to be a prayerful community, a community that listens to God and acts on God's message of justice for all.

Psalm 113:1–2, 4–6, 7–8 (see 1a, 7b) The psalmist praises God for helping the weak and needy. Using images reminiscent of Hannah's song in 2 Samuel, he celebrates God as a God of justice who does not tolerate inequality. Sooner or later, the psalmist says, God will right the scale, tossing those at the top of the ladder down from their positions of power and raising up those who have been oppressed and kept down.

The reality check that we are given here is twofold: First, the psalmist tells us that God is still God, no matter what it may look like in the political realm. Second, like Amos, the psalmist insists that the unjust social order we have become accustomed to will not last. In the end, those who are first will be last, and who are last will be first.

1 Timothy 2:1–8 With this reading, the author of 1 Timothy begins to instruct his young colleague. The themes he highlights differ from anything Paul himself might have said but are very characteristic of the pastoral epistles—a concern for the social order, an emphasis on truth, and a faith that is more fidelity to orthodoxy than a way of life.

The author calls us to be a community of prayer that lifts its hands to not only pray for but also help others. That is our vocation as people of faith, he says. We are to pray and serve so that by our intercession, the whole world might come to know the love and justice of Jesus Christ.

Luke 16:1–13 or 16:10–13 The parable of the dishonest steward is certainly a strange one. Did Jesus really mean to commend the steward's cheating, or as many commentators suggest, did he mean something else, perhaps to commend the steward's bold action. The early Church clearly struggled with this story, for Luke himself gives three different interpretations of it right in the passage itself (see 16: 8, 9, and 10–12).

When we look at this parable in the context of Luke's narrative, two possible interpretations present themselves. If we take the parable by itself and ignore the additions Luke made to it in verses 8 to 13, this story connects nicely to the parable of the prodigal son, which precedes it.

---
1. Genesis 1:26.

Both parables are challenges to the Pharisees. In this case Jesus is saying that their stewardship of God's people is being called into account and they had better act quickly and boldly to get God's approval.

If, on the other hand, we follow Luke's lead, this parable could just as easily connect to the rest of chapter 16, all of which has to do with the faithful use of one's possessions. In that case, this story is like the parable of the rich man and Lazarus, which follows. Both are warnings to handle our possessions in ways that will gain us eternal life.

 # Preparation

The prophet Amos lived in a period of prosperity, but not all members of the community prospered equally. Amos named the injustice he saw in how others took advantage of the poor and vulnerable. As we await the coming of the kingdom, we must participate actively and wisely in the world today. We must not only avoid outright cheating, but we must act justly and lovingly, including the ways we use our possessions and money. When we live in right relationship with God and one another, we are living the way Christ called us to live. The choices we make and the way we treat others matters absolutely. Living in right relationship highlights the importance of trustworthiness and honesty, and how such attributes are vital to Christian life.

Lectionary for Mass #135C

Amos 8:4–7

Psalm 113:1–2, 4–6, 7–8 (see 1a, 7b)

1 Timothy 2:1–8

Luke 16:1–13 or 16:10–13

Objectives

- To examine how choices about material things have moral implications and therefore play a role in our relationship with God.

- To introduce and explain the term *mammon*.

Preparation and Materials

- Read the Season Background, the lectionary readings, and the Scripture Background.

- Bookmark the appropriate readings (see page xiv) in the lectionary, children's lectionary, or Bible. Place the book in a convenient location for the leader.

- Write the words of dismissal on a card for the priest celebrant.

- Prepare the words of the song the children will sing as they gather in the space for the Liturgy of the Word.

- Select volunteers (older children or adults) to proclaim the readings.

- Display the responsorial psalm refrain lyrics.

- Display the Apostles' or Nicene Creed.

- Prepare intercessions for the Prayer of the Faithful adapted for the needs of the Church, world, oppressed or marginalized, and local community.

- Bring an actual balance scale and weights, or an image of one, to show the children.

Prayer Leader Reflection Questions

>> **What role does money play in your life? How do you ensure that your actions are always oriented toward God rather than earthly wealth?**

>> **How do you actively support just compensation for all who labor?**

Procession

Following the Collect of the Mass, the priest celebrant picks up the lectionary and invites those who would like to participate in the Liturgy of the Word with children to come forward and gather in the center aisle. The people who will lead the children out and facilitate the Liturgy of the Word also come forward at this time. Holding the lectionary so that all can see, the priest celebrant sends the children forth using his own words or the following:

> *Priest*: **Dear children, God uses the seasons to teach us many things, and in fall, God teaches us about letting go. As the trees lose their leaves and the world prepares for winter sleep, we too can focus on what we need to change and what we need to let go of in our lives. Go now with your prayer leader(s) to listen for what God might be asking of you. May peace be with all of you.**

The leader processes out holding the lectionary, and the children follow behind. The parish music minister may have selected a song of dismissal for the assembly to sing while the children leave. A good option is "The Word of God: Children's Dismissal" by M. D. Ridge and Timothy R. Smith (WLP/GIA).

Centering

Continue to sing the song of dismissal that the assembly sang as you left the church. Or sing the refrain from "The Cry of the Poor" (Foley), or "Whatsoever You Do" (Jabusch) or have instrumental music playing as the children gather in the space for the Liturgy of the Word.

Place the lectionary on the ambo or lectern. Light the candle placed by the ambo or lectern, and then lead the following prayer:

> **O God,**
> **you care for all those in need and invite us to do the same.**
> **Open our hearts to your Word**
> **so we might know you and follow you more fully.**
> **Through Christ our Lord.**

> *Children:* **Amen.**

First Reading

Amos 8:4–7

Responsorial Psalm

Psalm 113:1–2, 4–6, 7–8 *Sing the same musical setting that is used in your parish's celebration of the liturgy.*

Second Reading

1 Timothy 2:1–8

Sing the Gospel Acclamation used in your parish's celebration of the liturgy.

Gospel Reading

Luke 16:1–13 or 16:10–13

Homily/Reflection

> ≫ **Have you ever seen a balance scale?**

[Display the balance scale or image you brought.] Perhaps you have used one at school or you have seen a picture of one. A beam is balanced in the middle on a point, with a basket on each end. When something is put in one of the baskets and it tips, weights can be put on the other side to make it balance. This was an important tool for buying and selling things in the ancient world.

Scales are still important today to measure weight. When your mom or dad goes to the grocery store to buy bananas, they probably put the bananas in a scale and pay a price based on how much the bananas weigh, rather than the number of bananas. However, what if I was selling bananas and I put them in a balance scale, but I secretly hid an extra weight inside the banana basket? It would look like the bananas weighed more than they really did, wouldn't it? My customer would pay more than the bananas should cost. Would that be fair? No! That's cheating my customer.

In the first reading, we hear from the prophet Amos about people doing exactly this—cheating. Amos was a prophet long before the birth of Jesus. Amos saw how those who had enough to sell were saying "We will . . . fix our scales." This means they were adjusting their scales to look balanced, but actually, people paid too much for the products being weighed and the sellers got more money. The sellers chose money as most important, even when their cheating ways caused people to be hurt. Amos told them that this was not right, that God could see what they were doing. God cares about how we use money and the other things that belong to us.

We can learn from Amos about what is the wrong way, but what is the right way? In the Gospel, Jesus says, "The person who is trustworthy in small matters is also trustworthy in great ones; and the person who is dishonest in very small matters is also dishonest in great ones." What can this mean for us, even as young as we are? It means that God cares about how you use your belongings right now. Maybe it means taking care of the things your parents have provided for you, like putting your shoes away properly and not throwing them off when you come into the house. Or not dragging your backpack on the ground so that it doesn't rip at the bottom. Maybe it means that you share, like when you have two pencils and a friend has none, and you offer what you have. All of these are ways we can use our belongings as God asks us to.

Jesus didn't only talk about being trustworthy with money. He told us the reason why it so important that we use our money rightly. He used a word that might be new to us. He used the word *mammon*, which means "wealth." It is another way of referring to money. Jesus said, "No one can serve two masters. He will either hate one and love the other or be devoted to one and despise the other. You cannot serve God and mammon." We can only have one most important thing in our lives. Jesus wants us to choose God as most important, as who is most important. All our choices, including the choices we make about our money and belongings, can either show that God is most important, or not.

>> **What will you choose today?**

Profession of Faith

Following the homily or reflection, the prayer leader invites everyone to stand to profess our faith. Together, sing or recite the Apostles' or Nicene Creed. Refer the children to the words of the prayer that you have displayed.

Prayer of the Faithful

Leader: **Grateful for our faith, we now bring our prayers to God. Please respond, "O God, graciously hear us."**

May the Church faithfully serve God our Master who provides for all our needs, we pray: *O God, graciously hear us.*

May our wealth be shared among all who are in need around the world, and that God's notion of fairness and justice extend to all who labor, we pray: *O God, graciously hear us.*

May the sick be comforted and healed according to God's will, we pray: *O God, graciously hear us.*

May we be free to give ourselves to God and our neighbor, and never be possessed by our possessions, we pray: *O God, graciously hear us.*

Invite other intercessions from the children, or add intercessions based on the current needs of the Church, the world, the oppressed or marginalized, and the local community. Conclude each of the children's petitions with **"we pray"** and invite the response **"O God, graciously hear us."**

May those who have died see the fullness of justice and mercy in the presence of God, we pray: *O God, graciously hear us.*

**Heavenly Father,
you teach us how we should live.
May we share your blessings with all our brothers and sisters.
Hear us, we pray.
Through Christ our Lord.**

Children: **Amen.**

Quietly return with the children to the main assembly. Be mindful of children having difficulty finding their families.

September 25, 2022
Twenty-Sixth Sunday in Ordinary Time
Woe to the Complacent!

 ## Scripture Background

Connections to Church Teaching and Tradition

❋ "Man, through a life of fidelity to the one God, comes to experience himself as loved by God, and discovers joy in truth and in righteousness—a joy in God which becomes his essential happiness: 'Whom do I have in heaven but you? And there is nothing upon earth that I desire besides you . . . for me it is good to be near God'[1]" (DCE, 10).

❋ "Love of preference for the poor, and the decisions which it inspires in us, cannot but embrace the immense multitudes of the hungry, the needy. . . . It is impossible not to take account of the existence of these realities. To ignore them would mean becoming like the 'rich man' who pretended not to know the beggar Lazarus lying at his gate[2]" (SRS, 42).

❋ "The education of conscience is a lifelong task. . . . Prudent education teaches virtue; it prevents or cures fear, selfishness and pride . . . and feelings of complacency, born of human weakness and faults" (CCC, 1784).

Amos 6:1a, 4–7 Today's reading from the prophet Amos follows the same lines as last week's, only with stronger language and the announcement of an unambiguous day of reckoning. In this passage Amos seems to be describing a celebration that included a feast. He could hardly do more to emphasize the luxury enjoyed by the wealthy participants. The beds (couches) on which they lounged had ivory inlay and their meat was the choicest, from calves that had been kept tethered so that they would be the fattest and juiciest. They even drank from the bowls reserved for sacrificial use, demonstrating the height of their arrogance. Their complacency had roots in a variety of circumstances. They were wealthy, their social status gave them a feeling of unique importance, and they felt that God's choice of Israel was irrevocable (see 5:14, 6:1).

The people at this feast supposed that their celebration made them closer to God, but it had the opposite effect. Earlier, Amos had condemned their sacrifices saying in the name of God, "I despise your feasts / . . . take away from me / your noisy songs / . . . let justice surge like waters / and righteousness like an unfailing stream" (5:21–23). Because they did not do that, the self-satisfied revelers would soon be the first to go into exile.

Psalm 146:7, 8–9, 9–10 (1b) It may seem contradictory to follow God's guarantee of exile with praise of God's unwavering faithfulness, but as this psalm develops we come to understand more and more about what God's faithfulness entails. As we sang in last week's psalm, God is first and foremost faithful to the poor and the needy. Thus, we can also proclaim that the Lord loves the just. It is precisely that love for the little ones that leads God to thwart the way of the wicked. Only those who share God's care for the poor and pursue righteousness will rejoice in knowing that the Lord will reign forever.

1 Timothy 6:11–16 Paul tells Timothy to pursue righteousness, and we could understand the next few verses as an explanation of what he meant. To be righteous entails many things. It begins with conducting oneself in a way that is pleasing to God and fulfilling the law. It also means meeting one's obligations to others. Thus, Paul follows the injunction to pursue righteousness by mentioning "devotion" (6:11), or *piety*, a word which implies that one participates knowledgeably in worship and with the fear of the Lord that flows from awe at what God has wrought in creation and human history. *Faith*, as used here, involves two things: faithfulness to his vocation and the message he preaches, or the ongoing development of his own faith. In reality, the two are complementary: faithfulness to the mission will include growth in his own faith. Next, Paul uses the word *agape* for "love." That is a love that chooses to give preference to others; it is based in the will, not the emotions. Patience and gentleness also complement one another, as they are expressions of agape. Paul's injunction reminds Timothy that a man of God is one who continually pursues the fulfillment of his vocation to be pleasing to God. It is a reality and a process.

Luke 16:19–31 In this parable, unique to Luke's account of the Gospel, Jesus has Abraham remind the rich man, "They have Moses and the prophets. Let them listen to them" (16:29). Had the rich man paid attention to the prophet Amos? Had he prayed the psalms? Given his opulent life, what right did he have to call Abraham Father? There is an immense contrast between the two main characters here. The rich man is known only by his possessions while the poor man has a name—the only person to be named in any of Jesus' parables. While Lazarus lay outside,

---

1. Psalm 73 (72):25, 28.
2. Luke 16:19–31.

the rich man feasted in his own home. The rich man wore luxurious clothing and Lazarus was covered with sores. The rich man left scraps under his table while unclean dogs attended Lazarus. Death brought the reversal. The rich man simply died, and Lazarus is carried off by the angels. Lazarus is in the position of highest bliss while the rich man was confined to the place of the dead.

Jesus addressed this parable to the money-loving Pharisees who had mocked him for his teaching about the right use of material goods. He was critiquing their complacency in the face of the needs of others. The parable calls us, too, to consider how our own complacency might thwart our pursuit of righteousness.

Preparation

Each of the readings today speak of the dangers of complacency. The prophet Amos described a community of immense wealth who were well fed and entertained, and consequently were untroubled by the collapse of their country. The First Letter to Timothy makes clear that this kind of complacency must be avoided to give full and irreproachable testimony to Jesus Christ. Finally, in the Gospel, the effect of the rich man's complacency results in the painful torment of separation from God. We are exhorted to avoid the model of the rich man and serve as witnesses to the love and compassion of Jesus Christ with fortitude and perseverance.

Lectionary for Mass #138C

Amos 6:1a, 4–7

Psalm 146:7, 8–9, 9–10 (1b)

1 Timothy 6:11–16

Luke 16:19–31

Objectives

- To announce our invitation to eternal life as arising from Christ's crossing the great chasm between life and death on our behalf.

- To introduce *Dives* as a traditional name for the rich man in Luke's Gospel passage. Note: Possible pronunciations are "DAI-veez," "DEE-vays," or "DEE-ways," but not "DIVES" as pronounced in English. Contemporary translations do not generally use this name. Use your best judgment on whether this discussion benefits the children you are serving to hear a proper name, "Dives," or "the rich man."

Preparation and Materials

- Read the Season Background, the lectionary readings, and the Scripture Background.

- Bookmark the appropriate readings (see page xiv) in the lectionary, children's lectionary, or Bible. Place the book in a convenient location for the leader.

- Write the words of dismissal on a card for the priest celebrant.

- Prepare the words of the song the children will sing as they gather in the space for the Liturgy of the Word.

- Select volunteers (older children or adults) to proclaim the readings.

- Display the responsorial psalm refrain lyrics.

- Display the Apostles' or Nicene Creed.

- Prepare intercessions for the Prayer of the Faithful adapted for the needs of the Church, world, oppressed or marginalized, and local community.

Prayer Leader Reflection Questions

>> **When have you been complacent in your life of faith? How might you avoid becoming complacent?**

>> **How do you cultivate practices of virtue in your daily life, so that you might "compete well for the faith"?**

Procession

Following the Collect of the Mass, the priest celebrant picks up the lectionary and invites those who would like to participate in the Liturgy of the Word with children to come forward and gather in the center aisle. The people who will lead the children out and facilitate the Liturgy of the Word also come forward at this time. Holding the lectionary so that all can see, the priest celebrant sends the children forth using his own words or the following:

> *Priest*: **Dear children, God uses the seasons to teach us many things, and in fall, God teaches us about letting go. As the trees lose their leaves and the world prepares for winter sleep, we too can focus on what we need to change and what we need to let go of in our lives. Go now with your prayer leader(s) to listen for what God might be asking of you. May peace be with all of you.**

The leader processes out holding the lectionary, and the children follow behind. The parish music minister may have selected a song of dismissal for the assembly to sing while the children leave. A good option is "The Word of God: Children's Dismissal" by M. D. Ridge and Timothy R. Smith (WLP/GIA).

Centering

Continue to sing the song of dismissal that the assembly sang as you left the church. Or sing the refrain from "Whatsoever You Do" (Jabusch), or have instrumental music playing as the children gather in the space for the Liturgy of the Word.

Place the lectionary on the ambo or lectern. Light the candle placed by the ambo or lectern, and then lead the following prayer:

> **Loving God,**
> **we praise you and thank you for this time together.**
> **Help us hear your Word so our hearts may be changed by it.**
> **Through Christ our Lord.**

> *Children:* **Amen.**

First Reading

Amos 6:1a, 4–7

Responsorial Psalm

Psalm 146:7, 8–9, 9–10 (1b) *Sing the same musical setting that is used in your parish's celebration of the liturgy.*

Second Reading

1 Timothy 6:11–16

Gospel Acclamation

Sing the Gospel Acclamation used in your parish's celebration of the liturgy.

Gospel Reading

Luke 16:19–31

Homily/Reflection

In today's Gospel, we hear Jesus talk about two men who died. The two men in the story lived different lives, which led them to very different ends. The first man is a rich man. In Latin, the word for "wealthy" is *dives [see Objectives]* and people in the Church have sometimes called the rich man by this name. When we hear the description of his life, we know that he was very wealthy, indeed. He wore "fine linen," which is a kind of cloth that is very soft, and it was dyed purple, the color of royalty. His meals were "sumptuous," which means they were big meals of rich, delicious food. Lazarus, on the other hand, was very poor. Instead of his body described as being covered in soft and beautiful linen, his body was covered in sores. He would have liked to have eaten the scraps from the rich man's table, but perhaps he didn't even have that. This was someone who suffered greatly.

When both men died, each experienced a different afterlife. To see Lazarus in the "bosom of Abraham," where he had been carried off by angels, the rich man had to look up. Abraham called the space between them a "chasm," a space too deep and wide to cross. The rich man was separated not only from Lazarus, but also from God, and it was so painful that Jesus called it "torment."

Even in death, though, the rich man still thought of himself as more important than Lazarus. He wanted Lazarus to act as his servant. He never even talked directly to Lazarus, neither in life or nor after death. He instead talked to Abraham and asked him to send Lazarus. He wanted Lazarus to cross that great chasm, a task that would have seemed quite treacherous, just so he could give the rich man a drop of water. When Abraham explained this was not possible, the rich man still expected Lazarus to serve his family. The rich man didn't understand that his wealth and power did him no good in death, and the way he treated other people was what mattered more.

As listeners today, we know that after Jesus shared this, and told much more to those who would listen, that he died and then rose again. He was the one who *could* cross a chasm, to share eternal life in the presence of God with those who had died. Jesus wants to share this gift of eternal life with us.

>> **How might we pay attention to Jesus' teachings? How might we respond to the gift that he offers?**

We can respond to the gift by listening to the words of the Bible in order to understand more fully who God is and what God asks of us. We can respond to the gift by using our power and our things for the good of those who are most in need, instead of to make ourselves seem more important. We can respond to the gift by saying yes to Christ's invitation to love God, our neighbor and ourselves. We can learn not to be like the rich man, and we have the hope of one day joining Lazarus in the bosom of Abraham.

Profession of Faith

Following the homily or reflection, the prayer leader invites everyone to stand to profess our faith. Together, sing or recite the Apostles' or Nicene Creed. Refer the children to the words of the prayer that you have displayed.

Prayer of the Faithful

Leader: **Today we heard that the rich man sinned because he was not concerned with the poor man outside his door. Let us pray that our eyes and hearts be always open to the needs of others, especially those around us. Please respond, "Lord, hear our prayer."**

That the Church may always pursue righteousness, devotion, faith, love, patience, and gentleness, we pray: *Lord, hear our prayer.*

That all people of goodwill may never ignore the cries of those who suffer but use what we have to serve those in need, we pray: *Lord, hear our prayer.*

That the sick, especially those who suffer painful skin conditions, may be mindful of God's care and comfort, we pray: *Lord, hear our prayer.*

That our parish community may constantly give witness to the message of the Gospel, we pray: *Lord, hear our prayer.*

Invite other intercessions from the children, or add intercessions based on the current needs of the Church, the world, the oppressed or marginalized, and the local community. Conclude each of the children's petitions with **"we pray"** and invite the response **"Lord, hear our prayer."**

That those who have died may be welcomed into the bosom of Abraham, we pray: *Lord, hear our prayer.*

Mighty God,
we rejoice in your greatness and power,
your gentleness and love,
your mercy and justice.
Accept the prayers your children bring before you.
Through Christ our Lord.

Children: **Amen.**

Quietly return with the children to the main assembly. Be mindful of children having difficulty finding their families.

October 2, 2022
Twenty-Seventh Sunday in Ordinary Time
God Hears and Responds

 ## Scripture Background

Connections to Church Teaching and Tradition

● "Certain constant characteristics appear throughout the Psalms: . . . the distraught . . . believer who, in his preferential love for the Lord, is exposed to a host of enemies and temptations, but who waits upon what the faithful God will do, in the certitude of his love and in submission to his will" (CCC, 2589).

● "All . . . disciples of Christ, persevering in prayer and praising God . . . , should present themselves as a sacrifice, living, holy and pleasing to God. . . . They should everywhere on earth bear witness to Christ and give an answer to everyone who asks a reason for their hope of eternal life" (LG, 10).

● "Until the arrival of the new heavens and the new earth in which justice dwells . . . the pilgrim church, in its sacraments and institutions, which belong to this present age, carries the mark of this world which will pass, and it takes its place among the creatures which groan and until now suffer the pains of childbirth and awaits the revelation of the children of God" (LG, 48).

Habakkuk 1:2–3; 2:2–4   Habakkuk cries out to the Lord for help, but the Lord appears not to pay attention and is not responding. Violence, ruin, misery, destruction, strife, and clamorous discord envelop Habakkuk and God's people, yet the Lord appears distant and uncaring. In times of crisis, we, like Habakkuk, cry out to the Lord in frustration at our inability to do much about what is happening. Crying out is a way of affirming and trusting that only the Lord's care and response will get us through the crisis. Habakkuk is assured in a vision that the Lord knows and cares for the people and is going to do something about it. However, the resolution will be accomplished on God's time frame, not ours. Meanwhile, we wait on the Lord for the promised vision to be fulfilled. The rash, who cannot wait on the Lord, lack faith, trust, and integrity. The just, those who have faith and trust and wait upon the Lord, shall live and experience God's power on behalf of the people. God's covenant love is ever faithful and trustworthy and will never disappoint. All who claim covenant relationship with God must trust and wait upon the Lord, always assured that God does hear and respond.

Psalm 95:1–2, 6–7, 8–9 (8)   Psalm 95, which begins the morning office in the Liturgy of the Hours, contextualizes praise and worship of God within Temple liturgy, affirming God as "the Rock of our salvation" (95:1b), our creator and shepherd who protects and guides. With joyful songs of thanksgiving, the psalmist invites all to come into the Lord's presence, bow down, and kneel before our creator, shepherd, and Lord. Faithful covenant-love relationship demands that we attune ourselves to our shepherd who knows and guides us. The last stanza challenges all to pay attention to God's voice and not to harden hearts the way their ancestors did in the desert, even though God had done marvelous deeds on their behalf in liberating them from slavery in Egypt. The word "today" (95:7d) highlights the lived reality that God continues to do marvelous things today. We need to trust, wait on the Lord, and have attentive ears and open hearts. In this manner we will experience God's covenant love and see fruits of that love lived out in our everyday lives.

2 Timothy 1:6–8, 13–14   The author, writing as if he were Paul, exhorts Timothy, a disciple commissioned for ministry, to "stir into flame" (1:6) the original fervor that was his when appointed "through the imposition of my hands" (1:6). Ministry is not to be done in a spirit of cowardice but rather through God's gift of "power and love and self-control" (1:7). Amid the difficulty and challenge of proclaiming God's countercultural message, Timothy is asked to bear the hardship of the Gospel proclamation with the "strength that comes from God" (1:8). The sound words that were handed on to him by Paul and others are to be guarded and cherished and, with the help of the Spirit, are to be creatively handed on to others so that others may experience that "faith and love that are in Christ Jesus" (1:13). The challenge of ministry is to know and trust that God is always with us, no matter how difficult the journey.

Luke 17:5–10   Luke's Jesus uses his journey to Jerusalem as a curriculum for discipleship. In today's reading, Jesus responds to the disciples' request while providing another occasion for addressing different demands of discipleship. To the disciples' request to "increase our faith" (17:5), Jesus clarifies that having faith per se—and not its quantity—is what truly matters. If one truly believes, then faith as small as a mustard seed, the smallest of all seeds, will prove to be powerful enough to accomplish great or impossible things, like moving a large, strong-rooted tree into the sea.

The second instruction on discipleship is more involved but essentially examines the responsibilities of discipleship. Disciples called to serve others should not expect rewards or bonuses for doing what is required of them. The unsettling example of interaction between master and slave teaches that disciples do what is expected without seeking laurels. The expression at the end of the reading, "we are unprofitable servants" (17:10), is best translated as follows: "we are not owed anything; we have done what we were obliged to do." Like Habakkuk in the first reading and Timothy in the second reading, discipleship demands faith and trust, waiting upon the Lord and knowing that God hears and responds, thus affecting the good work to which we have been called. We are owed nothing else.

Preparation

In this week's Gospel reading, Jesus responds to the disciples' request for more faith by offering several images to invite listeners to understand the consequences of faith. With the children, we focus on the images of the mustard seed and the mulberry tree, which illuminate how even the smallest bit of faith in a powerful God can yield amazing and surprising results. Jesus also shares the tale of the unprofitable servant. We recognize that faith inevitably leads to service and the ultimate results do not belong to us, but to the one we serve.

Lectionary for Mass #141C

Habakkuk 1:2–3, 2:2–4

Psalm 95:1–2, 6–7, 8–9 (8)

2 Timothy 1:6–8, 13–14

Luke 17:5–10 (141)

Objectives

- To explore the image of a mulberry tree moving itself as a model of the amazing and surprising action of the power of God in whom we have faith.

- To explain the concept of having faith.

Preparation and Materials

- Read the Season Background, the lectionary readings, and the Scripture Background.

- Bookmark the appropriate readings (see page xiv) in the lectionary, children's lectionary, or Bible. Place the book in a convenient location for the leader.

- Write the words of dismissal on a card for the priest celebrant.

- Prepare the words of the song the children will sing as they gather in the space for the Liturgy of the Word.

- Select volunteers (older children or adults) to proclaim the readings.

- Display the responsorial psalm refrain lyrics.

- Display the Apostles' or Nicene Creed.

- Prepare intercessions for the Prayer of the Faithful adapted for the needs of the Church, world, oppressed or marginalized, and local community.

- If possible, provide various seeds and a photo of a fully grown mulberry tree to show the children.

Prayer Leader Reflection Questions

>> How deep is your faith? How are you cultivating a faith that grows?

>> Where do you see the miraculous actions of God? Is your faith big enough to recognize it when it is most amazing and surprising?

Procession

Following the Collect of the Mass, the priest celebrant picks up the lectionary and invites those who would like to participate in the Liturgy of the Word with children to come forward and gather in the center aisle. The people who will lead the children out and facilitate the Liturgy of the Word also come forward at this time. Holding the lectionary so that all can see, the priest celebrant sends the children forth using his own words or the following:

> *Priest*: **Dear children, God uses the seasons to teach us many things, and in fall, God teaches us about letting go. As the trees lose their leaves and the world prepares for winter sleep, we too can focus on what we need to change and what we need to let go of in our lives. Go now with your prayer leader(s) to listen for what God might be asking of you. May peace be with all of you.**

The leader processes out holding the lectionary, and the children follow behind. The parish music minister may have selected a song of dismissal for the assembly to sing while the children leave. A good option is "The Word of God: Children's Dismissal" by M. D. Ridge and Timothy R. Smith (WLP/GIA).

Centering

Continue to sing the song of dismissal that the assembly sang as you left the church. Or sing the refrain from "We Walk by Faith" (SHANTI) or have instrumental music playing as the children gather in the space for the Liturgy of the Word.

Place the lectionary on the ambo or lectern. Light the candle placed by the ambo or lectern, and then lead the following prayer:

> **All-powerful God,**
> **prepare our minds**
> **to hear and heed your holy word.**
> **May we always follow the example of Jesus Christ, your Son,**
> **in whose name we pray.**

> *Children*: **Amen.**

First Reading

Habakkuk 1:2–3, 2:2–4

Responsorial Psalm

Psalm 95:1–2, 6–7, 8–9 (8) *Sing the same musical setting that is used in your parish's celebration of the liturgy.*

Second Reading

2 Timothy 1:6–8, 13–14

Gospel Acclamation

Sing the Gospel Acclamation used in your parish's celebration of the liturgy.

Gospel Reading

Luke 17:5–10

Homily/Reflection

[Invite children to see and touch various seeds you brought.] Maybe you have held a kernel of corn, a lima bean, or an acorn in your hand. You could look at it and see its different parts: the seed coat, the baby root, and leaf inside. You could feel the weight of it. A mustard seed, especially one from Israel where Jesus lived, is so much smaller. It is about the size of a period at the end of a sentence. It is so small that, unless you are looking for it, you might never see it. If you blow on it too hard, it might blow away. That's how small a mustard seed is!

Yet somehow this tiny seed does what all seeds do. When it goes into the ground it begins to change and grow. It turns into a sprout that slowly peeks out of the earth, but it gets larger and larger until eventually it is a huge plant. Within the seed, there is power to grow.

>> **How many of you have ever planted a seed and watched it grow?**
> *[Invite children to share their experiences for one minute.]*

Some seeds even grow into huge trees. A mulberry tree might grow to be as tall as a house! *[Show photo of mulberry tree]* But have you ever seen a huge tree pull itself out of the ground and move to someplace new? Jesus spoke of a mulberry tree doing just that, and not only moving to someplace new, but into the sea. Trees like the mulberry tree normally need fresh water to live, and yet this tree that moves itself chooses salt water as a new home.

>> **Can you imagine how amazing and surprising this would be?**

>> **What kind of power could cause this to happen? Whose power is strong enough to make such a thing happen?**

We know the answer to this question: It is God's power. In today's Gospel, Jesus tells us that faith has power, too, even if it is only as small as a mustard seed. Our faith is in a God who can do surprising and amazing things. But we need to work to cultivate our faith. When we ask for faith, God hears us and God will give us what that we need. It takes time, it takes opening our hearts and listening for God's response, it takes prayer. Prayer brings us closer to God. God wants for us all to spend some time with him in prayer, growing closer to him. Imagine how lots of people with just a tiny bit of faith all come together and create something really beautiful, like our church community. When we put all of our little bits of faith together, our faith grows into the faith of the whole Church.

When we spend time with God—in prayer, by coming to Mass, by listening to the stories of the Bible, for example—all of this will strengthen our relationship with God and increase our faith. One thing that we can appreciate about the Apostles is that they asked Jesus to make their faith stronger. It is really special that when we love someone we want to get even closer to them. So when we love God, we can ask for our faith to be stronger. We can ask to get closer to God.

Profession of Faith

Following the homily or reflection, the prayer leader invites everyone to stand to profess our faith. Together, sing or recite the Apostles' or Nicene Creed. Refer the children to the words of the prayer that you have displayed.

Prayer of the Faithful

Leader: **Trusting in the love and mercy of Almighty God, we bring all our needs before him. Please respond, "Lord, hear us."**

May the leaders of our Church be strengthened in their trust in the amazing and surprising power of God, we pray: *Lord, hear us.*

May the leaders of our government seek God's wisdom to protect all of creation, especially those of us who are so tiny we can barely be seen, we pray: *Lord, hear us.*

May there be greater respect for the lives of the elderly, the disabled, and the sick, that God's Spirit of comfort be with them, and may that same Spirit guide those who help them, we pray: *Lord, hear us.*

May those whose work involves the care of seeds see God's presence in creation, we pray: *Lord, hear us.*

Invite other intercessions from the children, or add intercessions based on the current needs of the Church, the world, the oppressed or marginalized, and the local community. Conclude each of the children's petitions with **"we pray"** and invite the response **"Lord, hear us."**

May all who have died, like the seed that is planted in the earth, experience an abundance of new life in heaven, we pray: *Lord, hear us.*

**Eternal God,
with you nothing is impossible.
Accept the prayers of your children.
Through Christ our Lord.**

Children: **Amen.**

Quietly return with the children to the main assembly. Be mindful of children having difficulty finding their families.

October 9, 2022
Twenty-Eighth Sunday in Ordinary Time
God Offers Salvation to All

 ## Scripture Background

Connections to Church Teaching and Tradition

- "Its [the Church's] joy in communicating Jesus Christ is expressed both by a concern to preach him to areas in greater need and in constantly going forth to the outskirts of its own territory or towards new sociocultural settings" (EG, 30).

- "The salvation which God has wrought, and the Church joyfully proclaims, is for everyone. God has found a way to unite himself to every human being in every age. He has chosen to call them together as a people and not as isolated individuals" (EG, 113).

- "Whether it aids the world or whether it benefits from it, the church has but one sole purpose—that the kingdom of God may come and the salvation of the human race may be accomplished. Every benefit the people of God can confer on humanity during its earthly pilgrimage is rooted in the church's being 'the universal sacrament of salvation,' at once manifesting and actualizing the mystery of God's love for humanity" (GS, 45).

2 Kings 5:14–17   Naaman, an Aramean general, a Gentile, and a leper, comes to the Israelite prophet Elisha requesting a cure. Elisha asks him to plunge into the Jordan River seven times. While initially refusing to humiliate himself by so doing, Naaman changes his mind and finds himself cured. In thanksgiving for his cure, he offers Elisha a gift that the prophet refuses. This long-distance miracle in which the prophet was not even present is due to God's graciousness and not Elisha's efforts. Naaman comes to believe in Israel's God as the only God "in all the earth" (5:15). Desiring to worship only Israel's God, Naaman asks for earth from the land so that when he returns home he will still be connected to and worship only the God of Israel, the only God in all the earth. Naaman's healing and conversion is a rich example of God's gracious offer of salvation to all, Jew and Gentile alike.

Psalm 98:1, 2–3, 3–4 (see 2b)   This enthronement psalm, extolling the kingship of God over all creation, invites all to sing a new song to the Lord, who has done wonderful deeds and proved victorious over all the earth. Connecting it with both the first reading's cure of the Gentile leper Naaman and the Gospel reading's cure of the ten lepers, including a Samaritan, the psalm proclaims that God has made salvation known in the sight of all the nations. God's covenant love, expressed as "kindness and . . . faithfulness" (98:3) toward Israel, is all-inclusive, enabling God's victory over chaos and disorder, and resulting in the establishment of justice and right relationship with all. God's graciousness toward Naaman is a manifestation to all the earth of God's saving power. Such deep and abiding covenant love for all humanity moves the psalmist to invite all to "sing joyfully to the LORD, all you lands" (98:4).

2 Timothy 2:8–13   The author of 2 Timothy continues to exhort Timothy, the community's leader, to remember and thus make present in his ministry, the heart of the Gospel: that Jesus Christ, a descendant of David, is risen from the dead. The author refers to Paul's imprisonment on behalf of that Gospel, and to the "chains" (2:9) endured for the sake of proclaiming it, "But the word of God is not chained" (2:9). Therefore Timothy, in imitation of Paul, is exhorted to "bear with everything for the sake of those who are chosen, so that they too may obtain the salvation that is in Christ Jesus" (2:10). God's graciousness, so freely and abundantly gifted to us in Christ, is for all. The reading ends with a poetic hymn highlighting numerous baptismal themes. If we die with Christ we shall also live with him, and if we persevere in living the Gospel we shall reign with him. If we refuse to acknowledge the Lord, however, we cut ourselves off from covenant relationship always freely offered. Even when we are unfaithful, God's covenant love remains always faithful, enduring, and always welcoming.

Luke 17:11–19   As Jesus continues his journey to Jerusalem, he travels through Samaria, where he encounters ten lepers. Lepers were to stay away from villages and were to warn people with bells and sounds to stay away. People were not to approach lepers. These ten outcasts risk approaching Jesus and ask for pity and compassion. Jesus risks approaching and speaking to them, telling them to go show themselves to the priests who would determine if they were clean of their leprosy and fit to join the community. On the way, they are cleansed of their leprosy. Only one returns, "glorifying God . . . , and he fell at the feet of Jesus and thanked him" (17:15). He was a Samaritan, a foreigner and an outcast. Jesus, commenting on the others who did not return to give thanks, acknowledges the foreigner and says, "Stand up and go; your faith has saved you" (17:19). Like Naaman, the Samaritan leper is cured physically but, in the process, comes to deeper faith and enters into covenant love with God.

For Luke, Jesus is the savior of all humanity breaking down boundaries and sharing God's graciousness with all, most especially the outcast, the foreigner, and the marginalized. Naaman the Aramean and the Samaritan leper, both foreigners and outcasts, become models of faith and thanksgiving in response to God's all-inclusive gracious covenant love, singing of God's saving power that they have seen and experienced. Jesus reached out to all, regardless of the risk. As disciples we too are called to risk reaching out to the marginalized and outcasts of our day manifesting God's gracious love for them in all our encounters.

 # Preparation

In this Sunday's Gospel, we hear of Jesus giving the gift of healing to ten lepers, one of whom is a Samaritan. Exploring the social significance of identity as lepers and Samaritans helps children to appreciate the depth of the gift that is offered. We know that the beauty and greatness of the gift is a foretaste of the kingdom of God that will be experienced in full at the parousia.

Lectionary for Mass #144C

2 Kings 5:14–17

Psalm 98:1, 2–3, 3–4 (see 2b)

2 Timothy 2:8–13

Luke 17:11–19

Objectives

- To introduce and explain the terms *leprosy* and *Samaritan*.

- To consider together God's healing action and our capacity to express gratitude.

Preparation and Materials

- Read the Season Background, the lectionary readings, and the Scripture Background.

- Bookmark the appropriate readings (see page xiv) in the lectionary, children's lectionary, or Bible. Place the book in a convenient location for the leader.

- Write the words of dismissal on a card for the priest celebrant.

- Prepare the words of the song the children will sing as they gather in the space for the Liturgy of the Word.

- Select volunteers (older children or adults) to proclaim the readings.

- Display the responsorial psalm refrain lyrics.

- Display the Apostles' or Nicene Creed.

- Prepare intercessions for the Prayer of the Faithful adapted for the needs of the Church, world, oppressed or marginalized, and local community.

Prayer Leader Reflection Questions

≫ **Who in your community is on the outside? How might you reach out to them in an effort to be more inclusive?**

≫ **What healing have you experienced in your own life? How do you express gratitude for it?**

Procession

Following the Collect of the Mass, the priest celebrant picks up the lectionary and invites those who would like to participate in the Liturgy of the Word with children to come forward and gather in the center aisle. The people who will lead the children out and facilitate the Liturgy of the Word also come forward at this time. Holding the lectionary so that all can see, the priest celebrant sends the children forth using his own words or the following:

> *Priest*: **Dear children, God uses the seasons to teach us many things, and in fall, God teaches us about letting go. As the trees lose their leaves and the world prepares for winter sleep, we too can focus on what we need to change and what we need to let go of in our lives. Go now with your prayer leader(s) to listen for what God might be asking of you. May peace be with all of you.**

The leader processes out holding the lectionary, and the children follow behind. The parish music minister may have selected a song of dismissal for the assembly to sing while the children leave. A good option is "The Word of God: Children's Dismissal" by M. D. Ridge and Timothy R. Smith (WLP/GIA).

Centering

Continue to sing the song of dismissal that the assembly sang as you left the church. Or sing the refrain from "All My Days" (Schutte, Murray), or have instrumental music playing as the children gather in the space for the Liturgy of the Word.

Place the lectionary on the ambo or lectern. Light the candle placed by the ambo or lectern, and then lead the following prayer:

> **O Lord of Grace,**
> **help us to move into a deeper understanding of your truth.**
> **We ask that these words of life, truth, and hope**
> **help us grow into better followers of your Son,**
> **Jesus Christ our Lord.**

> *Children:* **Amen.**

First Reading

2 Kings 5:14–17

Responsorial Psalm

Psalm 98:1, 2–3, 3–4 (see 2b) *Sing the same musical setting that is used in your parish's celebration of the liturgy.*

Second Reading

2 Timothy 2:8–13

Gospel Acclamation

Sing the Gospel Acclamation used in your parish's celebration of the liturgy.

Gospel Reading

Luke 17:11–19

Homily/Reflection

>> **What does it feel like to be left out?**

At the time that Jesus walked and talked with his friends on the earth like you and I do now, people sometimes caught a disease called leprosy. It still exists, but we are blessed to live in a time when there is medicine to treat it. During Jesus' time, though, there was no medicine. Leprosy is highly contagious, so in Jesus' time, when someone was known to have leprosy, that person had to move away and live alone or with a few other people who were sick with the disease to protect everyone else. Having leprosy meant being left out of a life shared with the community.

When Jesus was on his way to Jerusalem, he came through a community of people who had leprosy. This community was in a particular place, near Samaria. The people who live in Samaria are called Samaritans. For the people of Israel, the Samaritans were enemies. They did some things like the people of Israel, but they did not worship God in Jerusalem. As Jesus passed, these lepers recognized that he might be able to help them. They called out and asked for his help. Jesus gave them an instruction common at that time: "Go and show yourselves to the priests." It was the job of the priest to decide whether a person had been healed and was safe enough to return to the community. The lepers obeyed Jesus' instructions and discovered on their way that they had indeed been healed!

» **Can you imagine receiving this gift of healing?**

» **What would it be like to have been so lonely and left out and to have expected to feel that way for the rest of your life, and then to discover that you were healthy and could come back to the community?**

» **When we have received a wonderful gift, is there something we might like to do, or perhaps to say?**

We might like to say thank you. When the lepers discovered they had been healed, only one out of the ten did that. But which one? For the people of Israel who followed Jesus, they might have found the answer most surprising. The one who came back to say thank you was a Samaritan. It was the outsider, the enemy of the people of Israel, who saw that the healing power that had saved him from his suffering came from Jesus and expressed gratitude to him.

» **What does this tell us about the kingdom of God?**

When we hear in the Word of God about miracles, we know what heaven must be like; we have a glimpse of when we will experience God's kingdom in fullness.

» **What will the kingdom be like? Who will be there?**

» **As we ponder the gift of the kingdom that God offers to us, how will we respond?**

Profession of Faith

Following the homily or reflection, the prayer leader invites everyone to stand to profess our faith. Together, sing or recite the Apostles' or Nicene Creed. Refer the children to the words of the prayer that you have displayed.

Prayer of the Faithful

Leader: **God gives us so much: the life of grace, healing, pardon. Sometimes we forget to thank him. Let us bring our needs before him today in a spirit of gratitude. Please respond, "Lord, hear our prayer."**

For the leaders of our Church, especially those who serve in places where Christians are outsiders, let us pray: *Lord, hear our prayer.*

For our political leaders, that they may protect those who suffer most, let us pray: *Lord, hear our prayer.*

For all the sick, that they might feel the healing power of Jesus, let us pray: *Lord, hear our prayer.*

For all who have experienced God's gift of salvation, that they may offer him thanks and spread the faith to others, let us pray: *Lord, hear our prayer.*

Invite other intercessions from the children, or add intercessions based on the current needs of the Church, the world, the oppressed or marginalized, and the local community. Conclude each of the children's petitions with **"let us pray"** and invite the response **"Lord, hear our prayer."**

For those who have died, that they may enter into the fullness of the kingdom of God, where there is no suffering and sickness, let us pray: *Lord, hear our prayer.*

Father,
we thank you for hearing us.
As you grant our prayers, help us to be faithful all our days
to our Lord Jesus Christ,
in whose name we pray.

Children: **Amen.**

Quietly return with the children to the main assembly. Be mindful of children having difficulty finding their families.

October 16, 2022
Twenty-Ninth Sunday in Ordinary Time

Prayer Opens Us to God

 ## Scripture Background

Connections to Church Teaching and Tradition

❀ "We only devote periods of quiet time to the things or the people whom we love; and here we are speaking of the God whom we love, a God who wishes to speak to us. Because of this love, we can take as much time as we need, like every true disciple: 'Speak, Lord, for your servant is listening'" (EG, 146).

❀ "Praying 'our' Father opens to us the dimensions of his love revealed in Christ" (CCC, 2793).

❀ "'The Lord's Prayer is truly the summary of the whole gospel,'[1] the 'most perfect of prayers.'[2] It is at the center of the Scriptures" (CCC, 2774).

Exodus 17:8–13   Joshua, mentioned for the first time in the Torah, is designated by Moses as leader of the ensuing battle with the Amalekites, a nomadic tribe that controlled southern trade routes to and from Egypt. The dispute probably centered on land or water rights, things essential for desert survival. Moses with Aaron, his brother, and Hur situate themselves on a hill to oversee the battle. Moses displays the staff of God that aided the people in their liberation from Egypt, and extends hands in a typical prophetic manner, mediating God's favor on behalf of the people. Whenever he got tired and let down his hands, the battle favored Amalek, so Aaron and Hur assist Moses by providing a seated place and by supporting his hands. In this manner, victory by Joshua on behalf of God's people was assured. God's power mediated through Moses, not human machinations, brings about the victory that God desired.

Psalm 121:1–2, 3–4, 5–6, 7–8 (see 2)   This psalm of trust and confidence in God's help assures the psalmist and the community that our creator God will never fail us. Amid dangerous travel through mountains or hills, our ever-attentive God will not cause our feet to slip. Our guardian God protects and shades us from the dangerous effects of both sun and moon, always at our right side and easily accessible. Our very life is in the hands of God, who will guard it always from evil and every other harm. Prayer enables us to develop a deeper knowledge of God, who initiates an eternal love relationship with us, and who is ever ready to be there in all our coming and going. Prayer also enables us to respond to that love invitation with mutual love that both satisfies and never ends.

2 Timothy 3:14 — 4:2   Timothy is encouraged to "remain faithful" (3:14) to what he has heard and come to believe not only from people like Paul but also from his family. Such "wisdom for salvation" (3:15) comes from being immersed in the Sacred Scriptures, now linked to faith in Jesus Christ. "Sacred Scriptures" refers to the Old Testament for there was no New Testament. Some Christians tend to see little value in the Old Testament, focusing almost exclusively on the New Testament. This passage states clearly that "all Scripture is inspired by God" (3:16), and useful throughout life as a guide to come to know God and what God desires.

Like Timothy, we are charged with sharing the "wisdom for salvation" (3:15) gained from immersion in Scripture and through faith in Christ Jesus. Reflecting prayerfully on the Scriptures opens us up to God, enabling us to know God more deeply. We are to proclaim this wisdom "whether it is convenient or inconvenient" (4:2). Even when challenged, discouraged, opposed, or rejected, we are to carry on "through all patience and teaching" (4:2). All prayer should be rooted in Scripture, allowing its "wisdom for salvation" (3:15) to suffuse all our actions and relationships.

Luke 18:1–8   Luke sets the parable of the widow and the unjust judge in the context of advising persistence in prayer. The parable characterizes the unjust judge as fearing neither God nor humans, and correspondingly devoid of feeling or compassion for anyone. The powerless widow who has been treated unjustly comes demanding justice. The uncaring judge delays judgment, but the widow's persistence breaks down the judge who finally relents and administers justice, ultimately fearing some retribution from the widow. Jesus uses the widow's persistent demand for justice as a model for a disciple's prayer posture toward an attentive and compassionate God.

1. Turtullian, *De orat.* 1: PL 1, 1251–1255.
2. St. Thomas Aquinas, *Summa Theologica,* II–II, 83, 9.

Prayer opens us up to God, enabling us to turn with confidence to a loving and compassionate God who listens and responds. However, the response comes on God's timeline, not ours. We are asked to trust and know that God will respond, no matter how long the wait. The passage ends with an end-time question concerning faith. When Jesus returns, will the disciple's faith and trust still be evident? Or will the disciple have given up on faith, thinking that God does not care and will never respond? The parables encourages all disciples to pray and have faith in a loving and compassionate God who cares, listens, and always responds.

 # Preparation

In today's Gospel, we hear Jesus share a parable in which we are invited to seek out God in prayer just as the widow sought justice from the unjust judge. The widow received what she asked from someone who cared nothing for her. How much more can we trust in God's answer to our requests when we know that God loves us without end and wants us to have abundant joy?

Lectionary for Mass #147C

Exodus 17:8–13

Psalm 121:1–2, 3–4, 5–6, 7–8 (see 2)

2 Timothy 3:14—4:2

Luke 18:1–8

Objectives

- To invite the children to a life of prayer without ceasing.
- To introduce and explain the term *widow* and the circumstances of the life of a widow in Jesus' time and place.

Preparation and Materials

- Read the Season Background, the lectionary readings, and the Scripture Background.
- Bookmark the appropriate readings (see page xiv) in the lectionary, children's lectionary, or Bible. Place the book in a convenient location for the leader.
- Write the words of dismissal on a card for the priest celebrant.
- Prepare the words of the song the children will sing as they gather in the space for the Liturgy of the Word.
- Select volunteers (older children or adults) to proclaim the readings.
- Display the responsorial psalm refrain lyrics.
- Display the Apostles' or Nicene Creed.
- Prepare intercessions for the Prayer of the Faithful adapted for the needs of the Church, world, oppressed or marginalized, and local community.

Prayer Leader Reflection Questions

>> **How are you nurturing your own prayer life in order to pray without ceasing? What prayer practices do you engage in regularly?**

>> **Who in your community has no one else to advocate for them to receive justice? How are you speaking up for those who are alone?**

Procession

Following the Collect of the Mass, the priest celebrant picks up the lectionary and invites those who would like to participate in the Liturgy of the Word with children to come forward and gather in the center aisle. The people who will lead the children out and facilitate the Liturgy of the Word also come forward at this time. Holding the lectionary so that all can see, the priest celebrant sends the children forth using his own words or the following:

> *Priest*: **Dear children, God uses the seasons to teach us many things, and in fall, God teaches us about letting go. As the trees lose their leaves and the world prepares for winter sleep, we too can focus on what we need to change and what we need to let go of in our lives. Go now with your prayer leader(s) to listen for what God might be asking of you. May peace be with all of you.**

The leader processes out holding the lectionary, and the children follow behind. The parish music minister may have selected a song of dismissal for the assembly to sing while the children leave. A good option is "The Word of God: Children's Dismissal" by M. D. Ridge and Timothy R. Smith (WLP/GIA).

Centering

Continue to sing the song of dismissal that the assembly sang as you left the church. Or sing the refrains from "There Is a Longing" (Quigley), or "Seek Ye First the Kingdom of God" (SEEK YE FIRST), or have instrumental music playing as the children gather in the space for the Liturgy of the Word.

Place the lectionary on the ambo or lectern. Light the candle placed by the ambo or lectern, and then lead the following prayer:

> **Loving God,**
> **prepare our minds**
> **to heed your holy Word.**
> **Open our hearts**
> **that we may hear more clearly your message of love**
> **and live more closely in accordance with your will.**
> **Through Christ our Lord.**

> *Children:* **Amen.**

First Reading

Exodus 17:8–13

Responsorial Psalm

Psalm 121:1–2, 3–4, 5–6, 7–8 (see 2) *Sing the same musical setting that is used in your parish's celebration of the liturgy.*

Second Reading

2 Timothy 3:14—4:2

Gospel Acclamation

Sing the Gospel Acclamation used in your parish's celebration of the liturgy.

Gospel Reading

Luke 18:1–8

Homily/Reflection

When Jesus walked and talked on this earth like you and I do, people noticed that Jesus was very different. Those who listened to him wanted to hear what he had to say and to learn about God. They listened to how Jesus talked about his heavenly Father and they wanted to know how they should talk to God, too.

In today's Gospel, Jesus shares a parable about praying always.

» Do you remember what a parable is?

A parable is a story with more than one meaning. Jesus used parables to teach us about God's kingdom.

This parable is about a widow. A widow is a woman whose husband has died. This widow needed a judge's help to get justice from someone who had harmed her. In Jesus' time, a woman would not typically go to court herself. Her husband or her son would go for her. Since this widow went to court on her own, we might guess that she had no son. It was likely that she was alone and didn't have anyone else on her side. Unfortunately, the judge in the court was selfish and wasn't interested in giving her justice for its own sake. But did the woman give up? No! She returned day after day to ask for what she needed until eventually the judge figured out that it would be better for him to give her what she wanted so she could stop bothering him. The judge didn't love the widow. He didn't care about doing what was right, and yet even this judge who cared nothing for the widow eventually did what she asked.

It might feel unusual or confusing to compare this person to God! One way we pray is to ask for what we need. In prayer, we ask God for help. We know that God is not like the selfish judge. God loves us fully. God is the very source of what is right. How much more would God answer our prayer requests when we ask?

» How then can we be more like the widow in our attitude toward prayer?

Jesus gave us the key to understanding how to do this. He said, "pray always without becoming weary." *Weary* means "tired." This widow didn't just ask once and give up. She went back to the judge over and over and over again for what she needed. She trusted that her requests would have an effect and she stuck with her effort. We can choose to be like the widow; we can keep praying without ever giving up.

Sometimes it may seem that God isn't granting our prayers. But have you ever thought that sometimes the answer to what we're asking for might be "not now"? God is not saying no, nor is he saying he doesn't love us, nor is he saying he's not going to give us what we want. God doesn't work that way. God might be saying that what we're asking for is not good for us right now. So this is all the more reason for us to keep having faith—just like the widow—and never give up asking.

Profession of Faith

Following the homily or reflection, the prayer leader invites everyone to stand to profess our faith. Together, sing or recite the Apostles' or Nicene Creed. Refer the children to the words of the prayer that you have displayed.

Prayer of the Faithful

Leader: **Today we hear that we must pray always and never lose heart. God always listens and responds to our needs. Encouraged by this, let us bring our prayers to God. Please respond, "Lord, hear and answer us."**

That Church leaders continue to encourage the faithful to nurture their faith and grow in their love of God, we pray: *Lord, hear and answer us.*

That government leaders may represent those in our community who have no one else to stand up for them and seek justice on their behalf, we pray: *Lord, hear and answer us.*

That all who are lonely may find comfort in God, we pray: *Lord, hear and answer us.*

That judges render just and fair decisions on behalf of the people they serve, we pray: *Lord, hear and answer us.*

Invite other intercessions from the children, or add intercessions based on the current needs of the Church, the world, the oppressed or marginalized, and the local community. Conclude each of the children's petitions with **"we pray"** and invite the response **"Lord, hear and answer us."**

That those who have died may enjoy God's unending love, we pray: *Lord, hear and answer us.*

Heavenly Father, please give us the strength to always turn to you in prayer. May we recognize all the ways that you answer our prayer. Through Jesus Christ our Lord.

Children: **Amen.**

Quietly return with the children to the main assembly. Be mindful of children having difficulty finding their families.

October 23, 2022
Thirtieth Sunday in Ordinary Time
The Lord Hears the Cry of the Poor

 ## Scripture Background

Connections to Church Teaching and Tradition

- "Christ's disciples are called to renew ever more fully in themselves 'the awareness that the truth about God who saves, the truth about God who is the source of every gift, cannot be separated from the manifestation of his love of preference for the poor and humble, that love which, celebrated in the Magnificat, is later expressed in the words and works of Jesus'" (CSDC, 59).

- "The preferential love for the poor represents a fundamental choice for the Church, and she proposes it to all people of good will" (CSDC, 3).

- "In all places and circumstances, Christians, with the help of their pastors, are called to hear the cry of the poor. This has been eloquently stated by the bishops of Brazil: 'We wish to take up daily the joys and hopes, the difficulties and sorrows of the Brazilian people, especially of those living in the barrios and the countryside—landless, homeless, lacking food and health care—to the detriment of their rights'" (EG, 191).

Sirach 35:12–14, 16–18 Sirach is part of Israel's wisdom literature dealing with the proper exercise of justice, or right relationship. Justice is an essential component of covenant relationship. God is just, impartially promoting right relationship with all. Those claiming to be in covenant relationships with God, both rich and poor, are called to act justly. The rich act justly when attuned to the needs of the poor and respond accordingly. The poor are to act justly as well. Keenly attuned to the demands of justice, God is biased in favor of those whose rights have been violated. This passage asserts that, though impartial toward all, God hears "the cry of the oppressed . . . [and] is not deaf to the wail of the orphan, / nor to the widow" (35:13, 14). Acting justly demands the recognition of one's humble status and dependence on God. Whoever does so will be heard when they cry out to God in need and God will respond speedily, judging justly and affirming the right. To be in covenant relationship is to be aware of God's justice demands toward all, and to know that God sees, hears, and responds to every demand for justice.

Psalm 34:2–3, 17–18, 19, 23 (7a) The antiphon for Psalm 34 sums up the psalm's principal focus, "the Lord hears the cry of the poor." Those who take refuge in the Lord, who acknowledge their dependence on God's mercy and justice will be heard when they cry out and God will rescue them "from all their distress" (34:18b). The psalmist invites all to bless and praise the Lord who is "close to the brokenhearted; / and those who are crushed in spirit" (34:19). God reaches out and saves them, "redeem[ing] the lives of his servants" (34:23a), once again establishing right relationship with all. The evildoers, those who neither act justly nor work toward right relationship, are not heard, and remembrance of them is blotted out. Fitting praise is due to our merciful, just, and loving God, who cares for all, especially the poor and lowly.

2 Timothy 4:6–8, 16–18 The author of 2 Timothy employs various images when speaking of Paul's approach to his imprisonment, trial, and coming death as a model for all disciples. Paul's suffering is first seen as a libation, a pouring out of his life in sacrificial offering for others, replicating the pouring out of a sacrificial animal's blood offered to God. Using a sports image, the author affirms that Paul has competed well in life's race, has kept the faith and has been faithful to God to the end. Having given his life for the Lord, the author is certain that Paul's reward will be eternal life, along with all those who longed for the Lord's final appearance. Paul asks forgiveness for all those who deserted him during his trial, knowing that the Lord was with him, giving him strength to complete his mission, the spreading of the word to Gentiles. Paul is confident of the Lord's help in all his trials, trusting that the Lord will rescue him from all evil, and welcome him home. For all this, Paul humbly gives praise and glory to God.

Luke 18:9–14 The context of Luke's parable of the Pharisee and the tax collector going up to the Temple to pray is crucial to the lesson Jesus wants to teach all disciples. The parable addresses those who are "convinced of their own righteousness and despised everyone else" (18:9). Righteousness can lead to arrogance, setting itself up as the criterion for justice and right relationship while despising all who think and act differently. In their arrogance, the self-righteous are convinced that their way of thinking and acting is God's way.

Jesus' parable reverses this very common way of thinking among righteous people. The Pharisee, beyond exemplary in all his actions, is so caught up with his own righteousness that he despises the tax collector. Convinced that God is pleased only with him and not the tax collector, the Pharisee violates the key covenant requirement of care and concern, justice and right relationship, with all of God's people. The tax collector, through humble words and posture, acknowledges his sinfulness and asks God for mercy. Jesus asserts that the tax collector went away justified, not the Pharisee. Such reversal must have shocked his audience, as it continues to shock all whose arrogance and righteousness blinds them to their own need for God. Blind also to the need of others, especially the poor and sinners, they violate their covenant responsibility to them as members of God's family. God hears the cry of the poor, the materially as well as the spiritually poor. Do we?

Preparation

All of today's readings provide insight into the nature and purpose of prayer. Sirach and Psalm 34 echo each other, telling us that God hears the prayers of those who suffer. When we encounter realities that transcend our own ability to save ourselves, our stance before God becomes starker and we may know that God's greatness far exceeds anything we can do for ourselves. In the Second Letter to Timothy, today's second reading, Paul speaks of the sufferings that have laid bare his dependence on God. Paul's example reminds us that while God's answer to our prayers might not always be what we would choose for ourselves, God will always respond in ways that lead us to the kingdom of heaven. The parable of the Pharisee and the tax collector in Luke's Gospel invites us to note that all prayer, properly ordered, means placing ourselves humbly before God who is the source of all blessings.

Lectionary for Mass #150C

Sirach 35:12–14, 16–18

Psalm 34:2–3, 17–18, 19, 23 (7a)

2 Timothy 4:6–8, 16–18

Luke 18:9–14

Objectives

- To consider together the proper spiritual posture before God in prayer.

- To introduce and explain the words *exalt* and *humble* to the children.

Preparation and Materials

- Read the Season Background, the lectionary readings, and the Scripture Background.

- Bookmark the appropriate readings (see page xiv) in the lectionary, children's lectionary, or Bible. Place the book in a convenient location for the leader.

- Write the words of dismissal on a card for the priest celebrant.

- Prepare the words of the song the children will sing as they gather in the space for the Liturgy of the Word.

- Select volunteers (older children or adults) to proclaim the readings.

- Display the responsorial psalm refrain lyrics.

- Display the Apostles' or Nicene Creed.

- Prepare intercessions for the Prayer of the Faithful adapted for the needs of the Church, world, oppressed or marginalized, and local community.

Prayer Leader Reflection Questions

≫ **How do you respond to the cries of the poor? How do you practice the corporal and spiritual works of mercy?**

≫ **When do you notice yourself acting most like the Pharisee and relying on your own abilities to lift yourself up? How might you trust in God's power more fully?**

Procession

Following the Collect of the Mass, the priest celebrant picks up the lectionary and invites those who would like to participate in the Liturgy of the Word with children to come forward and gather in the center aisle. The people who will lead the children out and facilitate the Liturgy of the Word also come forward at this time. Holding the lectionary so that all can see, the priest celebrant sends the children forth using his own words or the following:

> *Priest*: **Dear children, God uses the seasons to teach us many things, and in fall, God teaches us about letting go. Go now with your prayer leader(s) to listen for what God might be asking of you. May peace be with all of you.**

The leader processes out holding the lectionary, and the children follow behind. The parish music minister may have selected a song of dismissal for the assembly to sing while the children leave. A good option is "The Word of God: Children's Dismissal" by M. D. Ridge and Timothy R. Smith (WLP/GIA).

Centering

Continue to sing the song of dismissal that the assembly sang as you left the church. Or sing the refrains from "I Want to Walk as a Child of the Light" (Houston), or "Gather Us In" (Haugen), or have instrumental music playing as the children gather in the space for the Liturgy of the Word.

Place the lectionary on the ambo or lectern. Light the candle placed by the ambo or lectern, and then lead the following prayer:

> **Lord Jesus,**
> **we are humble before you and we praise you.**
> **Open our hearts to your Word so we might know you and**
> **follow you more fully.**
> **Who live and reign with God the Father**
> **in the unity of the Holy Spirit, God for ever and ever.**

> *Children:* **Amen.**

First Reading

Sirach 35:12–14, 16–18

Responsorial Psalm

Psalm 34:2–3, 17–18, 19, 23 (7a) *Sing the same musical setting that is used in your parish's celebration of the liturgy.*

Second Reading

2 Timothy 4:6–8, 16–18

Gospel Acclamation

Sing the Gospel Acclamation used in your parish's celebration of the liturgy.

Gospel Reading

Luke 18:9–14

» When do you pray? Where do you pray?

Prayer is such an important part of our life with God. Sometimes we pray in church at Mass, or when we gather around the dinner table with our family before meals and bless our food. Sometimes we might pray alone before bedtime or when we pass a holy water font and bless ourselves. We could also say specific prayers like the Hail Mary and the Our Father, or we could use our own words to thank God or to ask him for something. Is that all there is, though? Our Church helps us to understand that prayer is more than that. Prayer is communication that goes both ways: between us and God, back and forth. We don't do all the talking; prayer must also involve *listening* for God's voice. All of the readings today all can tell us something about prayer. The first reading and the psalm both remind us that the Lord hears the cry of those who suffer. They speak about orphans and widows, the poor, the weak, and the oppressed. The psalm gives us a name we might use to describe these people: "the brokenhearted." Our God cares for those who are hurting and listens to them.

In the Gospel, Jesus told a parable about a Pharisee and a tax collector. In Jesus' time, a Pharisee was someone who cared very much about God's Word, studied it very closely and tried to do everything that God's Word instructed. Because the people of Israel were governed by the Romans, who were outsiders, people called "tax collectors," those who collected money to give to the government, were despised because were hurting the people of Israel. When we look at how each prayed, though, we notice something surprising. Let's listen again to their prayers. The Pharisee said, "O God, I thank you that I am not like the rest of humanity—greedy, dishonest, adulterous—or even like this tax collector. I fast twice a week, and I pay tithes on my whole income." What was the Pharisee's prayer really about? Listen to his words, what he spoke most often: "I," "I," "I," "I." If we compare this to how many times he talks about God, we hear that he only says, "O God" and "you" twice. He talks about himself twice as much as he talks about God.

>> **For the Pharisee, then, who is most important in the prayer?** [*It is the Pharisee. He is naming all the things that* **he** *has done.*]

The tax collector, the one who is considered an outsider, says, however, "O God, be merciful to me a sinner." How many times does the tax collector talk about himself? He says the word *me* once. When he refers to himself, he is asking God to direct mercy to him. Mercy is compassion or forgiveness specifically from someone who has power. Even when the tax collector is talking about himself, he is also acknowledging that God is powerful and merciful.

What does God ask of us in prayer? Jesus says, "whoever exalts himself will be humbled, and the one who humbles himself will be exalted." To be humble is to be small before one who is great. To be exalted is to be lifted up. When the Pharisee listed all the things that he had done, he was lifting himself up. He even showed this with his body. Jesus said, "he took up his position," but another way to say this is that he "stood up," perhaps even in front of the temple, but certainly apart from everyone else. The tax collector, on the other hand, "would not even raise his eyes to heaven." The tax collector humbled himself before God who is great.

At every Mass, we pray "Hosanna in the highest." God is the highest. We can jump up or even climb a mountain, but we will never reach as high as the highest heavens on our own. When we pray, we can show with our bodies, with our words, with our whole selves that we are humble before God who is great.

Profession of Faith

Following the homily or reflection, the prayer leader invites everyone to stand to profess our faith. Together, sing or recite the Apostles' or Nicene Creed. Refer the children to the words of the prayer that you have displayed.

Prayer of the Faithful

Leader: **Grateful for our faith, we now bring our prayers to God. Please respond, "Lord, hear our cry."**

May the Church always offer God's comfort to those most in need, we pray: *Lord, hear our cry.*

May world leaders care for those who do not have enough food, shelter, or protection, we pray: *Lord, hear our cry.*

May widows, orphans, and all who mourn know God's consolation, we pray: *Lord, hear our cry.*

May those in prison, and those who minister to them know that God rescues, redeems, and remembers them, we pray: *Lord, hear our cry.*

Invite other intercessions from the children, or add intercessions based on the current needs of the Church, the world, the oppressed or marginalized, and the local community. Conclude each of the children's petitions with **"we pray"** and invite the response **"Lord, hear our cry."**

May all who have died be exalted with God in the highest heavens, we pray: *Lord, hear our cry.*

God of life, give us more faith, hope, and love in order to do what you command. At the end of our lives, lift us up to you forever in heaven. Hear our cry, through Christ our Lord.

Children: **Amen.**

Quietly return with the children to the main assembly. Be mindful of children having difficulty finding their families.

October 30, 2022
Thirty-First Sunday in Ordinary Time
The Lord Is Gracious and Merciful

 Scripture Background

Wisdom 11:22—12:2   This passage from Wisdom, written during the first century BC, fuses both Greek and Jewish concepts of God, as it focuses on God's mercy and love of all creation. God, seen through Greek lenses, is all knowing, all powerful, and beyond all things. Yet the all-powerful God loves, cares for, and sustains all creation. God, whose "imperishable spirit is in all things" (11:26c), works in and through the created world. The all-powerful God is also full of mercy and compassion, "overlook[ing] people's sins that they may repent" (11:23b). God's love relationship with the world is exercised in sparing all things "because they are yours" (11:26a). It also leads God to "rebuke offenders little by little, / warn them and remind them . . . / that they may abandon their wickedness" (12:2). Our all-powerful God is truly gracious and merciful, faithful to all creation, and compassionate toward all. God's love and compassion are made real and are experienced whenever we exercise the same love and compassion for all.

Psalm 145:1–2, 8–9, 10–11, 13, 14 (see 1)   The psalmist extols, blesses, and praises God "forever and ever" (145:1c) because "the LORD is gracious and merciful, / slow to anger and of great kindness" (145:8–9). Both "gracious" and "kindness" translate the Hebrew word *hesed* meaning "ever-faithful," "enduring," and "all-giving" covenant love. For the psalmist, God's *hesed* or covenant love is manifested in the Lord being "good to all and compassionate towards all" (145:9c) of God's creation. In response, the psalmist calls upon all creation to thank the Lord. The "faithful ones" (145:10b) those who enter into covenant relationship with God, are also to thank and bless the Lord, and speak of God's power and might manifested in all creation. God is faithful and holy, lifting up "all who are falling / and raises up all who are bowed down" (145:14). God's faithful covenant love is good to all, especially those in distress, pain, or anguish. Let us thank, praise, and bless the Lord always.

2 Thessalonians 1:11—2:2   Paul prays for his Thessalonian community that God's grace active in them may "powerfully bring to fulfillment every good purpose and every effort of faith" (1:11). For Paul, it is God's grace and gift of faith that activates ethical living and all good works. Belief in God through Jesus is primary, and through that faith we are gifted with the power to live in fidelity to God's love and presence. In this manner, God is glorified in them as they become more closely bonded with God in Christ. Paul also addresses the distress that some seem to be experiencing over the imminent return of the Lord. Either by some proclamation through a "spirit" (2:2), or possibly a letter falsely attributed to Paul, some in the community believe that the Lord will soon return. Anxiety could have resulted from lack of readiness for some, or from a relaxation of the demands of discipleship, thus doing nothing until Christ returns. Paul says that neither stance is a fitting response for a believer. One is to continue trusting in the Lord and living ethically through God's grace, so that whenever the Lord returns, all will be ready and will have nothing to fear or be anxious about.

Luke 19:1–10   The Zacchaeus narrative, unique to Luke, highlights a key element of Jesus' ministry, namely, to seek out and save the lost and marginalized, welcoming them to God's table of mercy and love. As chief tax collector, the wealthy Zacchaeus was despised by fellow Jews for cheating people, typical of tax collectors, and for collaborating with Roman occupiers. However, Zacchaeus' desire to connect with Jesus, even setting himself up for shame and ridicule by climbing a tree, causes Jesus to connect with him and to invite himself to Zacchaeus' house for dinner. "Today, I must stay at your house" (19:9) connotes a necessity on Jesus' part to seek the lost and welcome them back to God and community. God's covenant love is experienced in the person and ministry of Jesus.

Zacchaeus enthusiastically responds to Jesus' invitation to experience God's mercy and love by offering to give half his possessions to the poor and by restoring fourfold anyone he has cheated. Using the word "today" (19:9) a second time, Jesus affirms that Zacchaeus has taken advantage of his saving offer and reestablished himself as a "descendent of Abraham" (19:9). God's gracious and merciful love activated by Jesus has accomplished what Jesus was sent to do, "to seek and to save what was lost" (19:10). As Jesus' disciples, we too are called to activate Jesus' covenant love in all our encounters.

Preparation

God loves all of creation. There is nothing we can do to make God stop loving us. God invites us continually to return to him when we have strayed from his love. Our reconciliation with God leads to an intimacy in which the high point is a shared meal together, and the food is God's very self, the Eucharist. Children can relate to today's Gospel story of the small Zacchaeus being noticed by Jesus.

Lectionary for Mass #153C

Wisdom 11:22—12:2

Psalm 145:1–2, 8–9, 10–11, 13, 14 (see 1)

2 Thessalonians 1:11—2:2

Luke 19:1–10

Objectives

- To introduce the meaning and social significance of the tax collector in Jesus' time.

- To invite consideration of acts of repentance and restoration as responses to the abundant and enduring love that God has for us.

Preparation and Materials

- Read the Season Background, the lectionary readings, and the Scripture Background.

- Bookmark the appropriate readings (see page xiv) in the lectionary, children's lectionary, or Bible. Place the book in a convenient location for the leader.

- Write the words of dismissal on a card for the priest celebrant.

- Prepare the words of the song the children will sing as they gather in the space for the Liturgy of the Word.

- Select volunteers (older children or adults) to proclaim the readings.

- Display the responsorial psalm refrain lyrics.

- Display the Apostles' or Nicene Creed.

- Prepare intercessions for the Prayer of the Faithful adapted for the needs of the Church, world, oppressed or marginalized, and local community.

Prayer Leader Reflection Questions

>> **When has an experience of God's love changed you?**

>> **How do you take care of the poor, both in your own community and the world? What would it look like to give away half of everything you have to those in need?**

Procession

Following the Collect of the Mass, the priest celebrant picks up the lectionary and invites those who would like to participate in the Liturgy of the Word with children to come forward and gather in the center aisle. The people who will lead the children out and facilitate the Liturgy of the Word also come forward at this time. Holding the lectionary so that all can see, the priest celebrant sends the children forth using his own words or the following:

Priest: **Dear children, God uses the seasons to teach us many things, and in fall, God teaches us about letting go. As the trees lose their leaves and the world prepares for winter sleep, we too can focus on what we need to change and what we need to let go of in our lives. Go now with your prayer leader(s) to listen for what God might be asking of you. May peace be with all of you.**

The leader processes out holding the lectionary, and the children follow behind. The parish music minister may have selected a song of dismissal for the assembly to sing while the children leave. A good option is "The Word of God: Children's Dismissal" by M. D. Ridge and Timothy R. Smith (WLP/GIA).

Centering

Continue to sing the song of dismissal that the assembly sang as you left the church. Or sing the refrains from "Hosea" (Norbet), or "We Are the Light of the World" (Greif), or have instrumental music playing as the children gather in the space for the Liturgy of the Word.

Place the lectionary on the ambo or lectern. Light the candle placed by the ambo or lectern, and then lead the following prayer:

**Lord Jesus,
because you love us so much, you seek us out and call us to your banquet.
Open our hearts to your Word
so we might know you and follow you more fully.
Who live and reign with God the Father
in the unity of the Holy Spirit, God for ever and ever.**

Children: **Amen.**

First Reading

Wisdom 11:22—12:2

Responsorial Psalm

Psalm 145:1–2, 8–9, 10–11, 13, 14 (see 1) *Sing the same musical setting that is used in your parish's celebration of the liturgy.*

Second Reading

2 Thessalonians 1:11—2:2

Gospel Acclamation

Sing the Gospel Acclamation used in your parish's celebration of the liturgy.

Gospel Reading

Luke 19:1–10

Homily/Reflection

>> **Have you ever felt too small? Have you ever felt like you wanted to be seen but couldn't get noticed?**

In today's Gospel, we hear about Jesus meeting someone who really was small. His name was Zacchaeus, and he wanted so badly to connect with Jesus that he climbed a tree to see him.

>> **Zacchaeus was a "chief tax collector." Do you know what taxes are?**

In the Book of Genesis, we hear about a kind of tax that Joseph, son of Jacob and Rachel, asked for from people in Egypt. Joseph asked people to give one fifth of the grain they produced so that it could be saved for a time when the crops didn't grow. It was a way for everyone to help respond to a shared need. It isn't always easy to see what taxes are used for, though, so sometimes people don't like paying them. During Zacchaeus' time, the people who collected the taxes also took some of what they collected for themselves. People thought they were dishonest and hurtful to their own community. So tax collectors weren't liked very much and were called sinners. They were on the outside of the community. Because Zacchaeus was the "chief tax collector," some people might have thought of him as the chief sinner!

But even though Zacchaeus had made choices that hurt other people and even though he was on the outside and small, he still recognized that Jesus was someone he wanted to see. When Jesus was passing through Jericho, Zacchaeus found a way to be able to see him, and Jesus did notice him! He told Zacchaeus to come down from the tree because he was going to stay at Zacchaeus' house. For the Jewish people, coming into someone's house was very special. It was shocking to the crowd that Jesus would eat with someone who was a sinner.

>> Why would Jesus want to spend time with someone people thought was a sinner?

We might find the answer in the first reading, which says about God: "you love all things . . . that you have made." Zacchaeus was made by God and God loved Zacchaeus. When Jesus said he would come to Zacchaeus' house, I wonder if this reminded Zacchaeus of how much God loved him and who God made him to be.

Zacchaeus was inspired to change for the better. He said he would repay anyone he had unjustly taken money from, but not just what he had taken. He said he would pay four times what he had taken. He also said he would give half of what he owned to the poor. Zacchaeus responded to the gift of God's overflowing love with an overflowing offering to others.

We, too, were made by God and we know that God loves us completely. God won't stop loving us. We can get lost, though. We can wander away from the path God calls us to follow, just like the lost sheep in the parable we heard just a few weeks ago. Like Zacchaeus up in the tree, Jesus invites us to be close to him, and to share a very special meal with him, the meal of his abundant love—the Eucharist. Now, right here, is when we are most particularly close to Jesus. When we are reminded of this overflowing love that God has for us, we can be like Zacchaeus in another way. We can admit when we were wrong and we can change, not only repaying exactly what we hurt, but making things even better than they were before.

Profession of Faith

Following the homily or reflection, the prayer leader invites everyone to stand to profess our faith. Together, sing or recite the Apostles' or Nicene Creed. Refer the children to the words of the prayer that you have displayed.

Prayer of the Faithful

Leader: **Grateful for our faith, we now bring our prayers to God. Please respond, "Lord, be merciful to us."**

For the Church, that she may always seek and be the model of the reconciliation and restoration that is a true response to God's limitless love, we pray: *Lord, be merciful to us.*

For world nations to care for God's beloved creation, we pray: *Lord, be merciful to us.*

For sinners to be reconciled to God and receive his mercy in the sacrament of reconciliation, we pray: *Lord, be merciful to us.*

For the gifts of our community to be used in the service of the poor, we pray: *Lord, be merciful to us.*

Invite other intercessions from the children, or add intercessions based on the current needs of the Church, the world, the oppressed or marginalized, and the local community. Conclude each of the children's petitions with **"we pray"** and invite the response **"Lord, be merciful to us."**

For all who have died, that they may join the heavenly banquet in the household of God, we pray: *Lord, be merciful to us.*

**God of mercy,
everything we have comes from you.
Help us to follow in your path, and help us call to you when we
need to return.
Through Christ our Lord.**

Children: **Amen.**

Quietly return with the children to the main assembly. Be mindful of children having difficulty finding their families.

November 1, 2022
Solemnity of All Saints

Longing to See God's Face

 ## Scripture Background

Connections to Church Teaching and Tradition

⚜ "They are . . . to live 'as is fitting among saints,' (Ephesians 5:3), and 'as God's chosen ones, holy and beloved, to show compassion, kindness, lowliness, meekness, and patience' (Colossians 3:12) to have the fruits of the Spirit for their sanctification" (LG, 40).

⚜ "All who in obedience to Christ seek first the kingdom of God will derive from it a stronger and purer motivation for helping all their brothers and sisters and for accomplishing the task of justice under the inspiration of charity" (GS, 72).

Revelation 7:2–4, 9–14   The Book of Revelation offers hope, courage, strength, and consolation to disciples who suffer persecution and death for fidelity to Jesus' values and lifestyle. Two vision scenes are pictured. The first addresses the disciples still struggling on earth as the angel seals the "foreheads of the servants of our God" (7:3). When destruction of their evil persecutors occurs according to God's plan, they will be marked with God's seal and be spared, for they belong to God. The symbolic number 144,000 represents the twelve tribes of Israel squared multiplied by the perfect number one thousand indicating an incalculable totality. The second vision recounts the heavenly liturgy of worship and honor given to God and the Lamb (John's symbol for the Risen Christ) by "a great multitude, which no one could count" (7:9). These are the ones who have remained faithful despite suffering persecution and death, those who remained pure and faithful even to death, modeling themselves on Christ who shed his blood on the cross for all.

Revelation richly expresses their identity as those who have "washed their robes and made them white in the Blood of the Lamb" (9:14). Their longing to see God's face motivated them to model themselves on Jesus, and to live the values of the Beatitudes proclaimed in today's Gospel.

Psalm 24:1–2, 3–4, 5–6 (see 6)   The psalm's refrain captures well the Solemnity of All Saints as it invites us to acknowledge to God that "this is the people that longs to see your face." This Temple processional psalm declares that our God is the creator of the earth and all who dwell in it, establishing it by bringing order to the chaotic watery powers. Our powerful creator God who created and ordered the universe has chosen to enter into loving covenant relationship with us. The psalm's other verses use a dialogue question and answer method to acquaint the people to the demands of covenant relationship for anyone desiring to see the Lord's face, usually understood as experiencing the Lord's intimate presence in the Temple. Purity of heart and mind, and covenant love actualized in right relationship with all are the heart of covenant fidelity. These people do and will continue to experience God's intimate love relationship forever.

1 John 3:1–3   John calls disciples "children of God" (3:1) expressing the intimacy and the longing that covenant relationship through Jesus and the Holy Spirit engenders. However, fidelity to covenant living leads to rejection and persecution because covenant values challenge the typical manner of operating of the "world" (3:1). Just as the world rejected ("did not know" [3:1]) Jesus, so they reject and persecute his followers. Yet no matter what happens, we are beloved children of God here and now. What that love relationship will look like for all eternity in full intimacy with God we do not know. We do know that those who have "this hope" (3:3), this longing for full intimacy with God, strive to adhere faithfully to covenant love ("makes himself pure" [3:3]) modeled by Jesus, and will ultimately experience God's face and loving embrace for all eternity.

Matthew 5:1–12a   The Beatitudes introduce Matthew's Sermon on the Mount, chapters 5 through 7. They are guidelines for disciples, encapsulating the values that Jesus came to proclaim both in his own life and in his preaching on the kingdom of God. On the Solemnity of All Saints, we claim that the lifestyle embedded in the Beatitudes is the essence of sainthood. The universal call to holiness in chapter 5 of *Lumen gentium* reminds us that all are called to sainthood. We accomplish this with the Spirit's help by taking on the mind and heart of Jesus as expressed in the Beatitudes' values.

These values form the core of right relationship with God and others, while challenging the ordinary patterns of people's lives. Can it be that the poor, the sorrowful, the meek, and those who hunger and thirst for righteousness are truly blessed? Do the merciful, the clean of heart, the peacemakers, and those persecuted for righteousness truly acquire blessedness in this world and the next? Often such a lifestyle leads not to blessedness but worries, troubles, and conflicts. Maybe that is why the Beatitudes end with a realistic assessment that such living results in insults and persecution.

Yet Jesus stresses that living these values brings about the kingdom of God on earth and results in eternal life with God. Longing to see God's face demands living out the Beatitudes daily, thus establishing right relationship with God and others that will last for all eternity.

Preparation

On All Saints' Day we recall all those whose lives were illuminated by the Gospel, and we recall our own calling to sainthood. The Christian life is not a simple one, as the saints can attest. One of the Beatitudes is "Blessed are the clean of heart, for they shall see God." We celebrate the witness of all these beautiful hearts, the saints, who show us what it looks like to dedicate our lives to God.

Lectionary for Mass #667

Revelation 7:2–4, 9–14

Psalm 24:1–2, 3–4, 5–6 (see 6)

1 John 3:1–3

Matthew 5:1–12a

Objectives

- To teach children about sainthood and heaven.

- To help children understand our calling to be saints also.

Preparation and Materials

- Read the Season Background, the Lectionary readings, and the Scripture Background.

- Bookmark the appropriate readings (see page xiv) in the Lectionary, children's Lectionary, or Bible. Place the book in a convenient location for the leader.

- Write the words of dismissal on a card for the priest celebrant.

- Prepare the words of the song the children will sing as they gather in the space for the Liturgy of the Word.

- Select volunteers (older children or adults) to proclaim the readings.

- Display the responsorial psalm refrain lyrics.

- Display the Apostles' or Nicene Creed.

- Prepare intercessions for the Prayer of the Faithful adapted for the needs of the Church, world, oppressed or marginalized, and local community.

Prayer Leader Reflection Questions

>> Which Beatitude stands out to you, and why?

>> Who has gone before you, leaving you with a guideline for living a good Christian life? (Say a prayer of thanks for their intercession in your life.)

Procession

Following the Collect of the Mass, the priest celebrant picks up the Lectionary and invites those who would like to participate in the Liturgy of the Word with children to come forward and gather in the center aisle. The people who will lead the children out and facilitate the Liturgy of the Word also come forward at this time. Holding the Lectionary so that all can see, the priest celebrant sends the children forth using his own words or the following:

> *Priest:* **Dear children, we send you with your leader(s) to listen carefully to God's Word. Pay attention to what God is saying to you today. May the Holy Spirit help you understand and live this Good News. Go now in peace.**

The leader processes out holding the Lectionary, and the children follow behind. The parish music minister may have selected a song of dismissal for the assembly to sing while the children leave. A good option is "The Word of God: Children's Dismissal" by M. D. Ridge and Timothy R. Smith (WLP/GIA).

Centering

Continue to sing the song of dismissal that the assembly sang as you left the church. Or sing the refrain from "We Are the Light of the World" (Greif), or "Sing with All the Saints in Glory" (Hymn to Joy), or have instrumental music playing as the children gather in the space for the Liturgy of the Word.

Place the Lectionary on the ambo or lectern. Light the candle placed by the ambo or lectern, and then lead the following prayer:

> **Loving God,**
> **we praise you and thank you for this time together.**
> **Help us hear your Word so our hearts may be changed by it.**
> **May we always follow the example of Jesus Christ, your Son,**
> **who lives and reigns with you**
> **in the unity of the Holy Spirit,**
> **God for ever and ever.**

> *Children:* **Amen.**

First Reading

Revelation 7:2–4, 9–14

Responsorial Psalm

Psalm 24:1–2, 3–4, 5–6 (see 6) *Sing the same musical setting that is used in your parish's celebration of the liturgy.*

Second Reading

1 John 3:1–3

Gospel Acclamation

Sing the Gospel Acclamation used in your parish's celebration of the liturgy.

Gospel Reading

Matthew 5:1–12a

Homily/Reflection

Today's holyday, the Solemnity of All Saints, is when we remember all the saints in heaven. Some saints are very well known, like St. Francis of Assisi, St. Patrick, and St. Nicholas, but many saints are not as well known. In fact, most saints in heaven have names not known on earth because they went to heaven long ago, or haven't yet been recognized as saints in heaven.

(Share an anecdote like the following.) One of my favorite saints is St. Teresa of Kolkata. During her life Mother Teresa cared for the poorest people in India. She would go out and look for the poor and sick, even dying people on the streets. She would take them to her hospital and made sure that they were fed, clothed, and had medicines. But during her life, St. Teresa also had struggles with her faith. She wasn't afraid to admit her challenges, and by her example and life, she inspired others who struggled with their faith, too.

» Which saints do you admire? Why do you admire them?

Did you know that we are all called to sainthood? Yes, every person in this room, and every one of your parents, your siblings, friends, and anyone you have ever met in your entire life. What makes a person become a saint? Simply put, a saint is a human soul who has gone to heaven. People go to heaven by the grace of God, through Christ's death and Resurrection. Saints are people who lived the Beatitudes.

In today's Gospel reading we heard the Beatitudes, which are promises from Jesus. These promises are about the hardships and challenges we will face in life, and that these struggles will not overcome us. Jesus said blessed are the poor in spirit, those who mourn, the meek, those who hunger and thirst for righteousness, the merciful, the clean of heart, the peacemakers, the persecuted, and those who are insulted.

>> **What does it mean to be "clean of heart"? What are some qualities of being clean?**

Clean things are in order. Clean things are healthy. Clean things are good for the environment. When things are clean, there is space for good things to happen. So when we have a clean heart, it means that we have put God first in our lives. Once God is first in our lives, everything else that follows will be in the correct order. When we have a clean heart, our lives will be healthy. We will strive to make healthy choices, which is a sign of valuing all of the gifts our God has given to us. When we have a clean heart, we want not only our bodies to be clean, but also our environment. We want to take care of the earth and protect it from pollution or garbage, because we want our outsides to match our insides! When we have a clean heart, we have prepared a space for God to come and live. We want to honor God with our lives, so keeping ourselves pure of heart makes room for God.

Is it always easy to live the way Jesus has called us to live? No, Christianity is not an easy religion to live by. But the Christian life is a wonderful challenge from our Lord: how we choose to live the Gospel teachings in our everyday lives is a choice we make with every person in our lives. If sainthood is our goal, we must do our very best to follow Jesus' teachings. In the Beatitudes, Jesus gave people hope in their future with him.

Profession of Faith

Following the homily or reflection, the prayer leader invites everyone to stand to profess our faith. Together, sing or recite the Apostles' or Nicene Creed. Refer the children to the words of the prayer that you have displayed.

Prayer of the Faithful

Leader: **As God's people on earth, let us unite our prayers with all the saints in heaven. Please respond, "Lord, help your people."**

For all who lead and guide the Church, especially those who help us follow the Beatitudes and live as children of God, we pray: *Lord, help your people.*

For our country's leaders, may they hunger and thirst for righteousness, we pray: *Lord, help your people.*

For those in our parish community who mourn, who are meek and poor in spirit, and who are clean of heart and are peacemakers, we pray: *Lord, help your people.*

Invite other intercessions from the children, or add intercessions based on the current needs of the Church, the world, the oppressed or marginalized, and the local community. Conclude each of the children's petitions with, **"we pray,"** and invite the response, **"Lord, help your people."**

For all of our ancestors and family members who have died, and for the intercession of all of the saints who live in heaven with God, we pray: *Lord, help your people.*

Holy God, our most loving Father, we offer our petitions with the prayers of the Blessed Mother, her spouse Joseph, and all the saints, confident in your mercy revealed in their heroic lives. Through Jesus Christ our Lord.

Children: **Amen.**

Quietly return with the children to the main assembly. Be mindful of children having difficulty finding their families.

November 6, 2022
Thirty-Second Sunday in Ordinary Time
God Gives Us the Strength We Need

 ## Scripture Background

Connections to Church Teaching and Tradition

❋ "But in truly great trials, where I must make a definitive decision to place the truth before my own welfare . . . we need witnesses—martyrs—who have given themselves totally, so as to show us the way—day after day. We need them if we are to prefer goodness to comfort, even in the little choices we face each day—knowing that this is how we live life to the full" (SS, 39).

❋ "The local Churches should do everything possible to ensure that the memory of those who have suffered martyrdom should be safeguarded[1]" (EIA, 15).

❋ "Christ will raise us up 'on the last day'; but it is also true that, in a certain way, we have already risen with Christ. For, by virtue of the Holy Spirit, Christian life is already now on earth a participation in the death and Resurrection of Christ" (CCC, 1002).

❋ "Those who die in God's grace . . . and are perfectly purified . . . are like God for ever for the 'see him as he is'[2]" (CCC, 1023).

1. No. 37: AAS, 87 (1995), 29; cf. *Propositio, 31*.
2. 1 John 3:2; cf. 1 Corinthians 13:12; Revelation 22:4.

2 Maccabees 7:1–2, 9–14   The history of the mother and seven brothers who were martyred for refusing to betray their faith follows on the account of the willing martyrdom of the elderly Eleazar who refused even to pretend that he was eating pork and thereby abandoning the covenant. His reasoning was that feigning apostasy would scandalize the young, which to him was worse than death. The full martyrdom narrative is found in 6:18—7:42.

The word *martyr* comes from the Greek word for "bearing witness," and that is precisely what each of these nine people did, awakening both astonishment and wrath in the king. These faithful people witnessed to a faith that no threat, persecution, or even the sight of their loved ones being tortured could sway. As a matter of fact, the influence of seeing each brother tortured and killed only strengthened the resolve of the ones remaining near their mother. When the last brother's turn came, the king ordered the mother to advise him to avoid death. Instead, she encouraged him, reminding him of the power of the Creator who had given him life and would return him to her in the future. We see here the same dynamic that the Church Father, Tertullian, expressed when he said, "The blood of martyrs is the seed of the Church." God indeed gave them strength, not only in grace but also through each one's witness and encouragement.

Psalm 17:1, 5–6, 8, 15 (15b)   Those who pray this psalm begin by maintaining the rightness of their cause. The parts we pray insist on that and also express resolute and persistent faith. Following the message of 2 Maccabees, we trust that, despite setbacks or persecution, we are destined to be in the eternal presence of God.

2 Thessalonians 2:16—3:5   The key concept in this selection is prayer. Paul begins with a prayer for the community that reminds them of God's love for them. As in last week's readings, this prayer reminds us that the Christian life is a process that depends on grace. Paul also asks the community to pray for him so that he may accomplish his mission. His desire for deliverance is not to save himself, but to be able to continue evangelizing. Finally, he stresses that no matter what, they can count on God's faithfulness, even when they may be called to demonstrate the very "endurance of Christ" (3:5).

Luke 20:27–38 or 20:27, 34–38   This interaction between Jesus and the Sadducees can be read in several ways. On one hand, it is a critique of the idea that the value of a woman is determined by her childbearing, or by her providing descendants for husband, but that is only a side issue. Like the Pharisees who mocked Jesus for his attitude toward material goods (see 16:14), this group of Sadducees ridiculed the idea of eternal life. The sayings of Moses to which they refer are from Deuteronomy 25:5–10, which includes the precept that if a man refuses to marry his brother's widow, even after the elders have admonished him to do so, she has the right to strip him of his sandal and to spit in his face, thereby releasing herself from all obligation to the family and leaving him known as "the man stripped of his sandal" (25:10).

Nearing the climax of his mission, Jesus refused their bait and instead used their absurd example to speak of the resurrection of the dead as something that even Moses had tacitly acknowledged. In that, he used their own sources of authority to annul their argument. The key point here, as in the reading from 2 Maccabees, is the teaching about the Resurrection.

In Maccabees, the promise of eternal life supported the decision of the martyrs to face death rather than be unfaithful; they judged their present on the basis of their hope for the future. In this scene, Jesus describes the "children of this age" (Luke 20:34) as those whose sights are set on material and biological concerns. The others are those who live in such a way that it is the "coming age" (20:35) that determines their activity. The latter are the ones who recognize that all that they are comes from and will find fullness in the God of the living.

 # Preparation

Today's readings affirm that there is indeed life beyond death. In Jesus' time, this was not a belief that was universally shared, even within the Jewish community. The Sadducees in particular saw no basis for this belief and therefore challenged it. Jesus offered both to them and to us today that God is the God of the living, that those righteous who have gone before us share in new life with God and that new life will ultimately include our physical bodies.

Lectionary for Mass #151C

2 Maccabees 7:1–2, 9–14

Psalm 17:1, 5–6, 8, 15 (15b)

2 Thessalonians 2:16—3:5

Luke 20:27–38

Objective

- To introduce and explain bodily resurrection as a part of our faith that Jesus himself affirmed with his words and actions.

Preparation and Materials

- Read the Season Background, the lectionary readings, and the Scripture Background.

- Bookmark the appropriate readings (see page xiv) in the lectionary, children's lectionary, or Bible. Place the book in a convenient location for the leader.

- Write the words of dismissal on a card for the priest celebrant.

- Prepare the words of the song the children will sing as they gather in the space for the Liturgy of the Word.

- Select volunteers (older children or adults) to proclaim the readings.

- Display the responsorial psalm refrain lyrics.

- Display the Apostles' or Nicene Creed.

- Prepare intercessions for the Prayer of the Faithful adapted for the needs of the Church, world, oppressed or marginalized, and local community.

Prayer Leader Reflection Questions

>> **How do you respect the dignity of your own body and the bodies of others? How is care of creation reflected in the choices that you make about your body and those of others?**

>> **How do you pray for those who have died?**

Procession

Following the Collect of the Mass, the priest celebrant picks up the lectionary and invites those who would like to participate in the Liturgy of the Word with children to come forward and gather in the center aisle. The people who will lead the children out and facilitate the Liturgy of the Word also come forward at this time. Holding the lectionary so that all can see, the priest celebrant sends the children forth using his own words or the following:

> *Priest*: **Dear children, God uses the seasons to teach us many things, and in fall, God teaches us about letting go. As the trees lose their leaves and the world prepares for winter sleep, we too can focus on what we need to change and what we need to let go of in our lives. Go now with your prayer leader(s) to listen for what God might be asking of you. May peace be with all of you.**

The leader processes out holding the lectionary, and the children follow behind. The parish music minister may have selected a song of dismissal for the assembly to sing while the children leave. A good option is "The Word of God: Children's Dismissal" by M. D. Ridge and Timothy R. Smith (WLP/GIA).

Centering

Continue to sing the song of dismissal that the assembly sang as you left the church. Or sing the refrain from "Sing with All the Saints in Glory" (Hymn to Joy), or have instrumental music playing as the children gather in the space for the Liturgy of the Word.

Place the lectionary on the ambo or lectern. Light the candle placed by the ambo or lectern, and then lead the following prayer:

> **Heavenly Father,**
> **you have made our bodies and souls out of love.**
> **We know that you want us to share in your unending love**
> **now and in heaven.**
> **Open our hearts to your Word**
> **so we might know you and follow you more fully.**
> **Through Christ our Lord.**

> *Children:* **Amen.**

First Reading

2 Maccabees 7:1–2, 9–14

Responsorial Psalm

Psalm 17:1, 5–6, 8 and 15 *Sing the same musical setting that is used in your parish's celebration of the liturgy.*

Second Reading

2 Thessalonians 2:16—3:5

Gospel Acclamation

Sing the Gospel Acclamation used in your parish's celebration of the liturgy.

Gospel Reading

Luke 20:27–38

Homily/Reflection

≫ **Have you ever wondered what happens when we die?**

This is a question that people have asked since the very beginning of history. People of Jesus' time asked Jesus this very question. This could feel like a difficult question to talk about because none of us here have experienced death and could tell others what happens or what it's like. It might seem natural to think that because we no longer see and talk to someone who has died, that this person disappears and no longer exists. Some people believed this to be true. When we consider difficult questions, we can turn to find answers in God's Word, the Bible. We can listen to how God has responded to questions like this in order to think about what that might mean for us now and in the future.

To answer the people who asked, "What happens when we die," Jesus turned to the words of Moses. Moses is a very important person for the people of Israel. It was Moses who first received the gift of the Law and it was Moses who came into the presence of God who spoke to him in the burning bush. Moses was in close relationship with God, so what he said about God could be trusted to be true. He called God "the God of Abraham, Isaac, and Jacob," and yet when Moses said this, Abraham, Isaac, and Jacob had already died. What could this mean? Why would Moses say this? How could God still be the God of Abraham, Isaac, and Jacob if they were no longer living on the earth?

Jesus recognized that Moses' words spoke about what happens when we die. He understood that those who have died still existed. They had not disappeared and become nothing. Indeed, they had become something more. They have a life that is stronger than death. God wants us to share in a life that is more, not less, than this life that we live on the earth. Jesus said that "the dead will rise"; he wanted us to know that this "something more" isn't only for our souls, but it is also for our bodies. All parts of us, all that has God has made, is made for the resurrected life. The people who listened to this first conversation didn't know yet that Jesus himself would die and rise and that people would see his resurrected body after he had risen from the dead. We know. We have heard the testimony of those who saw him and touched him and ate with him. Jesus did all these things after his resurrection to help us understand what we have in store for us. This is the life that is stronger than death that he shares with us in baptism when we receive the light of life and are called "children of God."

We know too that we must live as "children of light," as "children of God." We must choose to follow God's law of love. We show who we are by the way we live our life on the earth. We also become more of who we are. We help others to see this beautiful gift that God wants to share with all of us. We help the light spread. We know that God wants us to live forever in heaven and we prepare now for the end of our lives, that we will come to share in this "something more," that we will receive our resurrected bodies and live in eternal life forever with God.

Profession of Faith

Following the homily or reflection, the prayer leader invites everyone to stand to profess our faith. Together, sing or recite the Apostles' or Nicene Creed. Refer the children to the words of the prayer that you have displayed.

Prayer of the Faithful

Leader: **We turn to our heavenly Father in prayer to ask him for what we need. Please respond, "Lord, hear our prayer."**

That the Body of Christ might live more and more as children of God, walking in righteousness, let us pray to the Lord: *Lord, hear our prayer.*

That world leaders may secure religious liberty for people of every nation, let us pray to the Lord: *Lord, hear our prayer.*

That those who do not yet know the hope of the resurrection may come to understand the beautiful gift of eternal life that God wants all of us to share, let us pray to the Lord: *Lord, hear our prayer.*

That people's disagreements can still yield a way to peace and harmony, let us pray to the Lord: *Lord, hear our prayer.*

Invite other intercessions from the children, or add intercessions based on the current needs of the Church, the world, the oppressed or marginalized, and the local community. Conclude each of the children's petitions with **"let us pray to the Lord"** and invite the response "**Lord, hear our prayer.**"

That all who have died may join the company of Abraham, Isaac, and Jacob and live forever in God's presence, let us pray to the Lord: *Lord, hear our prayer.*

**God of mercy,
protect our bodies and our minds from the things
that get in the way of following you,
so that we might do your will with our whole hearts.
May we always trust you
and serve you faithfully.
Through Christ our Lord.**

Children: **Amen.**

Quietly return with the children to the main assembly. Be mindful of children having difficulty finding their families.

November 13, 2022
Thirty-Third Sunday in Ordinary Time
Various Challenges in a Lifetime

 Scripture Background

Connections to Church Teaching and Tradition

- "Jesus venerated the Temple by going up to it for the Jewish feasts of pilgrimage, and with a jealous love he loved this dwelling of God among men. The Temple prefigures his own mystery. When he announces its destruction, it is as a manifestation of his own execution and of the entry into a new age in the history of salvation, when his Body would be the definitive Temple" (CCC, 593).

- "The Church is called the building of God. . . . On this foundation the Church is built by the apostles and from it the Church receives solidity and unity. This edifice has many names to describe it: the house of God in which his family dwells; the household of God in the Spirit; the dwelling-place of God among men; and, especially, the holy temple. This temple . . . is compared in the liturgy to the Holy City, the New Jerusalem" (CCC, 756).

- "Christ's disciples hope to render to others true witness of Christ, and to work for their salvation" (AG, 12).

Malachi 3:19–20a   To our ear, this passage, heard alongside the Gospel passage in which Jesus speaks of the end times to his disciples, may feel like a prediction or forecast. Yet the Old Testament does not work like a fortune teller predicting the future. Rather, the words that were often spoken by a prophet (like *Malachi* whose name translated from Hebrew means "my messenger") speak of the real-life situations that challenge God's people and stress the importance for them to be faithful once again to the covenant. Malachi presents a contrast between those who are proud evildoers and those who fear the Lord. Earlier in the chapter he cites particular evil ways the people have chosen to act: "I will draw near to you for judgment, / and I will be swift to bear witness / Against sorcerers, adulterers, and perjurers, / those who deprive a laborer of wages, / Oppress a widow or an orphan, / or turn aside a resident alien, / without fearing me, says the Lord of hosts" (3:5). God's prophet and messenger invites listeners to return to God. When they do, they will be blessed and prosperous, and "they shall be mine, says the Lord" (3:17). Destruction will come to the wicked and justice and healing will come to the faithful and righteous.

Psalm 98:5–6, 7–8, 9 (see 9)   Psalm 98 is an enthronement psalm that celebrates God as the Lord of all creation. In fact, Psalms 86, 97, and 98 all celebrate rejoicing in the face of God's power and glory. Psalm 98 can be proclaimed because truly all the ends of the earth have seen God act to save his people. Therefore, all peoples as well as all of creation clap, sing, and shout with joy for God comes to rule with justice and equity. Next Sunday as we end our liturgical year on the Solemnity of Christ the King, we remember this psalm of praise for God's saving power that rescues the powerless of the world not only in the present moment but for all time to come.

2 Thessalonians 3:7–12   Often the epistles were written not only to teach about faith in Christ but also to correct misunderstandings. Paul writes to the community of Thessalonica, where some believed they did not need to work or plan for the future because they could simply wait for Christ to come again. This attitude had become a burden on others in the community. In his letter, Paul reminds them that "we always pray for you, that our God may make you worthy of his calling and powerfully bring to fulfillment every good purpose and every effort of faith, that the name of our Lord Jesus may be glorified in you" (1:11–12). There would be many challenges both for the community and for believers, but Paul prays that "the Lord of peace himself give you peace at all times and in every way" (2 Thessalonians 3:16). Their faithful perseverance to that message is what is required of disciples and would bring them peace.

Luke 21:5–19   Like Malachi, Luke sets up a contrast for his readers. There will be those who will harm, persecute, and imprison disciples and there will be those who testify to their God. Those who give witness, though they may be hated and even killed, will not be harmed. Their perseverance, strength, and resolve will render their persecutors powerless in the face of God's power. This is Jesus' last appearance in the Temple. By setting this story in the Temple, which only Luke does, Luke reminds his community of the other times the Temple was significant in Jesus' life. He was presented to the Lord in the Temple and recognized by Simeon and Anna (see 2:22–38). He was found by his parents as he did his Father's bidding (see 2:49). He drove out the money changers and taught the Good News (see 19:45—20:1). After his Ascension, the disciples returned to the Temple to give praise (see 24:52–53). The destruction of the Temple will not matter, it is Jesus' words to his disciples that will. Their rootedness in Christ and their willingness to give testimony will be all that is necessary.

The disciples who followed Jesus would face many challenges as they stayed faithful to his teaching and instructions. However, they are deeply rooted in Jesus and therefore grounded in their inheritance as people of God's covenant. No matter the trials or tribulations that confronted them, no matter the persecutions or sufferings "by your perseverance you will secure your lives" (21:19).

Preparation

As the earth in the northern hemisphere begins to ready for the sleep of winter and the fruits of the earth become ready for harvest, our Church turns attention to the slumber of our own deaths and the harvest of souls at the end of time, which we call the parousia. We stand in awe at God's power and the inevitability of God's ultimate victory, but we recognize that the time approaching the parousia will involve struggle. All that is not of God will be burned away. In the meantime, as we await God's kingdom, we do not stand idle, but instead seek to be models of God's justice until it arrives in fullness.

Lectionary for Mass #159C

Malachi 3:19–20a

Psalm 98:5–6, 7–8, 9 (see 9)

2 Thessalonians 3:7–12

Luke 21:5–19

Objectives

- To explain God's justice to the children.

- To inspire joyful anticipation at the coming of God's justice in the parousia.

Preparation and Materials

- Read the Season Background, the lectionary readings, and the Scripture Background.

- Bookmark the appropriate readings (see page xiv) in the lectionary, children's lectionary, or Bible. Place the book in a convenient location for the leader.

- Write the words of dismissal on a card for the priest celebrant.

- Prepare the words of the song the children will sing as they gather in the space for the Liturgy of the Word.

- Select volunteers (older children or adults) to proclaim the readings.

- Display the responsorial psalm refrain lyrics.

- Display the Apostles' or Nicene Creed.

- Prepare intercessions for the Prayer of the Faithful adapted for the needs of the Church, world, oppressed or marginalized, and local community.

Prayer Leader Reflection Questions

>> How does your faith in God help to calm fears and anxieties about the future?

>> What injustices do you see in your own community? How might you help to bring healing and harmony for those who do not have what they need for the fullness of life?

Procession

Following the Collect of the Mass, the priest celebrant picks up the lectionary and invites those who would like to participate in the Liturgy of the Word with children to come forward and gather in the center aisle. The people who will lead the children out and facilitate the Liturgy of the Word also come forward at this time. Holding the lectionary so that all can see, the priest celebrant sends the children forth using his own words or the following:

Priest: **Dear children, God uses the seasons to teach us many things, and in fall, God teaches us about letting go. As the trees lose their leaves and the world prepares for winter sleep, we too can focus on what we need to change and what we need to let go of in our lives. Go now with your prayer leader(s) to listen for what God might be asking of you. May peace be with all of you.**

The leader processes out holding the lectionary, and the children follow behind. The parish music minister may have selected a song of dismissal for the assembly to sing while the children leave. A good option is "The Word of God: Children's Dismissal" by M. D. Ridge and Timothy R. Smith (WLP/GIA).

Centering

Continue to sing the song of dismissal that the assembly sang as you left the church. Or sing the refrains from "Lord of All Hopefulness" (SLANE), or "Soon and Very Soon" (Crouch), or have instrumental music playing as the children gather in the space for the Liturgy of the Word.

Place the lectionary on the ambo or lectern. Light the candle placed by the ambo or lectern, and then lead the following prayer:

Lord of justice,
open our hearts to your Word
so we might know you and follow you more fully.
May we always follow the example of Jesus Christ, your Son,
in whose name we pray.

Children: **Amen.**

First Reading

Malachi 3:19–20a

Responsorial Psalm

Psalm 98:5–6, 7–8, 9 (see 9) *Sing the same musical setting that is used in your parish's celebration of the liturgy.*

Second Reading

2 Thessalonians 3:7–12

Gospel Acclamation

Sing the Gospel Acclamation used in your parish's celebration of the liturgy.

Gospel Reading

Luke 21:5–19

Homily/Reflection

This is the last week before the Solemnity of Our Lord Jesus Christ, King of the Universe. We sometimes call next Sunday the Feast of Christ the King, and it is the final Sunday of the liturgical year. As we come close to the end of the liturgical year, we also think about end times. Just as the liturgical year moves toward a conclusion, all of history is moving toward a conclusion that we call the parousia. It is the time when God will be "all in all" and God's kingdom will have no end. Jesus Christ will return in power and glory and the light of God will be so bright and full that we won't even need the sun and the moon for light.

The first reading and psalm speak about a particular quality of the fullness of God's kingdom: God's justice. Many might think *justice* is the same as *fairness*. If there is a tray of two donuts in front of me and a friend, I might say that what is fair is for each of us to have one donut. What is unfair is for my friend to eat both donuts and I have none, but that's not God's justice. God's justice is everyone living in relationships of love and harmony. Everyone gets what they need for the fullness of life together.

The prophet Malachi spoke about God's justice in the fullness of the kingdom when he said, "the sun of justice will arise with healing in its wings." We can imagine what that will feel like. We close our eyes and think about being outside on a cold day with the sun hidden behind clouds.

We can picture the clouds parting and a burst of heat and the light making our world better, warmer, more whole and healthy.

I think if I experienced that I would be so filled with joy that I would want to sing. The psalm says this, too. The psalm tells us to "sing praise to the Lord . . . who comes to govern the earth, to govern the world with justice and the peoples with fairness." But it is not only us who sing. All of creation belongs to God, is loved by God, and so all of creation sings at the Lord's just rule of the earth. Even the seas and the rivers and the mountains make music for God. There is so much joy that it overflows and is shared amongst everyone and everything that is good.

We await the parousia with hope, but we are still not there. We know that God's justice cannot totally be seen yet. Each of us might be able to think about places and times that lack harmony, of places and times in which people do not have what they need to lead fulfilling lives.

» So what do we do in the meantime?

We can look for the places where God's justice is shining through, and when we see it, we can name it, share our joy about it with others. We can practice the virtue of justice; we can be examples and models for others of what living in God's justice looks like, of making right choices. Sometimes we might be the ones causing the disharmony, keeping others from getting what they need. When that has happened, we can admit we were wrong, say we are sorry to those we have hurt and try to find a way to promote healing. For those of us who are old enough and prepared, we can do this is a most particular way in the sacrament of reconciliation. God can heal *us*, too. We know that what we most need is God. When we rejoin the assembly in just a few minutes, we'll gather around the altar to see, touch, and taste God's very self in the Eucharist. That includes seeing, touching, tasting God's justice. We'll join with all the angels and saints as we sing together, united with heaven. Together, we will have what we most need.

Profession of Faith

Following the homily or reflection, the prayer leader invites everyone to stand to profess our faith. Together, sing or recite the Apostles' or Nicene Creed. Refer the children to the words of the prayer that you have displayed.

Prayer of the Faithful

Leader: **The day of the Lord is coming when he will bring us the fullness of joy and salvation. We trust in his just and merciful response to what we ask. Please respond, "Lord, hear us."**

May the Church be a model of God's healing justice, we pray:
Lord hear us.

May all elected officials seek the wisdom of God to make just decisions, we pray: *Lord hear us.*

May those who suffer in the name of Jesus be consoled with the joy and peace of God's kingdom, we pray: *Lord hear us.*

May all who labor be paid justly for their work, we pray: *Lord hear us.*

Invite other intercessions from the children, or add intercessions based on the current needs of the Church, the world, the oppressed or marginalized, and the local community. Conclude each of the children's petitions with **"we pray"** and invite the response **"Lord, hear us."**

May those who have died join the angels and saints in heaven and sing God's glory together, we pray: *Lord hear us.*

O heavenly Father,
we wait in joyful hope for the coming of your Son, Jesus.
Until that day, let us not lose faith in you.
We ask this through Christ our Lord.

Children: **Amen.**

Quietly return with the children to the main assembly. Be mindful of children having difficulty finding their families.

November 20, 2022
Solemnity of Our Lord Jesus Christ, King of the Universe

Today You Will Be with Me

 ## Scripture Background

Connections to Church Teaching and Tradition

❖ "The goal of salvation, the Kingdom of God embraces all people and is fully realized beyond history, in God. The Church has received 'the mission of proclaiming and establishing among all peoples the Kingdom of Christ and of God, and she is, on earth, the seed and the beginning of that Kingdom'" (CSDC, 49).

❖ "Let us believe the Gospel . . . that the kingdom of God is already present in this world and is growing, here and there, and in different ways" (EG, 278).

2 Samuel 5:1–3 As we celebrate this last Sunday of the liturgical year, we focus on Jesus Christ as the King of the Universe, the Risen Lord who has conquered death and now lives in eternal union with the Father and Spirit. Christ's kingship as deliverer and shepherd of the whole universe is prefigured in the person of David, king of Israel's united kingdom and that of the holy city, Jerusalem. David's anointing by all the other tribes as king of Israel is actually David's third anointing. Samuel performed the first one while David was still a youth, setting God's approval on David as future king (see 1 Samuel 16:13). David's second anointing designates him king of Judah (see 2 Samuel 2:4). Here, all the tribes acknowledge their intimate kinship with David, "here we are, your bone and your flesh" (5:1); they are pleased with David's previous leadership under Saul. David's role as leader and shepherd of the people is God's doing, and the tribes fully approve and promise loyalty and fidelity. As king, David promises to care for God's people, exercising justice and right relationship, thus becoming the visible representative of God as shepherd of the people. Hence, David prefigures Christ's future kingdom and rule over all creation.

Psalm 122:1–2, 3–4, 4–5 (see 1) This pilgrimage psalm expresses the great joy of those who cherished the opportunity to go to the Temple, "the house of the LORD" (122:1) situated at the very pinnacle of Jerusalem, the holy city established by King David. Jerusalem, the focal worship center of all the tribes, was admired for its Temple, its beauty, and its adherence to the covenant promises and Torah regulations. Both king and city were understood to be the living embodiment of the Lord's intimate dwelling and covenant relationship with all the people. Thanksgiving to God for such marvels as the Temple and the city was the only fitting response any pilgrim could give. Thus Jerusalem, the Temple, and the unity therein expressed became a symbol for intimate covenant relationship with God for all time.

Colossians 1:12–20 The author of the Letter to the Colossians inserts a preexisting liturgical hymn at the beginning of the letter to exalt Christ's role as king over all creation. The author introduces the hymn by inviting disciples to offer praise and thanksgiving to God for the privilege "to share / in the inheritance of the holy ones" (1:12). Through Christ's passion, death, and Resurrection, God has gifted us with redemption, the forgiveness of sin, and "delivered us from the power of darkness / and transferred us to the kingdom of his beloved Son" (1:13). Jesus is praised and exalted above all creation—the "firstborn of all creation" (1:15) in whom all things were created. In Christ, "all things hold together" (1:17). He is "the head of the body, the church . . . in him all the fullness was pleased to dwell" (1:18). Through the blood of his cross, Christ reconciled all things, "making peace . . . / whether those on earth or those in heaven" (1:20). Such high Christology exalting Christ as the reconciling king of the universe is a fitting hymn for this last Sunday of the liturgical year.

Luke 23:35–43 Death by crucifixion is far removed from the human concept of kingship. Kings usually exercise power over others. Luke narrates this scene with irony and paradox, asserting that the world's ways are not God's ways. Jesus is the chosen one of God, the Christ (Messiah), the true king of the Jews in the line of David, who has come to establish God's kingdom, and through his self-gift on the cross is accomplishing his mission. However, the rulers, the soldiers, and one of the criminals crucified with him cannot understand the cosmic events happening before their eyes. Paradoxically, everything they are saying in mockery about him is true, which they fail to see. One of the crucified criminals does see. Luke uses him to assert Jesus' innocence and undeserved punishment. This crucified criminal also acknowledges Jesus' kingly status, humbly asking to be remembered by Jesus when "you come into your kingdom" (23:42). Jesus, eagerly welcoming the repentant sinner, "today" (23:43) welcomes this lost son into paradise with him. Luke's main Gospel themes manifest themselves. Jesus, the universal savior of all, shows special care and concern for the rejected and for all repentant sinners. As Davidic king, Jesus came to establish God's kingdom and to call all to repentance and mutual loving service. In so doing, we too can anticipate Jesus assurance that "today you will be with me in Paradise" (23:43).

 # Preparation

On this Solemnity of Our Lord Jesus Christ, King of the Universe, we honor and celebrate the reality that Jesus is Lord and ruler of all. We look to the history of kingship in Israel, and David as model and foretaste of the divine kingship of Christ. We recall the words of the Letter of Paul to the Colossians that offers us language for Christ's awesome transcendence. We encounter the reality presented in the Gospel of the surprising and terrible crowning of Christ on the cross that enabled our share in the inheritance of the kingdom.

Lectionary for Mass #162C

2 Samuel 5:1–3

Psalm 122:1–2, 3–4, 4–5 (see 1)

Colossians 1:12–20

Luke 23:35–43

Objectives

- To consider together the significance of Christ's kingship and the extent of God's kingdom.

- To introduce and explain the term *inheritance* to the children in the context of the second reading.

Preparation and Materials

- Read the Season Background, the lectionary readings, and the Scripture Background.

- Bookmark the appropriate readings (see page xiv) in the lectionary, children's lectionary, or Bible. Place the book in a convenient location for the leader.

- Write the words of dismissal on a card for the priest celebrant.

- Prepare the words of the song the children will sing as they gather in the space for the Liturgy of the Word.

- Select volunteers (older children or adults) to proclaim the readings.

- Display the responsorial psalm refrain lyrics.

- Display the Apostles' or Nicene Creed.

- Prepare intercessions for the Prayer of the Faithful adapted for the needs of the Church, world, oppressed or marginalized, and local community.

Prayer Leader Reflection Questions

» **How is Jesus Christ the king of your life? When is Christ your priority? Are there times you choose something or someone before Jesus?**

» **How have you educated yourself about the Church's teachings on capital punishment? How might you help to eliminate it in your community, your country, and your world?**

Procession

Following the Collect of the Mass, the priest celebrant picks up the lectionary and invites those who would like to participate in the Liturgy of the Word with children to come forward and gather in the center aisle. The people who will lead the children out and facilitate the Liturgy of the Word also come forward at this time. Holding the lectionary so that all can see, the priest celebrant sends the children forth using his own words or the following:

> *Priest*: **Dear children, God uses the seasons to teach us many things, and in fall, God teaches us about letting go. As the trees lose their leaves and the world prepares for winter sleep, we too can focus on what we need to change and what we need to let go of in our lives. Go now with your prayer leader(s) to listen for what God might be asking of you. May peace be with all of you.**

The leader processes out holding the lectionary, and the children follow behind. The parish music minister may have selected a song of dismissal for the assembly to sing while the children leave. A good option is "The Word of God: Children's Dismissal" by M. D. Ridge and Timothy R. Smith (WLP/GIA).

Centering

Continue to sing the song of dismissal that the assembly sang as you left the church. Or sing refrains from "Jesus, Remember Me" (Berthier), or "The King of Love My Shepherd Is" (St. Columba), or have instrumental music playing as the children gather in the space for the Liturgy of the Word.

Place the lectionary on the ambo or lectern. Light the candle placed by the ambo or lectern, and then lead the following prayer:

> **God of all life and all time,**
> **you rule us with justice, mercy, and love.**
> **Open our hearts to your Word**
> **so we might know you and follow you more fully.**
> **Through Christ our Lord.**

> *Children:* **Amen.**

First Reading

2 Samuel 5:1–3

Responsorial Psalm

Psalm 122:1–2, 3–4, 4–5 *Sing the same musical setting that is used in your parish's celebration of the liturgy.*

Second Reading

Colossians 1:12–20

Gospel Acclamation

Sing the Gospel Acclamation used in your parish's celebration of the liturgy.

Gospel Reading

Luke 23:35–43

Homily/Reflection

Today is the last Sunday of the liturgical year, which is something like New Year's Eve. It is a time to think about endings, beginnings, and what is most important. On this final Sunday, we gather to celebrate a great feast. Officially we call it the Solemnity of Our Lord Jesus Christ, King of the Universe, but we also call it the Feast of Christ the King. We honor that Jesus is our true King.

≫ When you think of a king, how would you describe him?

In some ways, Jesus Christ is like an earthly king. The first reading tells us about the most beloved king of Israel, King David. King David united the people of Israel, protected them, and ruled with justice. Later, when the people of Israel no longer had a king so well-loved, they waited and hoped for a new one like their ancestor David. The people of Israel spoke of one to come who would sit on the throne of David. The Gospels tell us that Jesus was of the house of David, or his descendant. We know that Jesus shares the qualities of kingship that David had, and we love and praise them.

Jesus Christ isn't only like an earthly king, though. Jesus Christ is more than an earthly king. He is a God-king. Jesus does not reign over one particular country and one particular people who live there, but all people, all the earth, all creation. In the second reading, we are reminded of who Jesus really is. All things were created *for* Jesus Christ but also *through* him. He was there at the start of creation because he was there *before* creation. Jesus Christ has no beginning. He is even the King of time itself. As the king of all creation and the king of all time, he is not bound by time, but is King of all creation that is, that ever was, that ever will be.

We hear in today's Gospel of Jesus on the cross. We know he died but he also rose again. Death did not rule over Jesus, but instead, Jesus was victorious over death. Jesus Christ is King of life. Jesus Christ shares this life that is stronger than death with us in baptism. We are named as children of God. That means that as family of the King, we are royal too.

In the second reading, St. Paul tells is that we share in an inheritance. The word *inheritance* usually refers to something of value that is passed on from an older family member to a younger family member. Our inheritance is what has the most value: the kingdom of God. We share in the eternal life that belongs to the King.

Today, as we think about endings and beginnings, let's also take a few moments of silence think about who comes first in our hearts, who rules our hearts.

Profession of Faith

Following the homily or reflection, the prayer leader invites everyone to stand to profess our faith. Together, sing or recite the Apostles' or Nicene Creed. Refer the children to the words of the prayer that you have displayed.

Prayer of the Faithful

Leader: **Christ our King reigns in his eternal kingdom with his heavenly Father, to whom we confidently present our needs. Please respond, "Lord God, hear our prayer."**

For the Church, that she might always look to Jesus Christ our King, to know what to do and how to do it, we pray: *Lord God, hear our prayer.*

For kings, queens, and other powerful rulers of this world, that they might govern wisely, we pray: *Lord God, hear our prayer.*

For those imprisoned in body or mind, and for those who love and care for them, that they may experience God's justice and mercy, we pray: *Lord God, hear our prayer.*

For all who teach and lead young people in the faith, that they may impart to their students the message of Christ with clarity and conviction, we pray: *Lord God, hear our prayer.*

Invite other intercessions from the children, or add intercessions based on the current needs of the Church, the world, the oppressed or marginalized, and the local community. Conclude each of the children's petitions with **"we pray"** and invite the response **"Lord God, hear our prayer."**

For all who have died, that they might be with Christ in paradise, we pray: *Lord God, hear our prayer.*

God of all life and all time, you want to bring all things to you through your Son, the King of the universe. We acclaim him as our King, for by his passion and death he delivered us from darkness. Receive our prayers and grant us mercy. Through Christ our Lord.

Children: **Amen.**

Quietly return with the children to the main assembly. Be mindful of children having difficulty finding their families.

Season Background for Advent

Understanding Advent

Most of us recognize Advent as the time when we prepare for Christmas. The pace of our lives seems to increase rapidly and become more hectic each year, especially right after the American Thanksgiving holiday. Yet the liturgical year presents us with the opportunity to slow down and reflect on the significance of what and whom we will celebrate on Christmas and throughout Christmas Time. Like Mary, as she prepared for the birth of her Son, Advent is a time for pause, reflection, and preparation for the gift of God's love coming to us through the baby Jesus. This liturgical season includes the four Sundays, and the weekdays in between, until Evening Prayer I of Christmas, which is prayed on Christmas Eve.

Advent is the time to prepare for when we remember Christ's first coming long ago, and it is also a time of joyful expectation as we ponder our belief in Christ's second coming in glory at the end of time. This latter dimension can be difficult for younger children to understand. Yet do not shy away from talking about Christ coming again. Start to move the children beyond an understanding of Christmas that focuses only on the infant lying in the manger years ago. Christ is alive in the hearts of all people now! As Catholics, we also live in the hope of Christ's coming again. These three dimensions are what we prepare to celebrate in the Church's liturgies of Christmas Time and in our lives.

As Advent progresses, the Advent wreath grows brighter as we light more candles each week. On the Third Sunday of Advent, Gaudete Sunday, we joyfully pause to mark the approach of Christmas. We light the rose candle on the Advent wreath and reflect on how, at the halfway point, a turning point in the season, we have kept the Advent season in our hearts and our homes.

Liturgical Environment

Advent requires subtlety and restraint in the environment. The liturgical color for Advent is violet. This is the same color as that of Lent. In order to distinguish between the two seasons, violet with deeper shades of blue is used for Advent. While both Advent and Lent are penitential seasons, Advent is the season of joyful expectation. In addition to using the liturgical color in your space, make use of the Advent wreath. The candles will help the children to mark the progression toward Christmas and focus on Christ's coming among us.

Overview of the Readings

As we begin the new liturgical year with the First Sunday of Advent, we also move into Year A of the Lectionary cycle of readings. In Year A, the Gospel according to Matthew is the primary account of the Gospel proclaimed in the Sunday liturgy. During Advent there are three prevalent themes: we long for the Messiah, are urged to be alert for Christ's Second Coming, and meditate on Christ's presence in our lives now. The Scripture readings for the four weeks of Advent and the Liturgy of the Hours revolve around the first two of these themes. They encourage proper preparation, point to the grace and humility of Mary, show us how to adore God in the Incarnation, and recognize the glory of Jesus Christ and how he frees us from sin and ingratitude. We hear from the prophet Isaiah and are drawn to the compelling message of John the Baptist in the Gospels.

As is the case each Sunday, continuity exists between the first reading and the selection from the Gospel. The more we listen carefully to the first reading and the Gospel throughout the seasons of Advent and Christmas Time, the more we come to understand that Jesus Christ is the fulfillment of the Old Testament prophecies. Indeed, he is the Messiah, the Son of Man and the Son of God, who comes to save us, the Lord's people. The passages from the New Testament in the second readings enhance our reflection on the great themes of joyful expectation and renewed hope in the future coming of the Lord in glory.

First Readings   During Advent the first reading is from the book of the prophet Isaiah on the Messiah and the Messianic age. The first reading sets the stage for the Gospel, which identifies Jesus as the one who fulfills the prophecies of the Messiah. Jesus, born of a virgin and named Emmanuel, is the Lord's sign of salvation for his people.

Responsorial Psalms   The new liturgical year begins on the First Sunday of Advent with the same responsorial psalm that was sung on the Solemnity of Christ the King to conclude the previous liturgical year, Year C. Psalm 122 encourages us to go rejoicing to the Lord's house. The psalms for the Second and Third Sundays of Advent speak of the Lord's justice and kingship (Psalms 72 and 146, respectively). On the Fourth Sunday of Advent, Psalm 24 speaks of going to "the mountain of the Lord." It calls us to prepare our hearts to receive the Lord's blessings and justice.

Second Readings   On three of the four Sundays of Advent in Year A, the second reading comes from Paul's Letter to the Romans. On the other Sunday, the Third Sunday of Advent, the Second Reading is from the Letter to James. The exhortations to awake from sleep, to welcome one another as Christ welcomes us, to be patient until the coming of the Lord, and to be obedient and firm in our faith in the Son of God are common Advent themes of the Second Readings.

Gospel Readings   During Advent of each of the three years of the Lectionary cycle of readings, the Gospel reading has a particular theme related to the meaning of the season. The Gospel on the First Sunday of Advent speaks of the Lord's coming at the end of time. In Year A, the year of Matthew, the Gospel on the First Sunday has Jesus teaching his disciples about staying awake for the coming day of the Lord. On the Second and Third Sundays of Advent, the Gospel reading involves John the Baptist; in particular, John the Baptist's call to repentance, Jesus' own affirmation of John as the messenger who prepared the way for him, and the followers of John querying Jesus as to whether or not he is the one to come.

The Gospel proclaimed on the Fourth Sunday of Advent each year always focuses on an event that immediately precedes the Lord's birth. In Year A, the Gospel on this Sunday involves Joseph, the foster father of Jesus, who appears infrequently in the Gospel readings proclaimed during the Church's liturgies. This Gospel is an intensely personal interaction between Joseph and an angel, who appears to him in a dream asking him to take Mary into his home because the child she bears has been conceived through the Holy Spirit.

November 27, 2022
First Sunday of Advent

Awaken!

 ## Scripture Background

Connections to Church Teaching and Tradition

- During Advent the Church presents the ancient expectancy of the Messiah and his coming in the flesh in the Incarnation. It is a season of preparation, worship, and service (CCC, 524).

- In Advent we await Christ's Second Coming at the end of time, described as "eschatological," which can happen at any moment (CCC, 673, 840, 2853).

- We pray for and anticipate God's promise of peace and justice in the world. Peace is God's gift, the fruit of the Holy Spirit and charity, the foundation of the common good (CCC, 736, 1828–1832, 1909).

Isaiah 2:1–5   Isaiah was a prophet in the eighth century BC. Chapter 2 is part of a collection of oracles against Jerusalem and the southern kingdom of Judah for their apostasy. The northern kingdom of Israel along with its capital, Samaria, was conquered by the Assyrians in 733 BC and was later destroyed in 722 BC. In the prophet Isaiah's time, King Hezekiah demolished the idolatry practiced on the "high places" (2 Kings 18:4) and tried to centralize worship in Jerusalem. Isaiah sees a time in the future when all nations shall stream to the Holy City to receive instruction from the Lord. It will be a time of world peace when people "beat their swords into plowshares and their spears into pruning hooks" (v. 4). All peoples will be attracted to the true worship offered by God on Mount Zion.

Psalm 122:1–2, 3–4, 4–5, 6–7, 8–9 (see 1)   Psalm 122 is a psalm of ascent, sung by pilgrims as they reached the gates of Jerusalem. According to God's decree, the tribes were to go up to the Holy City three times a year for the pilgrimage feasts of Passover, Pentecost, and Tabernacles. As they gathered for worship, the pilgrims prayed in thanksgiving for God's protection on their journey and for the peace and prosperity of Jerusalem. The city had been the religious and political capital of Israel from the time of David. Prayer for Jerusalem was a prayer for the good of the whole nation. In time, Jerusalem became the symbol of the Church, the New Jerusalem.

Romans 13:11–14   Paul stresses the urgency of the time. He declares that salvation is near and urges that "it is the hour now for you to awake from sleep" (v. 11). He and the early Church expected the Second Coming of Christ at any moment; they were to live ready for it to happen.

Paul's words in the last verses of this passage brought St. Augustine to conversion, as he describes in his autobiographical work *Confessions*. Augustine was walking in the garden, distressed because of his failure to live a life in Christ. Suddenly, he heard a child's voice saying, "Take and read; take and read." He snatched up a volume of Paul's writings and read the first passage on which his eyes fell: "The night is advanced, the day is at hand" (v. 12). Like Paul, Augustine shed his former way of life and "put on the Lord Jesus Christ" (v. 14). Now is the time for all Christians to wake and live in the light of the new life they have received in Jesus Christ.

Matthew 24:37–44   Chapters 24–25 form the fifth and final discourse in the Gospel according to Matthew. Jesus speaks both of the destruction of Jerusalem by the Romans in AD 70 and of his coming at the end of time. The early Christians eagerly anticipated the Second Coming, and they longed for the liberation from suffering that he would bring.

Jesus does not give them a timetable, but says that they will see warning signs of his return. He points to the fig tree and tells them to learn its lesson (v. 32). If a person can tell when summer is near by the signs of nature, so, too, the signs of the times will indicate when Christ is near. Yet no one knows the time of his coming, not the angels, not even Jesus himself. The exact time of his return is known to none but God. It is futile for Jesus' disciples to speculate; their duty is to prepare and to watch.

Jesus warns them that his coming will be similar to Noah's day. When "God saw how corrupt the earth had become," God determined to "bring the flood waters on the earth" (Genesis 6:12, 17). The perverse and lawless people had no concern about the future until it was too late and "the flood came and carried them all away" (Matthew 24:39). Noah was "a righteous man and blameless in his generation" (Genesis 6:9). Because he listened to God's warning, he and his family were saved from destruction. So, too, at the time of Christ's coming, men and women will be preoccupied with their ordinary activities. Those who are prepared for his arrival will be taken into God's Kingdom. Those who are unready will be left in their own sin. Jesus' followers must be vigilant for his return whenever it may occur.

Preparation

(We now begin a new lectionary cycle. Use Year A readings.)
In Advent, we wait and prepare for both Christmas, when we celebrate that Christ was born, and the time when Christ will return in fullness in the parousia. At the culmination of history, all peoples will draw near to the Lord and experience the fullness of God's light. Our response to this good news can only be joy. We do not know when this will happen, so we should keep ready. Wearing the armor of light helps us to do this.

Lectionary for Mass #1A

Isaiah 2:1–5

Psalm 122:1–2, 3–4, 4–5, 6–7, 8–9 (see 1)

Romans 13:11–14

Matthew 24:37–44

Objectives

- To present the parousia, the time when Christ will return in fullness, as a time we await.

- To offer the image of "armor of light" as way to think about our preparations for Christ's coming.

Preparation and Materials

- Read the Season Background, the lectionary readings, and the Scripture Background.

- Bookmark the appropriate readings (see page xv) in the lectionary, children's lectionary, or Bible. Place the book in a convenient location for the leader.

- Write the words of dismissal on a card for the priest celebrant.

- Prepare the words of the song the children will sing as they gather in the space for the Liturgy of the Word.

- Select volunteers (older children or adults) to proclaim the readings.

- Display the responsorial psalm refrain lyrics.

- Display the Apostles' or Nicene Creed.

- Prepare intercessions for the Prayer of the Faithful adapted for the needs of the Church, world, oppressed or marginalized, and local community.

Prayer Leader Reflection Questions

>> **If Jesus were to return today, would you be ready? Would he find you in shambles or in good order? What do you need to do to prepare your heart for Christ's return?**

>> **In what ways do you pursue the peacemaking that is a part of our movement toward the parousia?**

Procession

Following the Collect of the Mass, the priest celebrant picks up the lectionary and invites those who would like to participate in the Liturgy of the Word with children to come forward and gather in the center aisle. The people who will lead the children out and facilitate the Liturgy of the Word also come forward at this time. Holding the lectionary so that all can see, the priest celebrant sends the children forth using his own words or the following:

> *Priest*: **Children, watching and waiting for someone or something is not easy, but that is what we do in Advent. We watch and wait to celebrate the birth of Jesus at Christmas, and for Christ to come again. Go now in peace to listen to the Word of God. Listen to the ways we can be watchful as we await Christ's coming.**

The leader processes out holding the lectionary, and the children follow behind. The parish music minister may have selected a song of dismissal for the assembly to sing while the children leave. A good option is "The Word of God: Children's Dismissal" by M. D. Ridge and Timothy R. Smith (WLP/GIA).

Centering

Continue to sing the song of dismissal that the assembly sang as you left the church. Or sing "Litany of the Word" (Farrell), or the refrain from "Soon and Very Soon" (Crouch), or have instrumental music playing as the children gather in the space for the Liturgy of the Word.

Place the lectionary on the ambo or lectern. Light the candle placed by the ambo or lectern, and then lead the following prayer:

> **O Christ Jesus,**
> **you have promised the fullness of your light in the parousia.**
> **We long to hear your voice,**
> **to deepen and develop our understanding of who you are**
> **and what you have in store for our lives.**
> **We pray in your name, Lord Jesus, come.**

> *Children:* **Amen.**

First Reading

Isaiah 2:1–5

Responsorial Psalm

Psalm 122:1–2, 3–4, 4–5, 6–7, 8–9 (see 1) *Sing the same musical setting that is used in your parish's celebration of the liturgy.*

Second Reading

Romans 13:11–14

Gospel Acclamation

Sing the Gospel Acclamation used in your parish's celebration of the liturgy.

Gospel Reading

Matthew 24:37–44

Homily/Reflection

Today, we begin Advent, a season of waiting and preparing to celebrate the great feast of Christmas. We are getting ready to enjoy in a most particular way that Jesus came to be born to us. We know that the people of Israel waited and prepared for the coming of the Messiah. During this time, we also remember that we are waiting for when Jesus Christ will come again. We call this time that we look forward to the "parousia," when God will be "all in all" (1 Corinthians 15:28), when the light of the Lord will be so bright that we will no longer need the sun and moon (Isaiah 60:19), and Jesus Christ will return in glory.

» We hear from Isaiah in the first reading. Who was he?

Isaiah was a prophet of the Jewish people who listened deeply for God's voice and shared the Word of God with the people. For them, during this time, the place where God was most present was in the city of Jerusalem, on Mount Zion, inside the temple. God dwelled in the Holy of Holies, a place so holy, so set apart, that only one person, the high priest, could go inside it on one single day, the day of atonement. Isaiah described a beautiful time in the future when not just Jewish people, but all people would recognize God. Once they recognize God, they would want to draw near, to climb the holy mountain to be close to God, to hear God's voice and know God's law. Once they experience this, they would respond with peace, turning their swords and spears into tools for harvest and walking together in God's light. We wait with Isaiah and the Jewish people when all people will know God, when all wars will end and when we will all share in God's light.

» How can we respond, knowing that this time will come?

In knowing this announcement, on hearing this good news, we may want to respond with a prayer of joy. The writer of today's psalm responded in just this way! We hear "I rejoiced when they said to me, Let us go to the house of the LORD'" (Psalm 122:1). This writer speaks of being invited to go to Jerusalem to the "house of the Lord." This is a way of speaking about the temple, the place where God lives. Being together, close to the Lord, leads the psalm writer to pray for the peace that we will experience in fullness in the parousia.

Jesus knew these words. He prayed and listened to God's Word as a faithful Jewish person. He spoke, too, about the time when he would return, the day of the Lord. He warned us that as the time draws near, not everything will be easy and we won't know that the time is coming, so we should be always ready.

» How can we be ready?

We can stop choosing the things that separate us from the one who is Light, Jesus Christ. Instead, we can put on the armor of light. We can seek out what helps us to live as children of light. Praying, listening to God's Word, receiving the sacraments, caring for our neighbors . . . there are so many ways we can put on armor of light to be ready for the time when we will see Christ's own light in all its glory. *(If time permits, invite children to offer more ideas of getting ready.)*

Profession of Faith

Following the homily or reflection, the prayer leader invites everyone to stand to profess our faith. Together, sing or recite the Apostles' or Nicene Creed. Refer the children to the words of the prayer that you have displayed.

Prayer of the Faithful

Leader: **As we look toward the day when God will be all in all, we pray at this time for our needs and the needs of the world. Please respond, "Father forever, hear our prayer."**

For the Church, may she help prepare our hearts for the Son of Man when he comes again, we pray: *Father forever, hear our prayer.*

For our world, that leaders of all nations may seek peace, we pray: *Father forever, hear our prayer.*

For those who have lost their way, the poor, and the outcast, we pray: *Father forever, hear our prayer.*

For the children here, that their Advent journey may be a time of patient waiting and prayer, we pray: *Father forever, hear our prayer.*

Invite other intercessions from the children, or add intercessions based on the current needs of the Church, the world, the oppressed or marginalized, and the local community. Conclude each of the children's petitions with **"we pray"** and invite the response **"Father forever, hear our prayer."**

For those who have died, that they might live in the fullness of God's light and life, we pray: *Father forever, hear our prayer.*

Mighty God,
give us the strength to put on the armor of light
so that we might experience the fullness of your kingdom in
the parousia.
Hear our prayers through Christ our Lord.

Children: **Amen.**

Quietly return with the children to the main assembly. Be mindful of children having difficulty finding their families.

December 4, 2022
Second Sunday of Advent

Justice Shall Flourish

 ## Scripture Background

Connections to Church Teaching and Tradition

- "Many Jews and even certain Gentiles who shared their hope recognized in Jesus the fundamental attributes of the messianic 'Son of David,' promised by God to Israel"[1] (CCC, 439).

- "Love of preference for the poor, and the decisions which it inspires in us, cannot but embrace the immense multitudes of the hungry, the needy, the homeless, those without medical care and, above all, those without hope of a better future" (SRS, 42).

- "Action on behalf of justice and participation in the transformation of the world fully appear to us as a constitutive dimension of the preaching of the Gospel, or, in other words, of the Church's mission for the redemption of the human race and its liberation from every oppressive situation" (JM, 6).

Isaiah 11:1–10   Isaiah paints the possibility of a reign of justice and faithfulness where the spirit of wisdom and harmony will sprout and grow. The Israelites could imagine all the signs of a new springtime sprouting forth almost instantly, like seeing a flower bloom in time-lapse photography. In the previous chapter, Isaiah used natural images to tell of the destruction of unfaithful kings: "Now the Lord, the LORD of hosts, / is about to lop off the boughs with terrible violence; / The tall of stature shall be felled, / and the lofty ones shall be brought low; / He shall hack down the forest thickets with an ax, / and Lebanon in its splendor shall fall" (Isaiah 10:33–34). Isaiah brings to life the qualities a king was supposed to have and demonstrates what would happen under such a king's reign. Isaiah's description of the world that we hope for is reminiscent of the Garden of Eden.

Isaiah's listeners hoped for a political king to make this Kingdom of God possible. But Israel must remain firmly rooted in God, confident in their hope for such a Messiah. Believers have found in this passage a deeper meaning that has been revealed through the coming of Jesus Christ. Jesus Christ, the Messiah, the sign of God's fidelity to his people, is the fulfillment of Isaiah's prophecy.

Psalm 72:1–2, 7–8, 12–13, 17 (see 7)   A perfect world where justice and peace and abundance will flourish forever. This sounds incredible and perhaps even impossible, yet Psalm 72 imagines just such a world. All people— especially the poor, the afflicted, and the lowly—will be rescued and saved. All will have what they need, and because of this, justice will flourish and peace will reign.

This royal psalm prays for blessings upon the reign of the anointed king. In an ideal world, this king, who as God's representative was to care for the weaker members of the community, was also to govern with justice and release God's blessings upon his people. But earthly kings fell short of this work, and when the rule of kings ended in the sixth century BC, God's people continued to hope for this kind of intervention. They believed in the possibility of God's Kingdom of peace and justice and expressed it in their hope for the coming of a Messiah. This Advent, we, too, can pray this psalm in longing for a world that will bring about God's reign, full of the fruits of justice and peace. As we pray, we prepare ourselves to do our part that justice and peace might flourish.

Romans 15:4–9   In his Letter to the Romans, Paul makes it clear that there are no special rights to salvation that come with being either a Jew or Gentile. Rather, the righteous are saved because Jesus Christ died and rose for all, Jew and Gentile alike. God's action in Christ has brought salvation. For Paul, followers of the Messiah are called to respond to his call by the way they live. In these verses, which are part of Paul's response to an argument begun in chapter 14, he advises his listeners to think in harmony, praise God in one voice, and welcome others as Christ did. Despite conflict, tensions, or divisions, believers must act like Christ because they have been shown mercy, grace, and salvation by God's astounding action in Christ.

Matthew 3:1–12   We may wonder why Matthew spends so much time describing John the Baptist's strange clothes and odd diet. By describing his camel-hair clothing and leather belt, Matthew links John to prophets before him, such as Elijah and Samuel, who preached against injustice and called for social transformation. John's clothing indicates that he, too, will preach

---

1. Cf. Matthew 2:2; 9:27; 12:23; 15:22; 20:30; 21:9, 15.

about the coming of a reign of justice and the need to reform one's life and heart. Repentance is a necessary part of baptism, and producing good fruits demonstrates a repentant heart.

In Luke's version of this scene, the Baptist speaks to the multitudes, but in Matthew, John directs his words to the Pharisees and Sadducees, the religious leaders of his time. His point seems to challenge them with the question, "What made you think you could escape this call to produce good fruit?" They cannot claim that their religious superiority or legacy exempts them from this condition of repentance. Perhaps this is a good question for us to ask ourselves as believers this Advent. We can claim nothing in the face of God's judgment except how we have changed our lives, believed in the Messiah, and helped build up the Kingdom of God.

 # Preparation

Sin and death have entered our world. We recognize and experience suffering. Christ's coming is the presence of new life where before there was destruction and death. The fullness of that new life will be experienced in the parousia. This new life will be for all of humanity and even beyond when all of creation will be at peace. Today, we listen to the ancient prophecies of Isaiah and are reminded of how long the Hebrew people had been waiting for a savior to rescue them. Their hope was in a messiah who would introduce a new reign where justice would flourish.

Lectionary for Mass #4A

Isaiah 11:1–10

Psalm 72:1–2, 7–8, 12–13, 17 (see 7)

Romans 15:4–9

Matthew 3:1–12

Objectives

- To introduce the peace of the parousia for humanity and all of creation.

- To explore the image of the prophesied Messiah as judge and warrior.

Preparation and Materials

- Read the Season Background, the lectionary readings, and the Scripture Background.

- Bookmark the appropriate readings (see page xv) in the lectionary, children's lectionary, or Bible. Place the book in a convenient location for the leader.

- Write the words of dismissal on a card for the priest celebrant.

- Prepare the words of the song the children will sing as they gather in the space for the Liturgy of the Word.

- Select volunteers (older children or adults) to proclaim the readings.

- Display the responsorial psalm refrain lyrics.

- Display the Apostles' or Nicene Creed.

- Prepare intercessions for the Prayer of the Faithful adapted for the needs of the Church, world, oppressed or marginalized, and local community.

Prayer Leader Reflection Questions

» How do you allow the gifts of the Holy Spirit to guide your life?

» As you prepare your heart for the coming of the Lord, have you considered your own repentance? Consider celebrating the sacrament of reconciliation during Advent.

Procession

Following the Collect of the Mass, the priest celebrant picks up the lectionary and invites those who would like to participate in the Liturgy of the Word with children to come forward and gather in the center aisle. The people who will lead the children out and facilitate the Liturgy of the Word also come forward at this time. Holding the lectionary so that all can see, the priest celebrant sends the children forth using his own words or the following:

> *Priest*: **You will hear wondrous things in the Scriptures today, children! The wolf and the lamb will be friends. The calf and young lion will be guided by a child. A man wearing camel's hair and eating locusts tells us about the Lord's coming. Go now and listen to God's Word speaking wonderful things to you.**

The leader processes out holding the lectionary, and the children follow behind. The parish music minister may have selected a song of dismissal for the assembly to sing while the children leave. A good option is "The Word of God: Children's Dismissal" by M. D. Ridge and Timothy R. Smith (WLP/GIA).

Centering

Continue to sing the song of dismissal that the assembly sang as you left the church. Or sing "The King Shall Come When Morning Dawns" (Brownlie) or the refrain from "Ready the Way" (Hurd), or have instrumental music playing as the children gather in the space for the Liturgy of the Word.

Place the lectionary on the ambo or lectern. Light the candle placed by the ambo or lectern, and then lead the following prayer:

> **God of mercy,**
> **help us to prepare the way for your coming.**
> **Allow our hearts to be open to your Word.**
> **We pray in the name of your Son, Lord Jesus, come.**

> *Children:* **Amen.**

First Reading

Isaiah 11:1–10

Responsorial Psalm

Psalm 72:1–2, 7–8, 12–13, 17 (see 7) *Sing the same musical setting that is used in your parish's celebration of the liturgy.*

Second Reading

Romans 15:4–9

Gospel Acclamation

Sing the Gospel Acclamation used in your parish's celebration of the liturgy.

Gospel Reading

Matthew 3:1–12

Homily/Reflection

(This homily/reflection focuses on the first reading.)

As we wait and prepare for Christmas, we also wait and prepare for the parousia, the time when Christ will come again. The prophet Isaiah speaks today about this beautiful moment, this time that will come later. Isaiah begins by speaking about a "stump" and a "shoot." Imagine a large tree, a plant full of life, reaching high in the sky toward the sun and protected by a strong trunk covered in thick bark, with branches spreading out full of green leaves. But this mighty tree is cut down. Most of what is left of the tree is buried in the ground and what is above is cut open for all to see. It is a sign of death.

>> **What's left when you cut a tree down?** *[a stump]*

>> **Isaiah says that something has come forth from this stump—a "shoot." What is a shoot?**

When a plant begins to grow, a tiny little stem, perhaps with one little leaf, comes up green and soft. It doesn't look mighty or tall, but in this case, this shoot is a sign of new life coming out of destruction and death.

The next verse calls this "shoot" a "him." Who is this person whose new life will come from what seemed like death? Isaiah said that it will be someone who has the Spirit of the Lord resting upon him. This person has all the gifts of the Holy Spirit: wisdom, understanding, counsel, strength, knowledge, piety, and fear of the Lord. I wonder if these gifts are named because they help him to do the job that Isaiah described him doing. This "shoot" is a judge. He is a judge who doesn't decide just by how people look or what other people say, but instead he judges with justice, and that justice will be a band around his waist. We wear bands, or belts, around our waists. They hold us in tight. This "shoot" is also a warrior. He has a weapon, a "rod," but this weapon is his mouth, his breath. The effects of the weapon are for those who have harmed the poor and the afflicted. Isaiah called these people who do harm "ruthless" and "wicked."

>> **When you imagine a judge and warrior who does these things, what do you imagine this judge and warrior looking like?**

Isaiah also said that when the "shoot" comes, the "wolf shall be a guest of the lamb." Would a lamb want a wolf so close by? A wolf is a threat to the lamb because normally the wolf wants to eat the lamb. But something is different here. Again, we hear "the leopard shall lie down with the young goat. The calf and the young lion shall browse together." *Browse* means "to eat grass." Why are all these animals that normally would not get along suddenly together? Some of them have found a new food and none of the animals are attacking each other. Who is the judge and warrior who leads them? It is a child. Can you imagine this scene? This new life of peace shared by all of creation will be led by a child. Isaiah let us know where all this will happen: "They shall not harm or destroy on all my holy mountain," which is in Jerusalem and is the place where the temple, the place where God dwells most intensely. When this happens, "for the earth shall be filled with knowledge of the LORD, as water covers the sea." This knowledge will be not only for the Jewish people but also for the Gentiles, the non-Jews. In the parousia, this new life of peace from God will be complete.

Profession of Faith

Following the homily or reflection, the prayer leader invites everyone to stand to profess our faith. Together, sing or recite the Apostles' or Nicene Creed. Refer the children to the words of the prayer that you have displayed.

Prayer of the Faithful

Leader: **Called to "prepare the way of the Lord" and to build God's kingdom, we bring our needs to God. Please respond, "Prince of Peace, hear our prayer."**

That the Body of Christ may always be in harmony with the Church and with one another, we pray: *Prince of Peace, hear our prayer.*

That world leaders may always seek justice and peace, we pray: *Prince of Peace, hear our prayer.*

That those who are sick may be restored to health and wholeness, and may welcome the compassion of those who care for them, we pray: *Prince of Peace, hear our prayer.*

That we may embrace hardships with hope and encourage one another with confident faith, we pray: *Prince of Peace, hear our prayer.*

Invite other intercessions from the children, or add intercessions based on the current needs of the Church, the world, the oppressed or marginalized, and the local community. Conclude each of the children's petitions with **"we pray"** and invite the response **"Prince of Peace, hear our prayer."**

That all who have died may know the Lord in fullness, we pray: *Prince of Peace, hear our prayer.*

Mighty God,
remove every block in our path toward your kingdom
so that we may be brought closer to you.
Accept the prayers of your children through Christ our Lord.

Children: **Amen.**

Quietly return with the children to the main assembly. Be mindful of children having difficulty finding their families.

December 8, 2022
Solemnity of the Immaculate Conception of the Blessed Virgin Mary

Mary's Response to God's Will

 ## Scripture Background

Connections to Church Teaching and Tradition

- "The Solemnity of December 8 . . . is a joint celebration of the Immaculate Conception of Mary, of the basic preparation (cf. Isaiah 11:1, 10) for the coming of the Savior and of the happy beginning of the Church without spot or wrinkle" (MC, 3).

- "In order for Mary to be able to give the free assent of her faith to the announcement of her vocation, it was necessary that she be wholly borne by God's grace. . . . By the grace of God Mary remained free of every personal sin her whole life long" (CCC, 490, 493).

- "When we read that the messenger addresses Mary as 'full of grace,' the Gospel context . . . enables us to understand that among all the 'spiritual blessings in Christ' this is a special 'blessing.' . . . In an entirely special and exceptional way Mary is united to Christ. . . . As the Council teaches, Mary 'stands out among the poor and humble of the Lord, who confidently await and receive salvation from him'" (RM, 8).

Genesis 3:9–15, 20 This passage begins at the point of encounter between Adam and God, following the Fall. It bears typical characteristics of the J (Yahwist) tradition. God is presented anthropomorphically, and Adam's sin is portrayed in all its brash stupidity. Though Adam initially speaks, the key characters are Eve and the serpent. She is tempted by the serpent and falls victim to his wiles. God addresses him first with the divine curse.

Adam and Eve had previously held mastery over animals, but their sin has subverted this order. Now there will be hostility between humans and animals, continuing throughout time. Christian tradition has read these verses as the protoevangelium, a first announcement of the Gospel, asserting the eventual conquest of evil by Christ, offspring of Mary.

The closing line, naming Eve as "the mother of all the living" (Genesis 3:20), has a connection with the Gospel for the solemnity of the Immaculate Conception. In contrast with Eve's negative response to God's command, Mary responds with obedient faith. Through Mary's response, the tide of human history turns.

Psalm 98:1, 2–3, 3–4 (1a) Psalm 98 belongs to a collection within the Book of Psalms known as Hymns of the Lord's Kingship, or Enthronement Psalms (Psalms 95—99). These psalms tell of the Lord's kingship over Israel and the whole world. The "right hand" and "holy arm" (Psalm 98:1) of the Lord has brought about victory for God's people, accomplishing wondrous deeds. The opening call to "sing to the LORD a new song" (Psalm 98:1) suggests that this marvelous, divine feat calls for a concomitant response that offers to God something new, distinct, creative, and wonderful.

In the context of this solemnity honoring Mary's Immaculate Conception, the antiphon opening the psalm presents a call both to Mary and to all who celebrate this day. When Mary is called to bear the Son of the Most High, she is invited to sing a new song to the Lord for what God is about to accomplish in her, and through her, for the world. Mary's yes overturns the avalanche of sin that has followed Eve's no to God. A new day dawns in the history of salvation, and the community of believers lifts up praise to God for what has been accomplished in Mary for the world's redemption.

Ephesians 1:3–6, 11–12 Here we are given what is believed to be an early Christian hymn for the liturgy, extolling the ineffable plan of God to bring redemption to the world through Jesus Christ. The text praises God for the election offered to the human race, to be made "holy and without blemish before him" (Ephesians 1:4). Though we know ourselves to fall painfully short of the grace and blessing offered us, the fact of our own inadequacy pales beside the gift of God's love bestowed upon us.

When Paul declares "In love he destined us for adoption to himself through Jesus Christ" (Ephesians 1:5), he affirms that God's will for our salvation flows forth in divine love. One element of this surpassing love of God may be discerned in the singular grace bestowed on Mary, from the moment of her conception, to be free of original sin. It is important for us to note that even this grace comes to her through Christ, who brings all of us up into the fullness of divine life.

Luke 1:26–38 Two important themes converge in this passage from the Gospel according to Luke: the moment of the turning of the ages and Mary's faith-filled response. Recalling 2 Samuel 7, where God promises that the Messiah is to come from the house of David, we see that this passage brings that prophesied salvific moment to full reality. It is presented in contrasting terms of utter fragility (the young and inexperienced maiden) and divine strength ("you shall name him Jesus" [the Lord saves] "and of his kingdom there will be no end") (vv. 31–33).

Mary is immediately addressed as "favored" (full of grace). She already possesses grace from God, which sets her apart, and though she initially demurs from the angel's announcement, saying, "How can this be?" (v. 34), she listens to the continuing explanation of a plan quite different from her own. In the end, her wholehearted response, "May it be done to me according to your word" (v. 38), quietly, and with profound nobility, sets off the turn of the ages.

Preparation

Today's solemnity celebrates that Mary was conceived without any sin. It celebrates that from the beginning of Mary's life, God loved her. From the beginning, she found favor with God. Her ability to do God's will and to say yes is a direct result of God's grace. Because she is the Mother of God, she holds a special place in salvation history. She is the first of all saints and the model of true discipleship—one who does the will of God.

Lectionary #689

Genesis 3:9–15, 20

Psalm 98:1, 2–3, 3–4 (1a)

Ephesians 1:3–6, 11–12

Luke 1:26–38

Objectives

- To help children know that the Immaculate Conception is about the beginning of Mary's life.

- To understand how we may also say yes to God.

Preparation and Materials

- Read the Season Background, the Lectionary readings, and the Scripture Background.

- Bookmark the appropriate readings (see page xv) in the Lectionary, children's Lectionary, or Bible. Place the book in a convenient location for the leader.

- Write the words of dismissal on a card for the priest celebrant.

- Prepare the words of the song the children will sing as they gather in the space for Liturgy of the Word.

- Select volunteers (older children or adults) to proclaim the readings.

- Display the responsorial psalm refrain lyrics.

- Display the Apostles' or Nicene Creed.

- Prepare intercessions for the Prayer of the Faithful adapted for the needs of the Church, world, oppressed or marginalized, and local community.

Prayer Leader Reflection Questions

» **In what ways do you see Mary as the model for us?**

» **Consider your own faith in God's plan. Do you give yourself over to God even when it might not make sense?**

Procession

Following the Collect of the Mass, the priest celebrant picks up the Lectionary and invites those who would like to participate in the Liturgy of the Word with children to come forward and gather in the center aisle. The people who will lead the children out and facilitate the Liturgy of the Word also come forward at this time. Holding the Lectionary so that all can see, the priest celebrant sends the children forth using his own words or the following:

> *Priest:* **Dear children, we practice waiting during this time of Advent. Waiting for something special takes practice and patience. But when we are patient, we will eventually rejoice at Christmas, and celebrate that time when there will be no more tears and sadness, only joy in God's Kingdom. Go now to hear God's Word.**

The leader processes out holding the Lectionary and the children follow behind. The parish music minister may have selected a song of dismissal for the assembly to sing while the children leave. A good option is "The Word of God: Children's Dismissal" by M. D. Ridge and Timothy R. Smith (WLP/GIA).

Centering

Continue to sing the song of dismissal that the assembly sang as you left the church. Or sing "Mary Said 'Yes!,'" or "Fill Ev'ry Valley" (Mangan), or have instrumental music playing as the children gather in the space for the Liturgy of the Word.

Place the Lectionary on the ambo or lectern. Light the candle placed by the ambo or lectern and then lead the following prayer:

> **God of all creation,**
> **touch our hearts with the fire of your love as we listen to your Word.**
> **We wait in hope for the coming of your Son,**
> **who lives and reigns with you in the unity of the Holy Spirit,**
> **God, for ever and ever.**

> *Children:* **Amen.**

First Reading

Genesis 3:9–15, 20

Responsorial Psalm

Psalm 98:1, 2–3, 3–4 (1a) *Sing the same musical setting that is used in your parish's celebration of the liturgy.*

Second Reading

Ephesians 1:3–6, 11–12

Gospel Acclamation

Sing the Gospel Acclamation used in your parish's celebration of the liturgy.

Gospel Reading

Luke 1:26–38

Homily/Reflection

Today is a very special day! Today is the day when we celebrate the Immaculate Conception of the Blessed Virgin Mary. The Immaculate Conception is the holy day when we remember the very beginning of the Virgin Mary's life. The reason this day is so special is that we remember that God preserved Mary from sin! God made sure she would never commit sins or even have Original Sin. So from the very beginning of Mary's life, she was pure and sinless. That is what we mean by the Immaculate Conception. What a very special way to prepare her to be the Mother of God!

In the Gospel today, God sends the angel to ask Mary a big favor.

>> **What is the favor?** (*to be Jesus' Mother*)

In today's Gospel, God sends an angel to Mary to ask her if she will be the mother of God. Mary had a choice. She could say no.

>> **Have you ever said no to someone who loves you?**

>> **Have people you love ever said no to you?**

Sometimes we do say no because it is the right thing to do, but usually we say yes to the people who love us. When people love us, they do not ask us to do things that are bad for us, but sometimes they do ask us to do things that will be hard for us. The hard things are the ones we sometimes feel like saying no to. For example, when your mom asks you to apologize to your sibling after a fight, you might feel like saying no. When the angel said God wanted Mary to be the Mother of his Son, Mary did not know if it would be easy or hard. She was not sure how it would happen.

》 Do you think it would be hard to say yes to something when you don't know what will happen?

Mary knew God loved her and cared about her, and the angel reminded her of that. Mary had a choice. She could say yes or no. Mary chose to say, "Yes, I will bring Jesus into the world." Mary said yes because she wanted to do something really good out of her love for God and because she had faith. God is not asking us the same things he asked of the Virgin Mary, but he does ask us to say yes to him. God wants each of us to keep bringing the message of Jesus' love into the world.

》 How many of you want to say yes to that today?

Profession of Faith

Following the homily or reflection, the prayer leader invites everyone to stand to profess our faith. Together, sing or recite the Apostles' or Nicene Creed. Refer the children to the words of the prayer that you have displayed.

Prayer of the Faithful

Leader: **We wait in joyful hope for Christ to come again, and so we turn to him in prayer. Please respond, "Come, Lord, hear our prayer."**

For the leaders of the Church, may they have the courage to lead by example in saying yes to the Lord, we pray: *Come, Lord, hear our prayer.*

For our elected officials, local leaders, and those who have authority in our communities, may they ensure the protection of the most vulnerable, especially the poor, the aged, and the unborn, we pray: *Come, Lord, hear our prayer.*

For those who feel alone or friendless, may they find a spirit of hope and justice in our local community, we pray: *Come, Lord, hear our prayer.*

For each of us to avoid the allure of material desires this Advent, and focus on preparing the Lord's way, we pray: *Come, Lord, hear our prayer.*

Invite other intercessions from the children, or add intercessions based on the current needs of the Church, the world, the oppressed or marginalized, and the local community. Conclude each of the children's petitions with, **"we pray,"** and invite the response, **"Come, Lord, hear our prayer."**

For all those who have died, that they may live with God forever, we pray: *Come, Lord, hear our prayer.*

**Good and gracious God,
we bring our prayers to you and ask your blessing
on all of us who are preparing our hearts
to celebrate the birth of your Son, Jesus.
We ask you to grant our prayers if it is your will.
Through Christ our Lord.**

Children: **Amen.**

Quietly return with the children to the main assembly. Be mindful of children having difficulty finding their families.

December 11, 2022
Third Sunday of Advent
The Lord Comes to Save

 ## Scripture Background

Connections to Church Teaching and Tradition

- "Jesus accompanies his words with many 'mighty works and wonders and signs,' which manifest that the kingdom is present in him and attest that he was the promised Messiah[1]" (CCC, 547).

- "By freeing some individuals from the earthly evils of hunger, injustice, illness, and death,[2] Jesus performed messianic signs. Nevertheless he did not come to abolish all evils here below,[3] but to free men from the gravest slavery, sin" (CCC, 549).

- "God blesses those who come to the aid of the poor and rebukes those who turn away from them. . . . It is by what they have done for the poor that Jesus Christ will recognize his chosen ones.[4] When 'the poor have the good news preached to them,' it is the sign of Christ's presence[5]" (CCC, 2443).

Isaiah 35:1–6a, 10 On this Third Sunday of Advent, also called *Gaudete* ("Rejoice") Sunday, Isaiah speaks of great joy in the realization that our loving God comes to restore and save us. Isaiah speaks of the anticipated return of the people from exile through God's mighty hand. God's saving actions will be evident in both the natural and the human world. All of nature will exult and rejoice. The desert, the parched land, and the steppe all will bloom abundantly and burst into joyful song. The fertile and life-giving qualities of the most enviable lands will be theirs.

All the weak, those without hope, and those who fear God's abandonment, are challenged to "be strong, fear not," for "[God] comes with vindication" (v. 4). The blind, the deaf, the lame, and the mute will be healed of their infirmities and will experience God's great care. All that is debilitated, limited, and without life will be restored and renewed. Those returning home from exile will experience God's life-giving and restoring work. God has willingly paid the ransom for their return. Restored and renewed in hope and spirit, they "will return and enter Zion singing" and "sorrow and mourning will flee" (35:10). Christians understand and experience Christ's coming to renew and restore all humanity in this same rich fashion of joy and renewed life.

Psalm 146:6–7, 8–9, 9–10 (see Isaiah 35:4) The psalm's refrain repeats and continues Isaiah's focus of renewal and restoration by calling upon the Lord to "come and save us." Assured of God's affirmative response, the psalmist breaks into praise of the Lord who "keeps faith forever" (v. 6). God's continued care and enduring love are manifested in very concrete and specific terms. The oppressed, the hungry, and the captives have their needs met. The blind are given sight and the "bowed down" are raised up (v. 8). Working for justice is especially endearing to God, who "protects strangers" and sustains "the fatherless and the widow," while the "way of the wicked" is thwarted (v. 9). Thus "the Lord shall reign forever" (v. 10). God's saving work among us becomes the model of how we are called to deal with one another.

James 5:7–10 James' advice to his community stresses the need for patience whenever anxiety and fear surface because of delayed expectations. The Lord has come to save us and upon his return, all will be brought to fulfillment. In the meantime, we are to live life in the concrete, facing the challenges of living together in community and the impulse to complain and judge, along with misunderstanding and possible persecution by others for our beliefs. Throughout these challenges James counsels patience, for "the coming of the Lord is at hand" (v. 8).

Just as the farmer patiently waits for rain in hope of a fruitful harvest, so we are to wait for the Lord in hope of complete fulfillment. We are challenged to be patient, make our hearts firm, and resist the temptation to judge others. James offers the prophets as models of "hardship and patience" (v. 10). They remained faithful during the many difficulties they encountered for speaking "in the name of the Lord" (v. 10), and we are to be patient in our hardships for the Lord, too. Advent, the season of joyful anticipation of the Lord's return, helps us cultivate patience as we strive to carry on the Lord's work until he comes again.

Matthew 11:2–11 This dialogue between Jesus and John the Baptist's disciples reveals Matthew's theological affirmation that in Jesus, God's saving action is now being accomplished. In response to John's inquiry concerning "the one who is to come" (v. 3), namely, the Messiah, Jesus responds by pointing to all the signs that the Scripture specified as indicators of the presence of the Messiah: concern for the poor and all those who are in need of God's healing touch.

---

1 Acts 2:22; cf. Luke 7:18–23.
2 Cf. Jn 6:5–15; Lk 19:8; Mt 11:5.
3 Cf. Lk 12:13–14; Jn 18:36.
4 Cf. Mt 25:31–36.
5 Mt 11:5; cf. Lk 4:18.

This somewhat different messianic concept from the one anticipated has Jesus conclude his response by asserting, "[B]lessed is the one who takes no offense at me" (v. 6). The messianic times are full of God's saving actions on behalf of the poor and needy, and not displays of military might. This neglected messianic image would cause some to take offense at Jesus and challenge his messianic claims.

Jesus praises John as a prophet who prepared for his coming as Messiah. Jesus also affirms, though, that those who accept him as the Messiah and carry on his work will do greater things than John. The power of God's saving action will be evident in all those who choose to model themselves on Jesus' messianic mission.

Preparation

In the parousia, when the kingdom of God is no longer hidden, all creation will be full of life and all maladies will be healed. Jesus inaugurated the in-breaking of the kingdom of God and announced it with his words and deeds throughout his earthly ministry. We wait with patience for the healing and joy of the parousia and have confidence that while it remains concealed, it continues to grow and like ripe fruit, it will be fully revealed at harvest.

Lectionary for Mass #7A

Isaiah 35:1–6a, 10

Psalm 146:6–7, 8–9, 9–10 (see Isaiah 35:4)

James 5:7–10

Matthew 11:2–11

Objectives

- To announce the kingdom of God as something that is hidden but already here.

- To explain miracles as restoration to the goodness and life of the original state of creation.

Preparation and Materials

- Read the Season Background, the lectionary readings, and the Scripture Background.

- Bookmark the appropriate readings (see page xv) in the lectionary, children's lectionary, or Bible. Place the book in a convenient location for the leader.

- Write the words of dismissal on a card for the priest celebrant.

- Prepare the words of the song the children will sing as they gather in the space for the Liturgy of the Word.

- Select volunteers (older children or adults) to proclaim the readings.

- Display the responsorial psalm refrain lyrics.

- Display the Apostles' or Nicene Creed.

- Prepare intercessions for the Prayer of the Faithful adapted for the needs of the Church, world, oppressed or marginalized, and local community.

Prayer Leader Reflection Questions

>> **Today's Gospel is full of questions about whether Jesus is the one who comes to save. Do you have expectations of Jesus Christ? What are they?**

>> **How can you help the children to experience this week's liturgy as a sign of joy?**

Procession

Following the Collect of the Mass, the priest celebrant picks up the lectionary and invites those who would like to participate in the Liturgy of the Word with children to come forward and gather in the center aisle. The people who will lead the children out and facilitate the Liturgy of the Word also come forward at this time. Holding the lectionary so that all can see, the priest celebrant sends the children forth using his own words or the following:

> *Priest*: **Dear children, sometimes it feels that good things, like Christmas, are so far away that they'll never get here. We need to be patient, like the farmer who waits for the precious fruit of the earth. But know that Jesus, whose birth we will soon celebrate, is already here with you now. Go and listen to him speak to you in the readings.**

The leader processes out holding the lectionary, and the children follow behind. The parish music minister may have selected a song of dismissal for the assembly to sing while the children leave. A good option is "The Word of God: Children's Dismissal" by M. D. Ridge and Timothy R. Smith (WLP/GIA).

Centering

Continue to sing the song of dismissal that the assembly sang as you left the church. Or sing the refrains from "Proclaim the Joyful Message" (Marchionda/Schutte), or "Ready the Way" (Hurd), or have instrumental music playing as the children gather in the space for the Liturgy of the Word.

Place the lectionary on the ambo or lectern. Light the candle placed by the ambo or lectern, and then lead the following prayer:

> **O God,**
> **how we wait with faith for the feast of Christmas!**
> **Allow our hearts to be open to your Word**
> **so that we may serve you completely.**
> **We pray in the name of your Son Lord Jesus, come.**

> *Children:* **Amen.**

First Reading

Isaiah 35:1–6a, 10

Responsorial Psalm

Psalm 146:6–7, 8–9, 9–10 (see Isaiah 35:4) *Sing the same musical setting that is used in your parish's celebration of the liturgy.*

Second Reading

James 5:7–10

Gospel Acclamation

Sing the Gospel Acclamation used in your parish's celebration of the liturgy.

Gospel Reading

Matthew 11:2–11

Homily/Reflection

Jesus' favorite thing to talk about was the kingdom of God. He talked about God's kingdom more than anything else because he wanted people to be able to recognize it. Jesus set in motion the breaking in of the kingdom of God to this world. It is hidden, but it is here. Jesus showed this not only with his words, but also with his actions. In a most particular way, he showed this when he performed miracles. When miracles happen, they seem to break the rules of nature. But what Jesus really did when he performed miracles was to make things as they had always meant to be.

In the beginning when God created everything, all of it was good. The world was full of life. There was love and joy and friendship with God among people, creatures, and all of God's creation. But the first sin of human beings damaged that. With the choice of the first human beings to disobey God, suffering and pain entered the world. The world is not always full of love and joy. Nature is not always in harmony. There is suffering and sickness and death.

The people of Israel recognized this. They waited and longed for a time when creation would be restored, when there would be no more suffering and death, when friendship with God would be full and complete for all people. The prophet Isaiah spoke about what that would be like. He told of how creation itself would be full of life, when even the desert would bloom. He spoke in a most particular way about what would happen to people. Those who were blind would see; those who were deaf would hear; those who couldn't talk would be able to sing; those who couldn't walk would be able to jump! There would be an end to suffering, and there would be healing and joy, and it would be God who would save.

John the Baptist was another prophet, one who lived when Jesus lived. John also waited for the coming of the kingdom of God. When he heard about what Jesus was doing, he wanted to know whether the kingdom of God had arrived. Jesus answered him, not by saying yes or no, but by reminding him of Isaiah's prophecy: "the blind regain their sight, the lame walk, lepers are cleansed, the deaf hear, the dead are raised, and the poor have the good news proclaimed to them" (Matthew 11:5).

» Can you name some of the miracles in the Bible that Jesus did?

When Jesus walked and talked on this earth, he performed miracles. Just as Isaiah had described, when Jesus met a blind person, he healed him so he could see. When Jesus met someone who could not hear or speak, he healed him so that he could do both. He restored people to health and community, but we also know that there are people today who still cannot hear and there are others who still cannot see. The kingdom of God has come because Jesus Christ has redeemed us. But the kingdom is also not yet here in fullness—Christ will come again and transform everyone and everything. During this season of Advent, we wait for the time when God will be "all in all," when "sorrow and mourning flee" (Isaiah 35:10). We know that that there will be everlasting joy. It is not always easy to wait for this time, especially when we are the ones who are suffering, but we have faith, and we have patience.

Profession of Faith	Following the homily or reflection, the prayer leader invites everyone to stand to profess our faith. Together, sing or recite the Apostles' or Nicene Creed. Refer the children to the words of the prayer that you have displayed.

Prayer of the Faithful	*Leader:* **God tells us to patiently await all the good things that the Savior brings. As we wait, we make our needs known to him. Please respond, "Wonderful Counselor, hear our prayer."**

May the Church teach the world the patience it needs to await the coming of the parousia, we pray to the Lord: *Wonderful Counselor, hear our prayer.*

May world leaders prepare the way for the coming of the Lord by fostering harmony, dialogue, and sincere concern for their people, we pray to the Lord: *Wonderful Counselor, hear our prayer.*

May the blind see, the lame walk, the diseased be cleansed, the deaf hear, the dead be raised to new life, and the poor have the words of the Gospel opened to them, we pray to the Lord: *Wonderful Counselor, hear our prayer.*

May good relationships be restored among us, and may we return to the Lord with all our hearts, we pray to the Lord: *Wonderful Counselor, hear our prayer.*

Invite other intercessions from the children, or add intercessions based on the current needs of the Church, the world, the oppressed or marginalized, and the local community. Conclude each of the children's petitions with **"we pray to the Lord"** and invite the response, **"Wonderful Counselor, hear our prayer."**

May all who have died see the glory of the Lord, we pray to the Lord: *Wonderful Counselor, hear our prayer.*

O God,
help us to know the joy of the coming of Christ and to celebrate it.
Accept the humble prayers of your children through Christ our Lord.

Children: **Amen.**

Quietly return with the children to the main assembly. Be mindful of children having difficulty finding their families.

December 18, 2022
Fourth Sunday of Advent

Promise Is Given Birth

 ## Scripture Background

Connections to Church Teaching and Tradition

- Jesus Christ is the incarnate love of God (DCE, 12).

- Mary is Mother of the Church and the model for us all (NDC, 74).

- Mary shows us what love is, its origin, and constantly renewed power (DCE, 42).

- Mary submitted to God's will to conceive by the Holy Spirit (LG, 55–56; CCC, 484–507, esp. 484–486 and 494).

Isaiah 7:10–14 In 736 BC, Assyria is threatening to take over the whole region. Some counsel the king, Ahaz, to join in a coalition against Assyria, while others, most notably Isaiah, tell him to lay low. It would be better for him and for Judah not to do a thing. Ahaz himself is leaning toward conciliation with Assyria in hopes of saving himself and his country.

Through Isaiah, God offers Ahaz a sign of hope, but Ahaz is not sure he wants one. In a false show of piety, he refuses the offer. God, however, is not dissuaded that easily. God tells Ahaz that Jerusalem shall be saved. The threat he fears shall be averted, and the sign of this hope is the birth of a child. This child, Isaiah says, will be God's concrete sign of compassion, for through the child, Ahaz's line will continue in spite of the Assyrian threat.

No wonder the Church associates this passage with the birth of Jesus. Just as the birth of Emmanuel was a sign of promise to Ahaz, the birth of Jesus is a concrete sign of God's compassion for the world.

Psalm 24:1–2, 3–4, 5–6 (7c, 10b) Psalm 24 was originally composed as a processional liturgy and was used as such for years in the Second Temple, sung antiphonally by priest and people. It celebrates the entrance of the Ark, which represented the presence of God, into the Temple. The most striking feature of this psalm is the connection it makes between ethical behavior and worship.

This psalm celebrates the entrance of the promised child, God's Own Begotten, into this earthly tabernacle to be with us and dwell among us.

Romans 1:1–7 Paul had not yet visited the Church in Rome, so he begins his letter with a whirlwind summary of his Gospel. He describes himself as a personal slave of Christ. He then launches into a long exposition on who Christ is and what that means to the world in general and to the believers in Rome in particular. Paul's readers, no doubt, would have recognized at least part of this, for Paul deliberately wove familiar traditions into his own interpretation of the Gospel.

Although it is clear that the birth of the Christ child is not nearly as important to Paul as the life of the man Jesus, Paul makes several points that befit our celebration of Advent. First, he reminds us that the promise fulfilled in the coming of Christ is the culmination of an age-old hope first sounded by the prophets. Second, by emphasizing the Spirit and the power of God at work in Jesus, Paul points us to the larger implications of the child of promise we await this Advent. He reminds us that the coming of Christ involves not just his birth but his life, Death, and Resurrection as well.

Matthew 1:18–24 To appreciate this reading on its own terms, we must first separate it from the more familiar account in Luke. Here, Joseph is the primary player, not Mary. As the head of the household, Joseph is the one who receives the annunciation. There are no shepherds, no angels (except the one in the dream), and no trips to Bethlehem.

Once Matthew's and Luke's accounts are distinguished, one can see that they address similar issues but with different approaches. The Messiah was expected to be a descendant of King David, but Jesus' only claim to the Davidic line was through Joseph, who was not his natural father. While Luke sidesteps the issue by emphasizing Mary, Matthew's account shows that it was God's will that Joseph be regarded as Jesus' legitimate, if adoptive, father.

Likewise, both evangelists knew the Messiah was supposed to be from Bethlehem. Jesus, however, was from Nazareth. Luke's version has Jesus born while his parents are visiting Bethlehem, but in Matthew, the Holy Family already lives in Bethlehem and moves to Nazareth later.

Most of all, both Luke and Matthew want to emphasize that even though it seems that Jesus was born illegitimately, his birth was God's doing and thus quite legitimate, even purposeful. Matthew's account gives us still another important insight into the birth we await this Advent: it did not happen according to human convention. Indeed, it broke many of those human conventions that God's will might become manifest.

 # Preparation

In the season of Advent, we join with the people of Israel listening closely to God's words about the Messiah. We recognize that these words spoke of Jesus Christ long before his coming. We celebrate that the promise has been fulfilled. The proper response to this gift is one of holy obedience. Joseph is a consummate model of that kind of response because he obeys the commands of the angel of God, fulfilling his commitment to Mary by remaining her husband.

Lectionary for Mass #10A

Isaiah 7:10–14

Psalm 24:1–2, 3–4, 5–6 (7c and 10b)

Romans 1:1–7

Matthew 1:18–24

Objectives

- To ponder Jesus' identity as the one Isaiah prophesied as born of the virgin and "God-with-us."

- To invite the children to consider their holiness and obedience as a response to the gift of Emmanuel.

Preparation and Materials

- Read the Season Background, the lectionary readings, and the Scripture Background.

- Bookmark the appropriate readings (see page xv) in the lectionary, children's lectionary, or Bible. Place the book in a convenient location for the leader.

- Write the words of dismissal on a card for the priest celebrant.

- Prepare the words of the song the children will sing as they gather in the space for the Liturgy of the Word.

- Select volunteers (older children or adults) to proclaim the readings.

- Display the responsorial psalm refrain lyrics.

- Display the Apostles' or Nicene Creed.

- Prepare intercessions for the Prayer of the Faithful adapted for the needs of the Church, world, oppressed or marginalized, and local community.

Prayer Leader Reflection Questions

» **What signs in your life help you to see Emmanuel and to recognize that God is with you?**

» **When do you recognize God's signs and obey like Joseph did? When do you avoid God's signs like King Ahaz did?**

Procession

Following the Collect of the Mass, the priest celebrant picks up the lectionary and invites those who would like to participate in the Liturgy of the Word with children to come forward and gather in the center aisle. The people who will lead the children out and facilitate the Liturgy of the Word also come forward at this time. Holding the lectionary so that all can see, the priest celebrant sends the children forth using his own words or the following:

> *Priest*: **Dear children, sometimes God asks difficult things of us. When that happens, we might be afraid that we are not strong enough, or smart enough, or good enough. Joseph and Mary must have had similar fears, but they had faith that God would give them the grace they needed. Their fears turned to joy when Jesus was born. The time when we will celebrate his birth is very close now. Christmas is almost here! Go now and listen to God encouraging you in the Scriptures.**

The leader processes out holding the lectionary, and the children follow behind. The parish music minister may have selected a song of dismissal for the assembly to sing while the children leave. A good option is "The Word of God: Children's Dismissal" by M. D. Ridge and Timothy R. Smith (WLP/GIA).

Centering

Continue to sing the song of dismissal that the assembly sang as you left the church. Or sing "O Come, O Come Emmanuel" (Veni, veni Emmanuel), or the refrain from "Soon and Very Soon" (Crouch), or have instrumental music playing as the children gather in the space for the Liturgy of the Word.

Place the lectionary on the ambo or lectern. Light the candle placed by the ambo or lectern, and then lead the following prayer:

> **God of all creation,**
> **we know about the coming Christ your Son**
> **because of the message of an angel.**
> **Allow our hearts to be open to your Word**
> **so that we may serve you completely.**
> **Through Christ our Lord.**

> *Children:* **Amen.**

First Reading

Isaiah 7:10–14

Responsorial Psalm

Psalm 24:1–2, 3–4, 5–6 (7c and 10b) *Sing the same musical setting that is used in your parish's celebration of the liturgy.*

Second Reading

Romans 1:1–7

Gospel Acclamation

Sing the Gospel Acclamation used in your parish's celebration of the liturgy.

Gospel Reading

Matthew 1:18–24

Homily/Reflection

Today is the Fourth Sunday, the last Sunday, of Advent. Our season of preparation is coming to an end and Christmas is so close—only a few days away! As we near the time when we celebrate Jesus' birth, the Church invites us to listen and to ponder together about who it is that was born.

» Who was it that the people of Israel were waiting for? Who is it that came?

In the letter to the Romans, Paul reminded his audience of Jesus' identity. Jesus was promised by the prophets. The people of Israel waited and longed for and prepared for the Messiah. The prophets told of signs to look for when he came. The greatest king of Israel was King David. The prophets told the people that the Messiah would be a king like David, from his own family. Paul reminded the Romans as well that, though Jesus was from the family of David, his power did not come from earthly kingship, but from God, through the work of the Holy Spirit, who is a Spirit of holiness.

Paul was recalling the words of many prophets, but in particular, Isaiah. We heard Isaiah's own words today too. Isaiah was speaking to another king of Israel, King Ahaz. King Ahaz was not like

King David. King Ahaz did not want to listen to God's Word from Isaiah and did not want to see God's power. Isaiah told him that even if he didn't want to see it, there would be a sign of God's power: A young woman would come to be pregnant and have a son whose name would be Emmanuel. We have seen this sign ourselves! We know that the young woman was Mary, who would have a baby who is "God-with-us."

In the Gospel reading, though, Joseph had not yet recognized the sign. He was to be married to Mary, but they had not yet begun to live together as husband and wife. It was during that time that Joseph found out that Mary was pregnant. This was very surprising! He did not know yet how this could happen. An angel, a messenger from God, came to him in a dream to help him to understand. The angel explained that this happened by the power of the Holy Spirit and this child was the one that Isaiah had spoken about to King Ahaz. The angel told Joseph to keep his promise to live with Mary as husband and wife and to name the child Jesus, which means "one who saves."

As we consider the signs that help us to recognize that Jesus is God-with-us and the one who saves, what do we do? Do we try not to see, like King Ahaz? Or do we recognize and obey God's voice like the holy ones that we are called to be? Joseph belonged to God. He was obedient and holy. When Joseph awoke, he kept his promise to Mary just as the angel had told him.

>> **How can we listen more closely to God's Word like those that Isaiah spoke?**

>> **How can we be holy like Joseph?**

Profession of Faith

Following the homily or reflection, the prayer leader invites everyone to stand to profess our faith. Together, sing or recite the Apostles' or Nicene Creed. Refer the children to the words of the prayer that you have displayed.

Prayer of the Faithful

Leader: **Relying on a God who is with us always, we pray for our needs and those of the world. Please respond, "Emmanuel, hear our prayer."**

For our Holy Father, Pope N., all bishops, priests, and deacons as they seek to give themselves in faithful love to the Church, we pray to the Lord: *Emmanuel, hear our prayer.*

For the rulers of our world, that they might recognize the ways that God is leading them and follow the Spirit, we pray to the Lord: *Emmanuel, hear our prayer.*

For all who are facing difficult decisions and those preparing for life transitions, that they may be as trusting as Joseph, we pray to the Lord: *Emmanuel, hear our prayer.*

For all fathers, that they may be loving and righteous like Joseph, we pray to the Lord: *Emmanuel, hear our prayer.*

Invite other intercessions from the children, or add intercessions based on the current needs of the Church, the world, the oppressed or marginalized, and the local community. Conclude each of the children's petitions with **"we pray to the Lord"** and invite the response **"Emmanuel, hear our prayer."**

For those who have died, may they live with God forever, we pray to the Lord: *Emmanuel, hear our prayer.*

**Emmanuel, "God-with-us,"
as we wait in joyful hope for your coming once more,
guide and direct your Church in the way of your love.
Hear the prayers of the children, we pray.
Who live and reign for ever and ever.**

Children: **Amen.**

Quietly return with the children to the main assembly. Be mindful of children having difficulty finding their families.

Season Background for Christmas Time

Understanding Christmas Time

Advent leads us to Christmas Time. For Catholics, Christmas is more than just one day, it is an entire season! The fact that Christmas is a whole season teaches us how sacred the memorial of Christ's birth and early manifestations as the Savior of the World are to believers. Next to the yearly celebration of the Paschal Mystery during the sacred Triduum and Easter Time, these are the days that the Church holds most sacred. Christmas Time goes from Evening Prayer I of Christmas until the Sunday after Epiphany, the Feast of the Baptism of the Lord. During these days, we celebrate all that we have prepared for during Advent. The lights in the church are bright to reflect the brightness of the Lord's glory shining throughout the world. Through his birth, life, death, and Resurrection he has once and for all overcome darkness.

After the liturgies for the Nativity of the Lord (Christmas), the Church celebrates the Feast of the Holy Family of Jesus, Mary, and Joseph (Friday, December 30) to encourage families to live out their faith. On the eighth day of the Octave of Christmas, January 1, the Church celebrates the Solemnity of Mary, the Holy Mother of God. This is the oldest designation given to Mary by the Church. She is the image of the Church and the model of discipleship and holiness. This is also the day on which the Church celebrates the naming of Jesus, hence its association with circumcision, which was traditionally celebrated eight days after the birth of a male Jewish child.

The next solemnity celebrated during Christmas Time is the Epiphany of the Lord. Most of the children whom you serve will be familiar with Epiphany as the day when the three Wise Men (also known as Magi) follow the star and visit Jesus, bringing him gifts as a sign of homage to him. Epiphany, which means "manifestation," also offers us an opportunity to reflect deeply on the mystery of the Incarnation. Jesus, in his coming as man, manifested God to us. He was, is, and forever will be Emmanuel—God-with-us—our Savior and the Savior of the World. For this, we too praise and honor him.

Christmas Time concludes with another manifestation feast, the Feast of the Baptism of the Lord (Monday, January 9). In the event of Jesus' baptism, proclaimed this year from Matthew's account of the Gospel, the Spirit of God descends on Jesus and a voice from heaven identifies him as "my beloved Son, with whom I am well pleased" (Matthew 3:17). Jesus' identity as Son of God and Messiah is made known in this event. Moreover, just as Jesus' baptism marks the beginning of his public ministry, our Baptism marks the beginning of our life in the world as his disciples.

Liturgical Environment

White is the predominant color for Christmas Time. Depending on fire safety regulations, consider incorporating a Christmas tree in your environment that mirrors the tree in your parish's worship space. Use a white cloth to cover the table on which you place the Lectionary or Bible. Use gold as an accent color on the table or as ribbons on the tree. Remember, Christmas Time continues through the Feast of the Baptism of the Lord, so refresh any Christmas plants you have as part of your environment.

Overview of the Readings

During Christmas Time, the Gospel readings introduce Jesus who is Emmanuel—God-with-us—who comes to instruct his disciples and us today about what it means to be his followers. Through the readings, we come to understand that Jesus is the fulfillment of the Old Testament prophecies.

First Readings   In Christmas Time, we continue to hear often from the prophet Isaiah. His proclamation of salvation—the truth that the Lord does not forsake his people and that the Lord redeems—resounds in beautiful, poetic language. On the Solemnity of the Epiphany of the Lord, Isaiah's exhortation to Jerusalem to rise up in splendor calls us, as recipients of the Lord's salvation, to let our own light shine today. By our example, we, like Jerusalem, reflect the Lord's glory such that other nations and peoples will walk by our light.

Responsorial Psalms   During Christmas Time, the responsorial psalms emphasize the light, salvation, and saving power of the Lord. On the Feast of the Holy Family of Jesus, Mary, and Joseph, the Solemnity of Mary, the Holy Mother of God, and the Feast of the Baptism of the Lord, the psalm refrains share the idea of blessing. Specifically on the Solemnity of Mary, the Holy Mother of God, the psalm states the belief that the Lord will bless his people with peace.

Second Readings   During Christmas Time, the second readings are the same for all three years of the Lectionary cycle of readings except on the feasts of the Holy Family and the Baptism of the Lord. The Second Readings for the four Christmas Masses proclaim how God has fully spoken to us through his Son to whom we are to bear witness, as the Apostle Paul did. On the ensuing feasts and solemnities of Christmas Time, the Second Readings come from Colossians, Galatians, Ephesians, and Acts. In turn, they speak of the virtues of family life, God's Son born of a woman and the Spirit of his Son, the sharing of Gentiles and all who believe in the promise of the Gospel, and Peter's testimony to how God anointed Jesus with the Holy Spirit.

Gospel Readings   The Solemnity of the Nativity of the Lord (Christmas), which marks the beginning of Christmas Time, has four distinct sets of readings which are the same for each of the three years of the Lectionary cycle of readings. Each Gospel account assigned to a specific Christmas Mass reflects a particular dimension of the Incarnation—the event of God becoming human in Jesus. The Gospel for the Christmas Vigil, the genealogy in Matthew, recalls Jesus' ancestry. During the Christmas Mass during the Night, the Gospel reading is Luke's account of the angels announcing the birth of Jesus in Bethlehem. The Gospel for the Mass at Dawn is Luke's description of the shepherds finding Mary, Joseph, and the infant lying in the manger. In this Gospel, we hear of Mary's reflective nature and the shepherds' ecstasy as they return home in awe, praising God because of what they saw. During the fourth Mass of the solemnity, the Mass during the Day, the Gospel is a selection from the prologue of John. This passage, deeply theological in nature, proclaims the profound truth that the Word became flesh and made his dwelling among us. We hear that the glory of the Word shines in the darkness, never allowing the darkness to overcome it. The Gospel on the Solemnity of the Epiphany of the Lord is the same each of the three years and is the time-honored narrative of the Wise Men following the star to find Jesus and pay him homage.

December 25, 2022
Solemnity of the Nativity of the Lord
There Is Nothing to Fear, God Is with Us

 ## Scripture Background

Connections to Church Teaching and Tradition

- "It is vitally important for the Church today to go forth and preach the Gospel to all: to all places, on all occasions, without hesitation, reluctance or fear. The joy of the Gospel is for all people: no one can be excluded. That is what the angel proclaimed to the shepherds in Bethlehem: 'Be not afraid'" (EG, 23).

- "The primary reason for evangelizing is the love of Jesus which we have received, the experience of salvation which urges us to ever greater love of him. What kind of love would not feel the need to speak of the beloved, to point him out, to make him known? If we do not feel an intense desire to share this love, we need to pray insistently that he will once more touch our hearts" (EG, 264).

- "The Church's mission derives not only from the Lord's mandate but also from the profound demands of God's life within us" (RMI, 11).

Isaiah 9:1–6 When hearing this reading, some will undoubtedly recall the words sung in George Frederic Handel's *Messiah*, a tribute to the evangelizing power of music. The words are Isaiah's, somewhat influenced by other cultures' descriptions of an ideal ruler. The historical circumstances surrounding this composition, however, were far from ideal: the people were undergoing deportation and enslavement. The only way for them to describe themselves was as living in a land of gloom. The horror of their abject darkness included their captors' brutality, which involved putting out the eyes of some of them, both as a warning and as a way to debilitate and humiliate would-be leaders.

When Isaiah speaks of light, he is not talking about the decorations that offset the dark of winter in December in the northern hemisphere. For Isaiah, light is a symbol of desperately needed salvation and liberation. The light is coming from God in person and in a person, a child to be born who would deliver the people. In Isaiah's day, that presaged a king. But no king lived up to the promise. Rather than abandon hope, the people came to understand the prophecy as referring to a Messiah to come. For the early Church, the prophecy fit the person of Jesus perfectly, who came offering light and liberation.

Psalm 96:1–2, 2–3, 11–12, 13 (Luke 2:11) This psalm, so appropriate for Christmas, sings out a core message of the psalter: Rejoice, for God reigns! The song celebrates and recalls Israel's many experiences of rescue. For us it sings the joy of the Nativity and invites us to ask how the Good News of Christ's birth sheds new light on our lives today. When we strive to let our daily lives be permeated with Christ's presence, we will know how to "announce his salvation, day after day" (v. 2).

Titus 2:11–14 This short reading reminds us that the coming of Christ at Christmas was only the beginning. The Epiphany has happened; God has appeared definitively in our history. As a result, Christ's presence enables us to live a new way. Even more, we look toward that future when Isaiah's prophecy of peace will come true; not only will there be peace, but every person will know the love of God that Christians have found in Christ. We proclaim that belief with the Lord's Prayer in every liturgy, as we remember the "blessed hope" (v. 13) we share as we await the coming of our Savior, our Lord Jesus Christ. This perspective on Christ's presence invites us to let that hope be the guiding beacon of our entire life.

Luke 2:1–14 This selection from Luke's account of the Gospel portrays three distinct scenes. In the first we hear of Mary and Joseph, who undertook a journey of approximately ninety miles in the last days of Mary's pregnancy. That journey was necessary because the people of occupied Israel had to register for the purpose of taxation. The opening scene depicts a time of oppression for God's people.

In the second scene, Luke uses very few words to announce the birth of the Messiah. He simply tells us that Mary's time was completed and she gave birth to her son. There is no great drama, no miracles, just a simple birth. To emphasize the ordinariness of it all, Luke mentions that the baby was wrapped in swaddling clothes—a sign as spectacular as someone today saying that the baby was diapered. Finally, as if the birth were not unostentatious enough, Luke adds a crucial detail and the rationale for it. The child was laid in a manger because there was no room for him among his own people. In those few lines, Luke orients us to the entire Gospel he is about to recount. God's son comes among us unobtrusively, in adverse conditions, and not even the members of God's own people make room for him.

The third scene underlines the simplicity of God's involvement in human history. The first to hear of the birth of the child are poor shepherds—either hired hands or those who had not the means to hire others to work the night shift for them. They were often stigmatized as dishonest and for being unable to fulfill the strict requirements of the law. It was to them that the announcement came, with the assurance that they had nothing to fear from this great event that God was working among them.

Preparation

The prophet Isaiah foretold a Messiah who would be both mighty King and child. The manner of Jesus' coming demonstrated his identity as both ordinary and extraordinary. Aspects of his birth were typical and humble, and yet it was also heralded by choirs of angels. The arrival of the Messiah was witnessed by shepherds who told the good news of what they had seen and heard.

Lectionary for Mass #14A

Isaiah 9:1–6

Psalm 96:1–2, 2–3, 11–12, 13 (Luke 2:11)

Titus 2:11–14

Luke 2:1–14

Objectives

- To show children how the birth of Jesus Christ was both ordinary and extraordinary.

- To draw a connection between the singing of the choirs of angels and our singing of the Gloria at Mass.

Preparation and Materials

- Read the Season Background, the lectionary readings, and the Scripture Background.

- Bookmark the appropriate readings (see page xv) in the lectionary, children's lectionary, or Bible. Place the book in a convenient location for the leader.

- Write the words of dismissal on a card for the priest celebrant.

- Prepare the words of the song the children will sing as they gather in the space for the Liturgy of the Word.

- Select volunteers (older children or adults) to proclaim the readings.

- Display the responsorial psalm refrain lyrics.

- Display the Apostles' or Nicene Creed.

- Prepare intercessions for the Prayer of the Faithful adapted for the needs of the Church, world, oppressed or marginalized, and local community.

Prayer Leader Reflection Questions

>> When you consider that you are a child of God, beloved by him, what thoughts come to mind?

>> How is your participation in the sacramental life of the Church giving glory to God?

Procession

Following the Collect of the Mass, the priest celebrant picks up the lectionary and invites those who would like to participate in the Liturgy of the Word with children to come forward and gather in the center aisle. The people who will lead the children out and facilitate the Liturgy of the Word also come forward at this time. Holding the lectionary so that all can see, the priest celebrant sends the children forth using his own words or the following:

> *Priest*: **Children, the birth of the Lord is announced to shepherds, those whose job it is to keep watch over their flocks. God's message of peace falls upon the hearts of the world. Go forth in peace to hear about the love of God.**

The leader processes out holding the lectionary, and the children follow behind. The parish music minister may have selected a song of dismissal for the assembly to sing while the children leave. A good option is "The Word of God: Children's Dismissal" by M. D. Ridge and Timothy R. Smith (WLP/GIA).

Centering

Continue to sing the song of dismissal that the assembly sang as you left the church. Or sing the refrains from "Go, Tell It on the Mountain" (Go TELL IT), or "Away in a Manger" (MUELLER), or have instrumental music playing as the children gather in the space for the Liturgy of the Word.

Place the lectionary on the ambo or lectern. Light the candle placed by the ambo or lectern, and then lead the following prayer:

> **We praise you, O God,**
> **as we welcome your son Jesus Christ as our Savior.**
> **Allow our hearts to be open to your Word**
> **so that we may serve you completely.**
> **Through Christ our Lord.**

> *Children:* **Amen.**

First Reading

Isaiah 9:1–6

Responsorial Psalm

Psalm 96:1–2, 2–3, 11–12, 13 (Luke 2:11) *Sing the same musical setting that is used in your parish's celebration of the liturgy.*

Second Reading

Titus 2:11–14

Gospel Acclamation

Sing the Gospel Acclamation used in your parish's celebration of the liturgy.

Gospel Reading

Luke 2:1–14

Homily/Reflection

For the four weeks of Advent, we have been waiting and preparing. Now the time has come for us to enjoy the great feast of Christmas—we celebrate that Jesus has been born! The people of Israel waited and watched and heard the words of the prophets promising a Messiah. The Messiah has come. God's love is so great for his people that he sent his son to be born among humanity.

» What details of Christ's birth can you recall?

The actual moment when Jesus was born seems so ordinary. Jesus was born to a mother just like every other baby. Since Mary and Joseph were traveling, the child Jesus was laid in an animal's feeding trough instead of a cradle. Somewhere else, though, the full glory of the Lord, the majesty of this moment was announced. Shepherds in a field were taking care of their sheep when an angel appeared to them.

» Can you imagine what this might have been like for the shepherds, seeing an angel, knowing that they were in the presence of the glory of the Lord?

The shepherds were afraid! But the angel told them not to be afraid, that a Savior has come who is Christ the Lord, and that they would find this Savior, who was a baby wrapped in swaddling clothes and lying in a manger.

» What can a newborn baby do? What are some things a newborn cannot do? *(Ask children to share their thoughts, especially if they have baby brothers or sisters at home.)*

The child Jesus is different. He is the Savior, the anointed one, the Lord who is God. The prophet Isaiah had already told something about this baby, long before he was born. The first reading tells us that "a child is born to us, a son is given to us; upon his shoulder dominion rests" (Isaiah 9:5). *Dominion* refers to all that a king has, perhaps a whole country. This baby could somehow carry the dominion of a king. The dominion of this king is no small amount—it is huge and it is forever. This must be an extraordinary child!

After the angel made the announcement about the baby, other angels appeared, and they sang together. The words they sang are words you have heard at Mass. Let's sing them together. *(Sing the first line of a setting of the* Gloria, *ideally the Mass setting used most often at your parish, or perhaps the refrain of "Angels We Have Heard on High." The children who regularly attend Mass will be able to help with this singing so a high level of singing ability will not be necessary; however, if you prefer, invite a confident singer to lead this.)* This is a beautiful way to announce and to praise the glory of this king, this Messiah, this Savior, this Lord who is God.

When the shepherds heard the announcement of Jesus' birth, the angel called it "good news of great joy that will be for all the people" (Luke 2:10). This message was not only for the shepherds, but for all. This message is for us too. When the shepherds heard these words, they went to see the baby in swaddling clothes lying in the manger. We can seek out and be close to Jesus, too. We do this in prayer, in serving others, in coming to the table of the Lord. After the shepherds saw that the angel's words were true, they could not keep it to themselves. They told everyone. We, too, can share the good news! *(Ask children to offer ways.)*

Profession of Faith

Following the homily or reflection, the prayer leader invites everyone to stand to profess our faith. Together, sing or recite the Apostles' or Nicene Creed. Refer the children to the words of the prayer that you have displayed.

Prayer of the Faithful

Leader: **With abundant joy, we lift up our prayers to our God, who manifests his glory to all the world. Please respond, "Savior of the World, hear us."**

That the Church may share the good news that the Savior has been born with the joy of the shepherds, we pray: *Savior of the World, hear us.*

That peace may reign on earth, that the song of the angels may inspire those who govern nations and guide armies to seek peaceful resolutions to all disagreements, we pray: *Savior of the World, hear us.*

That the sick and the homebound, especially those who have no family with them this Christmas, may find companionship in the kindness of neighbors, we pray: *Savior of the World, hear us.*

That each of us might announce the good news of salvation to others by our actions and words, we pray: *Savior of the World, hear us.*

Invite other intercessions from the children, or add intercessions based on the current needs of the Church, the world, the oppressed or marginalized, and the local community. Conclude each of the children's petitions with **"we pray"** and invite the response **"Savior of the World, hear us."**

That all who have died may join with all the angels and saints in giving eternal praise and glory to God, we pray: *Savior of the World, hear us.*

O God,
we praise you this day for the Prince of Peace, your Son, comes to us as the hope of every nation.
Grant the humble prayers of your children.
Through Christ our Lord.

Children: **Amen.**

Quietly return with the children to the main assembly. Be mindful of children having difficulty finding their families.

January 1, 2023
Solemnity of Mary, the Holy Mother of God
Mary, Blessed of God

 ## Scripture Background

Connections to Church Teaching and Tradition

* "Jesus was born in a humble stable, into a poor family.[1] Simple shepherds were the first witnesses to this event. In this poverty heaven's glory was made manifest.[2] The Church never tires of singing the glory of this night" (CCC, 525).

* "To become a child in relation to God is the condition for entering the kingdom.[3] For this, we must humble ourselves and become little. Even more: to become 'children of God' we must be 'born from above' or 'born of God'[4]" (CCC, 526).

* "Mary is acclaimed by Elizabeth . . . as 'the mother of my Lord.'[5] In fact, the One whom she conceived as man . . . was none other than the Father's eternal Son, the second person of the Holy Trinity. Hence the Church confesses that Mary is truly 'Mother of God' (*Theotokos*)[6]" (CCC, 495).

---

1 Cf. Luke 2:6–7.
2 Cf. Luke 2:8–20.
3 Cf. Matthew 18:3–4.
4 John 3:7; 1:13; 1:12; cf. Matthew 23:12.
5 Luke 1:43; John 2:1; 19:25; cf. Matthew 13:55; et al.
6 Council of Ephesus (431): DS 251.

Numbers 6:22–27   Aaron's blessing probably goes back to the time of Moses (1250 BC). It is believed to be one of the oldest biblical poems. Its setting is most likely the Temple and the priestly blessings upon the people. The sacred name of God, always abbreviated Yhwh and translated into English as *Lord,* is used three times. The threefold blessing invokes God to enfold the people, to allow intimacy and graciousness to dominate the relationship, and to look upon us with kindness and grant us peace.

Peace entails a sense of wholeness in which everyone has what is needed for fullness of life. Peace demands that justice abound in all our dealings. As we begin the New Year, it is fitting to ask God to bless us so that we might live lives of justice that lead to peace. Mary, God's blessed, is our model as we begin a New Year. Her devotion and dedication to God brought abundant blessings upon her and upon all who follow the Son she brought into the world.

Psalm 67:2–3, 5, 6, 8 (2a)   This psalm of praise is a prayer of thanks to God for a bountiful harvest. Such concrete realities are obvious indicators of God's blessing upon the people and the land. The beginning verses are similar to the Aaronic blessing from today's reading from Numbers. God's blessing is not just for the people, but also serves as a way of making God's way and salvation known among all the nations. The care lavished on the people, along with the just and loving manner in which God guides and sustains them, causes other nations to be glad, to exult, and to praise the God of Israel.

God's blessings on the people have a far greater purpose and effect. By invoking God to bless us, we are seeking to secure God's blessings, not only for ourselves, but for all of creation as well. Through us, others will come to know and experience God's goodness, love, and mercy. As we celebrate a new year, we call upon God to bless us. Mary, who was blessed by God in a unique and singular way, is a sign of God's blessings for us all. Through God's blessings upon Mary, we come to know God's graciousness more clearly, and come to the realization that God blesses all people in the same rich, lavish way he blessed Mary.

Galatians 4:4–7   Paul's "fullness of time" (v. 4) refers to the time God deemed appropriate to become one of us. God became fully one of us—"born of a woman" (v. 4), and a Jew—"born under the law" (v. 4), while still fully retaining divinity as God's Son. Jesus' mission was to ransom us from the law and to make us adopted sons and daughters of God. Paul does not repudiate the law, but sees it as a tutor for one not yet of age. With Christ and the gift of the Spirit given through him, the law can be set aside for we have come of age and have been brought into a mature and intimate relationship with God.

Proof of this new mature status is God's gift of the Spirit, sent into our hearts, empowering us to call God "Abba," our loving Father. We are no longer slaves subject to the law, but are God's adult sons and daughters. Through Baptism into Christ, we become intimate members of God's family and heirs to all of God's love and blessings. Mary was among the first to experience that intimate and deep relationship to God in and through the Person of her Son, the second Person of the Holy Trinity. For this special gift, we honor her today as we thank God for the same rich gift that we have all received in Christ.

Luke 2:16–21   The shepherds, usually social outcasts, are the first to see and experience God in this lowly birth in a stable. They come to believe the divine presence in this ordinary child and are the first evangelizers. Like the nations in today's psalm, they come to see God's gracious blessings in the ordinary events of this birth, as they go forth "glorifying and praising God for all they had heard and seen" (v. 20). Their lives changed through this experience of God's blessings. We, too, are called to hear, see, and believe in God's great love for us, manifested in life's ordinary events.

Both the shepherds and Mary model what such seeing and hearing entails. The shepherds are invited to hear, come, see, believe, and praise God for such rich blessings. Mary keeps all these things in her heart, reflecting on them as they invite her to deeper understanding and belief. Like the shepherds, we are invited to hear, come, see, believe, and praise God. Like Mary, we are asked to ponder God's ways in our hearts, so that we may attune our lives to God's many blessings.

Preparation

Today's solemnity honoring our Blessed Mother falls during Christmas Time in the liturgical year and on New Year's Day in the secular calendar. Christmas Time is the season of celebrating the birth of Christ and New Year's Day celebrates the birth of a new calendar year. How appropriate to honor our spiritual mother Mary during this season of new beginnings! Filled with God's grace, she is our example for contemplating the greatness of God. In all the events surrounding her holy child's birth, Mary reflected on them in her heart. In his wisdom, God sent angels to the shepherds, who in turn greeted the child Jesus with shouts of joyful praises to God. We recall in this reading the great devotion our Lord has to the poorest and most humble people who walk this earth.

Lectionary for Mass #18A

Numbers 6:22–27

Psalm 67:2–3, 5, 6, 8 (2A)

Galatians 4:4–7

Luke 2:16–21

Objectives

- To explain to children Mary's unique identity as the Mother of God.

- To encourage children to trust, as Mary did, that God will help them understand things kept in their hearts.

Preparation and Materials

- Read the Season Background, the Lectionary readings, and the Scripture Background.

- Bookmark the appropriate readings (see page xv) in the Lectionary, children's Lectionary, or Bible. Place the book in a convenient location for the leader.

- Write the words of dismissal on a card for the priest celebrant.

- Prepare the words of the song the children will sing as they gather in the space for the Liturgy of the Word.

- Select volunteers (older children or adults) to proclaim the readings.

- Display the responsorial psalm refrain lyrics.

- Display the Apostles' or Nicene Creed.

- Prepare intercessions for the Prayer of the Faithful adapted for the needs of the Church, world, oppressed or marginalized, and local community.

Prayer Leader Reflection Questions

>> **How do you ponder God's gift of the Messiah in your heart?**

>> **Consider praying the Rosary (or a decade) reflecting on today's Gospel reading.**

Procession

Following the Collect of the Mass, the priest celebrant picks up the Lectionary and invites those who would like to participate in the Liturgy of the Word with children to come forward and gather in the center aisle. The people who will lead the children out and facilitate the Liturgy of the Word also come forward at this time. Holding the Lectionary so that all can see, the priest celebrant sends the children forth using his own words or the following:

> *Priest:* **My dear children, Christmas Time helps us remember that God loves us, is near to us, and is always with us. As you go to hear God's Word, listen carefully, God is speaking to you. Find the light that Jesus shares with us. Then be that light for everyone you meet. Go now in peace.**

The leader processes out holding the Lectionary, and the children follow behind. The parish music minister may have selected a song of dismissal for the assembly to sing while the children leave. A good option is "The Word of God: Children's Dismissal" by M. D. Ridge and Timothy R. Smith (WLP/GIA).

Centering

Continue to sing the song of dismissal that the assembly sang as you left the church. Or sing the refrain from "Hail Mary, Gentle Woman" (Landry), or "Away in a Manger" (MUELLER), or have instrumental music playing as the children gather in the space for the Liturgy of the Word.

Place the Lectionary on the ambo or lectern. Light the candle placed by the ambo or lectern, and then lead the following prayer:

> **We praise you and bless you, O God.**
> **We thank you for the gift of Jesus' mother, Mary.**
> **Open our hearts and ears so we will believe as she did.**
> **Through Christ our Lord.**

> *Children:* **Amen.**

First Reading

Numbers 6:22–27

Responsorial Psalm

Psalm 67:2–3, 5, 6, 8 (2a) *Sing the same musical setting that is used in your parish's celebration of the liturgy.*

Second Reading

Galatians 4:4–7

Gospel Acclamation

Sing the Gospel Acclamation used in your parish's celebration of the liturgy.

Gospel Reading

Luke 2:16–21

Homily/Reflection

Today is the Solemnity of Mary, the Holy Mother of God. It is a special day when we honor our Blessed Mother, and are grateful that she is the Mother of God.

Did you hear what was said about her in today's Gospel reading? There weren't very many words about her today, but what we heard is very important! We heard that Mary "kept all these things, reflecting on them in her heart." This means that Mary listened to everything the shepherds said about God sending them to see the Messiah. Hearing the praises and the message by the shepherds must have brought about wonder in Mary's heart. She thought about the greatness and goodness of God to bring about the miracle of Jesus. Also knowing the Jewish tradition and understanding that God's promise to the people was fulfilled in her son, Mary reflected on that too in her heart.

When Mary reflected in her heart that means she was thinking deeply or carefully about something. All moms and dads keep many things in their hearts, especially things about their children. Moms and dads think deeply and carefully about whether they are doing a good job as a parent. Moms and dads think deeply and carefully about how their children are different—one may love music and the other may be good at baseball, one is serious and one is more outgoing. Mother Mary may have been reflecting on all the amazing things that had happened to her recently. For example, she might have been thinking back to when the angel Gabriel asked her to be Jesus' mother. She might have felt unsure about the request but she was certain she trusted God. She might have been thinking about the trip to Bethlehem and not having a warm place to have her baby. She might have wondered why she ended up having to give birth in a stable and having to lay her baby in a manger. It was likely very hard on her but she kept her trust in God. And now, shepherds have come to see little Jesus because angels told them he was the Messiah. So there was a lot that Mother Mary could think deeply and carefully about. She might not have fully understood why everything was happening but she left everything up to God. She had complete trust in God that everything was happening as it should.

Mary is a good example for us. We might have things we keep in our hearts to reflect on, things we don't understand. We might be reflecting on why some people are bullies and seem to like hurting others. We might be reflecting on why some people are so good in math and others find it so very hard. We might reflect on why someone we love is very sick. Even when we cannot understand everything we, like Mother Mary, can trust God to be with us and help us. We can also ask Mother Mary for help by saying "Mary, Mother of God, pray for us." Or, we can pray a Hail Mary or the Rosary.

Let's try to follow Mother Mary's example as we reflect on whatever we hold in our hearts. Let's remember to trust, as Mary did, that God will always help us.

Profession of Faith

Following the homily or reflection, the prayer leader invites everyone to stand to profess our faith. Together, sing or recite the Apostles' or Nicene Creed. Refer the children to the words of the prayer that you have displayed.

Prayer of the Faithful

Leader: **A great light shines in the darkness! As we turn to our God in prayer, please respond, "Lord, hear our prayer."**

For the Church, and all Christians, that we may boldly meet our call to love all of God's people, let us pray to the Lord: *Lord, hear our prayer.*

For peace on earth, that the announcement of God's favor to the world may open the hearts of civil leaders to seek peaceful resolutions to global and domestic conflicts, let us pray to the Lord: *Lord, hear our prayer.*

For the poor and those who suffer in our world, that they may find consolation in our Blessed Mother's powerful protection, let us pray to the Lord: *Lord, hear our prayer.*

For all mothers to look to Mother Mary as a role model and to trust in God completely; and for us all to enjoy the blessings of health and happiness as we celebrate the arrival of a new year, we pray to the Lord: *Lord, hear our prayer.*

Invite other intercessions from the children, or add intercessions based on the current needs of the Church, the world, the oppressed or marginalized, and the local community. Conclude each of the children's petitions with, **"we pray to the Lord,"** and invite the response, **"Lord, hear our prayer."**

For those who have died, that they may live with God forever, we pray to the Lord: *Lord, hear our prayer.*

Heavenly Father,
you gave us Mary as a mother who loves and guides her children.
May we look to her as our model and guide.
Grant these prayers in accordance with your holy will.
Through Jesus Christ our Lord.

Children: **Amen.**

Quietly return with the children to the main assembly. Be mindful of children having difficulty finding their families.

January 8, 2023
Solemnity of the Epiphany of the Lord
Light in Darkness

 ## Scripture Background

Connections to Church Teaching and Tradition

⚜ "Christ is the light of nations and consequently this holy synod, gathered together in the holy Spirit, ardently desires to bring to all humanity that light of Christ . . . by proclaiming his Gospel to every creature.[1] . . . The Church, in Christ, is a sacrament—a sign and instrument, that is, of communion with God and of the unity of entire human race" (LG, 1).

⚜ "The white garment symbolizes that the person baptized has 'put on Christ,'[2] has risen with Christ. The *candle*, lit from the Easter candle, signifies that Christ has enlightened the neophyte. In him the baptized are 'the light of the world'[3]" (CCC, 1243).

Isaiah 60:1–6 This Epiphany reading was selected for its reference to camels coming to Jerusalem bringing the wealth of nations, gold, and frankincense. Along with Psalm 72, it provides the backdrop to the account in the Gospel of Matthew of the Magi following the star to the newborn king of the Jews. Isaiah's historical setting is the Babylonian exile, with the land ravaged and the people dispersed. Isaiah consoles Jerusalem and all its inhabitants with a vision of light in darkness. While it appears that despoiled and ravaged Jerusalem is in darkness, God has not abandoned her. God's glory and light shines upon Israel, rescuing her from darkness to new light, from slavery to freedom, as it did at the Exodus.

God's glory and light shine on Jerusalem with such splendor that all its exiled inhabitants, young and old, return to experience it. The wealth of nations shall be brought to Jerusalem, both to rebuild and to pay homage to the Lord. Jerusalem, so richly manifesting God's light, glory, and presence, is the beacon that guides all nations to the Lord. Today, we celebrate the revelation and manifestation of God's glory to all nations in the birth of Jesus, the Light of the World.

Psalm 72:1–2, 7–8, 10–11, 12–13 (see 11) The psalm describes the ideal qualities that people hope their newly crowned king might manifest. The psalmist prays that God might endow the new king with right judgment, just decisions, and concern for the afflicted and the poor. Such a king would be remembered always, and would become the model of kingship for all the nations. Such a rule would be desired by all. God's ways would be incarnated in the king, with all nations admiring and honoring such a king with riches, tribute, honor, homage, and service.

Such manifestation of God's wisdom and right judgment by the king would lead all nations to acknowledge and honor God. Such ways of acting would be desired by all and for all time. Epiphany celebrates the manifestation of just such a king in the person of the child Jesus, true God and true man. All nations, represented by the Magi from the east, come to honor and offer homage, praying that his kingship would last forever.

Ephesians 3:2–3a, 5–6 The author of Ephesians notes that through God's revelation, a mission—stewardship—was given for the benefit of all. God's mystery, the hidden plan of God from the beginning, was revealed by the Spirit to the author, as well as to the "holy apostles and prophets" (v. 5). The essence of that mystery is that the Gentiles are coheirs, members, and copartners "in the promise of Christ Jesus through the Gospel" (v. 6).

In Jesus, and through the power of the Spirit, God's mystery was revealed to the Jews. Correspondingly, a new way of thinking and acting was demanded of all Jews. No longer were they God's only Chosen People. Rather, God's plan from the beginning was that all would share in God's intimacy and blessings that they now enjoyed. The essence of Jesus' Good News is that Jews and Gentiles share equally in God's intimacy, blessings, and promises. Jesus' presence illuminates our minds and hearts; the Spirit's power enables us to be that same light to all the world.

Matthew 2:1–12 The Magi narrative, unique to the Gospel according to Matthew, developed out of several biblical and extrabiblical references intended to communicate beliefs concerning the identity and mission of Jesus. These post-Resurrection beliefs were projected into the early life of Jesus. The Magi represent the Gentiles who, guided by God's light, the star, come to Jerusalem to worship and honor the newborn king of the Jews. Herod and the Jewish leaders assert that the Messiah is to come from David's line and be born in David's town,

1 Cf. Mark 16:15.
2 Galatians 3:27.
3 Matthew 5:14; cf. Philippians 2:15.

Bethlehem. Herod, a Jewish king, represents those who are threatened by the new king and a new way of exercising kingship. Such people scheme to do away with Jesus and the values he manifests.

The Magi continue to follow God's light and are rewarded with an opportunity to recognize and honor the child Jesus as king with a completely different concept of kingship and ruling. Through this narrative, Matthew's wanted his to understand that Jesus came for all humanity. We who claim to be disciples of Jesus are called to bring that same insight, wisdom, and light to all the world. We are to manifest God's light to all, making certain that no one is excluded from membership in God's Kingdom. Epiphany celebrates Jesus' manifestation to the world, and our call to continue that mission in our lives.

 # Preparation

Today's reading from Isaiah foretells a time when all people will know the glory of Lord and will respond to this knowledge with joy and the giving of very particular gifts. God's presence will be light to all. In the Gospel of Matthew, we hear the fulfillment of Isaiah's prophecy in which people from afar see a most particular light, a star in the sky, and recognize the light of God in the child of Bethlehem. They respond with joy, humility, and offering gifts. We can follow the example of the Magi and respond to the gift of the incarnation as they did.

Lectionary for Mass #20C

Isaiah 60:1–6

Psalm 72:1–2, 7–8, 10–11, 12–13 (see 11)

Ephesians 3:2–3a, 5–6

Matthew 2:1–12

Objectives

- To announce that the gift of the incarnation that was foretold by Jewish prophets is a gift not only for Israel but for all.

- To introduce a connection between biblical images of the "glory" of God and light.

Preparation and Materials

- Read the Season Background, the lectionary readings, and the Scripture Background.

- Bookmark the appropriate readings (see page xv) in the lectionary, children's lectionary, or Bible. Place the book in a convenient location for the leader.

- Write the words of dismissal on a card for the priest celebrant.

- Prepare the words of the song the children will sing as they gather in the space for the Liturgy of the Word.

- Select volunteers (older children or adults) to proclaim the readings.

- Display the responsorial psalm refrain lyrics.

- Display the Apostles' or Nicene Creed.

- Prepare intercessions for the Prayer of the Faithful adapted for the needs of the Church, world, oppressed or marginalized, and local community.

Prayer Leader Reflection Questions

>> **How do you humble yourself before the one who is great? What gifts do you bring to Jesus?**

>> **What realizations or epiphanies have you experienced in your faith life? Did they change you? How?**

Procession

Following the Collect of the Mass, the priest celebrant picks up the lectionary and invites those who would like to participate in the Liturgy of the Word with children to come forward and gather in the center aisle. The people who will lead the children out and facilitate the Liturgy of the Word also come forward at this time. Holding the lectionary so that all can see, the priest celebrant sends the children forth using his own words or the following:

Priest: **Dear children, the beauty and wonders of creation can show us the way to God. In today's Gospel you will hear of the star that led the Magi to the newborn Jesus. While they gave him gifts of gold, frankincense, and myrrh, Jesus gives us far more precious gifts: the grace to be called his brothers and sisters and children of God, and the gift of everlasting life. Go forth to meet him!**

The leader processes out holding the lectionary, and the children follow behind. The parish music minister may have selected a song of dismissal for the assembly to sing while the children leave. A good option is "The Word of God: Children's Dismissal" by M. D. Ridge and Timothy R. Smith (WLP/GIA).

Centering

Continue to sing the song of dismissal that the assembly sang as you left the church. Or sing the refrains from "We Three Kings" (Kings of Orient), or "What Star Is This" (Puer Nobis), or have instrumental music playing as the children gather in the space for the Liturgy of the Word.

Place the lectionary on the ambo or lectern. Light the candle placed by the ambo or lectern, and then lead the following prayer:

**O God,
shine your light on our hearts,
so that we can follow you to reach the brightness of our eternal home.
May we be open to your Word
so that we may serve you completely.
Through Christ our Lord.**

Children: **Amen.**

First Reading

Isaiah 60:1–6

Responsorial Psalm

Psalm 72:1–2, 7–8, 10–11, 12–13 *Sing the same musical setting that is used in your parish's celebration of the liturgy.*

Second Reading

Ephesians 3:2–3a, 5–6

Gospel Acclamation

Sing the Gospel Acclamation used in your parish's celebration of the liturgy.

Gospel Reading

Matthew 2:1–12

Homily/Reflection

We have been enjoying our great feast of Christmas. We celebrate that Jesus was born. The Messiah has come. On Christmas Day, we heard about special visitors at Jesus' birth. The angel announced good news to shepherds that Jesus had been born and they went to see this for themselves. When they arrived, they found Jesus wrapped in swaddling clothes and lying in a manger just as the angel had told them. They were filled with joy. But these were not the only visitors who came. Today, we hear about others who came to see Jesus. In the Gospel reading today, we hear about the Magi. Sometimes we refer to them as "kings" or "wise men." You may have heard songs about them.

》 What songs have you heard that refer to these special visitors?

Now these visitors weren't kings, as far as we know, but they were from the East. They were from someplace far from Israel. They studied the stars to find out what God might be telling them, and they discovered something amazing. They saw new light. They found a new star and they realized that a new king had been born. The people of Israel knew about light. They sometimes spoke of the "glory" of the Lord. They understood that God is so great that we cannot fully see or understand God, but when people were near God and could experience the glory, it "shone." Yet it was not someone from Israel who followed the star and understood what it meant. It was the Magi, people who were not Jewish.

The Magi knew that this newborn King was special, someone who is a gift. When they went to visit the child, they were filled with joy, too, and they did some surprising things. When they arrived, they prostrated themselves. They laid down and made themselves small in front of Jesus. Jesus was a little child, but these grown-ups showed with their bodies that they understood Jesus' true greatness. They gave him gifts of gold, frankincense, and myrrh. These were very precious and expensive gifts; they were not toys that a child would play with.

Why these? Gold is precious. When it is formed and polished, it can capture and reflect light in a beautiful way. This is a gift for a king. Burning frankincense produces smoke that smells like perfume as it rises to the heavens. This is a gift for worshipping God. Myrrh was often made as oil that also smelled like perfume, but one of the ways the oil was used was to prepare the bodies of those who had died so they could be buried. This was a gift for a human being who would die.

Even though the Magi hadn't heard the Word of God in the Bible, even though they weren't people of Israel who knew God's name, they understood some important things about who Jesus is. Jesus is not only a gift for the people of Israel, but is also for others, for the whole world. That means Jesus is a gift for us!

>> **How can we respond to the gift of Jesus like the Magi responded?**

We can be humble before God, like when we genuflect before the tabernacle, but also following God's law. We can offer gifts to God, like during the offertory at Mass and when we serve those who are in need. We can enjoy Jesus with us in a most particular way when we come so close to him in receiving the Eucharist.

Profession of Faith

Following the homily or reflection, the prayer leader invites everyone to stand to profess our faith. Together, sing or recite the Apostles' or Nicene Creed. Refer the children to the words of the prayer that you have displayed.

Prayer of the Faithful

Leader: **God's love is made known to us in Christ Jesus, in whose name we pray for ourselves and others. Please respond, "King of Kings, hear our prayer."**

May all who are called to be ministers of the Gospel manifest the power of God's Word to both the powerful and the powerless, we pray: *King of Kings, hear our prayer.*

May world leaders govern with the humility and self-giving love of Jesus Christ who is king of all, we pray: *King of Kings, hear our prayer.*

May those searching for work and those who cannot work become productive in other ways, we pray: *King of Kings, hear our prayer.*

May those in our family of faith who are thinking about their future, especially young adults, have the courage to rely on God's wisdom, we pray: *King of Kings, hear our prayer.*

Invite other intercessions from the children, or add intercessions based on the current needs of the Church, the world, the oppressed or marginalized, and the local community. Conclude each of the children's petitions with **"we pray"** and invite the response **"King of Kings, hear our prayer."**

May all who have died live in the light of the Lord, we pray: *King of Kings, hear our prayer.*

O God, you are light for the whole world. Accept the prayers of your children through Christ our Lord.

Children: **Amen.**

Quietly return with the children to the main assembly. Be mindful of children having difficulty finding their families.

Season Background for Ordinary Time during Winter

Understanding Ordinary Time during Winter

Jesus' entry into public life, begun at his baptism, also helps move us toward the season of Ordinary Time. Unlike the seasons of Advent, Christmas Time, Lent, and Easter Time, Ordinary Time does not have its own distinctive character. During this season, we do not celebrate a particular aspect of the mystery of Christ. Rather, the Sundays of Ordinary Time focus on the entirety of the mystery of Christ in all its dimensions.

The season of Ordinary Time includes two periods: the Sundays and weekdays after the feast of the Baptism of the Lord through the Tuesday before Ash Wednesday, and the Sundays and weekdays after Pentecost Sunday until Evening Prayer I on the First Sunday of Advent. The shorter period of Ordinary Time is the first: Ordinary Time during winter. With its accompanying Gospel readings, the liturgies of this period provide ample opportunity for us to speak of our life as the Lord's disciples and to relate Jesus' instructions on the commandments and the moral life to the Church's teachings in these areas. This is a time to step back and relax in our faith. The name of this season is "Ordinary Time" because the Sundays are counted, or ordered, not because it is ordinary in any sense of the word. These Sundays provide us an extraordinary opportunity to ponder and live out the extraordinary truth of Christ's Paschal Mystery, the salvific events of his birth, life, death, and Resurrection. While winter's days may seem to drag on during this time, the Church's liturgy gifts us with a sense of celebration because of our call to be followers of the Savior.

Liturgical Environment

With the beginning of Ordinary Time, the liturgical color changes to green. The life and hope symbolized by the color green contrasts with the barrenness of winter and the increased darkness of winter's days in many parts of North America. Let simplicity characterize the environment during Ordinary Time. Allow simple green banners and draping, along with a few plants around the prayer table, to point to the life that comes from the Word of the Lord in the Lectionary.

Overview of the Readings

As Christmas Time ends and Ordinary Time begins, the Second Readings from the Apostle Paul address the practical concerns of the Christian community for unity within itself. While the first reading and the Gospel will help us consider the Lord's call and our formation as disciples of the Great Teacher, the Second Reading instructs us in how we are to live together as a community of his disciples, a task which is often challenging given the many expectations that society and peer pressure often seem to place on children and adults alike. The one table of the Word (the Liturgy of the Word and its Lectionary readings) and the Eucharist (the Liturgy of the Eucharist, which includes the reception of Holy Communion) strengthens us in our faith in Christ and, through the workings of the Holy Spirit, gives us the grace to respond to these expectations as followers of the one who is God-with-us.

First Readings   Over the course of the Sundays of Ordinary Time in winter, we hear from Isaiah, Zephaniah, Sirach, and Leviticus. At the beginning of the liturgical year, the first readings carry forward the theme of light and salvation that marked Christmas Time. In the latter part of the period, the first readings also begin to speak of keeping the commandments and being holy. With Lent on the horizon, the first readings also begin to include words of sin and repentance.

Responsorial Psalms   The beginning of Ordinary Time brings with it a variety of responsorial psalms. The psalm for the Second Sunday in Ordinary Time sets the tone for the journey through the season as we begin to learn what it means to be disciples of the Lord. First, we have to accept the Lord's call as Isaiah did and learn what it means to be disciples of the Lord. Trusting in God's mercy and kindness that is reflected in other psalms of Ordinary Time, we are called to respond with our dedication to do the Lord's will.

Second Readings   In this year's period of Ordinary Time before Lent, the Second Readings come from Paul's First Letter to the Corinthians. Beginning with an opening address and greeting to the Corinthians on the Second Sunday in Ordinary Time, which can be understood as an address to us today, the Second Readings urge the Corinthians, a people divided on questions of faith and morality, as well as who should be a part of the community of faith, to agree to be united with one another in the same mind, the mind of Christ. The strong in the community are to take care of the weak. The strong are to make sure that their actions do not negatively influence the faith of the weak. All are to be brothers and sisters in Christ.

Gospel Readings   With the onset of Ordinary Time in winter, we hear first from John's account of the Gospel on the Second Sunday in Ordinary Time. This Gospel helps transition us from Christmas Time to Ordinary Time because it continues the focus on the manifestation of Jesus' identity. In the Gospel reading for Year A, the focus is John's proclamation of Jesus as the Lamb of God. Then, beginning with the Third Sunday in Ordinary Time of each year, there is a semicontinuous proclamation of the synoptic account of the Gospel assigned to the current liturgical year. We hear about Jesus' call of his disciples, his instruction on following the commandments and the Law, and his directive to be perfect as the Father is perfect. Through these Gospel passages, we learn how to be faithful disciples of the Lord according to his Word. These Gospel readings give us the basis from which we can reflect on both our fidelity and infidelity to the Lord and his teachings during the coming season of Lent.

January 15, 2023
Second Sunday in Ordinary Time
You Are My Servant

 ## Scripture Background

Connections to Church Teaching and Tradition

✸ "By his loving obedience to the Father, 'unto death, even death on a cross' (Philippians 2:8), Jesus fulfills the atoning mission (cf. Isaiah 53:10) of the suffering Servant" (CCC, 623).

✸ "The teaching and spreading of her social doctrine are part of the Church's evangelizing mission. And since it is a doctrine aimed at guiding people's behavior, it consequently gives rise to a 'commitment to justice,' according to each individual's role, vocation and circumstances" (SRS, 41).

✸ "The members of the Church are impelled to engage in this [missionary] activity because of the charity with which they love God and by which they desire to share with all people the spiritual goods of both this life and the life to come" (AG, 7).

Isaiah 49:3, 5–6   This passage from Isaiah speaks either to an individual servant or to all of Israel as a servant of the Lord. Regardless of the addressee, the first verse we hear from Isaiah sounds like a commission: the servant is called and sent. The following verses indicate an even greater trust: "I will make you a light to the nations, / that my salvation may reach to the ends of the earth" (v. 6). The servant is called to go among the Gentiles and offer God's welcome, grace, salvation, and justice. Whoever the servant is, the servant has a role in history to live and offer the reign of God to all. Jesus Christ accepted the mission to spread the Good News of salvation to all by obediently submitting to the Father's will. His life, Death, and Resurrection invite his followers to do the same.

Psalm 40:2, 4, 7–8, 8–9, 10 (8a, 9a)   Psalm 40 almost seems to be two different psalms. The first verses (2–11), a part of the psalm for this Sunday, are a song of thanksgiving; the second set of verses (14–18) are a song of lament. It differs somewhat from the typical psalm form, in which lamentations are usually sung first. Perhaps the author is reminding the servant of the Lord about his dependence on God. The psalmist reminds the servant that God wants more than offerings—he wants an obedient heart. This theme is heard from several Old Testament prophets. The psalm verses speak of the actions of an obedient servant and the Lord's response to that servant. The Lord hears the servant's cry and gives him a new song. The Lord also gives ears open to obedience and sends the servant forth to proclaim and announce justice to the vast assembly. The psalm speaks plainly of God's actions and the servant's response.

1 Corinthians 1:1–3   Paul's opening verses in his first Letter to the Corinthians seem to set the tone for a glowing affirmation of their community and witness, if only we did not know what followed in the letter. The Corinthians have splintered into various rival groups. Paul writes to correct and address mistakes among them, including moral disorders and divisions in the community, offerings to idols, and problems in the liturgical assemblies. He reminds them that the Spirit is the source of all gifts and admonishes them about envy or rivalry with the striking image of the body and its interconnected parts. Paul later makes it clear that love is the greatest gift of all in the often-quoted verses about love in chapter 13.

Paul begins this letter, saying, "I give thanks to my God always on your account for the grace of God bestowed on you in Christ Jesus" (1 Corinthians 1:4). Knowing that all of these admonitions and concerns are addressed in the following chapters makes it touching that Paul begins his letter with an offering of grace, peace, and thanksgiving to the community at Corinth.

John 1:29–34   Last Sunday, we heard Matthew's account of Jesus' baptism by John (unless the Feast of the Baptism of the Lord falls on a Monday). This Sunday's Gospel provides the Baptist's testimony from the Gospel according to John. Throughout this Gospel, John the Baptist is mentioned almost twenty times. We hear about the places he preached, his discussions with followers, his testimony about Jesus, and even Jesus' own words to his opponents about John: "He was a burning and shining lamp, and for a while you were content to rejoice in his light" (John 5:35). John the Baptist is a strong witness to Jesus.

In today's passage he says he comes to testify about the one to come after him. He speaks of Jesus as the light to come and says that he came to give witness so that others may believe (John 1:7). John clearly states in this passage that the Baptist saw the Spirit come down on Jesus. He is bold and clear in his testimony that this is the Son of God. He speaks and acts so that others may come to know and believe that the Son of God will take away the sins of the world, bringing God's salvation to all. John himself is obedient to his call to testify, but he points out unmistakably Jesus' willingness to be obedient in giving himself to the Father's will, sacrificing his life for all of humanity. Jesus is the living expression of this Sunday's psalm refrain: "Here I am, Lord, I come to do your will" (Psalm 40:8a–9a).

Preparation

The readings today provide us with many models of serving God. Living as servants of God includes a call from God who made us for a purpose from our first beginnings and continues to sanctify us through Jesus Christ. The work of serving God entails announcing what is known with our senses and our minds, and through intimate relationship, that Jesus Christ is the Lamb of God who takes away the sins of the world. In praying today's psalm, we make the words of the psalmist our own. We present ourselves as open and ready, asking to do God's will.

Lectionary for Mass #64A

Isaiah 49:3, 5–6

Psalm 40:2, 4, 7–8, 8–9, 10 (8a, 9a)

1 Corinthians 1:1–3

John 1:29–34

Objectives

- To explore together the image of "servant of God" through the models of the prophet Isaiah, St. Paul, and St. John the Baptist, to consider together how we might be "servants of God" ourselves.

- To explain "knowing" of the Bible as cognitive knowledge, but also living in intimate relationship.

Preparation and Materials

- Read the Season Background, the lectionary readings, and the Scripture Background.

- Bookmark the appropriate readings (see page xv) in the lectionary, children's lectionary, or Bible. Place the book in a convenient location for the leader.

- Write the words of dismissal on a card for the priest celebrant.

- Prepare the words of the song the children will sing as they gather in the space for the Liturgy of the Word.

- Select volunteers (older children or adults) to proclaim the readings.

- Display the responsorial psalm refrain lyrics.

- Display the Apostles' or Nicene Creed.

- Prepare intercessions for the Prayer of the Faithful adapted for the needs of the Church, world, oppressed or marginalized, and local community.

Prayer Leader Reflection Questions

» **How have you heard God's call to serve?**

» **What are the particular ways that God has called you to serve?**

Procession

Following the Collect of the Mass, the priest celebrant picks up the lectionary and invites those who would like to participate in the Liturgy of the Word with children to come forward and gather in the center aisle. The people who will lead the children out and facilitate the Liturgy of the Word also come forward at this time. Holding the lectionary so that all can see, the priest celebrant sends the children forth using his own words or the following:

> *Priest:* **Children, in today's Scriptures you will hear of a lamb and a dove, and this is one way of telling us that Jesus is gentle, that the Holy Spirit is gentle with us, that God is peace. Go and listen for what else Jesus is telling you, and when you return, we will continue our celebration with great joy. Go in peace.**

The leader processes out holding the lectionary, and the children follow behind. The parish music minister may have selected a song of dismissal for the assembly to sing while the children leave. A good option is "The Word of God: Children's Dismissal" by M. D. Ridge and Timothy R. Smith (WLP/GIA).

Centering

Continue to sing the song of dismissal that the assembly sang as you left the church. Or sing the refrains from "Here I Am, Lord" (Schutte), or "I Say 'Yes,' My Lord" / "Digo 'Sí,' Señor" (Peña), or have instrumental music playing as the children gather in the space for the Liturgy of the Word.

Place the lectionary on the ambo or lectern. Light the candle placed by the ambo or lectern, and then lead the following prayer:

> **Everlasting God,**
> **you have called each of us by name to be your servants.**
> **Allow our hearts to be open to your Word**
> **so that we may serve you completely.**
> **In Christ's name we pray.**

> *Children:* **Amen.**

First Reading

Isaiah 49:3, 5–6

Responsorial Psalm

Psalm 40:2, 4, 7–8, 8–9, 10 (8a, 9a) *Sing the same musical setting that is used in your parish's celebration of the liturgy.*

Second Reading

1 Corinthians 1:1–3

Gospel Acclamation

Sing the Gospel Acclamation used in your parish's celebration of the liturgy.

Gospel Reading

John 1:29–34

Homily/Reflection

We have spent many weeks preparing for and celebrating Christmas Time and now we have come to Ordinary Time. Another way of thinking about this season of Ordinary Time is that we are counting time. It is time we spend moving forward, getting older, learning, and growing, especially as we become better disciples. Today, we are listening together about how we can move forward and grow in a particular way during this time: as servants of God.

≫ What do you think it means to be a servant?

We have some beautiful examples of those who serve God. In the readings today, we hear about the prophet Isaiah, St. Paul, and St. John the Baptist, who lived their lives as God asked them to. We hear Isaiah's words about being a servant of God "who formed me as his servant from the womb" (Isaiah 49:5). A *womb* is where a baby grows in the mother before being born. From the very beginning of their lives, God knew each of these servants and called them by name to a particular purpose (even if they didn't know it right away!). It was through the work of God that they were able to fulfill their purpose. John the Baptist spoke about Jesus as someone who ranked ahead of him. John recognized that Jesus Christ is greater and he was lesser. On their own, these servants of God would not be able to do great work. But through God's work of sanctification, of making them holy, these people could be able to do the work that belongs to God.

Servants of God are not alone in their work. When Isaiah described being called as a servant by God, he was not only speaking about himself. God called the people of Israel as a country, together as one, each person to be part of a community. St. Paul echoed this in the second reading when he spoke about being "with all those everywhere who call on the name of our Lord" (1 Corinthians 1:2). What binds servants together is calling on the Lord, Jesus Christ.

John the Baptist was very clear on what his work was as a servant of God. He served God so "that [Jesus] might be made known" (John 1:31). John understood that Jesus is truly the Lamb of God who takes away the sin of the world and that he is the Son of God. He saw with his own eyes how the Spirit came down and rested on Jesus and he heard the Father's words saying that Jesus was the one who would baptize with the Holy Spirit. This knowledge was so great, so important, so beautiful that he could not keep it to himself. He had to tell others. This is what he meant when he said that he "testified."

For the Jewish people, to "know" someone or something does not only mean to think correctly about it. When the Bible speaks about "knowing," it means to be very close and to be connected. When John spoke about Jesus being known, he didn't just want to tell people about what Jesus' title was, or facts about him. He wanted people to have a relationship with Jesus.

In the psalm today, we sang the words "Here am I Lord; I come to do your will." When we speak or sing these words, we make them our own prayer. We are telling God that we are also willing to be servants of God. We recognize that God has made us and called us by name for a purpose since before we were born. God makes us holy and sanctified so that we can be ready to do his work. Through our words and actions, we can do the particular work of testifying to others that Jesus is the Lamb of God, who takes away the sins of the world. We can see Jesus Christ with our own eyes and know him in a most particular way in the Eucharist.

>> **What are some ways we can serve God?**

Profession of Faith

Following the homily or reflection, the prayer leader invites everyone to stand to profess our faith. Together, sing or recite the Apostles' or Nicene Creed. Refer the children to the words of the prayer that you have displayed.

Prayer of the Faithful

Leader: **Like John the Baptist, who testifies that Jesus is the Lamb of God, we look forward to the salvation of the just, and we present to God our needs and concerns. Please respond, "Lamb of God, hear our prayer."**

For those in positions of Church authority to be models of servant leadership, we pray: *Lamb of God, hear our prayer.*

For leaders of the world to use their power with humility, we pray: *Lamb of God, hear our prayer.*

For those who are hungry and poor, we pray: *Lamb of God, hear our prayer.*

For our community of faith, we pray: *Lamb of God, hear our prayer.*

Invite other intercessions from the children, or add intercessions based on the current needs of the Church, the world, the oppressed or marginalized, and the local community. End each of the children's petitions with **"we pray"** and invite the response **"Lamb of God, hear our prayer."**

For all who have died, that they be made glorious in the sight of God, we pray: *Lamb of God, hear our prayer.*

O Lamb of God, you come to take away the sin of the world.
Help us to seek your will in all that we do.
Who live and reign with God the Father, in the unity of the Holy Spirit God, for ever and ever.

Children: **Amen.**

Quietly return with the children to the main assembly. Be mindful of children having difficulty finding their families.

January 22, 2023
Third Sunday in Ordinary Time
The Kingdom of Heaven Is at Hand

 ## Scripture Background

Connections to Church Teaching and Tradition

⚙ "The apostolate of the Church and of all of its members is primarily designed to manifest Christ's message by words and deeds and to communicate his grace to the world" (AA, 6).

⚙ "Divine providence works also through the actions of creatures. To human beings God grants the ability to cooperate freely with his plans" (CCC, 323).

Isaiah 8:23 — 9:3 This reading includes the well-known and inspiring line "The people who walked in darkness have seen a great light" (9:1). What was this darkness? The lands of Zebulun and Naphtali were the northernmost tribes of Israel and were geographically close to Assyria. They were the first captured when the Assyrians invaded Israel, and the last restored.

The great light that Isaiah proclaims to the Hebrews is a hymn of thanksgiving (9:1–6) for their deliverance from their captors. However, Isaiah also expresses concern for the Hebrews who remain under Assyrian power.

Psalm 27:1, 4, 13–14 (1a) "The Lord is my light and my salvation." The theme of this psalm, which we sing only a part of today, is confidence and trust in the Lord (27:1–3). Light is a biblical image for life and happiness. "The Lord is my light and my salvation; / whom should I fear?" (v. 1). In verses 4–6, the psalmist expresses confidence in the Lord, wishing to dwell in God's house, away from enemies. The Temple shines as God's house and is the perfect refuge. With the psalmist, we pray that we may gaze on the loveliness of God, who is our light and salvation.

1 Corinthians 1:10–13, 17 Paul's preaching of the Kingdom was built on the common union of all believers, a union nourished and centered in the Eucharist. Paul is very sensitive to the lack of this unity, and addresses it here. It was clear that the Corinthians did not all share the same vision but were, in fact, hostile to one another.

To help make his point, Paul asks: "Is Christ divided?" In this question, "Christ" means the community of believers (1 Corinthians 6:15, 12:12). He asks why the community is divided according to who baptized them. Was it Paul, Apollos, or Cephas? He reminds them they are baptized into Christ. Paul also teaches them that his vocation is not to baptize, but to preach. To preach is to release the power of the Gospel (2 Corinthians 4:7–12). Authentic preaching builds up the Body of Christ.

Matthew 4:12–23 or 4:12–17 After John the Baptist was handed over, Jesus came to Capernaum by the sea, on the northwest shores of the Sea of Galilee in the tribal land of Zebulun and Naphtali. This was to indicate that the beginning of Jesus' public ministry in Galilee was in accord with the Scriptures, as we hear in the first reading. Jesus began his public preaching saying, "Repent, for the kingdom of heaven is at hand" (v. 17). He begins his preaching with the words of the Baptist, but now with the difference that the Kingdom is near and has begun to be present. This Kingdom of Heaven indicates that time when God's power and judgment are made fully manifest and acknowledged by all.

The Sea of Galilee was large, and was an important trade route and home to a major fishing industry. In Matthew's account of the beginning of Jesus' public ministry, Jesus introduces the key disciples of his inner circle. These first disciples, Simon and Andrew, were fishermen and brothers. They owned their nets and boats, but left behind their possessions and source of income when Jesus called them to follow him in a new mission to become "fishers of men." James and John, two other brothers, who worked with their father, Zebedee, were also called that day.

Their immediate response highlights Jesus' attractiveness and persuasiveness. They had no understanding of what this invitation would mean or how it would change their lives. Yet, each of them immediately dropped their nets, left their boats, and followed Jesus.

Jesus went all over Galilee teaching the Good News of the kingdom. He taught and preached this Good News to all: the rich and poor, the learned and unschooled, the sinner and pious. Furthermore, he acted as a healer and exorcist for their ills and sufferings. What did the disciples learn and question as they walked the dusty paths of Galilee? What did this "fishing for men" mean in their daily lives? How are we called to "fish for men" today?

Preparation

The image of God as light pervades the Old Testament and the New. Isaiah prophesied the coming of the light as a comfort to a suffering people. The Gospel of Matthew ties this prophecy to Jesus' own suffering at the news of the arrest of John the Baptist. After Jesus withdrew at this news, he entered a new period of his ministry in which he began to preach publicly that the kingdom of God was at hand. He invited disciples to share in this work and we recognize that this invitation extends to us as disciples as well.

Lectionary for Mass #67A

Isaiah 8:23—9:3

Psalm 27:1, 4, 13–14 (1a)

1 Corinthians 1:10–13, 17

Matthew 4:12–23 or 4:12–17

Objectives

• To lift up the image of God as light and as one of comfort for all people.

• To invite the children to respond positively to the invitation of Jesus Christ to "come and follow me."

Preparation and Materials

• Read the Season Background, the lectionary readings, and the Scripture Background.

• Bookmark the appropriate readings (see page xv) in the lectionary, children's lectionary, or Bible. Place the book in a convenient location for the leader.

• Write the words of dismissal on a card for the priest celebrant.

• Prepare the words of the song the children will sing as they gather in the space for the Liturgy of the Word.

• Select volunteers (older children or adults) to proclaim the readings.

• Display the responsorial psalm refrain lyrics.

• Display the Apostles' or Nicene Creed.

• Prepare intercessions for the Prayer of the Faithful adapted for the needs of the Church, world, oppressed or marginalized, and local community.

Prayer Leader Reflection Questions

» **When has God been a light that brought you out of darkness and gloom?**

» **What are you willing to leave behind to follow Jesus?**

Procession

Following the Collect of the Mass, the priest celebrant picks up the lectionary and invites those who would like to participate in the Liturgy of the Word with children to come forward and gather in the center aisle. The people who will lead the children out and facilitate the Liturgy of the Word also come forward at this time. Holding the lectionary so that all can see, the priest celebrant sends the children forth using his own words or the following:

> *Priest*: **Beloved children, we send you now to listen carefully to the Word of God. Think about how you can be more like Jesus. May you open your hearts wide to the truth of the Scriptures. Go in peace.**

The leader processes out holding the lectionary, and the children follow behind. The parish music minister may have selected a song of dismissal for the assembly to sing while the children leave. A good option is "The Word of God: Children's Dismissal" by M. D. Ridge and Timothy R. Smith (WLP/GIA).

Centering

Continue to sing the song of dismissal that the assembly sang as you left the church. Or sing "You Call to Us, Lord Jesus" (Patterson) or the refrain from "Here I Am, Lord" (Schutte), or have instrumental music playing as the children gather in the space for the Liturgy of the Word.

Place the lectionary on the ambo or lectern. Light the candle placed by the ambo or lectern, and then lead the following prayer:

> **Loving God,**
> **help us to remember and understand your message today.**
> **Give us the strength and courage to love others as Jesus showed us.**
> **Through Christ our Lord.**

> *Children:* **Amen.**

First Reading

Isaiah 8:23—9:3

Responsorial Psalm

Psalm 27:1, 4, 13–14 (1a) *Sing the same musical setting that is used in your parish's celebration of the liturgy.*

Second Reading

1 Corinthians 1:10–13, 17

Gospel Acclamation

Sing the Gospel Acclamation used in your parish's celebration of the liturgy.

Gospel Reading

Matthew 4:12–23 or 4:12–17

Homily/Reflection

[This homily/reflection focuses on the longer Gospel reading, Matthew 4:12–23.]

» What is it like to be in darkness?

Maybe you woke up in your bedroom in the middle of the night when the light was off. It can be scary. Did you try to get around to find the door? You might have stubbed your toe on your way because you couldn't see where you were walking.

» What does it mean to be in gloom?

We sometimes describe weather as gloomy when it is cold and wet and the clouds cover the sun. Sometimes fog makes it hard to see where we are going. In the first reading today, the prophet Isaiah described what it was like for a whole country to be in darkness and gloom. In the Gospel, we hear that Jesus himself experienced darkness and gloom when he learned that John the Baptist had been taken away.

We know what it is like to come into the light as well, don't we? We can see where we are going. We don't have to be afraid. The psalm today tells us where true light comes from, not only the light we see with our eyes, but also the light we feel in our hearts and souls, the light we know with our minds. It is from the Lord. Jesus was human just as we are human, and he experienced emotions like sadness, hurt, and fear. The Gospel tells us that amid Jesus' darkness and gloom when he learned John had been taken, he withdrew. He went away to a place called Capernaum. Matthew also reminds us of Isaiah's words, that the Lord would bring light. Jesus knew these words. He knew that the kingdom of God was at hand. It was then that Jesus began in a new way his great work of preaching about the kingdom of God. He told people to repent, to turn from their old ways to do as God would have them do. He wanted people to look for the light who is God.

Jesus began also to invite others to share in this work. Capernaum was a place on the Sea of Galilee that is full of fish. There were many fishermen in Capernaum. He called Simon Peter and Andrew while they were casting their nets into the sea to catch fish. He called James and John while they were still on their boats. He invited them to a new way of life, not catching fish but catching people, bringing them toward the kingdom of God, helping people to recognize the light who is God. All of these men, Simon Peter, Andrew, James, and John stopped what they were doing, left it behind, and followed Jesus.

Jesus invites us to share in the work also. He wants us to be a part of a new way of life. He wants us to turn from old our ways to do as God would have us do. Jesus is calling our names and saying, "Follow me."

>> **Imagine if Jesus came here now and invited you to follow him as he did those first disciples. How would you respond?**

Remember that this liturgical season, Ordinary Time, is a time when we grow as good disciples. Jesus calls each of us to follow him. We might not all do the same things to be a follower of Jesus. Some might help a neighbor, while others might help at a food pantry. Some might donate some money to charity, others might give a homeless person a bottle of water. Some might pray more.

>> **What might be one way you can follow Jesus today?**

Profession of Faith

Following the homily or reflection, the prayer leader invites everyone to stand to profess our faith. Together, sing or recite the Apostles' or Nicene Creed. Refer the children to the words of the prayer that you have displayed.

Prayer of the Faithful

Leader: **As a people who walk in Christ's light, we place our prayers before the God of all creation. Please respond, "Lord, hear our prayer."**

That all who minister in the Church may rely upon the help of the Lord to strengthen them in times of need, let us pray: *Lord, hear our prayer.*

That world leaders guide their people to true freedom, let us pray: *Lord, hear our prayer.*

That all those who labor may be treated justly and receive fair compensation for their work, let us pray: *Lord, hear our prayer.*

That we each may listen closely for God's invitation to follow him and say yes, let us pray: *Lord, hear our prayer.*

Invite other intercessions from the children, or add intercessions based on the current needs of the Church, the world, the oppressed or marginalized, and the local community. Conclude each of the children's petitions with **"let us pray"** and invite the response **"Lord, hear our prayer."**

That all who have died may live in the fullness of God's light forever, let us pray: *Lord, hear our prayer.*

**Mighty God,
you are our light and our salvation.
Help us as we grow to be good disciples.
We humbly offer our petitions.
Through Christ our Lord.**

Children: **Amen.**

Quietly return with the children to the main assembly. Be mindful of children having difficulty finding their families.

January 29, 2023
Fourth Sunday in Ordinary Time
Blessed Be

 ## Scripture Background

Connections to Church Teaching and Tradition

● The closest we can get to knowing God's wisdom is in following Jesus' obedient example, as taught in the Beatitudes (NDC, 25, 45; CCC, 1716–1729).

● God created everything as an expression of divine wisdom (CCC, 295, 302–305, 315).

Zephaniah 2:3, 3:12–13 The prophet Zephaniah addressed Judah during the seventh century BC. Politically, the Mediterranean world shifted from a power base in Assyria to one in Mesopotamia. The northern kingdom of Israel had been destroyed in 721 BC; a similar fate faced the tiny nation of Judah. Judah, as a vassal of the Assyrians, participated in the worship of Assyria's gods.

Zephaniah believed that Judah, too, would suffer from the enemy's hand, but like Isaiah, he believed that God's hand would save Judah. The "day of the LORD's anger" refers perhaps to the threat of conquest on the political horizon. Faithfulness to God, expressed as obedience, justice, and humility (v. 3), is the means to salvation.

The reading for this week skips down to 3:12–13. These verses describe the aftermath of the day of the Lord. A few people will survive and these few will live according to the ways of God. Their life will be as peaceful as sheep that graze.

Zephaniah's words are both a consolation and a warning. Those who trust in God will survive, but for those who live unfaithfully, the future cannot be guaranteed.

Psalm 146:6–7, 8–9, 9–10 (Matthew 5:3) The Gospel for today provides the antiphon for the psalm response. Like the psalm, it celebrates God's care for the needy. Psalm 146 is a hymn of praise of God, the source of justice. Faithful and true, God protects all those who have no hope of protection. The psalm names what would be considered the least important of society: widows, orphans, strangers, the imprisoned. Israel knows that God gave food to the hungry in the desert, set the captive slaves free, and continues to care for the needy. The mercy and compassion of God is their motive for praise.

1 Corinthians 1:26–31 Paul addresses the wisdom and foolishness of faith by reminding the Corinthians of their status. If the Corinthians think that their new faith makes them superior to others, Paul is quick to deflate their egos. He reminds them that before becoming believers they were among the lowly of their society. In fact, their lowliness was the very thing that enabled them to receive the gift of faith in Christ.

Through the lowly, God's reign is established. God, not the wise, not the powerful, not the wellborn, is the greatest. God gives the Corinthians life through faith in Christ Jesus. He is the true source of wisdom and the way to a right relationship with God. If the Corinthians find it necessary to boast of anything, Paul asks them to boast about God, not about their own wisdom or status. God is the source of all life.

Matthew 5:1–12a Like a rabbi instructing his students, Jesus teaches the disciples and the crowds what the reign of God is like. The mountain setting (unlike the plain in Luke's Gospel) evokes another important mountain, Sinai, where the Law was given to Israel.

Who are the truly happy, the truly blessed? In the reign of God, they are those who have moved beyond themselves to recognize their need for God. Those who care enough to grieve will find themselves healed of their grief. The meek, who place others ahead of themselves, will dwell in God's land. Those whose passion for justice cannot be quenched will be satisfied. People who forgive readily and easily will find this action extended to them in God's reign. Those who can focus on God to the exclusion of all else will be rewarded with a vision of God. People who care for the community, who try to bring reconciliation and peace, will be honored by God. Those willing to die for what they believe are already within the reign of God. Finally, those who forego honor and the acclaim of others in order to proclaim Christ will find themselves honored and acclaimed.

True happiness is found easily but not without great cost. Disciples must be willing to put their lives on the line for others. They must move beyond a "Me first!" mentality to an altruistic spirit empowered by compassion, courage, and faith.

 # Preparation

Throughout salvation history, God has exhibited a preference for smallness: the humble of the earth, the weak and lowly of Corinth, the poor in spirit among Jesus' audience. In the smallness of those God chose, he allows a reversal to take place, in which the smallest can do the greatest work. Those with the least are most blessed. As disciples of Jesus Christ, we can embrace our own smallness, having confidence that our work is all the more effective because God's power is made plain. We stand in solidarity with others in their own smallness, knowing God's deep care and participating in making it known to others.

Lectionary for Mass #70A

Zephaniah 2:3, 3:12–13

Psalm 146:6–7, 8–9, 9–10 (Matthew 5:3)

1 Corinthians 1:26–31

Matthew 5:1–12a

Objectives

- To name and identify humility as describing those for whom God has a particular love and care.

- To invite the children to participate in God's care for those who are small, lowly, or lacking.

Preparation and Materials

- Read the Season Background, the lectionary readings, and the Scripture Background.

- Bookmark the appropriate readings (see page xv) in the lectionary, children's lectionary, or Bible. Place the book in a convenient location for the leader.

- Write the words of dismissal on a card for the priest celebrant.

- Prepare the words of the song the children will sing as they gather in the space for the Liturgy of the Word.

- Select volunteers (older children or adults) to proclaim the readings.

- Display the responsorial psalm refrain lyrics.

- Display the Apostles' or Nicene Creed.

- Prepare intercessions for the Prayer of the Faithful adapted for the needs of the Church, world, oppressed or marginalized, and local community.

Prayer Leader Reflection Questions

≫ **Which Beatitude stands out to you and why?**

≫ **How do you take care of those who are suffering or lacking?**

Procession

Following the Collect of the Mass, the priest celebrant picks up the lectionary and invites those who would like to participate in the Liturgy of the Word with children to come forward and gather in the center aisle. The people who will lead the children out and facilitate the Liturgy of the Word also come forward at this time. Holding the lectionary so that all can see, the priest celebrant sends the children forth using his own words or the following:

> *Priest*: **Dear children, we send you with your leader(s) to listen carefully to God's Word. Pay attention to what God is saying to you today. May the Holy Spirit help you understand and live this good news. Go now in peace.**

The leader processes out holding the lectionary, and the children follow behind. The parish music minister may have selected a song of dismissal for the assembly to sing while the children leave. A good option is "The Word of God: Children's Dismissal" by M. D. Ridge and Timothy R. Smith (WLP/GIA).

Centering

Continue to sing the song of dismissal that the assembly sang as you left the church. Or sing "We Are the Light of the World" (Greif) or have instrumental music playing as the children gather in the space for the Liturgy of the Word.

Place the lectionary on the ambo or lectern. Light the candle placed by the ambo or lectern, and then lead the following prayer:

> **Lord God,**
> **help us to honor you and truly love everyone.**
> **Allow our hearts to be open to your**
> **Word so that we may serve you completely.**
> **Through Christ our Lord.**

> *Children:* **Amen.**

First Reading

Zephaniah 2:3, 3:12–13

Responsorial Psalm

Psalm 146:6–7, 8–9, 9–10 (Matthew 5:3) *Sing the same musical setting that is used in your parish's celebration of the liturgy.*

Second Reading

1 Corinthians 1:26–31

Gospel Acclamation

Sing the Gospel Acclamation used in your parish's celebration of the liturgy.

Gospel Reading

Matthew 5:1–12a

Homily/Reflection

During these first few weeks of Ordinary Time, we listen and think about the beginning of Jesus' ministry. Last week we heard some of Jesus' very first public instructions when he told his listeners to repent because the kingdom of God is at hand and to "come and follow" him. Those who say yes to these instructions are called "disciples." You don't have to have lived in the time when Jesus was walking the earth to be a disciple. We also can say yes to Jesus today. We can be disciples.

» Once we have said yes, what do we do next?

In today's readings, we hear about what it means to be humble. To be humble is to be small. We know that God is great, far greater than us, and so we are humble before God. What about before each other? The prophet Zephaniah spoke about the "humble of the land" (Zephaniah 2:3). This does not only mean those who are small before God, but also small in an earthly way. Perhaps this might mean those who are poor and do not have enough to eat or to live. It could mean those who don't have a family to protect them, people like widows and orphans. It might be those who are weak or sick or who can't physically do what others can. Being humble means that we depend on God, for we can't do everything alone.

Jesus spoke of the humble as well. He named the "poor in spirit," "those who mourn," "the meek," and "those who hunger and thirst for righteousness." Some of these words might not be familiar to us. We probably already know that people who are "poor" do not have enough. We might know that people who "mourn" are those who are deeply sad because someone they love has died. Those who are "meek" don't have power. I'm sure we've all hungered and thirsted, if only for a short time. What does it mean to hunger and thirst for righteousness? Perhaps this means to have a need for goodness that is so strong that one suffers for it. Each of these experiences are from those who are missing something so gravely important, but Jesus called them "blessed."

>> **What does it mean to be blessed?**

Blessed can mean both happy and set apart for God. Why would people be happy if they are missing something important? Jesus preached that the kingdom of God is at hand. In the fullness of the kingdom of God, there will be no suffering and everyone will have what they need. How much joy would someone who lacks what they need have, knowing this is coming?

Jesus did not only name those who suffer. He also said those who help suffering people are also blessed. He named people who show mercy, who are clean of heart, who are peacemakers, and who are persecuted for righteousness' sake. Showing mercy can mean having compassion or forgiving. To have a clean heart is to love the things that we should. We probably know about making peace. Being persecuted means that someone is making us suffer and Jesus said this suffering is on behalf of goodness. Jesus said all of these people are blessed as well.

>> **What does this tell us about being blessed?**

What we have comes from God, rather than from ourselves. Maybe it could also mean that we should be close to those who do not have enough. One of the ways God takes care of people in need is through disciples, through people who say yes to God's call to serve. Paul also told the Corinthians that even though they were not powerful or wise or rich, these were the people that God chooses to act through so that his greatness is more easily seen. We are small, aren't we? We can rejoice that God's invitation to serve is for us too and that our own smallness might make us able to serve God even better than if we were big!

Profession of Faith

Following the homily or reflection, the prayer leader invites everyone to stand to profess our faith. Together, sing or recite the Apostles' or Nicene Creed. Refer the children to the words of the prayer that you have displayed.

Prayer of the Faithful

Leader: **God has called us to be his faithful followers. With confidence we pray for our needs and those of the world. Please respond, "Lord, hear us."**

May the Church always show God's special love for the smallest among us, we pray: *Lord, hear us.*

May world leaders serve the needs of all people with wisdom and compassion, we pray: *Lord, hear us*

May the poor and the downtrodden be blessed in God's kingdom of justice and righteousness, we pray: *Lord, hear us.*

May our nation's Catholic schools be strengthened in their spiritual and educational mission, we pray: *Lord, hear us.*

Invite other intercessions from the children, or add intercessions based on the current needs of the Church, the world, the oppressed or marginalized, and the local community. Conclude each of the children's petitions with **"we pray"** and invite the response **"Lord, hear us."**

May those who have died rejoice in the kingdom of God, we pray: *Lord, hear us.*

Father,
hear our prayers and draw us closer to you.
May we grow in faith and serve you more generously each day.
We ask this through Christ our Lord.

Children: **Amen.**

Quietly return with the children to the main assembly. Be mindful of children having difficulty finding their families.

February 5, 2023
Fifth Sunday in Ordinary Time
Taste and See

 ## Scripture Background

Isaiah 58:7–10 Isaiah, writing to the returned exiles from Babylon, answers the question, What will restore God's favor to us? The people are disillusioned and unhappy in their devastated environment. In the verses just prior, the people complain that they have tried fasting as they did in the days of old and still they have no positive response from God (58:3).

Isaiah condemns their unjust business practices and querulous behavior (vv. 3–4). Perhaps in the depressing days following the return, the sight of the ruined land and cities robbed the returnees of their faith. They imagined they could control God's responses to them through religious observances. Instead, Isaiah gives them the challenge: care for your neighbors, attend to their needs, and you will find God quick to respond to you. The people have ignored the poor and homeless and have turned against each other, speaking falsely about their neighbors. Isaiah does not look sympathetically on their plight. He forces the people to face their behavior as the source of their alienation from God. Caring for their neighbors both physically and socially is the way to God.

Psalm 112:4–5, 6–7, 8–9 (4a) The praise of the just person is the psalm response. The just are rooted in God and have nothing to fear from either life's circumstances or from evil itself. God is a steadfast companion to the person who treats the poor and weak with compassion. Like light, the just person is a source of hope and consolation to those who seek God (v. 4). Immortality of a sort is given to the just; the memory of kindness and generosity will live on.

1 Corinthians 2:1–5 In an antithesis to the "wisdom" the Corinthians want to claim, Paul claims weakness. Paul does not want the Corinthians to think that they have acquired a new kind of wisdom in the same way that other philosophical systems of the day promoted wisdom.

Unlike other preachers and philosophers of the first century, Paul tells the community that he came as a weak human being with a message about weakness—a crucified Christ. That they were convinced by his message had nothing to do with the power of his person, but rather was a result of the power of the Spirit.

Matthew 5:13–16 The faith of the Corinthians is not based on human wisdom, but on a far greater wisdom, the wisdom of God (v. 5). The danger of treating Christianity as another philosophical fad must have been great for the Corinthians.

Like the prophets who were themselves persecuted (5:12), the disciples have a responsibility to fulfill. Jesus uses two images, salt and light, to explain how his followers are to relate to the world.

Salt, an important preservative and seasoning, was a valuable commodity in the first century. It also had other meanings. In Numbers 18:19 salt was used in a covenant ceremony. Salt was also offered with sacrifices (Leviticus 2:13). The disciples, therefore, are important. They are what seasons and preserves life, they are signs of covenant and friendship between peoples, and they are signs of God's relationship with humanity.

The second part of verse 13 contains a warning: enthusiasm and commitment are required, and if that is lacking, they are as useless as salt that has lost its flavor. How salt loses its flavor has a variety of interpretations: salt used in Jewish rituals can become unclean; the impure salt from the Dead Sea can lose its taste; the salt used to fire the baking ovens can lose its ability to season food. The message is that the salt changes from useful to useless. The disciples, unless they preach the reign of God, are not really disciples. Like the people Isaiah addressed in the first reading, those who do not bring God's message of mercy and love to others are worthless.

Connections to Church Teaching and Tradition

⚜ "It is necessary, then, . . . to keep a watchful eye on this our world . . . whose . . . affairs pose problems and grave difficulties. . . . This is the field in which the faithful are called to fulfill their mission . . . to be the 'salt of the earth' and the 'light of the world' (cf. Matthew 5:13–14)" (CL, 3).

⚜ "The church, the salt of the earth and the light of the world (see Matthew 5:13–14), is even more urgently called upon to save and renew every creature, so that all things might be restored in Christ, and so that in him men and women might form one family and one people of God" (AG, 1).

⚜ "The disciples of Christ . . . hope to offer . . . an authentic Christian witness. . . . They seek to enhance the dignity of women and men . . . so people are helped to attain salvation by love of God and love of humanity; the mystery of Christ begins to shine out" (AG, 12).

Light, another necessity of life, is the second image Jesus uses to explain to his followers their role in the world. Light is often associated with the saving acts of God (Isaiah 2:5, Psalm 44:4) and with the suffering servant of God (Isaiah 42:6, 49:6). God's intent is to bring salvation to all peoples through those who are faithful.

The good works done by Jesus' followers are not to be hidden away but are to shine forth. God's salvation is made known through the actions of the disciples. The praise and glory their works will receive is part of the praise and glory of God. In other words, to act justly, to care for the weak and needy, is another form of praise. To "be salt" or to "be light" is to heal, to teach, to forgive, and to love.

Preparation

In today's Gospel reading from Matthew, Jesus spoke to his disciples about two images: salt and light. Jesus offered these images as metaphors for the identity of the Christian community. Salt preserves and flavors. Light provides comfort and the ability to find one's way safely. When salt or light are inside of something, they transform it. The Christian community is a part of the larger world and if the community is truly itself, it will change the larger world by the loving words and actions of its members.

Lectionary for Mass #73A

Isaiah 58:7–10

Psalm 112:4–5, 6–7, 8–9 (4a)

1 Corinthians 2:1–5

Matthew 5:13–16

Objectives

- To explore Jesus' metaphors of salt and light as the community of disciples.

- To invite the children to make loving choices to effect positive change in the larger world around them.

Preparation and Materials

- Read the Season Background, the lectionary readings, and the Scripture Background.

- Bookmark the appropriate readings (see page xv) in the lectionary, children's lectionary, or Bible. Place the book in a convenient location for the leader.

- Write the words of dismissal on a card for the priest celebrant.

- Prepare the words of the song the children will sing as they gather in the space for the Liturgy of the Word.

- Select volunteers (older children or adults) to proclaim the readings.

- Display the responsorial psalm refrain lyrics.

- Display the Apostles' or Nicene Creed.

- Prepare intercessions for the Prayer of the Faithful adapted for the needs of the Church, world, oppressed or marginalized, and local community.

- Use a liturgical calendar to show the children during the homily/reflection.

Prayer Leader Reflection Questions

>> **How are you being salt and light in your community?**

>> **Consider what it means to be Christ's disciple as you prepare the homily or reflection. Keep in mind that you are letting your light shine for children who are growing disciples.**

Procession

Following the Collect of the Mass, the priest celebrant picks up the lectionary and invites those who would like to participate in the Liturgy of the Word with children to come forward and gather in the center aisle. The people who will lead the children out and facilitate the Liturgy of the Word also come forward at this time. Holding the lectionary so that all can see, the priest celebrant sends the children forth using his own words or the following:

> *Priest*: **Dear children, God has given us gifts of grace so that we may do good in the world, especially for those who are most in need of help. This is what Jesus is telling us in today's Gospel. Go and learn from him, and when you return, we will praise God together.**

The leader processes out holding the lectionary, and the children follow behind. The parish music minister may have selected a song of dismissal for the assembly to sing while the children leave. A good option is "The Word of God: Children's Dismissal" by M. D. Ridge and Timothy R. Smith (WLP/GIA).

Centering

Continue to sing the song of dismissal that the assembly sang as you left the church. Or sing verse 3 and refrain of "City of God" (Schutte) or "Lead Me, Lord" (Becker) or have instrumental music playing as the children gather in the space for the Liturgy of the Word.

Place the lectionary on the ambo or lectern. Light the candle placed by the ambo or lectern, and then lead the following prayer:

> **O Lord,**
> **help us to remember and understand the good news.**
> **Increase our faith and help us to be your light in the world.**
> **Through Christ our Lord.**

Children: **Amen.**

First Reading

Isaiah 58:7–10

Responsorial Psalm

Psalm 112:4–5, 6–7, 8–9 (4a) *Sing the same musical setting that is used in your parish's celebration of the liturgy.*

Second Reading

1 Corinthians 2:1–5

Gospel Acclamation

Sing the Gospel Acclamation used in your parish's celebration of the liturgy.

Gospel Reading

Matthew 5:13–16

Homily/Reflection

We continue in Ordinary Time, a time of counting forward and growing as Jesus' disciples. There are two periods of Ordinary Time, one between Christmas and Easter and another between Easter and Christmas.

>> **Which period of Ordinary Time are we in now?** *(Display a liturgical calendar if you have one.)*

During this shorter and first part of Ordinary Time, we listen and think about Jesus' ministry, the first people who said yes to his call to be disciples, and how Jesus teaches us to live as his disciples, too. In today's Gospel, we heard Jesus compare his disciples to two things that are not normally said about people: salt and light.

During the time that Jesus walked and talked on this earth like you and I do, salt was important. Refrigerators had not yet been invented, so people used salt to preserve food like meat. Salt was also used to flavor food. Have you ever made popcorn from scratch? Maybe a grown-up helped you to cook the kernels so they popped in a pot and then you tasted a popped kernel or two. Do you remember what it tasted like? It was probably pretty dry and bland. But as soon as you add salt to popcorn, it tastes so much better and helps bring out the flavor that was there all along in the corn.

>> **What could Jesus have meant when he said, "You are salt"?**

Another comparison that Jesus made is light. We know that Jesus is the light of the world, and we hear a lot about God's light all throughout the Church year. Today, we hear Jesus speak about light in a different way, telling his disciples to *be* light. Jesus described how a lamp would be used in a home. It would be placed up high so that it could light as much of a room as possible. Today we can think about the electric lights that we often in have in our ceilings and on our tables. Would you turn on a light in your house and then cover the light with a bucket? No!

» What could Jesus have meant when he said, "You are the light of the world"?

When we say yes to being Jesus' disciples, we say yes to being salt and light. Jesus talked about salt and light as being inside of something else, changing it and making it better. We are in the world. We live in a community with other people. We might be a part of a neighborhood, a school, a music group, a sports team. We are meant to bring something to what we're part of and make it better. The words of the prophet Isaiah in the first reading today say to take care of those who do not have enough: people who are homeless, hungry, who don't have enough clothes. Isaiah also said to avoid saying unkind words and saying things that aren't true. If we do this, "then your light shall break forth like the dawn" (Isaiah 58:8).

Salt and the light of a lamp work best when they are inside of something, working to bring out goodness. A light that is hidden under a bucket won't shine brightly. If you don't add salt to food, the flavor of the dish won't change. Jesus wanted his disciples to really be in the world. When we shine our light and flavor our world for Jesus Christ, we are not only helping others, we also are changing the world.

**» Light gives people comfort and joy and helps them to see where they are going.
How can we give people comfort and joy and help them to see where they are going?**

» What are some other ways we can do positive things in the world?

Profession of Faith

Following the homily or reflection, the prayer leader invites everyone to stand to profess our faith. Together, sing or recite the Apostles' or Nicene Creed. Refer the children to the words of the prayer that you have displayed.

Prayer of the Faithful

Leader: **As the "salt of the earth" and the "light of the world," we pray to bring positive change for ourselves and for others. Please respond, "God of light and love, hear us."**

For our priests and all who serve the Church, that they seek to share the light of Christ, we pray: *God of light and love, hear us.*

For our world, that everyone may have what they need, we pray: *God of light and love, hear us.*

For those who live in fear, especially the sick and dying, that they may trust in God's power, we pray: *God of light and love, hear us.*

For those who are coming to know Jesus Christ for the first time, especially those who are looking forward to baptism at Easter, that their faith continue to grow, we pray: *God of light and love, hear us.*

Invite other intercessions from the children, or add intercessions based on the current needs of the Church, the world, the oppressed or marginalized, and the local community. End each of the children's petitions with **"we pray"** and invite the response **"God of light and love, hear us."**

For those who have died, that they may join in glorifying our heavenly Father forever with the angels and saints, we pray: *God of light and love, hear us.*

**Father of us all,
you are this world's radiant light and our hope is in your grace.
Accept the prayers of your children through Christ our Lord.**

Children: **Amen.**

Quietly return with the children to the main assembly. Be mindful of children having difficulty finding their families.

February 12, 2023
Sixth Sunday in Ordinary Time
Fulfillment of the Law

 ## Scripture Background

Connections to Church Teaching and Tradition

✦ "The Law of the Gospel fulfills the commandments of the Law. . . . Far from abolishing or devaluing the moral prescriptions of the Old Law . . . it reveals their entire divine and human truth" (CCC, 1968).

✦ "The gift of the commandments and of the Law is part of the covenant God sealed with his own. . . . Man's moral life has all its meaning in and through the covenant" (CCC, 2060–2061).

✦ "The Church proclaims human rights. . . . There is a temptation to feel that our personal rights are fully maintained only when we are free from every restriction of divine law. But this is the way leading to the extinction of human dignity, not its preservation" (GS, 41).

✦ "The Church feels the duty to defend the human dignity which belongs to every person, and 'denounces discrimination, sexual abuse and male domination as actions contrary to God's plan'¹" (EIA, 45).

Sirach 15:15–20   The selection we proclaim from Sirach today is part of a larger discussion of human responsibility addressed to people who held God to blame for the conduct of the wicked. In a religious milieu in which God was seen as the ultimate author of every action, some people held God responsible for evil and suffering, thereby undercutting faith in God's goodness. Sirach responds to that with a resounding affirmation of personal responsibility, emphasizing that those who choose to do so can keep the commandments. He insists that each of us account for our own choices, reminding us that God's commandments offer the path of true life.

Psalm 119:1–2, 4–5, 17–18, 33–34 (1b)   With 176 verses, Psalm 119 is by far the longest prayer in the psalter. Focusing on God's law, it uses eight synonyms for the law which, when added together, equal 174 references to God's Law. In spite of its focus on the Law, the psalm is not legalistic. Rather, it is a loving meditation on the blessings offered to those who set their hearts on God's way, seeking, loving, and following the Law. The author and any who spend time praying this psalm immerse themselves in the wonders of God's Law.

1 Corinthians 2:6–10   It is hard to know whether Paul is being tongue-in-cheek when he addresses himself to the "mature" Corinthians. Other parts of this letter indicate that he had little esteem for their current state of spiritual development (3:1, 5:1–2, 6:1–6). Here, however, the word he uses singles out people who have reached their goal, whose lives are fulfilling their deepest meaning. That they are Christians would indicate they are living the truth of the mystery God has revealed. As he continues talking to the Corinthians about true wisdom, Paul puts together citations from Isaiah 64:3 and Jeremiah 3:16, fashioning a beautiful image of God's indescribable revelation. This is a mystery, something that God has been working out since the beginning of the world (see Ephesians 1:3–14).

According to Paul, God's mystery, like his wisdom, is unlike anything of this world, which is in the process of passing away. Although this passage does not mention the Law, as it speaks of the mystery of God it draws our attention to the wonders of God's plan for humanity.

Matthew 5:17–37 or 5:20–22a, 27–28, 33–34a, 37   The part of the Gospel that we call the Sermon on the Mount is a collection of Jesus' teachings that Matthew wove together in one carefully constructed discourse. In this section, Jesus expresses profound respect for his Jewish tradition, which he both interprets and fulfills.

Although the sayings introduced with "You have heard" and "But I say" are often considered antitheses, implying that Jesus is abrogating the Jewish law, that is not necessarily the case. In some instances, he takes a teaching and goes to its root meaning. He demonstrates that the sin of murder has its roots in anger and disrespect of another. Adultery, which was understood at that time as an offense against the husband whose property had been abused by another, has its roots in looking at someone as an object of self-gratification rather than as a person and image of God. Thus, it is better to lose an eye or hand than disdain another person.

That teaching leads directly to the prohibition of divorce. Under traditional law, only the man could initiate a divorce, and, according to some interpretations, he was free to do so for the slightest of provocations. Jesus, however, promotes the dignity of women, saying they cannot simply be handed off as property.

---

1 *Propositio* 11.

Regarding interpersonal relationships and religion, Jesus calls his disciples to seek reconciliation with anyone who is angry with them. Otherwise, their sacrifice is hollow. So, too, since their word should be their bond, there is no reason to swear an oath. People can control their own behavior, but they are powerless over heaven, Jerusalem, or even something as trivial as their natural hair color.

Taken together, this Sunday's readings sound a call to deep integrity. Those who have been called by God have the freedom to choose obedience to God and the wonders of his Kingdom. To choose anything less than the unfolding of God's mystery is to tie your fate to that which is already passing away.

Preparation

The commandments are a gift that aids in our ability to remain in loving relationship with God and God's people. Our moral choices are a response to the gifts God has given us and they have consequences for our ability to live in intimacy with God now and in the fullness of time. Jesus invited his disciples to live their lives in such a way that they would make clear that the goodness God both desires and offers is complete.

Lectionary for Mass #76A

Sirach 15:15–20

Psalm 119:1–2, 4–5, 17–18, 33–34 (1b)

1 Corinthians 2:6–10

Matthew 5:17–37 or 5:20–22a, 27–28, 33–34a, 37

Objectives

- To explain moral decision-making as rooted in relationship with God and others.

- To invite the children to move beyond morality of prohibition to a morality of abundant loving response.

Note that if your group includes children younger than six, they are yet not concerned, nor will they be able to be concerned, with moral considerations, as they are still growing in spirituality. You may wish to focus on the idea of laws and rules as a gift from God.

Preparation and Materials

- Read the Season Background, the lectionary readings, and the Scripture Background.

- Bookmark the appropriate readings (see page xv) in the lectionary, children's lectionary, or Bible. Place the book in a convenient location for the leader.

- Write the words of dismissal on a card for the priest celebrant.

- Prepare the words of the song the children will sing as they gather in the space for the Liturgy of the Word.

- Select volunteers (older children or adults) to proclaim the readings.

- Display the responsorial psalm refrain lyrics.

- Display the Apostles' or Nicene Creed.

- Prepare intercessions for the Prayer of the Faithful adapted for the needs of the Church, world, oppressed or marginalized, and local community.

Prayer Leader Reflection Questions

» **As a Christian, when are you called to go beyond the minimum adherence to the Ten Commandments?**

» **How do you seek out God's wisdom and let it guide your life?**

Procession

Following the Collect of the Mass, the priest celebrant picks up the lectionary and invites those who would like to participate in the Liturgy of the Word with children to come forward and gather in the center aisle. The people who will lead the children out and facilitate the Liturgy of the Word also come forward at this time. Holding the lectionary so that all can see, the priest celebrant sends the children forth using his own words or the following:

Priest: **Children, like a compass that always points to the north, there is something inside us that wants to do good, just as we want to eat when we are hungry or drink when we are thirsty. That is the Holy Spirit teaching us and calling to us. That same Spirit calls in today's readings. Go now and listen to him.**

The leader processes out holding the lectionary, and the children follow behind. The parish music minister may have selected a song of dismissal for the assembly to sing while the children leave. A good option is "The Word of God: Children's Dismissal" by M. D. Ridge and Timothy R. Smith (WLP/GIA).

Centering

Continue to sing the song of dismissal that the assembly sang as you left the church. Or sing the refrains from "Your Words Are Spirit and Life" (Farrell) or "They'll Know We Are Christians" (Scholtes) or have instrumental music playing as the children gather in the space for the Liturgy of the Word.

Place the lectionary on the ambo or lectern. Light the candle placed by the ambo or lectern, and then lead the following prayer:

**Lord of glory,
you have given us commandments and we want to obey you.
Allow our hearts to be open to your Word
so that we may serve you completely.
Through Christ our Lord.**

Children: **Amen.**

First Reading

Sirach 15:15–20

Responsorial Psalm

Psalm 119:1–2, 4–5, 17–18, 33–34 (1b) *Sing the same musical setting that is used in your parish's celebration of the liturgy.*

Second Reading

1 Corinthians 2:6–10

Gospel Acclamation

Sing the Gospel Acclamation used in your parish's celebration of the liturgy.

Gospel Reading

Matthew 5:17–37 or 5:20–22a, 27–28, 33–34a, 37

Homily/Reflection

[This reflection is intended to accompany the shorter Gospel reading. Note that you may need to adjust this script to focus more on God's gift if your group includes very young children (younger than six).]

>> **Have you ever drawn a picture and then given it to someone you love to show how much you care about that person?**

We sometimes give gifts to others to show the importance of the relationship between us. When the gift is something that we have made, we have put our own imprint on our work. Offering our work as gift is a way to give something of ourselves to others. God has given us so many gifts. All of creation is a gift to us. The people in our lives, who have been made by God and have God's imprint in a most particular way, have been given to us by God who made them.

>> **What other gifts has God given us?**

>> **Imagine that you made me a picture and gave it to me as a gift. How would you want me to treat it?**

>> **How would you feel if I tore it up?**

>> **How do we treat the gifts God has given us?**

God reaches out to us and invites us to live in loving relationship. We can say yes and enjoy that relationship, and we can also do more. Choosing a relationship with God means choosing God's will. This happens through our loving choices. God made all of creation, including our fellow human beings who, like us, are made in God's image and likeness. How we treat God's creation is an expression of how we treat God the Creator.

God has given us instructions for how to receive these gifts in a loving way. Our choices to do or not do things can make our relationship with God real but they can also harm that relationship. God has helped us to know how make loving choices by giving us commandments. Jesus told us that the greatest commandment has two parts: love God and love your neighbor as yourself. Jesus also reminded his disciples about other commandments that the people of Israel knew well: do not kill, do not commit adultery, do not take a false oath (or lie or make a promise you will not keep). Doing these things makes a relationship so damaged that it can no longer be repaired.

If I have killed another person, I cannot un-kill him. There is no way I can return my relationship with that person back to being good. An oath is a promise to do something in the future. A pinky-promise is a kind of oath. In the United States, when someone is elected to government, that person often takes an oath of office, promising to follow the law and to help the community. If I tell someone that something is as true and real as it can possibly be, and then it turns out to be a lie, can that person ever trust me again? It would be very hard!

When Jesus reminded his disciples of these commandments, though, he also invited them to see that we can go beyond protecting relationships from being broken beyond repair. We can protect our relationships with others and with God so that they aren't harmed. Jesus told us that we could do more than just not kill. We could keep our anger in control so that we wouldn't even hurt another person. Jesus told us that we could do more than just not break an oath. We could always speak the truth and say what we mean. We don't just keep the gifts God has given us from being destroyed. We act in ways that show we treasure all the gifts God has given us because we treasure God, and we know God treasures us.

Profession of Faith

Following the homily or reflection, the prayer leader invites everyone to stand to profess our faith. Together, sing or recite the Apostles' or Nicene Creed. Refer the children to the words of the prayer that you have displayed.

Prayer of the Faithful

Leader: **The wisdom of God's law guides our steps and so we bring our prayers to the Lord. Please respond, "Lord, hear us."**

That Church leaders may be guided by God's wisdom, we pray:
Lord, hear us.

That earthly laws of nations and governments may be in harmony with God's laws, we pray: *Lord, hear us.*

That those who are sick and suffering may be free of what binds them, we pray: *Lord, hear us.*

That those who have broken promises and have made false oaths may make amends for their failures, we pray: *Lord, hear us.*

Invite other intercessions from the children, or add intercessions based on the current needs of the Church, the world, the oppressed or marginalized, and the local community. Conclude each of the children's petitions with **"we pray"** and invite the response **"Lord, hear us."**

That all who have died may live forever in the fullness of the Kingdom of heaven, we pray: *Lord, hear us.*

Heavenly Father,
help us to live according to your commandments.
Accept the prayers of your children through Christ our Lord.

Children: **Amen.**

Quietly return with the children to the main assembly. Be mindful of children having difficulty finding their families.

February 19, 2023
Seventh Sunday in Ordinary Time
How Should I Act?

 ## Scripture Background

Connections to Church Teaching and Tradition

* "Jesus, the Good Shepherd, wishes to communicate his life to us and place himself at the service of life. . . . He likewise invites his disciples to reconciliation . . . love for enemies . . . and to opt for the poorest" (*Aparecida*, 353).

* "The Word became flesh *to be our model of holiness*" (CCC, 459).

* "Although the Church possesses a 'hierarchical' structure, nevertheless this structure is totally ordered to the holiness of Christ's members. And holiness is measured according to the 'great mystery' in which the Bride responds with the gift of love to the gift of the Bridegroom" (MD, 27).

Leviticus 19:1–2, 17–18   Today's passage from Leviticus summarizes the intent of all God's laws: "Be holy, for I, the LORD, your God, am holy" (v. 2). Our vocation is to imitate God. The passage ends with a synopsis of what that implies "You shall love your neighbor as yourself" (v. 18).

This reading invites an examination of the kind of God our behavior proclaims. Are we like the God we meet in Scripture, slow to anger and rich in compassion, or does our behavior give witness to a false god of success, beauty, or materialism? Are we more apt to proselytize for our sports team or political party than for the Gospel?

Psalm 103:1–2, 3–4, 8, 10, 12–13 (8a)   The *New American Bible* includes the subscript that this is a psalm of David. Whether or not it is of Davidic origins, it fits his experience.

In the context of our first reading, we sing this psalm remembering what God has done for us. The psalm also describes what our God is like. God pardons sin and heals us, redeems us from destruction and treats us with kindness and compassion. By forgiving us, God makes our transgressions the opposite of our self-definition: "as far as the east is from the west" (v. 12). This is the God who offers compassion and mercy to us, and whom we are called to imitate.

1 Corinthians 3:16–23   In this selection we are reminded of our intimate relationship with God. We, each and all of us, are the temple in which the Holy Spirit dwells. As a community, we replace the Temple where the people used to seek God's presence. In this context, the destruction of that Temple implies doing harm to the community.

Verses 18–23 of this reading summarize all that Paul has so far said. It reprises his themes of true wisdom versus human wisdom, and of the importance of remembering that the Corinthians do not belong to their favorite teacher. Rather, all belongs to them through Christ who belongs to God, and who brings them and us along with him to the Father.

Matthew 5:38–48   The last line of this reading looks back to the message of the first reading. "So be perfect, just as your heavenly Father is perfect" (v. 48) is another expression of "Be holy, for I, the LORD, your God, am holy" (Leviticus 19:2). This section of the Gospel according to Matthew has been misinterpreted by many over the years, who think that it means that those who suffer great injustice should just acquiesce to it, without doing anything to try to change things. In Jesus' environment, this was more a call to justice than to suffer in silence. To understand the passage well, we must remember that the people in Jesus' time lived in a class system. There was a great distinction between slaves and masters, the occupying army and the nationals, and the rich and poor.

When Jesus tells the people to turn the other cheek, note that he says to do this "when someone strikes you on your right cheek" (v. 39). A right-handed person can only strike the right cheek of another with the back of the hand, a gesture that a master would use with a slave. By turning the other cheek, the person is essentially challenging the attacker to hit him or her squarely, like an equal. This recalls the civil rights marchers' commitment to avoid retaliation, but to remain strong in demonstrating their own humanity in an attempt to challenge their oppressors' prejudices and sense of righteousness.

The tunic and cloak that Jesus mentions were the primary garments of his day. Typically, when a poor person had nothing left with which to pay a debt, his tunic and cloak would be offered as collateral. According to the law, the lender had to return the cloak in the evening, because it was also the debtor's blanket. Handing over both cloak and tunic would be a persuasive sign demonstrating that the economics of the day left the poor naked.

The saying "Go the extra mile" has its origin in this passage and is understood with some context. In Jesus' time, it was legal for a Roman soldier to force a local person to carry the soldier's heavy pack for just one mile—any more, and he would be subject to punishment. One can imagine the confusion and embarrassment a Roman soldier would feel trying to wrest his pack away from the Jew who is offering to carry it further. In all of these cases, loving the enemy comes down to asserting one's own humanity and attempting to call forth the humanity of the other. It is creative nonviolence, the most genuine way to love one's enemy.

 # Preparation

Today's Gospel reading describes Jesus subverting the wisdom of the world. "An eye for an eye and a tooth for a tooth" prevents escalation and vengeance and so it seems like good advice, but God's wisdom is greater and asks more of us. Jesus pointed to God's desire for our love to be for all, even those who are our enemies, and for us to offer a love that not only deescalates but also disrupts and defeats violence itself. Although we do not have the power to do this on our own, God does have this power and offers it to us.

Lectionary for Mass #79A

Leviticus 19:1–2, 17–18

Psalm 103:1–2, 3–4, 8, 10, 12–13 (8a)

1 Corinthians 3:16–23

Matthew 5:38–48

Objective

- To name God's wisdom as a wisdom embodied in love.

Preparation and Materials

- Read the Season Background, the lectionary readings, and the Scripture Background.

- Bookmark the appropriate readings (see page xv) in the lectionary, children's lectionary, or Bible. Place the book in a convenient location for the leader.

- Write the words of dismissal on a card for the priest celebrant.

- Prepare the words of the song the children will sing as they gather in the space for the Liturgy of the Word.

- Select volunteers (older children or adults) to proclaim the readings.

- Display the responsorial psalm refrain lyrics.

- Display the Apostles' or Nicene Creed.

- Prepare intercessions for the Prayer of the Faithful adapted for the needs of the Church, world, oppressed or marginalized, and local community.

Prayer Leader Reflection Questions

» **How are you holy and set apart for God? Where have you seen God's gift of holiness in yourself? How do your own actions affirm holiness?**

» **How do you show love to your enemies, or those who are not your friends, but rather strangers?**

Procession

Following the Collect of the Mass, the priest celebrant picks up the lectionary and invites those who would like to participate in the Liturgy of the Word with children to come forward and gather in the center aisle. The people who will lead the children out and facilitate the Liturgy of the Word also come forward at this time. Holding the lectionary so that all can see, the priest celebrant sends the children forth using his own words or the following:

Priest: **Beloved children, we send you now to listen carefully to the Word of God. Think about how you can be more like Jesus. May you open your hearts wide to the truth of the Scriptures. Go in peace.**

The leader processes out holding the lectionary, and the children follow behind. The parish music minister may have selected a song of dismissal for the assembly to sing while the children leave. A good option is "The Word of God: Children's Dismissal" by M. D. Ridge and Timothy R. Smith (WLP/GIA).

Centering

Continue to sing the song of dismissal that the assembly sang as you left the church. Or sing the refrain from "They'll Know We Are Christians" (Scholtes), or "Prayer of St. Francis" (Temple), or have instrumental music playing as the children gather in the space for the Liturgy of the Word.

Place the lectionary on the ambo or lectern. Light the candle placed by the ambo or lectern, and then lead the following prayer:

Heavenly Father,
we want to know your wisdom
and we want to please you with all that we say and do.
Allow our hearts to be open to your Word
so that we may serve you completely.
Through Christ our Lord.

Children: **Amen.**

First Reading

Leviticus 19:1–2, 17–18

Responsorial Psalm

Psalm 103:1–2, 3–4, 8, 10, 12–13 (8a) *Sing the same musical setting that is used in your parish's celebration of the liturgy.*

Second Reading

1 Corinthians 3:16–23

Gospel Acclamation

Sing the Gospel Acclamation used in your parish's celebration of the liturgy.

Gospel Reading

Matthew 5:38–48

Homily/Reflection

We want to be wise, don't we? We want to know and understand what is right. The Bible has a lot to say about wisdom. There is even a whole book on Wisdom! The people of Israel heard God's wise instruction about how we should live by loving our neighbor as ourselves. They understood that God wanted them to be united as one people, one community together in love before the Lord. Loving one another and avoiding anything that would harm others in the community meant that they could stay together and be who God called them to be.

Jesus also talked about wisdom. He named some of the things that the world often tries to call wise. He reminded his disciples of "an eye for an eye and a tooth for a tooth." Another way to say this was "*only* an eye" or "*only* a tooth." It meant if someone harmed you, you could expect that person to pay you back for what had been harmed. However, you could only harm them back equally as much as you were hurt, and no more. This rule keeps an argument from getting worse and prevents the harm to each person from getting worse.

» Does it sound fair?

Jesus also reminded his disciples that "You shall love your neighbor and hate your enemy." Our enemies are people who want to do us harm. The wisdom of the world would tell us that it makes sense to hate those who want to hurt you. Perhaps this even might protect you, but God's wisdom is not like the wisdom of the world. In the second reading, St. Paul told the Corinthians, "the wisdom of this world is foolishness in the eyes of God" (1 Corinthians 3:19). We know that God loves all people, even our enemies. God cares for all people. The sun rises and the rain falls whether we are good or bad and God is the one who makes sure this keeps happening. Jesus gave his disciples instructions that might seem foolish to the world, but really reflect God's love for all people. Jesus gave us a new rule: "love your enemies" and "pray for those who persecute you." It isn't easy to love a person who is your enemy or someone who harms you for no good reason, is it? Jesus also said, "be perfect, just as your heavenly Father is perfect" (Matthew 5:48). How can we strive to be perfect? With the help of God. God gives us the power and strength to love our enemies and to pray for those who persecute us.

The love that Jesus described wasn't the kind of love that means putting up with people who harm us or suffering in silence. Jesus didn't want his disciples to be hurt. Instead he gave his disciples instructions on how to stop the hurt without hurting back. When he said, "turn the other cheek," he did not mean that we should let others keep hurting us. Jesus is talking about standing up for what is right but not react with violence or negative words or actions. Sometimes, when we feel we are being treated badly, we can remember to pray for the people who are being unfair. We don't have to agree with what they are doing, but we can ask God to show them his love. Maybe they wouldn't treat others so unfairly if they knew and felt God's love.

Jesus wanted to turn the wisdom of the world upside down. He wanted people to see that God's wisdom is so much more. God's wisdom is about uniting people into one community of love. Jesus wants us to recognize that everyone deserves God's love, even though we sin. Jesus shows compassion to those who make mistakes; God forgives us and welcomes us back into new life.

Profession of Faith

Following the homily or reflection, the prayer leader invites everyone to stand to profess our faith. Together, sing or recite the Apostles' or Nicene Creed. Refer the children to the words of the prayer that you have displayed.

Prayer of the Faithful

Leader: **God our Father, as we celebrate the love you have given us, we confidently make our prayers to you. Please respond, "Holy God, hear our prayer."**

May the Church grow in holiness, that her priests, deacons, and lay ministers fulfill the work to which God has called them, we pray to the Lord: *Holy God, hear our prayer.*

May the world be freed from vengeance and hatred, we pray to the Lord: *Holy God, hear our prayer.*

May all who suffer from poverty, injustice, or abuse find healing in God and find love and support in a community of faith, we pray to the Lord: *Holy God, hear our prayer.*

May all have courage to love others as God has loved us, unconditionally and without expectation, we pray to the Lord: *Holy God, hear our prayer.*

Invite other intercessions from the children, or add intercessions based on the current needs of the Church, the world, the oppressed or marginalized, and the local community. End each of the petitions with **"we pray to the Lord"** and invite the response "**Holy God, hear our prayer.**"

May those who have died enjoy forever the presence of the most holy God, we pray to the Lord: *Holy God, hear our prayer.*

Heavenly Father,
as we are blessed to receive your love, gifts, and mercy, may we share them with others.
We make this prayer through Jesus Christ our Lord.

Children: **Amen.**

Quietly return with the children to the main assembly. Be mindful of children having difficulty finding their families.

Season Background for Lent

Understanding Lent

We begin the season of Lent, a journey of forty days. Forty is a symbolic number in Scripture, found in stories such as Noah and the flood, the Israelites wandering in the desert, and the time Jesus prayed and fasted in the desert before he began his ministry. It represents a long period of time focused on an important life experience. Like any journey, we begin in one place and end in another. The people who are preparing for Baptism and we who have been baptized begin with the story of temptation, our own weakness and sin. With the woman at the well, the man born blind, and Lazarus, we begin to see more clearly who Jesus is and where he is leading us. We experience the Triduum and discover anew that we are called to serve others and this sometimes leads to suffering and death. We arrive at Easter transformed and filled with God's new life. Lent is a journey of faith that leads to the font of rebirth.

Liturgical Environment

In creating your Lenten liturgical environment, take your cue from the church itself. There, the environment is sparse and the predominant color is violet, the color of repentance. In your space, a crucifix should be the main focus. Cover your lectern and other surfaces with violet cloth. If there are people in your parish who will be baptized at Easter, write their names on a card and keep it with this book so that you can pray for them in the Prayer of the Faithful each week.

Overview of the Readings

As we prepare to grow spiritually during the season of Lent, take time to pray with the readings of each Sunday. Since we are in Year A of the Lectionary cycle of readings, you will not need to worry about which readings your parish will use for the Third, Fourth, and Fifth Sundays of Lent. All of the Masses will use the Year A readings, which include some of the great conversion stories of Scripture.

First Readings   During Lent, the Old Testament readings are about the history of salvation, a theme that coincides with the season of Lent. The progression of the readings from the First through Fifth Sundays presents the main aspect of salvation history from its beginning through the promise of the New Covenant fulfilled in Jesus Christ.

Beginning with the second creation story, the creation of man out of dust and from the breath of the Lord (the First Sunday of Lent) to the call of Abraham (Second Sunday of Lent) to the gift of water from the rock at Massah and Meribah (Third Sunday of Lent) to the anointing of David as Israel's king (Fourth Sunday of Lent) to the Lord promising to put his Spirit in the Israelites (Fifth Sunday of Lent), our faith becomes rooted in the wondrous life the Lord has given his people from the very beginning of time, despite their occasional lack of faith in him.

Responsorial Psalms   Throughout Lent, the responsorial psalms repeatedly speak of the Lord's mercy. Whether it is a simple statement of the psalmist's and our confidence in the merciful nature of God (Psalm 130), a call to praise and worship God (Psalm 95), or a personal prayer to the Lord asking him to shower his mercy upon us (Psalms 51 and 33), the idea of God's loving kindness is a primary theme of the Lenten psalms. The Lord's forgiveness and care for his people is so deep and constant that on the Fourth Sunday of Lent, the responsorial psalm is the beloved Psalm 23, in which the psalmist confesses that because the Lord is his shepherd he is in want of nothing. On Palm Sunday, the responsorial psalm in each of the three years is Psalm 22, with the accompanying plea of one in need heard in the refrain: "My God, my God, why have you abandoned me?"

Second Readings   Unlike those of Ordinary Time, the Second Readings of Lent do correspond with both the first reading and the Gospel. To the extent to which it is possible, the Second Readings also provide a connection between these two readings. During Year A, the Second Readings on the First, Third, and Fifth Sundays of Lent come from Paul's Letter to the Romans, his great treatise on justification by faith and the peace that comes from this grace. On the Second Sunday of Lent, we hear a selection from the pastoral letter 2 Timothy, which reinforces the truth that suffering for the sake of the Gospel comes with being a disciple of Christ. On the Fourth Sunday of Lent, the Second Reading is a passage from the letter to the Ephesians, a letter considered by Scripture scholars to be deutero-Pauline. This means it contains themes common to Paul, but was written by someone other than Paul who was learned in his teachings. On Palm Sunday, the Second Reading is the same in each year of the three-year cycle. It presents Christ's humanity and divinity in the form of a beautiful hymn. This hymn climaxes in the exaltation of Christ and the call to every tongue to confess him as Lord because of his obedience to the point of death on a cross.

Gospel Readings   The Gospel readings of Lent provide some of the richest words with which people of all ages can pray, study, and grow spiritually as individuals and in relation to the Christian community. Year A of the Lectionary cycle of readings, in particular, gives us the great narratives of conversion on the Third, Fourth, and Fifth Sundays of Lent. These are the stories from John's account of the Gospel of the woman at the well, the man born blind, and the raising of Lazarus. The Gospel reading for the Second Sunday of Lent is always one of the synoptic accounts of Jesus' Transfiguration on the mountain. The temptation account sets us on the road to Easter, as we ponder those areas in our lives in which we give in to temptation and are in need of the saving grace of the one who did not. Hearing the account of Jesus' Transfiguration calls us to pause and remain in awe at his glory, just as the disciples who went up the mountain did.

February 26, 2023
First Sunday of Lent

Create in Me a Clean Heart

 ## Scripture Background

Connections to Church Teaching and Tradition

✦ "[Reason] becomes human only . . . if it looks beyond itself. Otherwise, man's situation, in view of the imbalance between his material capacity and the lack of judgment in his heart, becomes a threat for him and for creation" (SS, 23).

✦ "There are still others whose hopes are set on a genuine and total emancipation of humankind through human effort alone and look forward to some future earthly paradise where all the desires of their hearts will be fulfilled" (GS, 10).

✦ "But the world's Creator has stamped man's inmost being with an order revealed to man by his conscience. . . . Men 'show the work of the law written in their hearts. Their conscience bears witness to them.'[1] And how could it be otherwise? All created being reflects the infinite wisdom of God. It reflects it all the more clearly, the higher it stands in the scale of perfection[2]" (PT, 5).

Genesis 2:7–9; 3:1–7 In Genesis 2, God first creates the man out of the earth. After watching the creature, God says, for the first time in the Bible, "It is not good" (2:18). What was not good was that the human was alone. In the beginning, the man into whose nostrils God had blown the breath of life could just as well have been called "earth creature," for until the creation of Eve he had been unique and alone. Although he could name everything around him including the animals (a sign of domination), the man's loneliness did not go away. Finally, God created a companion who could converse with him and call him by name. Now both of them knew what it meant to be human.

Immediately after, we hear the account of sin's entry into the world via temptation by the serpent. What the prince of lies told them was that they would be like gods if they eat of the forbidden fruit. They had forgotten that they were made in the image of God and, via their relationship with God and one another, they were already like gods. They who had been made in the image of God thought they could make themselves gods and, in their disobedience, they obeyed one who was not the true God.

Psalm 51:3–4, 5–6, 12–13, 17 (see 3a) Psalm 51 is the most well-known penitential psalm. Like Psalm 103, which appears a number of times in the Lectionary, it is called a psalm of David, and it fits his experience. The psalm recognizes that every sin, no matter the victim, is also a sin against God. The key to this prayer is that it recognizes God as the center and ruler of the universe, the only one who can forgive and restore. And so we look to God, begging for mercy and renewal.

Romans 5:12–19 or 5:12, 17–19 Paul's Letter to the Romans is the only extant Pauline letter that was not written to a community that Paul knew well. Thus, in the beginning of the letter he introduces himself and the themes and topics he will treat, which include the early Church's basic teaching.

In today's liturgy we proclaim what he says in regard to the mysteries of sin and salvation. Paul contrasts Adam, counted as the first sinner, with Christ, the one who brought acquittal to all sinners who would accept him. Paul does not blame all sin on Adam, but rather recognizes Adam as the originator of sin and therefore of death. The point is not so much to teach about Original Sin and Adam, but rather to focus on Christ, who brings an abundance of grace, justification, and the promise that faithful disciples will reign with Christ.

Matthew 4:1–11 The account of Jesus' temptation in the desert occurs in all three synoptic accounts of the Gospel. The temptations that the devil puts before Jesus reprise the history of Israel. The first, creating bread for himself, recalls the trek through the wilderness, and is a temptation to use his power for himself. As if they were in a rabbinical debate, Jesus responds to the tempter with a Scripture quotation, citing Deuteronomy 8:3.

When the devil took him to the parapet of the temple and challenged him to jump, both the devil and Jesus quoted Scripture. The devil was asking Jesus to see if God really would care for him, and Jesus' response was to refuse to test God as the Israelites did in the desert (Deuteronomy 6:16).

Finally, the devil shows Jesus all the kingdoms of the world and offers them to Jesus if only he will worship him. This is the temptation that most closely resembles the Genesis account, because the devil is promising something that is not his to give. Not only that, but he is promising

1 Romans 2:15.
2 Cf. Psalm 18:8–11.

the kingdoms of the world, not the Kingdom of God. Jesus' reply summarizes his vocation and his call to disciples: "The Lord, your God, shall you worship / and him alone shall you serve" (v. 10). For the rest of the Gospel, Jesus will be living that vocation and trying to get it across to his disciples. His message is that, with the grace of God, all disciples can make God the center of their worship and live in a way that gives witness to God's grace.

Preparation

Immediately before the beginning of Jesus' earthly ministry, Jesus prayed and fasted in the desert. At the conclusion, the devil tried to tempt Jesus to abandon the will of God for more comfortable things. Jesus is the consummate example of resisting temptation and refused each of three attempts by the devil. Although the devil quoted Scripture, Jesus knew it better and knew its significance in light of the whole of salvation history. During Lent, we enter into the practices that Jesus engaged in—those of prayer and fasting. We hope and pray that we too can resist temptation to sin. Even when we fail, we trust in the love of God who forgives. We know when we ask for clean hearts, God will answer our prayer.

Lectionary for Mass #22A

Genesis 2:7–9, 3:1–7

Psalm 51:3–4, 5–6, 12–13, 17 (see 3a)

Romans 5:12–19 or 5:12, 17–19

Matthew 4:1–11

Objectives

- To consider together with the children how Jesus resisted temptation to sin.
- To offer the children definition of the word *sin* that is rooted in Scripture.

Preparation and Materials

- Read the Season Background, the lectionary readings, and the Scripture Background.
- Bookmark the appropriate readings (see page xvi) in the lectionary, children's lectionary, or Bible. Place the book in a convenient location for the leader.
- Write the words of dismissal on a card for the priest celebrant.
- Prepare the words of the song the children will sing as they gather in the space for the Liturgy of the Word.
- Select volunteers (older children or adults) to proclaim the readings.
- Display the responsorial psalm refrain lyrics.
- Display the Apostles' or Nicene Creed.
- Prepare intercessions for the Prayer of the Faithful adapted for the needs of the Church, world, oppressed or marginalized, and local community.

Prayer Leader Reflection Questions

>> What practices of prayer and fasting do you intend to commit to this Lent?

>> What do you need to ask forgiveness for? When will you experience the sacrament of reconciliation to receive a clean heart?

Liturgy Guide

FEBRUARY 26, 2023

Procession

Following the Collect of the Mass, the priest celebrant picks up the lectionary and invites those who would like to participate in the Liturgy of the Word with children to come forward and gather in the center aisle. The people who will lead the children out and facilitate the Liturgy of the Word also come forward at this time. Holding the lectionary so that all can see, the priest celebrant sends the children forth using his own words or the following:

Priest: **Children, many things promise to give us life, but Jesus reminds us that only God's Word gives true life. Go now and listen to this Word, and when you return to us, we will joyfully continue our celebration.**

The leader processes out holding the lectionary, and the children follow behind. The parish music minister may have selected a song of dismissal for the assembly to sing while the children leave. A good option is "The Word of God: Children's Dismissal" by M. D. Ridge and Timothy R. Smith (WLP/GIA).

Centering

Continue to sing the song of dismissal that the assembly sang as you left the church. Or sing "From Ashes to the Living Font" (Hommerding) or the refrain from "Take, O Take Me As I Am" (Bell) or have instrumental music playing as the children gather in the space for the Liturgy of the Word.

Place the lectionary on the ambo or lectern. Light the candle placed by the ambo or lectern, and then lead the following prayer:

Mighty God,
help us to grow in our understanding of all that Christ offers us during Lent.
Allow our hearts to be open to your Word
so that we may serve you completely.
Through Christ our Lord.

Children: **Amen.**

First Reading

Genesis 2:7–9, 3:1–7

Responsorial Psalm

Psalm 51:3–4, 5–6, 12–13, 17 (see 3a) *Sing the same musical setting that is used in your parish's celebration of the liturgy.*

Second Reading

Romans 5:12–19 or 5:12, 17–19

Gospel Acclamation

Sing the Gospel Acclamation used in your parish's celebration of the liturgy.

Gospel Reading

Matthew 4:1–11

Homily/Reflection

We have gathered together today in a new season of our church year.

>> **Did anyone notice a new color in the church today?**

It is the color we sometimes call purple, but the Church calls violet. When we see this color in the church, we know that we are getting ready for something very special. The season we have begun is called Lent. This is the time we get ready for the great feast of Easter, the greatest of all feasts, the celebration of Jesus Christ rising from the dead.

On Easter, we remember that Christ has triumphed over sin and death. As we get ready for this celebration, we reflect on what sin is, and how much greater Christ's triumph over sin is. We may ask ourselves, "What is sin?" It means "missing the mark." Imagine an archer with a bow and arrow shooting at a target. When the archer has hit something other than the target, he has missed the mark. The arrow has taken the wrong path and ended in the wrong place. The Letter to the Romans uses the word *transgressions*. This means crossing a line into a place we do not belong. We want to be close to God and God wants us to be close to him as well. God has given us a path to follow. God's laws keep us from facing the wrong direction, keep us from leaving the right path.

Jesus always followed the path to his Father. He always followed the law and did what his Father asked of him. Although Jesus did this perfectly, that does not mean it was easy for him. When sin attracts us, when choosing something other than God's laws seem better than following the path to God, we call this "temptation." We hear about Jesus being tempted in the desert in the Gospel.

First Sunday of Lent • 127

The devil offered Jesus things that seemed appealing: riches, power, and protection from suffering. We can understand why someone might want to choose those things. In order for Jesus to have them, he would have had to turn away from God's path for him. Jesus was able to say no and to choose God's path.

Jesus also knew Scripture with his mind and with his heart. When Jesus was confronted with a choice, he responded with God's Word. The devil also knew God's Word, but he twisted it to mean something different than what God really wants. When Jesus used Scripture as a response to temptation, he understood its true purpose and how it fit into the whole story of God's love.

Jesus had spent forty days in the desert fasting. Fasting is to give something up that we really love or really want, as a way of prayer, to help us to be closer to God. Fasting was a way for Jesus to tell God, "I love you even more than food." He could really feel in his body the longing for food as a reminder of the longing his soul felt to be close to God.

During Lent, we are invited to pay special attention to saying no to temptation. We can follow Jesus' example. We can fast from food or from other things we love to remind us how much we need God, and to say to God that our love is greater than the desire we have for earthly things. We can think of resisting temptation like a muscle. When we practice saying no to achieve something better, it helps us to know how to say no to the things that aren't good even when they seem really appealing. Knowing God's Word can help us to recognize and resist temptation. To understand the specific words of Scripture, we need to know how they are a part of the one plan of God that is a plan of love. We trust in the wisdom and guidance of the Church to do this well. Ultimately, the power to resist temptation lies in the power of the Holy Spirit. We can ask God to care for us, to send angels to minister to us too. Even when we have failed, when we have sinned, we know that God's forgiveness is greater than anything we can do. We can ask God to clean our hearts.

Profession of Faith

Following the homily or reflection, the prayer leader invites everyone to stand to profess our faith. Together, sing or recite the Apostles' or Nicene Creed. Refer the children to the words of the prayer that you have displayed.

Prayer of the Faithful

Leader: **Christ's obedience sets us free from sinful ways. Longing to return to the Father's love, we lift up our prayers to him. Please respond, "Merciful Father, hear us."**

For the Church during this time of Lent, that she may help us prepare our whole selves to recognize and know the salvation of Jesus Christ, we pray: *Merciful Father, hear us.*

For world leaders to work for love rather than for self-interest, we pray: *Merciful Father, hear us.*

For those who suffer from addiction, that they may receive the ministry of angels, we pray: *Merciful Father, hear us.*

For those who are hungry in body and spirit, we pray: *Merciful Father, hear us.*

Invite other intercessions from the children, or add intercessions based on the current needs of the Church, the world, the oppressed or marginalized, and the local community. Conclude each of the children's petitions with "**we pray**" and invite the response "**Merciful Father, hear us.**"

For all who have been called from this life, we pray: *Merciful Father, hear us.*

Father full of mercy and love, help us to resist all temptation and to do your will in our Lenten pilgrimage. Accept the prayers of your children through Christ our Lord.

Children: **Amen.**

Quietly return with the children to the main assembly. Be mindful of children having difficulty finding their families.

March 5, 2023
Second Sunday of Lent

Listen to Him

Scripture Background

Genesis 12:1–4a   Abraham is the chief figure in the first reading for the Second Sunday of Lent in all three years of the Lectionary cycle (A, B, C). In this year's reading, we meet Abram as the model of faith, hope, and obedience. He listened to God and believed that the impossible could happen. Accepting the incredible plan of God, he left everything behind. We can paraphrase Paul and say that by faith, Abram was transfigured. His life became something he never could have imagined, but he believed in the power of God more than in his own fortunes.

Psalm 33:4–5, 18–19, 20, 22 (22)   Following the account of the call of Abram and his faith-filled response, our psalm sings what might well have been in Abram's mind, even if the psalm itself was written in a future epoch. The refrain intimates that we stand with Abram as we place our trust in God. The body of the psalm proclaims our belief in the trustworthiness of the Lord, and recognizes that the kindness of the Lord fills all of creation. The final strophe, which is also the end of the psalm itself, reminds us that the Lord, our help and our shield, is our only source of hope; therefore, our best act of faith is to wait for the Lord with a listening heart.

2 Timothy 1:8b–10   Throughout Paul's second Letter to Timothy we encounter a very human Paul writing to his protégé, Timothy, as one would write to a beloved son. He uses his own experience to counsel Timothy about how to be a good minister of the Gospel. That, of course, will entail suffering, but the strength to bear it comes from God who, as Paul has said in other places, has called us from the beginning of time. That theme is reminiscent of Psalm 139 and Jeremiah 1:5, and it provides a follow-up to the story of Abraham's call. In the context of the other readings, Paul invites us to consider our own call to a holy life and how the grace and appearance of Christ Jesus enlightens and changes—transfigures—our life.

Matthew 17:1–9   The account of the Transfiguration follows Jesus' first prediction of his Passion and his explanation that discipleship entails taking up one's own cross. In some ways, the real subjects of the Transfiguration are the three disciples. The narrative speaks more about them than about Jesus, and only names Moses and Elijah as his conversation partners. We are not told of Jesus' own experience, but rather what the three saw and heard. We are not told whether or not this experience strengthened Jesus, but it was clearly meant to be a revelation to the disciples.

The description of the transfigured Jesus is almost like a Resurrection appearance. It happens after six days, as did God's revelation to Moses in Exodus 24:13–16. It happens on a mountain, a prototypical place for divine revelations. Jesus is described as having a face that shone like the sun while his clothes became "white as light" (v. 2), recalling John the Evangelist's description of Jesus as the Light of the World. The two Old Testament figures that appear with Jesus, Moses and Elijah, are two of the most important figures in Israel's history and represent the Law and the prophets. Jesus is solidly in line with his Jewish heritage.

Here, as at the time of his baptism, a voice comes from the heavens and now proclaims "This is my beloved Son, with whom I am well pleased; listen to him" (v. 5). The voice certainly unnerved the disciples, causing them to fall over in fear. In one of the classic Orthodox icons of the Transfiguration, the disciples' reaction is portrayed vividly: the three seem to be hiding in plain sight. Like a child who closes her eyes and thinks she has erased the object of her fear, they have fallen down and cannot bear to behold the vision before them. In addition, we see other disciples in the distance, seemingly in caves from which they can see, hear, and

Connections to Church Teaching and Tradition

- "Disciples must be formed in a spirituality of missionary action . . . based on docility to the impulse of the Spirit, to its life giving power which mobilizes and transfigures all dimensions of existence" (*Aparecida*, 284).

- "Proclaiming the death of the Lord . . . entails that all who take part in the Eucharist be committed to changing their lives. . . . It is his fruit of a transfigured existence and commitment to transforming the world in accordance with the Gospel which splendidly illustrates the eschatological tension inherent in the celebration of the Eucharist" (EE, 20).

understand even less than Peter, James, and John. The truth is that what Jesus and God are revealing about Jesus' nature as the Second Person of the Holy Trinity, is beyond their ability to comprehend. As time goes on, through the Passion and Resurrection, they will gradually come to understand more.

At the end, the gentle Jesus touches the three and tells them not to be afraid. He also tells them that they are not to report the vision to anyone. Obviously, they have not yet understood it. The central point is that in order to understand, they must listen to him.

 # Preparation

At the transfiguration, Jesus revealed the fullness of his identity to Peter, James, and John. Then, with the arrival of Moses and Elijah, their conviction that Jesus was the Messiah was confirmed. They did not understand the complete significance of Jesus' identity at the time, however. Jesus asked them to wait to share what they had witnessed until after his own death and resurrection. Only then would they know that God's glory would be fully manifested by Christ's death on the cross and his resurrection.

Lectionary for Mass #25A

Genesis 12:1–4a

Psalm 33:4–5, 18–19, 20, 22 (22)

2 Timothy 1:8b–10

Matthew 17:1–9

Objectives

- To explore the relationship between the experience of the paschal mystery as necessary for the disciples to understand Jesus' transfiguration.

- To introduce the children to the meaning of *transfiguration*.

Preparation and Materials

- Read the Season Background, the lectionary readings, and the Scripture Background.

- Bookmark the appropriate readings (see page xvi) in the lectionary, children's lectionary, or Bible. Place the book in a convenient location for the leader.

- Write the words of dismissal on a card for the priest celebrant.

- Prepare the words of the song the children will sing as they gather in the space for the Liturgy of the Word.

- Select volunteers (older children or adults) to proclaim the readings.

- Display the responsorial psalm refrain lyrics.

- Display the Apostles' or Nicene Creed.

- Prepare intercessions for the Prayer of the Faithful adapted for the needs of the Church, world, oppressed or marginalized, and local community.

Prayer Leader Reflection Questions

≫ **In moments of fear or anxiety, how often do you turn to God?**

≫ **Are you taking the time this Lent to listen more closely to the voice of God? How are your Lenten devotions or fasting faring?**

Procession

Following the Collect of the Mass, the priest celebrant picks up the lectionary and invites those who would like to participate in the Liturgy of the Word with children to come forward and gather in the center aisle. The people who will lead the children out and facilitate the Liturgy of the Word also come forward at this time. Holding the lectionary so that all can see, the priest celebrant sends the children forth using his own words or the following:

> *Priest*: **Dear children, Lent is a time for us to focus more on prayer, to make sacrifices for others, and to think about how Christ sacrificed himself on the cross for us. During this time, let us work on being as selfless and loving as Jesus Christ was. Go in peace to hear God's Word.**

The leader processes out holding the lectionary, and the children follow behind. The parish music minister may have selected a song of dismissal for the assembly to sing while the children leave. A good option is "The Word of God: Children's Dismissal" by M. D. Ridge and Timothy R. Smith (WLP/GIA).

Centering

Continue to sing the song of dismissal that the assembly sang as you left the church. Or sing the refrain from "Be Not Afraid" (Dufford) or have instrumental music playing as the children gather in the space for the Liturgy of the Word.

Place the lectionary on the ambo or lectern. Light the candle placed by the ambo or lectern, and then lead the following prayer:

> **O God,**
> **help us to see clearly so that we can recognize and enjoy your glory.**
> **Allow our hearts to be open to your Word**
> **so that we may serve you completely.**
> **Through Christ our Lord.**

> *Children:* **Amen.**

First Reading

Genesis 12:1–4a

Responsorial Psalm

Psalm 33:4–5, 18–19, 20, 22 (22) *Sing the same musical setting that is used in your parish's celebration of the liturgy.*

Second Reading

2 Timothy 1:8b–10

Gospel Acclamation

Sing the Gospel Acclamation used in your parish's celebration of the liturgy.

Gospel Reading

Matthew 17:1–9

Homily/Reflection

We have gathered today to celebrate the Second Sunday of Lent. We are getting ready for the great feast of Easter, the greatest of all feasts. At Easter we will celebrate that Jesus rose from the dead. When Jesus rose, he brought a light and a life that is stronger than death and he shares this light and life with us. We are so happy for this gift and want to be completely ready to receive it. We spend this time in Lent preparing our whole selves—our hearts, our minds, our bodies—to celebrate this great gift.

» How have you been preparing yourself for Easter?
[You may wish to ask children about prayer, fasting, and almsgiving.]

Jesus wanted his friends to be ready. He wanted them to be prepared to understand and receive this gift as well. He gave them opportunities to know who he really is. Today, we hear how Jesus allowed his friends see him in a different way that would help them to know him more. We call this the transfiguration, which refers to the way Jesus was changed to show that he was God.

Before the transfiguration of Jesus took place, Jesus had taken Peter, James, and John to a mountaintop. We often speak of God as in the highest heavens. For the Jewish people, mountains were holy places where the earth and the heavens almost touch. Some of the most important moments when God had reached out to people happened on a mountain.

>> **What are other examples in the Bible of something important happening on a mountain?** (*Moses received the Ten Commandments on a mountain; Noah's ark landed on a mountain; the stories of Abraham and Isaac and of Elijah took place on a mountain; Moses had met God in the burning bush on a mountain; Elijah had heard the whisper of God's voice on a mountain.*)

Jesus was revealing to his friends that when heaven and earth come close, he is the bridge between them.

When Jesus' appearance changed, his face shone and his clothes became "white as light."

>> **How would you have felt if you had seen Jesus' transfiguration?**

We might think about what it is like to look at the flash of lightning in a dark sky, or what happens when our eyes have been closed for a long time in sleep and then suddenly someone turns on the light. The light is so bright that it almost hurts to look at. If we look directly at the sun, our eyes could be damaged. So to look upon Jesus changed must have been beautiful but perhaps it was almost too much to bear. It must have been so amazing.

Then they heard God the Father's voice telling them, "This is my beloved Son . . . listen to him." Jesus said to keep the transfiguration a secret until after he died and rose. It was only through the experience of his death and resurrection that they would come to understand what Jesus' glory meant. They had to go back down the mountain because Jesus had to do the work that made it possible for all of us to share in a life that is stronger than death. This work would be hard and as much as Jesus might have wanted to hide from that hard work, he was willing to do it for us. He wanted us all to be able to share in his eternal life when we will be able to see his face shining like the sun, not just for a moment, but forever!

Profession of Faith

Following the homily or reflection, the prayer leader invites everyone to stand to profess our faith. Together, sing or recite the Apostles' or Nicene Creed. Refer the children to the words of the prayer that you have displayed.

Prayer of the Faithful

Leader: **We place our hope in God, as we open our hearts without fear in prayer. Please respond, "Lord, hear our prayer."**

That Church leaders seek to minister to their flock with love and compassion, we pray: *Lord, hear our prayer.*

That we may always recognize the beauty and goodness of each human being on this earth, no matter how small or hidden, we pray: *Lord, hear our prayer.*

That those in our faith community who are sick and that members of our families who experience daily hardship may trust in the Lord's kindness, we pray: *Lord, hear our prayer.*

That we may always recognize Jesus as the Father's beloved Son and listen to what he commands, we pray: *Lord, hear our prayer.*

Invite other intercessions from the children, or add intercessions based on the current needs of the Church, the world, the oppressed or marginalized, and the local community. Conclude each of the children's petitions with **"we pray"** and invite the response **"Lord, hear our prayer."**

That those who have died may share the joys of heaven, we pray: *Lord, hear our prayer.*

O God,
you told us that Jesus is your beloved Son
and that we should listen to him.
Help us to follow your command.
Accept the prayers of your children through Christ our Lord.

Children: **Amen.**

Quietly return with the children to the main assembly. Be mindful of children having difficulty finding their families.

March 12, 2023
Third Sunday of Lent

Christ the Living Water

 Scripture Background

Connections to Church Teaching and Tradition

- Christ creates the gift of faith in those who seek him (RM, Preface for the Third Sunday of Lent).

- The Lord Jesus is the fountain for whom catechumens thirst; through the Son, the Father has offered salvation to all sinners (RCIA, 154).

- The human virtues are rooted in the theological virtues of faith, hope, and charity (CCC, 1812).

- "The woman of Samaria is a symbol of the Church not yet made righteous but about to be made righteous" (LH, II:212, from a treatise on John by St. Augustine, bishop).

Exodus 17:3–7   As a squeaky wheel gets its grease, so a cranky people get their water. Moses and God react differently to the thirsty people strewing complaints across the desert. Moses is exasperated, but God comes up with a practical solution. This passage tells the classic story of Moses striking a rock with his staff, and God opening the rock with a burst of water. The elders of Israel witnessed the event, lending credibility to an otherwise implausible story. God invited the people into this journey, wanted them to complete it, and offered them every aid. This episode serves as a prelude to the Gospel of the day, which in turn foreshadows the mystery of Baptism.

Psalm 95:1–2, 6–7, 8–9 (8)   This psalm recalls the same event told in the first reading. Here, though, God's response is not as bemused as it seems to be in Exodus. Instead of casually cooperating with the people's request, God issues a different command to a later generation: "'Harden not your hearts . . . / as in the day of Massah in the desert, / Where your fathers . . . / tested me though they had seen my works' " (vv. 8, 9). Basically, the psalm is asking a later generation of beleaguered people to have a better attitude than their forebears had.

Romans 5:1–2, 5–8   Just as God poured forth water for the people in the desert, so God pours love into the hearts of Christians through the gift of the Holy Spirit. St. Paul's challenging letter to the Romans has some of its meatiest material in chapter 5. He explores what came to be known as the theological virtues: Christians are justified by faith, which gives them hope, because they have received the love of God. By comparing this gift of the Spirit to something "poured out" (v. 5), Paul uses a metaphor that the Lectionary puts to eloquent purpose. It links this passage with the love of God in the first reading and the Gospel's promise of the Spirit.

John 4:5–42 or 4:5–15, 19b–26, 39a, 40–42   A woman who comes to perform an ordinary task finds herself in an extraordinary conversation. The story is one of the most vivid in the Gospel according to John.

In the time of Christ, Jews and Samaritans did not get along, partly because many generations earlier, upon their release from the Babylonian captivity, the Jews rebuilt the Temple without inviting the Samaritans to help. So, when Jesus, a Jew, asks a woman, a Samaritan, for a drink, he was already testing boundaries. That their conversation climaxed in a discussion on places of true worship showed their willingness to step right into the heart of a centuries-old conflict, played out in the ordinary lives of two people needing water on a hot, sunny day. Jesus wants something more than water. He wants the woman's faith. He probes and parries, demonstrating his prophetic knowledge of her life and his willingness to satisfy the deepest thirst in her heart. He offers her living water. He is that water, the one who can so slake those who receive him that they will never be thirsty, lifeless, and aimless again. He wants her to drink him in.

The woman herself shifts the discussion to faith, as she identifies the unrewarded thirst of the ancients: the coming of the Messiah, the one called Christ. Already she is wondering, could this be the one? At a well of water, echoing words Moses heard at a bush of fire, Jesus says to her, "I am he." Now, the woman acts like an apostle. She invites others to believe in Jesus, and they do, not just because of her testimony, but because they come to know Christ.

This entire story has long been associated with the Third Sunday of Lent. There is strong circumstantial evidence that it was proclaimed with the scrutiny rites in the early Church, in order to prepare catechumens for Baptism. This story, then, provides a paradigm in which those seeking the waters of Baptism today can find hope in the woman's story. Lent is observed not just by catechumens but also by the faithful. Those who mark the disciplines of Lent in order to renew their commitment to Christ will come to the end of their spiritual journey when they renew their baptismal promises at the Easter Vigil. Then they will be sprinkled with the blessed water of Baptism, living water that enables them to tell the world that Jesus is the Christ.

Preparation

For us human beings, water has been a beautiful and natural sign long before we came to appreciate its elevated reality in the sacramental life of the Church. It signifies birth and the perpetual sustenance of life, even as it has the power to destroy. In the experience of the people of Israel being led out of the bondage of Egypt into freedom, their human need for water led to an expression of covenantal love through God's provision of water. Jesus' own human need for water facilitated an encounter with the woman at the well, where he made clear his identity as the source of living water. We receive this living water in a particular way in the sacrament of baptism.

Lectionary for Mass #28A

Exodus 17:3–7

Psalm 95:1–2, 6–7, 8–9 (8)

Romans 5:1–2, 5–8

John 4:5–42 or 4:5–15, 19b–26, 39a, 40–42

Objective

- To explore the significance of water in everyday life, in the liturgical life of the Church, and its roots in Scripture.

Preparation and Materials

- Read the Season Background, the lectionary readings, and the Scripture Background.

- Bookmark the appropriate readings (see page xvi) in the lectionary, children's lectionary, or Bible. Place the book in a convenient location for the leader.

- Write the words of dismissal on a card for the priest celebrant.

- Prepare the words of the song the children will sing as they gather in the space for the Liturgy of the Word.

- Select volunteers (older children or adults) to proclaim the readings.

- Display the responsorial psalm refrain lyrics.

- Display the Apostles' or Nicene Creed.

- Prepare intercessions for the Prayer of the Faithful adapted for the needs of the Church, world, oppressed or marginalized, and local community.

Prayer Leader Reflection Questions

>> **How are you helping to prepare those to be baptized to receive the fullness of new life at Easter?**

>> **The human heart is made to seek God. Consider looking into some resources that will help you deepen your faith.**

Procession

Following the Collect of the Mass, the priest celebrant picks up the lectionary and invites those who would like to participate in the Liturgy of the Word with children to come forward and gather in the center aisle. The people who will lead the children out and facilitate the Liturgy of the Word also come forward at this time. Holding the lectionary so that all can see, the priest celebrant sends the children forth using his own words or the following:

> *Priest*: **Dear children, the Lord is in our midst. He will go before you and speak to you in today's readings, and he will pour life-giving water into your hearts. Then he will lead you back to us, and together we will sing the praises of Jesus, the savior of the world. Go in peace.**

The leader processes out holding the lectionary, and the children follow behind. The parish music minister may have selected a song of dismissal for the assembly to sing while the children leave. A good option is "The Word of God: Children's Dismissal" by M. D. Ridge and Timothy R. Smith (WLP/GIA).

Centering

Continue to sing the song of dismissal that the assembly sang as you left the church. Or sing "I Heard the Voice of Jesus Say" (verse 2 / various publishers) or the refrain from "The Servant Song" (Gillard), or have instrumental music playing as the children gather in the space for the Liturgy of the Word.

Place the lectionary on the ambo or lectern. Light the candle placed by the ambo or lectern, and then lead the following prayer:

> **God be in our minds and hearts as we gather in this Lenten season.**
> **May these Scriptures help us repent and be ready for Easter.**
> **Through Christ our Lord.**

> *Children:* **Amen.**

First Reading

Exodus 17:3–7

Responsorial Psalm

Psalm 95:1–2, 6–7, 8–9 (8) *Sing the same musical setting that is used in your parish's celebration of the liturgy.*

Second Reading

Romans 5:1–2, 5–8

Gospel Acclamation

Sing the Gospel Acclamation used in your parish's celebration of the liturgy.

Gospel Reading

John 4:5–42 or 4:5–15, 19b–26, 39a, 40–42

Homily/Reflection

[This homily/reflection refers to shorter Gospel reading.]

>> **When you enter the church for Mass, do you dip your hand in holy water and make the Sign of the Cross on yourself? Why do you do that?**
> *[Reflect with the children on why we bless ourselves with holy water.]*

>> **Water is so important! In what ways is water needed in our everyday lives?**

More than half or our body is water, and we need to drink water to stay alive. We might be able to go a whole month without eating anything at all, but we can't go more than a few days without water. We also need water for cleaning. To remain healthy, we have to bathe. Washing our hands can keep us from getting sick. Water is also beautiful. Perhaps we enjoy looking at fluffy clouds in the sky that are really a large group of tiny little droplets of water. Similar beads of water in the sky help us to see rainbows. We might delight in going out to watch the waves crash on a beach or how the birds or boats roll on the swells of the tide. Water is so precious and, as with all good gifts, we recognize that it comes from God.

In the first reading, the Israelites who followed Moses into the desert knew how important water was. There is very little water in the desert. Moses led the people of Israel out of the suffering and slavery of Egypt into a place of freedom, but the place he led them to was a desert. When the people realized they didn't have water, they wondered what good freedom is without life. God told Moses to strike a rock and from out of it, new water flowed. Although the people followed Moses, it was truly God who had led them. God made them a promise to take care of them. He provided what was needed to lead the Israelites to a new life of freedom.

We heard about other people who were thirsty, too. As Jesus was traveling, he stopped by a well at noon, the time when the sun is highest, heating the ground below. For people who do not have running water, it is hard work to carry water to your home. In the time of Jesus, this is what people had to do. They walked to and from wells of water in order the get what they needed. Jesus went to a well and there he met a woman who was working hard in the heat of the day to make sure her own house had enough water. When Jesus told her he had living water, she thought at first this might be the kind of cool, running water that would satisfy the thirst of her body. Another way to say what Jesus was speaking about was that he has "the water of life." But Jesus wasn't just speaking of cool, running water. He was speaking of another kind of water and another kind of life.

» What do you think Jesus meant?

During this season of Lent, we are getting ready to celebrate the new life that Jesus offered to us through his death and resurrection. Some, perhaps even some of us here, are preparing in a very particular way. They will be receiving the gift of water that not only gives earthly life but also brings Jesus' life that is stronger than death. They are preparing to receive the waters of baptism in a few weeks. They will receive this living water and be reborn into Christ's everlasting life. As we await this beautiful gift, we hope and pray, together with all those preparing, for wisdom and strength so that we, like the woman at the well, can recognize the truth of Christ's Word, the gift he has to offer and to share that good news with others.

Profession of Faith

Following the homily or reflection, the prayer leader invites everyone to stand to profess our faith. Together, sing or recite the Apostles' or Nicene Creed. Refer the children to the words of the prayer that you have displayed.

Prayer of the Faithful

Leader: **The Lord provides streams of living water to quench our thirst and to renew us in spirit. Drawing deeply from this wellspring of life, we place our needs in God's hands. Please respond, "God of life, hear our prayer."**

May all who have not yet received the living waters of the Gospel be given that chance through the ministry of the Church, we pray: *God of life, hear our prayer.*

May all life on earth have access to safe and healthy water to drink, we pray: *God of life, hear our prayer.*

May the hungry be fed, the homeless sheltered, the unemployed find work, and the unwanted feel welcome, we pray: *God of life, hear our prayer.*

May those preparing to enter the Church this Easter discover the truth that "hope does not disappoint," we pray: *God of life, hear our prayer.*

Invite other intercessions from the children, or add intercessions based on the current needs of the Church, the world, the oppressed or marginalized, and the local community. Conclude each of the children's petitions with **"we pray"** and invite the response **"God of life, hear our prayer."**

May all who have died be welcomed to eternal life, we pray: *God of life, hear our prayer.*

O God,
we know we are young and small, but you lift us up to you.
May all your children be surrounded by care and love.
Grant what we ask in faith through Christ our Lord.

Children: **Amen.**

Quietly return with the children to the main assembly. Be mindful of children having difficulty finding their families.

March 19, 2023
Fourth Sunday of Lent
Christ the True Light

 ## Scripture Background

Connections to Church Teaching and Tradition

✸ "'This bath is called *enlightenment*, because those who receive this [catechetical] instruction are enlightened in their understanding.'[1]" (CCC, 1216).

✸ "The word 'Christ' comes from the Greek translation of the Hebrew *Messiah*, which means 'anointed.' . . . In effect, in Israel those consecrated to God for a mission that he gave were anointed in his name. This was the case for kings, for priests, and, in rare instances, for prophets"[2] (CCC, 436).

1 Samuel 16:1b, 6–7, 10–13a God chooses David as the king of Israel, and Samuel anoints him. This reading serves two purposes in today's liturgy. When lifted out of its context here, it can be placed in sequence with the other first readings of the season; it then becomes one in a series of markers in the history of Israel. One workable method of preaching and catechizing during Lent focuses just on the first readings of the six weeks, which together show how God was preparing for the salvation of the human race step by step throughout the generations of Israel. One of those milestones is the anointing of David.

The other reason this reading fits today's liturgy is its relationship to the Gospel account of the man born blind. Basically a story of how people who have physical sight may lack spiritual sight, this first reading carries a similar message. Those who were looking for a likely candidate to be king overlooked the best of them all.

Note how dramatically the writer of 1 Samuel keeps the reader in suspense. The name of the future king is not revealed until the very last lines. A skilled reader of this passage will pause before announcing the name, as if to say, "And the winner is [*pause for excruciating suspense*] . . . David!"

Psalm 23:1–3a, 3b–4, 5, 6 (1) Unquestionably the most popular psalm in the Bible, Psalm 23 appears today because of its idyllic picture of the shepherd with his peaceful sheep. It looks back to the first reading with reassuring confidence that David will shepherd God's people as no one has before. The psalmist at Mass can imagine David singing these words—he who is the shepherd acknowledging that the Lord is his shepherd. Then will come alive this phrase: "You anoint my head with oil" (v. 5).

This psalm has little to do with the theme of the Gospel, but matches up nicely with the story about the anointing of Israel's first king.

Ephesians 5:8–14 Addressing a Gentile community in words not complimentary about its past, Paul says, "You were once darkness, but now you are light in the Lord" (v. 8). Paul affirms the beautiful brightness that shines from the hearts of these believers and encourages them to shine their light upon others. The closing verses probably come from an early Christian hymn, summoning those who sleep—and those who have died—to greet Christ who gives them light.

Obviously, this passage is chosen for today's liturgy because of its strong link to the theme of the Gospel. Whereas the Gospel will tell of a man born blind, Paul refers to a people born blind, but who now see with the eyes of faith.

John 9:1–41 or 9:1, 6–9, 13–17, 34–38 Jesus gives sight to a man born blind. But that is not even half the story. The miracle is dispatched rather quickly in the early verses of this chapter, and the rest of today's proclamation explores the effect this miracle has on the family, acquaintances, and the very person of the man born blind.

John does not conceal his main point. He contrasts physical blindness with spiritual blindness. This miracle story lies behind the opening verse of the popular hymn "Amazing Grace": "I once was lost, but now am found, / was blind, but now I see."

Like last week's Gospel, this one has a long history associated with the catechumenate. As catechumens elected for the Easter sacraments make their final preparations for Baptism, they experience scrutiny rites intended to drive out whatever keeps them from Christ and to strengthen their resolve to follow him. As did the woman at the well, so does the man born

1 St. Justin, Apol. 1, 61, 12: PG 6, 421.
2 Cf. Exodus 29:7; Leviticus 8:12;
1 Samuel 9:16; 10:1; 16:1, 12–13;
1 Kings 1:39; 19:16.

blind. Surprisingly, the man never asked Jesus for this miracle. His gift of faith came after, not before, his healing. Yet, it comes in a powerful statement: "I do believe, Lord," he says.

This story still strengthens those preparing for Baptism, even as it reminds those already baptized that following Christ means removing blindness. At this stage of Lent, the faithful should be more aware of their weaknesses, their dependencies, their addictions, and their sin. They may not have asked for the healing that Lent offers, but here it is, ready to open their eyes, that they might believe.

Preparation

God is infinite and beyond all time, and yet has chosen to enter into time and space. He reveals more and more of the Divine Self in salvation history until the fullness of God's revelation in the person of Jesus Christ. God is the author of salvation history. Its unity and movement toward one ultimate conclusion in the parousia establishes a relationship between its various moments as well as the biblical texts that describe them. The call of King David and the Davidic kingship have a direct relationship with the incarnation and paschal mystery. As members of Christ's faithful we can turn to the faithfulness of David as a model for how our own faithfulness may be lived out.

Lectionary for Mass #31A

1 Samuel 16:1b, 6–7, 10–13a

Psalm 23:1–3a, 3b–4, 5, 6 (1)

Ephesians 5:8–14

John 9:1–41 or 9:1, 6–9, 13–17, 34–38

Objectives

- To introduce children to the historical context of the Davidic kingship.

- To offer a unified framework of salvation history for understanding the texts of the Bible.

Preparation and Materials

- Read the Season Background, the lectionary readings, and the Scripture Background.

- Bookmark the appropriate readings (see page xvi) in the lectionary, children's lectionary, or Bible. Place the book in a convenient location for the leader.

- Write the words of dismissal on a card for the priest celebrant.

- Prepare the words of the song the children will sing as they gather in the space for the Liturgy of the Word.

- Select volunteers (older children or adults) to proclaim the readings.

- Display the responsorial psalm refrain lyrics.

- Display the Apostles' or Nicene Creed.

- Prepare intercessions for the Prayer of the Faithful adapted for the needs of the Church, world, oppressed or marginalized, and local community.

Prayer Leader Reflection Questions

➤➤ How are you someone after God's own heart? What gets in the way of this being true? How can you live your life in greater faithfulness to God's will?

➤➤ You are part of the story of salvation history authored by God. What does that mean to you?

Procession

Following the Collect of the Mass, the priest celebrant picks up the lectionary and invites those who would like to participate in the Liturgy of the Word with children to come forward and gather in the center aisle. The people who will lead the children out and facilitate the Liturgy of the Word also come forward at this time. Holding the lectionary so that all can see, the priest celebrant sends the children forth using his own words or the following:

> *Priest*: **Dear children, today's first reading reminds us that God does not judge us according to appearances. Rather, God looks into our hearts and sees the goodness and strength and beauty that are there. Go now and listen to God, who looks upon you with great love.**

The leader processes out holding the lectionary, and the children follow behind. The parish music minister may have selected a song of dismissal for the assembly to sing while the children leave. A good option is "The Word of God: Children's Dismissal" by M. D. Ridge and Timothy R. Smith (WLP/GIA).

Centering

Continue to sing the song of dismissal that the assembly sang as you left the church. Or sing "I Heard the Voice of Jesus Say" (verse 3 / various publishers) or the refrain from "Walk in the Light" (Landry), or have instrumental music playing as the children gather in the space for the Liturgy of the Word.

Place the lectionary on the ambo or lectern. Light the candle placed by the ambo or lectern, and then lead the following prayer:

> **God be in our minds and hearts as we gather in this Lenten season.**
> **May these Scriptures help us repent and be ready for Easter.**
> **Through Christ our Lord.**

> *Children:* **Amen.**

First Reading

1 Samuel 16:1b, 6–7, 10–13a

Responsorial Psalm

Psalm 23:1–3a, 3b–4, 5, 6 (1) *Sing the same musical setting that is used in your parish's celebration of the liturgy.*

Second Reading

Ephesians 5:8–14

Gospel Acclamation

Sing the Gospel Acclamation used in your parish's celebration of the liturgy.

Gospel Reading

John 9:1–41 or 9:1, 6–9, 13–17, 34–38

Homily/Reflection

Lent helps us to remember salvation history. God is the author of time. God, who is bigger than time itself, has chosen to enter into time over and over, so that human beings could know God. Then they could walk and talk on earth with God's very self in the person of Jesus Christ, who showed the fullness of his glory in his death and resurrection. Each moment, woven together as one story, shows us that all of this is done out of God's great love for us.

During Lent, we listen each week to a first reading that speaks of encounters with God in salvation history. We hear these readings in order. A few weeks ago, we heard God's work in creation and sin coming into the world, then God's promise to Abraham to make of him a great nation, and then last week, of God's protection and care for the people of Israel who were led out of Egypt to freedom. Today, we heard about God choosing a king of the people of Israel, the king against whom all the other kings were measured: King David. The people of Israel wanted a king, and the first was King Saul. A king often becomes one because he is the son of a king. David was not King Saul's son, though. David was Jesse's son. When the prophet Samuel was told by God to anoint the son of Jesse as the King of Israel, Samuel thought Jesse's oldest son, Eliab, looked kingly. Yet God did not choose Eliab or any of Jesse's sons who were present. David, the youngest, was out taking care of the sheep. Jesse hadn't even brought David in from the fields to meet with Samuel. Despite all this, God told Samuel that David, the youngest, was the one to anoint as king.

» **We might wonder why David was chosen. Was it because he was a shepherd?**
Was it because he was the least likely of the sons to be chosen?

Perhaps knowing each sheep and caring for them so well might have helped David to know and care for God's people. Perhaps David learned from his older brothers how to act wisely and protect others. The prophet Samuel already knew why David was to be king: "The Lord has sought out a man after his own heart" (1 Samuel 13:14). King David would listen to the will of God and follow it. David did not always make perfect choices, but when he made mistakes, he confessed and received forgiveness. He was faithful to God. God promised that love and care for Israel would come to the Jewish people through the house of David, in the form of a future king who would be greatest of all kings and rule forever.

» Who is this great king?

It is Jesus Christ who is Lord. Jesus' faithfulness to God's will was so great that he suffered death on a cross so that we could rise with him to new life. We know that the fullness of the glory of Christ's kingship will be visible in the parousia, in the fullness of time when God will be "all in all" (1 Corinthians 15:28). In choosing a king for Israel, God did not choose the oldest or the biggest or strongest. We have already been chosen to be God's children. When we are baptized, we too are anointed. Even when we are young or small, we know God chooses us to play a role in the great work of salvation history.

» How can we be faithful like David?

We can listen closely to the word of God. Spending time in prayer can help us to recognize what God wants us to know. We can listen to and study the Bible and the Church's teaching about Scripture. When we sin, we can admit it, say that we are sorry, and ask for forgiveness. We too can be people after God's own heart.

Profession of Faith

Following the homily or reflection, the prayer leader invites everyone to stand to profess our faith. Together, sing or recite the Apostles' or Nicene Creed. Refer the children to the words of the prayer that you have displayed.

Prayer of the Faithful

Leader: **We journey with Jesus in prayer, sacrifice, and in service to others. With trust, let us bring our prayers before God our Father. Please respond, "Lord, hear us."**

For the Catholic Church to remain a beacon of hope, leading people away from sin and darkness, we pray: *Lord, hear us.*

For kings and queens and world leaders, that they may have the wisdom to govern for the good of all they are responsible for, we pray: *Lord, hear us.*

For those who are physically blind, that they may teach us how to trust in the guidance of others, we pray: *Lord, hear us.*

For those preparing for the waters of baptism at Easter, that their eyes be opened to the truth and that they may seek the compassionate touch of the Savior always, we pray: *Lord, hear us.*

Invite other intercessions from the children, or add intercessions based on the current needs of the Church, the world, the oppressed or marginalized, and the local community. Conclude each of the children's petitions with **"we pray"** and invite the response **"Lord, hear us."**

For those who have died, that may they hear Jesus calling them to eternal life, we pray: *Lord, hear us.*

**O God,
awaken us in the light of Christ.
Save us from darkness so that we may live as children of light,
now and forever.
Through Christ our Lord.**

Children: **Amen.**

Quietly return with the children to the main assembly. Be mindful of children having difficulty finding their families.

March 26, 2023
Fifth Sunday of Lent
Christ the Resurrection and the Life

 ## Scripture Background

Connections to Church Teaching and Tradition

- "The Christian Creed . . . culminates in the proclamation of the resurrection of the dead on the last day and in life everlasting" (CCC, 988).

- "For as true man he wept for Lazarus his friend / and as eternal God, raised him from the tomb" (RM, Preface for Fifth Sunday of Lent).

Ezekiel 37:12–14 Through the prophet Ezekiel, God announces to captive Israel that freedom will come, as surely and miraculously as the dead shall rise from their graves. This short passage concludes a famous prophecy in which Ezekiel sees dry bones in a field coming to life as a mighty army, stirred by spirit—and not just any spirit—by God's Spirit. This powerful conclusion places a mighty prophecy before a dispirited people. God's comparison would have stunned even the prophet: captive Israel's future resembles the liberty of the dead from their graves. On this particular Sunday, this passage lifts a veil from the miracle that caps Jesus' career in John's account of the Gospel: the raising of Lazarus from the dead.

Psalm 130:1–2, 3–4, 5–6, 7–8 (7) The psalm today carries a refrain about God's mercy that prophetically pairs it with the "fullness of redemption" (v. 7). God's mercy is not just a compassionate feeling of pain, but one that intervenes to offer complete salvation. The faint drumbeat of the coming Easter victory can already be heard. More importantly, this psalm opens with the famous line, "Out of the depths I cry to you, O LORD."

Well known by its Latin title, *De profundis,* this prayer for mercy stresses the depths from which the psalmist cries out. In the light of the other readings today, Psalm 130 brings to the ears of the faithful the chilling voice of the dead, calling out from the depths of the grave for forgiveness, confident that God will redeem. This psalm has a classic position in the Catholic funeral rites for the same reason. Although the original psalmist was alive but feeling lonely, the psalm can be heard as the voice of the souls of the faithful departed, expressing their confident plea for forgiveness and life.

Romans 8:8–11 The Spirit of Christ gives life to those who are dead. Paul applies this statement in two ways, both to the living and to the dead. Those who are "in the flesh" live in sin, but those in whom the Spirit of God dwells are "in the spirit" (8:9). So throughout a Christian's days, the Spirit bestows righteousness. It does not end with death. Through the Spirit, God, who raised Jesus from the dead, gives life to bodies claimed by death.

Throughout this central passage of the letter to the Romans, Paul is building his case about the triumph of spirit over flesh, life over sin and death. Because of the thematic content of the other readings today, this passage helps the Christian understand how the powers of Christ over death apply very personally to the lives of believers.

John 11:1–45 or 11:3–7, 17, 20–27, 33b–45 Jesus raises his friend Lazarus from the dead. John's dramatic account of this episode has Jesus appear indifferent to the sickness, but he is more interested in life than death, in preaching than in illness. When he tells the disciples that Lazarus has died, he adds, "I am glad for you that I was not there" (v. 15). Illness and death are merely the substance upon which Jesus builds the greatest prophetic stance of his career. This is the last of the great signs Jesus works in John's account of the Gospel. After showing his power over death here in chapter 11, the story of his Passion gets underway in chapter 12.

The conversation with Martha carries the most important teaching. Jesus tells her, "I am the resurrection and the life." The Resurrection is not just something that happened to him; he is the Resurrection, the one in whom all souls find hope.

This Gospel is the climax of three Johannine passages that build through the latter part of Lent. They were probably first associated with scrutinies in the early Church. The post–Vatican II lectionary recovered them, to be used even in Years B and C whenever there are elect present with whom to celebrate scrutinies. The images increase in drama: first water, the source of life; then light, the sign of faith; and now life, the fulfillment of the promise of birth. The elect can be brought to a deeper appreciation of the sacraments to which they are called, even as they leave behind whatever keeps them from Christ.

These readings also draw the faithful more deeply into the expectations of the Christian life. More aware of their sin, they seek God's forgiveness. Many will celebrate the Sacrament of Reconciliation before Easter. With today's reading they encounter the ultimate mysteries of life. God who summoned them through their birth now shows power over death. Those who repent die to their past, that they may rise as new people on Easter Day.

 # Preparation

In the Gospel of John, Jesus' raising of Lazarus is the final act that leads to the Jewish leaders' decision to pursue Jesus' execution. Jesus' ability to resuscitate Lazarus simply by commanding him to come out demonstrates his supreme divine power. Despite this power, Jesus still wept with Lazarus' sister, Mary. His humanity united our human suffering to his own. He stands in solidarity with us and saves us completely through the gift of eternal life.

Lectionary for Mass #34A

Ezekiel 37:12–14

Psalm 130:1–2, 3–4, 5–6, 7–8 (7)

Romans 8:8–11

John 11: 1–45 or 11:3–7, 17, 20–27, 33b–45

Objectives

- To meditate together on Jesus' power as extending even over death.

- To offer the words of Psalm 130:1 as our own prayer that Jesus answers.

Preparation and Materials

- Read the Season Background, the lectionary readings, and the Scripture Background.

- Bookmark the appropriate readings (see page xvi) in the lectionary, children's lectionary, or Bible. Place the book in a convenient location for the leader.

- Write the words of dismissal on a card for the priest celebrant.

- Prepare the words of the song the children will sing as they gather in the space for the Liturgy of the Word.

- Select volunteers (older children or adults) to proclaim the readings.

- Display the responsorial psalm refrain lyrics.

- Display the Apostles' or Nicene Creed.

- Prepare intercessions for the Prayer of the Faithful adapted for the needs of the Church, world, oppressed or marginalized, and local community.

Prayer Leader Reflection Questions

>> **How do you engage in the corporal and spiritual works of mercy, in particular, the works of burying the dead, comforting the sorrowful, and praying for the living and the dead?**

>> **In the midst of suffering and lament, how do you turn to God in prayer?**

Procession

Following the Collect of the Mass, the priest celebrant picks up the lectionary and invites those who would like to participate in the Liturgy of the Word with children to come forward and gather in the center aisle. The people who will lead the children out and facilitate the Liturgy of the Word also come forward at this time. Holding the lectionary so that all can see, the priest celebrant sends the children forth using his own words or the following:

> *Priest*: **Dear children, Jesus wept over the death of Lazarus, and he wants no one to die. So he gave himself for us that we might live forever with him. This is the message of the readings you will hear today. And when you come back to us, we will all celebrate together the joy of everlasting life.**

The leader processes out holding the lectionary, and the children follow behind. The parish music minister may have selected a song of dismissal for the assembly to sing while the children leave. A good option is "The Word of God: Children's Dismissal" by M. D. Ridge and Timothy R. Smith (WLP/GIA).

Centering

Continue to sing the song of dismissal that the assembly sang as you left the church. Or sing "I Heard the Voice of Jesus Say" (verse 1 / various publishers) or "With the Lord There Is Mercy" (Modlin), or have instrumental music playing as the children gather in the space for the Liturgy of the Word.

Place the lectionary on the ambo or lectern. Light the candle placed by the ambo or lectern, and then lead the following prayer:

> **Lord our God,**
> **please help us to love others with the great love that your Son showed**
> **when he died and rose for us.**
> **Allow our hearts to be open to your Word**
> **so that we may serve you completely.**
> **Through Christ our Lord.**

Children: **Amen.**

First Reading

Ezekiel 37:12–14

Responsorial Psalm

Psalm 130:1–2, 3–4, 5–6, 7–8 (7) *Sing the same musical setting that is used in your parish's celebration of the liturgy.*

Second Reading

Romans 8:8–11

Gospel Acclamation

Sing the Gospel Acclamation used in your parish's celebration of the liturgy.

Gospel Reading

John 11: 1–45 or 11:3–7, 17, 20–27, 33b–45

Homily/Reflection

We have come to the fifth week of Lent. Next week is Holy Week, the final week of our preparation for the great feast of Easter. During that week, we will think and pray about the last moments before Jesus suffered and died. Today, the Gospel was about the death of Jesus' friend, Lazarus. We know that when someone we love has died, we are no longer able to be with them physically. The death of someone we knew and loved is one of the saddest and hardest things we can experience. Jesus knew this to be true and he experienced it himself. When Jesus' beloved friend Lazarus died, he wept. He also did something more.

People had seen some of Jesus' power when he had healed others. One of those people was the man born blind whom we heard about last week. Jesus' friends knew he could restore people's health.

» What other miracles of Jesus can you remember?

Lazarus was sick and some people expected that Jesus would come and make him better. They were surprised and upset when he did not come before Lazarus died. When Jesus finally arrived at Bethany, Lazarus' sister, Mary, fell at his feet and told him "Lord, if you had been here, my brother would not have died" (John 11:21). She knew Jesus had power, but she did not yet understand how much. At Lazarus' tomb, the place where his body was laid, Jesus told his friends to remove the stone from the tomb. He commanded to Lazarus "Lazarus, come out!" (John 11:43). Lazarus rose and came out of the tomb, still wrapped in the cloth that had been used to prepare his dead body for burial. Jesus showed that his power was so great that it even extended over death.

This miracle of Jesus' helps us to understand in a very specific way what his own death would mean. Jesus had power over life and death. Not long after this, Jesus suffered and died before he rose. All that he experienced in the week we remember together during Holy Week, that special time that we recall the passion of the Lord, all happened because he chose it. He had the power to make something else happen, but he didn't do that. He followed the desire of the one who had sent him to experience terrible suffering, not because he had no other choice, but because he had made that choice to follow the will of God the Father.

In his own suffering, Jesus joined himself to our suffering. We do not have ultimate power like Jesus does. Some things make us sad and we do not have a choice about them. Sometimes our sadness is so great that we feel like we are in a deep, dark pit. The writer of the psalm we heard today felt that way. The first words of today's psalm are a prayer to God: "Out of the depths I call to you, Lord" (Psalm 130:1). We know that God hears our prayer. We might imagine God reaching down into the pit to help us out. Jesus did more than that, though. Jesus Christ has heard our cries from the depths of the pit and has joined us in order to lift us out. He lifts us so high that we can reach heaven.

Profession of Faith

Following the homily or reflection, the prayer leader invites everyone to stand to profess our faith. Together, sing or recite the Apostles' or Nicene Creed. Refer the children to the words of the prayer that you have displayed.

Prayer of the Faithful

Leader: **Confident that the Lord wants to transform death into new life, we pray for all in need this day. Please respond, "Merciful Lord, hear our prayer."**

That the Catholic Church may be an example of compassion to those who suffer, we pray: *Merciful Lord, hear our prayer.*

That those who govern nations and who lead corporations may be men and women of righteousness, we pray: *Merciful Lord, hear our prayer.*

That those who are sick may receive the care they need to be restored to health, we pray: *Merciful Lord, hear our prayer.*

That those who are suffering the loss of a loved one may trust that the Lord will heal their wounds and fill them with hope in the resurrection, we pray: *Merciful Lord, hear our prayer.*

That our parish community may be strengthened by the hope of rising to life with Christ, *Merciful Lord, hear our prayer.*

Invite other intercessions from the children, or add intercessions based on the current needs of the Church, the world, the oppressed or marginalized, and the local community. Conclude each of the children's petitions with **"we pray"** and invite the response **"Merciful Lord, hear our prayer."**

That those who have died may meet Jesus Christ, who is the resurrection and the life, we pray: *Merciful Lord, hear our prayer.*

**Lord our God,
you hear the cries of all those who suffer.
Accept the prayers of your children.
We ask this through Christ, our Lord.**

Children: **Amen.**

Quietly return with the children to the main assembly. Be mindful of children having difficulty finding their families.

April 2, 2023
Palm Sunday of the Passion of the Lord

Jesus the Son of David

 ## Scripture Background

Connections to Church Teaching and Tradition

- Christ died for all without exception (CCC, 605).

- "It is love 'to the end'[1] that confers on Christ's sacrifice its value as redemption and reparation, as atonement and satisfaction" (CCC, 616).

Matthew 21:1–11   Although we commonly speak of this day as Palm Sunday, its full title mentions the Passion of the Lord as well. Two Gospel passages are proclaimed on this day: one about the palms, the other about the Passion.

The first is proclaimed after the blessing of branches and before the entrance procession. In Matthew's account, the people recognize Jesus as the Son of David who comes in the name of the Lord. The word *hosanna* means something like "save us." It comes from the same Hebrew root as Jesus' own name, *Yeshua*, which means "savior."

The evangelist seems to have misunderstood Zechariah 9:9, where the prophet uses two different ways to express a humble king astride an animal. Matthew thought he meant two different animals, so he has Jesus straddling them both.

Isaiah 50:4–7   This is the third of Isaiah's four oracles of the servant of God. It poignantly foreshadows the suffering of Jesus as he approaches Calvary, giving his back to those who beat him, not shielding his face from buffets and spitting, yet confident that the Lord God will be his help.

This passage was newly added to the Palm Sunday Mass after the Second Vatican Council. There were very few Old Testament readings on Sundays prior to the Council. This passage broadens the Christian's appreciation of the role of the Son of God in the eternal plan of salvation.

Psalm 22:8–9, 17–18, 19–20, 23–24 (2a)   Perhaps the line in the Passion that most wrenches believers is Jesus' impassioned cry "My God, my God, why have you abandoned me?" He is quoting Psalm 22, which the Church sings for the responsorial today. The liturgy, however, does not rest on the quotation of that single agonizing line. It excerpts three stanzas of suffering: scoffing enemies, pierced hands and feet, and garments divided by a roll of the dice. It concludes with a powerful fourth stanza presupposing a faith that stabilizes amid terror: all the descendants of Israel should revere God.

Philippians 2:6–11   For as long as there have been lectionaries, possibly at least since the fifth century, this passage has always been associated with Palm Sunday. It perfectly captures the mission of the Son of God, who takes on human form, humbling himself to Death on a Cross, and then is exalted as Lord above all creation. The Palm Sunday Gospel will tell of the Death of Christ, but this passage reveals already the mystery that will be proclaimed more grandly next week.

Matthew 26:14 — 27:66 or 27:11–54   "Jesus cried out again in a loud voice, and gave up his spirit" (27:50). These are the words that galvanize the faithful today. Matthew's account of the Passion is a long, dramatic meditation on the final hours in the life of Jesus of Nazareth, but it all comes down to this line. If he had not died, there would be no meaning to his Resurrection. Because of his Death, believers who suffer from ailments, injury, and abandonment all know that they have an intercessor who understands.

Although all four Gospel accounts devote their largest section to the Passion and Death of Jesus, Matthew's account is the traditional one to be proclaimed on Palm Sunday. Prior to the publication of the lectionary revised after the Second Vatican Council, Catholics heard it at Mass every year. Matthew includes episodes with which every faithful Christian is familiar: Judas betrays Jesus for thirty pieces of silver, Jesus has a last supper with his disciples, Peter

---

1   John 13:1.

hears the prophecy that he will deny Jesus three times, Jesus prays in agony that the cup may pass from him, a violent mob descends on Jesus at his arrest, Caiaphas interviews Jesus, Judas hangs himself, Pilate questions Jesus, Barabbas is set free, soldiers mock and scourge Jesus, Jesus is crucified with two criminals and he dies on the Cross, the sanctuary veil is torn as the earth quakes, a centurion proclaims the divinity of Jesus, and Joseph of Arimathea reverently lays the body of Jesus to rest.

Even those who know this story well enter into its power every year. The proclamation of the Passion is more than a simple recitation of events. It is the Word of God thundering through the gathered assembly, making them present to the supreme sacrifice that even now saves.

 # Preparation

On Palm Sunday, the kingship of Christ is made plain, both in the people's acclamation of Jesus at his triumphant entry into Jerusalem and in the true manifestation of his power and glory on the cross. Jesus Christ's great power extends over individuals, peoples, all of creation, and even death itself. At Mass, we sing "Hosanna" in acknowledgement of the reality that Jesus Christ truly has the power to save and has offered the work of salvation through the paschal mystery.

Lectionary for Mass #37

Matthew 21:1–11

Isaiah 50:4–7

Psalm 22:8–9, 17–18, 19–20, 23–24 (2a)

Philippians 2:6–11

Matthew 26:14—27:66 or 27:11–54

Objectives

- To compare and contrast the kingship of Jesus with other concepts of kingship.

- To introduce and define the term *Hosanna*.

Preparation and Materials

- Read the Season Background, the lectionary readings, and the Scripture Background.

- Bookmark the appropriate readings (see page xvi) in the lectionary, children's lectionary, or Bible. Place the book in a convenient location for the leader.

- Write the words of dismissal on a card for the priest celebrant.

- Prepare the words of the song the children will sing as they gather in the space for the Liturgy of the Word.

- Select volunteers (older children or adults) to proclaim the readings.

- Display the responsorial psalm refrain lyrics.

- Display the Apostles' or Nicene Creed.

- Prepare intercessions for the Prayer of the Faithful adapted for the needs of the Church, world, oppressed or marginalized, and local community.

Prayer Leader Reflection Questions

>> **How are you spiritually preparing yourself for Holy Week?**

>> **How will you encourage and motivate the families you serve to participate in as many of the liturgies of Holy Week as possible?**

Procession

Following the Collect of the Mass, the priest celebrant picks up the lectionary and invites those who would like to participate in the Liturgy of the Word with children to come forward and gather in the center aisle. The people who will lead the children out and facilitate the Liturgy of the Word also come forward at this time. Holding the lectionary so that all can see, the priest celebrant sends the children forth using his own words or the following:

> *Priest*: **Beloved children of God, Jesus comes to us as king, but as a meek king, gentle and humble of heart. Everything you will hear him endure— his betrayal, suffering, and death—he endured for us. Go and listen to God's Word.**

The leader processes out holding the lectionary, and the children follow behind. The parish music minister may have selected a song of dismissal for the assembly to sing while the children leave. A good option is "The Word of God: Children's Dismissal" by M. D. Ridge and Timothy R. Smith (WLP/GIA).

Centering

Continue to sing the song of dismissal that the assembly sang as you left the church. Or sing "Hosanna, Son of God" (Marchionda), the refrain from "My God, My God" (Whitaker), or "Jesus, Remember Me" (Berthier), or have instrumental music playing as the children gather in the space for the Liturgy of the Word.

Place the lectionary on the ambo or lectern. Light the candle placed by the ambo or lectern, and then lead the following prayer:

> **God be in our minds and hearts as we gather in this Lenten season.**
> **May these Scriptures help us repent and be ready for Easter.**
> **Through Christ our Lord.**

> *Children:* **Amen.**

First Reading

Isaiah 50:4–7

Responsorial Psalm

Psalm 22:8–9, 17–18, 19–20, 23–24 (2a) *Sing the same musical setting that is used in your parish's celebration of the liturgy.*

Second Reading

Philippians 2:6–11

Gospel Acclamation

Sing the Gospel Acclamation used in your parish's celebration of the liturgy.

Gospel Reading

Matthew 26:14—27:66 or 27:11–54

Homily/Reflection

Today, unlike at almost any other Mass, we hear two Gospel readings. This is the first day of Holy Week. We remember together the moments before and up to when Jesus died. Listening to two different readings of the Gospel shows us two different ways we can look at Jesus as King, like two different vantage points from which to look at a painting or using two different telescopes to look at the same star. Jesus remains the same but our vision of him changes, and the different ways of seeing him help us to better see the whole. It also reminds us of two different days in the life of Jesus, the Sunday when he entered Jerusalem and the Friday when he died. We remember how in a matter of days, people in the city treated him in two very different ways.

You heard the first Gospel proclaimed at the beginning of Mass. As Jesus entered Jerusalem, people laid palm branches and even their own cloaks on the road in front of him. In Jesus' time, the roads were often made of dirt or perhaps of stones placed together. Walking on them would have made your feet dirty and dusty. The people saw how special Jesus was, and they would rather have their own clothes get filthy that Jesus' feet get dirty or dusty. They also shouted, "Hosanna in the highest." We have heard this word many, many times.

>> **Where have you heard this word before?** *[sung in church at the start of the Mass]*

This Hebrew word is often translated as, "Save us, please!" The people believed that Jesus had the power to save, the power that comes from the most high God.

In Jesus' time, many people expected that a king would come to their rescue, one who would look like the other kings of the world, only stronger and more powerful. They thought that the Kingdom would be a country that the king's army would protect so that no enemies could ever harm the people. The people of Israel experienced many years under others' domination. The Israelites were not always free to live peacefully and to worship God openly. We might be able to understand why someone would want a king to end this kind of oppression!

Jesus' kingship was different from what the people anticipated, though. Kings often wear crowns. Jesus wore a crown like other kings, but his crown had important differences. Jesus' crown was made of thorns. To others it looked ridiculous and to him it would have caused great pain. Kings often have a scepter, a staff that is a symbol of a king's great power, held in his strongest hand. Jesus was given a scepter. It was a reed. Reeds are hollow tall grass. They bend when they are pushed against, even if it is only by the wind. Jesus' scepter would have looked like no power at all.

When the people of the crowds saw what looked like Jesus' great weakness, as he hung on the cross, they said, "He saved others; he cannot save himself." What many did not know was that the very act of not saving himself was *how* he saved others. After he died, his true power showed itself. A great earthquake shook the ground and split rocks. Three days later, Jesus rose from the dead. His power is so great that it is over all the people, all the nations, all the earth and even over death itself.

Profession of Faith

Following the homily or reflection, the prayer leader invites everyone to stand to profess our faith. Together, sing or recite the Apostles' or Nicene Creed. Refer the children to the words of the prayer that you have displayed.

Prayer of the Faithful

Leader: **On this day we solemnly remember Jesus coming into the holy city of Jerusalem. We waved palm branches, sang Hosannas, and named Jesus as a servant of God. In trust, we turn to him in prayer. Please respond, "Lord, hear our prayer."**

May the Church always follow the example of Christ who gave himself selflessly and completely out of love, we pray: *Lord, hear our prayer.*

May all judges, lawmakers, and lawyers interpret the law with fairness, and work to protect the gift of life in all forms, we pray: *Lord, hear our prayer.*

May all who are imprisoned and those who have received an unjust sentence rely upon God's compassion, we pray: *Lord, hear our prayer.*

May those preparing for the waters of baptism at Easter spend this last week of preparation in prayer and contemplation, we pray: *Lord, hear our prayer.*

Invite other intercessions from the children, or add intercessions based on the current needs of the Church, the world, the oppressed or marginalized, and the local community. Conclude each of the children's petitions with **"we pray"** and invite the response **"Lord, hear our prayer."**

May all who have died accompany the Lord into Paradise, we pray: *Lord, hear our prayer.*

**Christ Jesus,
you suffered, died, and rose from the dead
so that we could share in the life that is stronger than death.
Grant the prayers that we offer with humble hearts.
Who live and reign with God the Father, in the unity of the
Holy Spirit,
God, for ever and ever.**

Children: **Amen.**

Quietly return with the children to the main assembly. Be mindful of children having difficulty finding their families.

Season Background for Easter Time

Understanding Easter Time

We are people of the Resurrection! We rejoice in the celebration of Jesus Christ's victory over death because we know it is the source of God's new life in us. This great feast continues for fifty days. Each Sunday during Easter Time we read about the first Christians and how their lives were dramatically changed by Christ's Resurrection. Ours are, too. Jesus promises that we will share in this life that is stronger than death. By his appearances to the disciples, we, too, are called to see Christ's presence in our own lives. His Ascension gives us our commission to spread the Good News to the ends of the earth. Pentecost is the reassurance that Jesus Christ does not leave us alone to do this work. The Spirit is always with us to comfort and guide us. Let us rejoice! Alleluia!

Liturgical Environment

We continue to focus on the image of the cross during Easter Time, but with new meaning. We rejoice that the cross is no longer a symbol of shame and death, but one of victory and new life! Keep the crucifix in your environment, perhaps surrounding its base with fresh flowers. Cover your lectern and other surfaces with white cloth. Display fresh flowers in your space throughout Easter Time. If some of the children are growing flowers in their gardens at home, you may want to invite them to bring flowers that can be placed in a special vase.

Overview of the Readings

First Readings   During Easter Time, you will notice a shift in the first readings. At this time of the liturgical year, they are from the New Testament Book of the Acts of the Apostles. The passages describe the life and growth of the early Church and how the Church witnessed to faith in Christ's Resurrection. On the Solemnity of the Ascension of the Lord, the first reading is always the account of the Ascension from Acts, which concludes with the question to the disciples about why they are still staring at the sky. This is a question that leads them to embrace the Spirit given to them at Pentecost and leads us today to discern how the Spirit leads us to live out our Christian mission. The first reading is one proclaimed in the Church on Pentecost for centuries. The account from the Acts of the Apostles narrates the dramatic coming of the Holy Spirit upon those gathered in the house, and how everyone, regardless of his or her native language, is able to hear everyone else speaking of God's mighty acts.

Responsorial Psalms   As Lent and Holy Week give way to Easter Time, the tone of the responsorial psalm changes. The joy of the Resurrection first celebrated at the Easter Vigil can be heard from Easter Sunday through Pentecost. Note that each Sunday of Easter Time, including Pentecost, includes the option for the refrain of the responsorial psalm to be "Alleluia." Choosing this option makes the celebration of the Resurrection palpable and obvious to the assembly.

The responsorial psalms as a whole during Easter Time communicate praise and thanksgiving for the works of God the Creator, joy for the Lord's Day, hope for seeing the goodness and the mercy of the Lord, and confidence that the Lord himself will show his followers the path to life and hear the prayers of his people. Interspersed with the joyful psalms is a repetition of Psalm 23 on the Fourth Sunday of Easter, also referred to as Good Shepherd Sunday, and a prayer for the Lord's mercy on the Fifth Sunday of Easter. On the Solemnity of the Ascension, Psalm 47 fittingly speaks of God mounting his throne and those around him shouting with joy. As the liturgical assemblies of today sing this psalm, they, too, shout for joy as they remember and celebrate Christ the Lord ascending to his throne at the right hand of the Father. The concluding responsorial psalm of Easter Time, sung on Pentecost, calls upon the Lord to send out his Spirit and renew the face of the earth. Our contemporary singing of this psalm gives voice to our belief that the Spirit the Lord sends will be present, always and everywhere, renewing the earth and her peoples.

Second Readings   Most of the Second Readings of Easter Time come from the pastoral letter 1 Peter. Written as an instruction to the newly baptized, its appropriateness to Easter Time is obvious. The Second Readings from 1 Peter are meant to carry forth the spirit of joyful faith and hope that is fundamental to Easter Time.

Only on the Solemnities of the Ascension and Pentecost do the Second Readings come from another New Testament work. On the Solemnity of the Ascension, the passage from Ephesians includes petitions for the Church as it spreads after Christ's Ascension. On Pentecost, the reading from 1 Corinthians leads those gathered as the Church today to reflect on the many diverse gifts that exist among them, and the unity that exists because of their common Baptism in Christ.

Gospel Readings   In the proclamation of the Gospel readings throughout Easter Time, we experience both joy and trepidation at the event of the Resurrection. As Easter Time progresses, our sense of joy continues while our awe and fear subside. We come to know the Risen Lord in the peace he brings, in the conversation on the way to Emmaus, in the meal he shares with two of his disciples, in the catch of a large number of fish, and in his call to Peter to tend his sheep. We learn from the readings from the Gospel according to John, interspersed with those from the Gospel according to Luke, that this Risen Lord is the gate and the Way, the Truth, and the Life. The excerpts from the Lord's discourse and prayer at the end of the Last Supper from John on the Fifth, Sixth, and Seventh Sundays of Easter show how deeply the Lord cares for those who follow him and will remain after him. He is the one who promises another Advocate on the Solemnity of Pentecost, when the Gospel tells of Jesus breathing the Holy Spirit upon the disciples.

April 9, 2023
Easter Sunday of the Resurrection of the Lord (Day)
Celebrate with Joy

 ## Scripture Background

Connections to Church Teaching and Tradition

- Jesus fulfills both the promises of the Old Testament and his promises (CCC, 652).

- Easter is the feast of feasts, the focal point of the church year (CCC, 1169–1171).

- Christ is alive in a new way after the resurrection (CCC, 554–556, 645–647, 999–1000).

Acts 10:34a, 37–43 Jesus' earthly ministry was limited mostly to Jews (see Matthew 15:24). At Jesus' Ascension, he commanded his followers to be his witnesses "to the ends of the earth" (Acts 1:8). In obedience to Christ's mandate, the Gospel moved beyond Israel's borders. Peter's offer of baptism to Cornelius, an uncircumcised Roman centurion, was a pivotal incident. Underlying the event were key questions: Did Christians have to obey Jewish dietary laws and practices? Could non-Jews become Christians without being circumcised? God prepared Peter to break through his narrow understanding of the law by giving him a vision of "unclean" animals that the Jews were forbidden to eat. God tells Peter, "What God has made clean, you must not call profane" (10:15). For the first time in Acts, Peter proclaims the kerygma to a non-Jew. As at the first Pentecost, the Spirit pours forth on all those listening.

Psalm 118:1–2, 16–17, 22–23 (24) Psalm 118 is the Great Hallel (Hebrew for "praise"), the last of the Hallel Psalms (Psalms 113–118), which recount God's deliverance of the Hebrew slaves from Egypt. Psalm 118 was sung at all major festivals. During the Feast of Tabernacles, it was a processional hymn on entering the Temple. The crowds that greeted Jesus as he entered Jerusalem sang, "Blessed is the one who comes in the name of the LORD" (v. 26, see Matthew 21:9). Jesus quoted Psalm 118: "The stone that the builders rejected has become the chief cornerstone" (v. 22) to describe his own rejection but ultimate victory. The Hallel Psalms were also sung during the Passover meal. Jesus and his disciples sang Psalm 118 before he went out to the garden of Gethsemane to face death.

Colossians 3:1–4 The early Christians regarded Baptism as a dying and a rising again. As the person was immersed in the waters, it was as if he or she were buried in death. As they emerged from the waters, it was like being resurrected to a new life. Therefore, Christians must rise from Baptism as different persons. Their thoughts must be set on the things of God and no longer concerned with the passing things of earth. This was not another worldliness in which Christians withdraw from the activities of this world; ethical principles follow that make it clear what was expected of newborn Christians (vv. 5–25). They would now view everything in light of eternity and no longer live as if this world was all that mattered.

Sequence: *Victimae paschali laudes* The Easter Sequence, *Victimae paschali laudes,* is a song of praise to the Paschal Victim that also reflects the Gospel account of Mary's encounter with the Risen Lord.

John 20:1–9 Two stories of the Resurrection were widely circulated in John's time. One story centered on the empty tomb; the other involved appearances of the Risen Lord. One of these stories involved Mary from Magdala, a fishing village on the Sea of Galilee. There is no basis for identifying her with the repentant sinner of Luke's Gospel (Luke 7:36–50). Mary was a faithful follower of Jesus and, along with Jesus' mother and other women, was a witness to his crucifixion and burial (John 19:25). In John's Gospel, she was the first to discover the empty tomb. She believed Jesus' body had been stolen, and she ran to report the news to Peter and John. Jewish law held that two men were required as witnesses; therefore, Mary could not serve as a witness. The two apostles rushed to the tomb. John arrives first, but out of respect for the elder apostle, waits for Peter to enter the tomb. They observe the burial clothes lying folded neatly, which refuted any claim that Jesus' body was stolen. Peter is slow to understand the meaning of the empty tomb, but John "saw and believed" (20:8). Even though they did not yet understand the Scripture that Jesus must rise from the dead, John served as the example for all "those who have not seen and yet have come to believe" (v. 29).

Matthew 28:1–10 Matthew's Gospel shows Mary Magdalene and "the other Mary" arriving at the tomb at a critical moment. An earthquake and an angel announce to the women, and to Matthew's audience, "He is not here, for he has been raised, as he said" (v. 6). The women are invited to see the emptiness of the tomb for themselves and then to "go quickly and tell his disciples" (v. 7). Like Mary in John's Gospel, the Marys in Matthew's account meet Jesus on their way, and he sends them forth as his messengers. Both the women and the disciples whom they tell are instructed to move beyond their immediate experience to the work Jesus still has for them to do in Galilee.

Preparation

The Gospel of Matthew describes the Easter morning scene as a drama that involves not only Jesus' followers, but also Roman soldiers and even creation itself. Regardless of the motivation of the women to return to Jesus' tomb, what they encountered was shocking and transformative. An earthquake and a dazzling angel announce that Jesus has risen. The women's initial fear did not trump their joy or prevent them from sharing the good news of this reality. Jesus shared his light and life with these women, with the disciples, and with us. We are invited to continue sharing this good news and to encounter the risen Lord ourselves.

Lectionary for Mass #42A

Acts 10:34a, 37–43

Psalm 118:1–2, 16–17, 22–23 (24)

Colossians 3:1–4 or 1 Corinthians 5:6b–8

Sequence: *Victimae paschali laudes*

John 20:1–9 or Matthew 28:1–10

Objectives

- To announce the very heart of the kerygma to the children: Jesus who died is risen! Alleluia!

- To situate the message that Jesus is risen in the context of a history of Christian testimony.

- To invite the children to share in the work of making this announcement to others.

Preparation and Materials

- Read the Season Background, the lectionary readings, and the Scripture Background.

- Bookmark the appropriate readings (see page xvi) in the lectionary, children's lectionary, or Bible. Place the book in a convenient location for the leader.

- Write the words of dismissal on a card for the priest celebrant.

- Prepare the words of the song the children will sing as they gather in the space for the Liturgy of the Word.

- Select volunteers (older children or adults) to proclaim the readings.

- Display the responsorial psalm refrain lyrics.

- Display the Apostles' or Nicene Creed.

- Prepare intercessions for the Prayer of the Faithful adapted for the needs of the Church, world, oppressed or marginalized, and local community.

Prayer Leader Reflection Questions

» **How does your belief that Jesus truly died and rose affect your life?**

» **What symbols of Easter resonate most with the children? Help them to differentiate from secular symbols of bunnies, chicks, and so on.**

Procession Following the Collect of the Mass, the priest celebrant picks up the lectionary and invites those who would like to participate in the Liturgy of the Word with children to come forward and gather in the center aisle. The people who will lead the children out and facilitate the Liturgy of the Word also come forward at this time. Holding the lectionary so that all can see, the priest celebrant sends the children forth using his own words or the following:

> *Priest*: **Dear children, today is a day of great joy! Jesus, who died, lives forever, and he gives us that same everlasting life. As you listen to the readings about his resurrection, remember that he is here and with you always. When you return to us, we will continue our celebration with great rejoicing. Go in the peace of Christ.**

The leader processes out holding the lectionary, and the children follow behind. The parish music minister may have selected a song of dismissal for the assembly to sing while the children leave. A good option is "The Word of God: Children's Dismissal" by M. D. Ridge and Timothy R. Smith (WLP/GIA).

Centering Continue to sing the song of dismissal that the assembly sang as you left the church. Or sing "Three Days" (M. D. Ridge), the refrain from "This Is the Day" (Haugen), or have instrumental music playing as the children gather in the space for the Liturgy of the Word.

Place the lectionary on the ambo or lectern. Light the candle placed by the ambo or lectern, and then lead the following prayer:

> **O God,**
> **you make this most holy feast full of the light of the glory of the**
> **Lord's resurrection.**
> **Allow our hearts to be open to your Word**
> **so that we may serve you completely.**
> **Through Jesus Christ our risen Lord.**

> *Children:* **Amen.**

First Reading Acts 10:34a, 37–43

Responsorial Psalm Psalm 118:1–2, 16–17, 22–23 (24) *Sing the same musical setting that is used in your parish's celebration of the liturgy.*

Second Reading Colossians 3:1–4 or 1 Corinthians 5:6b–8

Gospel Acclamation *Sing the Gospel Acclamation used in your parish's celebration of the liturgy.*

Gospel Reading John 20:1–9 or Matthew 28:1–10

Homily/Reflection [This reflection is intended to accompany the proclamation of Matthew 28:1–10.]

Alleluia! Praise God! Today is Easter Sunday, the most important day of our Church year, when we celebrate that Jesus is risen! He has brought his life and light, one that will never go out. As we celebrate this great feast together, we listen to the Gospel that tells us of the first people to discover this good news. They shared what they had heard and seen with others, who shared it with more and more people until today, when it has reached our own ears.

On that first Easter Sunday, Mary and Mary Magdalene came to the tomb. They came at dawn, the time when after the dark of night, the light of the sun begins to shine. Sometimes we speak of that time as when the light triumphs over the darkness.

≫ What happens to the darkness when a light shines?

Any place the light touches, the darkness disappears. It is destroyed. When Jesus rose, he brought with him a life that is stronger than death, a light that will never go out. This light and life transform everything. All of creation is affected; nothing is left out. As the women arrived at the tomb, there was an earthquake. The very earth itself shook. Then an angel appeared, whose appearance was like lightning.

» What might it be like to look at someone who shone like light?

We know how the people who were there that day felt. They were afraid! They did not know yet how meaningful what they were witnessing is. The angel told them: what Jesus said would happen has happened. He died and he has been raised. Today, as we hear and think about Christ's glorious resurrection at Mass, we have the benefit of so many people before us hearing and thinking about and sharing these words. But these women at the tomb were the first to hear this news! They were still afraid, but they were also joyful. When the angel instructed them to go and tell others this good news, their joy and courage were stronger than their fear and they were able to do just that. This message was not only for these women. It was meant to be shared. Later they met Jesus himself and he gave them the very same instruction. That message continued to be shared all over the world: Jesus who died is risen. Over time, the message was shared with more and more people until one day it reached our own ears. We have heard this good news and it is for us. Today, we understand what the disciples were witnessing over two thousand years ago. We know that the tomb was empty because our Lord did not let death hold him down. He was resurrected and glorified, as he promised. The disciples were seeing the first signs of Christ's resurrection from the dead. Our Lord had conquered death for all humanity. What Mary and the disciples witnessed that day is what we remember on this glorious Easter morning. By Christ's resurrection we too have hope in living forever with our God in heaven after our life on earth is complete.

Profession of Faith

Following the homily or reflection, the prayer leader invites everyone to stand to profess our faith. Together, sing or recite the Apostles' or Nicene Creed. Refer the children to the words of the prayer that you have displayed.

Prayer of the Faithful

Leader: **Christ is risen, and the power of his resurrection fills the world today with new life. Please respond, "Risen Lord, hear our prayer."**

For the Church, that she might always be a sign of the light and life of the risen Christ, we pray: *Risen Lord, hear our prayer.*

For the world, that everyone might experience the fullness of life that the risen Christ offers to us, we pray: *Risen Lord, hear our prayer.*

For all who live in fear, especially those who fear death, that hope in the resurrection may lead them to new life, we pray: *Risen Lord, hear our prayer.*

For all who have been baptized this Easter, that they may continue to grow in faith in our risen Christ, we pray: *Risen Lord, hear our prayer.*

Invite other intercessions from the children, or add intercessions based on the current needs of the Church, the world, the oppressed or marginalized, and the local community. Conclude each of the children's petitions with **"we pray"** and invite the response **"Risen Lord, hear our prayer."**

For all who have died, that they might enjoy the presence of the risen Christ, we pray: *Risen Lord, hear our prayer.*

**O Christ Jesus,
on the first Easter you defeated death
and unlocked for us the path to life forever with you.
Please make us new so that we would also rise up
in the light of life with you.
Who live and reign with God the Father,
in the unity of the Holy Spirit, God, for ever and ever.**

Children: **Amen.**

Quietly return with the children to the main assembly. Be mindful of children having difficulty finding their families.

April 16, 2023
Second Sunday of Easter/ Sunday of Divine Mercy

Christ Our Strength and Courage

 ## Scripture Background

Connections to Church Teaching and Tradition

- "The virtue of fortitude enables one to conquer fear, even fear of death, and to face trials and persecutions. It disposes one even to renounce and sacrifice his life in defense of a just cause. 'The Lord is my strength and my song.'[1] 'In the world you have tribulation; but be of good cheer, I have overcome the world'[2]" (CCC, 1808).

- "Spiritual progress tends toward even more intimate union with Christ. . . . God calls us all to this intimate union with him" (CCC, 2014).

Acts 2:42–47 This passage is one of four idealized descriptions of the early Christian communities that are present in Acts. Although they are idealized descriptions, they do highlight the ethical implications of what Jesus' mission and ministry demand. The communities "devoted themselves to the teaching of the apostles and to the communal life, to the breaking of bread and to the prayers" (v. 42). The teaching of the Apostles connected the communities with the eyewitness that Jesus instructed and guided. Communal life was integral to Jesus' ministry, a life of care and concern for the other, rooted in our common bond as members of God's family. Sharing of possessions was voluntary, not mandatory, and Christians were called to be mindful of the concern for those in need. The breaking of bread was a common designation for the Eucharistic meal that was held in homes, in which Jesus' presence and memory was kept alive. The prayers said in the Temple linked Jesus' Jewish roots with those of his followers. This was and still is a bold way to proclaim our new life in Christ. It attracted many new members then, and it should characterize Jesus' disciples to this day. In the Spirit, we make bold to live as Jesus modeled.

Psalm 118:2–4, 13–15, 22–24 (1) Psalm 118, also used on Easter Sunday, returns with a different refrain and a slightly different focus. We are invited to give thanks to the Lord, whose goodness and love are everlasting. This thanksgiving psalm of praise calls upon the liturgical assembly (house of Israel), the priests and liturgical ministers (house of Aaron), and all those who fear the Lord to acknowledge and affirm God's faithful and enduring covenant love (mercy). The psalmist has personally experienced God's love and saving help in times of trouble. Acknowledging God's saving help, the psalmist affirms the Lord as "my strength and my courage" (v. 14) leading to "joyful shout of victory" (v. 15). The one rejected was rescued by God and made the cornerstone. God's love and care have accomplished this, eliciting great joy. In its liturgical context, the community affirms that the Lord continues to love and save us this very day. We truly rejoice and are made glad in our loving God, who gives strength and courage today and always.

1 Peter 1:3–9 This passage begins with the "new birth to a living hope" (v. 3) that is ours in the Risen Christ. In Christ, we have salvation and an inheritance that lasts forever, kept for us in heaven till "the final time" (v. 5) when all will be revealed. Until then, the community's faith struggle with persecution and rejection is viewed as a time of testing and purification, ultimately producing a more genuine and purified faith to the glory of God. Even though the community has not seen the Lord, they love him and believe in him. This stance eventually leads to great joy and lasting hope as the community strives to attain the goal of their faith: ultimate union with God.

Easter Time celebrates this new birth in the Risen Christ with those baptized at the Easter Vigil, as well as with all the baptized. The Risen Christ is our strength and courage, enabling us to face any and all challenges to faith as we await ultimate union with God. Through our baptismal commitment, the Holy Spirit, the third Person of the Trinity, emboldens us to act in the Lord's name no matter the cost, living in love and enduring hope until the Lord returns.

John 20:19–31 This passage, proclaimed every Second Sunday of Easter, recounts two Easter appearances to the disciples. In both cases, the Risen Christ appears on the first day of

1 Psalm 118:14.
2 John 16:33.

the week. Fear and locked doors are dispelled by the Risen Christ, who stands in their midst and wishes them peace. Showing them his hands and his side, he assures them that it is he. Jesus commissions them just as the Father commissioned him, by breathing new life into them and emboldening them with the Holy Spirit. Their ministry is to be characterized by reconciliation and forgiveness.

Thomas is not present and refuses to believe until he sees and touches Jesus. This occasions Jesus' second appearance. Wishing them peace, the Risen Lord calls forth Thomas to touch, see, and believe. Thomas responds with the strongest affirmation of Jesus' identity in the entire Gospel: "My Lord and my God" (v. 28). Thomas believes because he has seen. Jesus blesses all those who have not seen and yet believe. We who have not seen and yet believe are made bold by the Risen Christ, through his gift of peace and the Spirit, to go out to the world and proclaim the Father's love, leading to forgiveness and reconciliation.

 # Preparation

Despite the testimony of other disciples, Thomas, who was not present, needed to experience the risen Christ with his own senses in order to believe. As Christians living two millennia from the time when Jesus walked the earth, we are like Thomas after that first Sunday. We have the opportunity to rely on testimony from those who have encountered the risen Christ. We can encounter him ourselves in a most particular way in the Eucharist. Living a life of faith changes us in these ways: living in loving community; being formed by the teaching that was handed on to us; serving others, and participating in prayer that includes liturgy and sacramental life.

Lectionary for Mass #43A

Acts 2:42–47

Psalm 118:2–4, 13–15, 22–24 (1)

1 Peter 1:3–9

John 20:19–31

Objectives

- To highlight the pattern in Scripture of God's announcements: beginning with fear in the presence of the divine, and then responding in joy, which leads to sharing the good news.

- To consider together how faith in the good news of Jesus Christ is marked by membership in loving Christian community, attentiveness to the Word of God and the teaching of the apostles, service, and prayer, which is most especially experienced in liturgy and sacraments.

Preparation and Materials

- Read the Season Background, the lectionary readings, and the Scripture Background.

- Bookmark the appropriate readings (see page xvi) in the lectionary, children's lectionary, or Bible. Place the book in a convenient location for the leader. Select volunteers to proclaim the readings.

- Write the words of dismissal on a card for the priest celebrant.

- Prepare the words of the gathering song the children will sing.

- Display the responsorial psalm refrain lyrics and display the Apostles' or Nicene Creed.

- Prepare intercessions for the Prayer of the Faithful.

- Note that the homily/reflection recalls the Gospel of Matthew, the Gospel ordinarily proclaimed at the Easter vigil, which has been selected in this work for the Gospel proclaimed last Easter Sunday. If the children remained in the assembly for Easter Sunday Mass, remember together the text of the Gospel of John in which Mary Magdalene, Peter, and the beloved disciple are the first witnesses of the resurrection.

Prayer Leader Reflection Questions

>> **How is your own life marked by membership in loving Christian community; attentiveness to the Word of God and the teaching of the apostles; service; and prayer, which is most especially experienced in liturgy and sacraments?**

>> **What would it be like to be able to touch the wounds of Christ?**

Procession

Following the Collect of the Mass, the priest celebrant picks up the lectionary and invites those who would like to participate in the Liturgy of the Word with children to come forward and gather in the center aisle. The people who will lead the children out and facilitate the Liturgy of the Word also come forward at this time. Holding the lectionary so that all can see, the priest celebrant sends the children forth using his own words or the following:

> *Priest*: **Children, blessed are those who have not seen Jesus but have believed. We have not seen him, but we can hear him speaking to us in the Scriptures. Hearing his voice helps us to have faith. Go now and listen to Jesus, who rose from the dead, that you may grow in faith.**

The leader processes out holding the lectionary, and the children follow behind. The parish music minister may have selected a song of dismissal for the assembly to sing while the children leave. A good option is "The Word of God: Children's Dismissal" by M. D. Ridge and Timothy R. Smith (WLP/GIA).

Centering

Continue to sing the song of dismissal that the assembly sang as you left the church. Or sing "This is the Feast of Victory" (various publishers), "Alleluia No. 1" (Fishel) or have instrumental music playing as the children gather in the space for the Liturgy of the Word.

Place the lectionary on the ambo or lectern. Light the candle placed by the ambo or lectern, and then lead the following prayer:

> **O God,
> each year as we celebrate this great feast of Easter,
> you light a fire of faith in your children.
> Allow our hearts to be open to your Word
> so that we may serve you completely.
> Through Christ our risen Lord.**

> *Children:* **Amen.**

First Reading

Acts 2:42–47

Responsorial Psalm

Psalm 118:2–4, 13–15, 22–24 (1) *Sing the same musical setting that is used in your parish's celebration of the liturgy.*

Second Reading

1 Peter 1:3–9

Gospel Acclamation

Sing the Gospel Acclamation used in your parish's celebration of the liturgy.

Gospel Reading

John 20:19–31

Homily/Reflection

Today, we gather together to celebrate this second week of Easter. The joy of the resurrection is so great that our celebration lasts more than one day. In fact, it lasts for forty-nine days, and on the fiftieth day, we will conclude our celebration of Easter with the great feast of Pentecost.

On Easter Sunday we heard from the Gospel of Matthew about that first morning when Mary and Mary Magdalene discovered that Jesus had indeed risen. Do you remember what we heard, how the earth itself shook and an angel appeared who was so bright and white that it would have been difficult to look? Nothing like this had ever happened before. These first witnesses were afraid, but they were also filled with so much joy! At first, though, it was only these few people who knew this great reality.

This week, we hear that more people saw and heard Jesus. The Gospel of John describes what happened on that evening, only a few hours after the tomb was discovered to be empty. The disciples had gathered together in a locked room, and Jesus appeared among them. But Jesus gave them a gift: "Peace be with you," he said and he breathed on them, giving them the gift of the Holy Spirit. Just like the first witnesses in the morning, the disciples were filled with so much joy to be with the Lord Jesus, whom they loved, once again. Just like the first witnesses in the morning had, these witnesses were given an instruction, too. They shared their testimony about this experience with others.

One person they told was Thomas. When he heard the other disciples telling him that Jesus had risen, he doubted them. He said he wanted to touch Jesus' wounds, to know it was truly him and that everything that had happened was real. The next week, when they were gathered again, Jesus appeared in the same way and Thomas now had the chance to see, to touch, to hear, and to believe. He called Jesus "my Lord and my God."

We are more like Thomas after that first Sunday than the second, aren't we? We cannot put our hands in Jesus' side. We cannot touch his hands and feet. Yet Jesus called us "blessed." After Thomas confessed Jesus as Lord and God, Jesus said, "Blessed are those who have not seen and have believed." That is referring to us. We have received the message, the good news that Jesus is risen, and like the witnesses at the tomb, like the disciples gathered on that first Sunday night, we also have great joy. The letter of Peter describes this by saying we "rejoice with an indescribable and glorious joy" (1 Peter 1:8).

Living as a person of faith changed Thomas. It made him able to see who Jesus really is and to announce it. Living as people of faith changes us, too. It changes anyone who can say like Thomas that Jesus is "my Lord and my God." How? Today's first reading tells us what our lives look like when we live as true believers. We live in loving community with one another. That means taking care of those around us and sharing with people who do not have enough. It means continuing to grow in knowledge about the one in whom we believe through the Word of God and Church teaching. It means praying regularly. We do this together in a most particular way in our celebration of the Mass, when we touch and taste the Body and Blood of Christ.

Profession of Faith

Following the homily or reflection, the prayer leader invites everyone to stand to profess our faith. Together, sing or recite the Apostles' or Nicene Creed. Refer the children to the words of the prayer that you have displayed.

Prayer of the Faithful

Leader: **As we continue to celebrate the resurrection, we are confident that our risen Lord intercedes for us. Please respond, "Risen Lord, hear our prayer."**

That the Church faithfully witness to the resurrection of Jesus Christ, we pray: *Risen Lord, hear our prayer.*

That Christ's gift of peace may settle in the hearts of all people, we pray: *Risen Lord, hear our prayer.*

That those who doubt or struggle with faith may know God's love and presence, we pray: *Risen Lord, hear our prayer.*

That all who have been baptized this Easter may continue to grow in faith in our risen Christ, we pray: *Risen Lord, hear our prayer.*

Invite other intercessions from the children, or add intercessions based on the current needs of the Church, the world, the oppressed or marginalized, and the local community. Conclude each of the children's petitions with **"we pray"** and invite the response **"Risen Lord, hear our prayer."**

That all who have died may live with God forever in heaven, we pray: *Risen Lord, hear our prayer.*

O Jesus,
your mercy lasts forever.
Help us to grow as your people and increase in our minds and hearts
the risen life we share with you.
Who live and reign with God the Father,
in the unity of the Holy Spirit, God, for ever and ever.

Children: **Amen.**

Quietly return with the children to the main assembly. Be mindful of children having difficulty finding their families.

April 23, 2023
Third Sunday of Easter
Recognized in Bread Broken

 ## Scripture Background

Connections to Church Teaching and Tradition

- Jesus' appearances after his Resurrection most clearly reveal the Trinity, the fundamental mystery, and our destiny (CCC, 65–66, 638–655).

- Jesus' Resurrection is both a historical and a transcendent event, a work of the Trinity offering salvation to all (CCC, 639, 648, 655).

- Church charitable organizations are responsible for reinforcing members so that through their words, silence, and example they may be witnesses to Christ (DCE, 31).

Acts 2:14, 22–33 Here is another summary of the early Christian Gospel, courtesy of Luke. Peter's first speech, given on the day of Pentecost, like the speech we read last week, is tailored to fit both Peter's audience (Jews from all over the empire who had made pilgrimages to Jerusalem for the festival) and Luke's readers (gentile Christians and Christian sympathizers). The summary resembles the summary we saw on Easter Day: God was at work in the ministry of Jesus. According to God's plan as laid out in Scripture, Jesus was handed over for execution and was raised on the third day, also according to God's plan. Now Jesus is at the right hand of the Father. The Apostles, Peter says, are witnesses to these things through the power of the Spirit they have just been given. To emphasize his point, Peter quotes Psalm 16, citing King David as another witness.

Peter's words point out two very different responses to Jesus. The religious leaders saw the mighty deeds of Jesus but did not recognize him. They believed Jesus to be a threat, and they conspired with the Romans to have him killed. The Apostles, on the other hand, not only saw Jesus but also recognized him. They even ate and drank with him following his Resurrection. Their response is faithful witness, full of the Holy Spirit. How will we respond to Jesus? What will our witness be?

Psalm 16:1–2, 5, 7–8, 9–10, 11 (11a) Tradition has attributed this psalm to King David, and Luke follows that tradition in our Gospel today. However, it is more likely that a Levite or other temple functionary wrote it. Either way, the psalm powerfully expresses trust in God's care. The psalmist does not request deliverance from what is clearly a life-threatening situation. Instead, he asks for God's protection. Using images that call to mind God's gift of the Promised Land, the psalmist proclaims trust in God. He recalls God's goodness to him and his own faithfulness to God and his Law. The psalmist is so confident of God's protection that he says God will never let him see corruption.

1 Peter 1:17–21 The author of 1 Peter again addresses his congregation of "exiles." This time, he is more explicit about their alienation. Believers are strangers to this world, he says. Having been redeemed (that is, brought out of slavery), they no longer belong to the world. Having been purified by the Blood of Christ, they no longer fit. Instead, their hope and faith are in God, who raised Jesus from the dead and glorified him.

In Christ, God has delivered us from the past. Christ's Death and Resurrection have forever freed us from the ways of life that once took us away from God. How shall we respond to this grace? We are to be a holy people. For 1 Peter, that means living our lives in reverence for God. It means remembering the high price Christ paid for our deliverance. It also means obeying the truth; and the truth, the author says, is love.

Luke 24:13–35 The story of the road to Emmaus illustrates how hard Jesus works to make us aware. No wonder he calls the disciples "slow of heart." They had read the Scriptures, which said the Messiah would suffer and then be vindicated. They had heard Jesus say he would return on the third day. They had heard the witness of the women. The Risen Christ was right there with them, explaining the Scriptures, yet they did not recognize him. Perhaps their grief kept them from seeing Jesus. Perhaps their fear blinded them. Or perhaps they did not recognize Jesus because they were looking for someone else, someone who would "restore Israel." But the minute Jesus broke bread, their eyes were opened. They saw their Risen Savior.

God has given us many opportunities to recognize the Risen Christ too. Like those disciples on the road to Emmaus, we also have the witness of Scripture to help us see. We have Jesus' own words to help us recognize him. Most of all, we have the Eucharist, where through the presence of the assembly, the proclamation and preaching of the word, and the breaking of the bread, the Risen Christ meets us. Grief and disappointment, fear and false expectations may blur our vision at times, but even then we can always be sure that Jesus is with us.

 # Preparation

The disciples were deeply sad was they walked on the road to Emmaus after the death of Jesus. They encountered a stranger, who seemed not to recognize the reason for their sadness. Nonetheless they listened to him breaking open Scripture for them. Then when he broke bread with them, they truly recognized that this stranger was in fact Christ the Lord. We too are disciples who can listen to the breaking open of the Word in order to understand more fully the good news of Jesus Christ. At Mass, we too experience the breaking of the bread and encounter Jesus' very self.

Lectionary for Mass #46A

Acts 2:14, 22–33

Psalm 16:1–2, 5, 7–8, 9–10, 11 (11a)

1 Peter 1:17–21

Luke 24:13–35

Objectives

- To lift up the Mass, where the bread is broken, as a place of most intimate encounter with Jesus Christ.

- To draw a connection between encountering Jesus in the Word (Liturgy of the Word) and encountering Jesus at the table (Liturgy of the Eucharist).

Preparation and Materials

- Read the Season Background, the lectionary readings, and the Scripture Background.

- Bookmark the appropriate readings (see page xvi) in the lectionary, children's lectionary, or Bible. Place the book in a convenient location for the leader.

- Write the words of dismissal on a card for the priest celebrant.

- Prepare the words of the song the children will sing as they gather in the space for the Liturgy of the Word.

- Select volunteers (older children or adults) to proclaim the readings.

- Display the responsorial psalm refrain lyrics.

- Display the Apostles' or Nicene Creed.

- Prepare intercessions for the Prayer of the Faithful adapted for the needs of the Church, world, oppressed or marginalized, and local community.

- Prepare an image of Sacred Heart of Jesus.

Prayer Leader Reflection Questions

>> **Have you ever felt alone, as if God was not with you? How would you help yourself or someone else with that struggle?**

>> **When have you noticed Christ's presence in your life?**

Procession

Following the Collect of the Mass, the priest celebrant picks up the lectionary and invites those who would like to participate in the Liturgy of the Word with children to come forward and gather in the center aisle. The people who will lead the children out and facilitate the Liturgy of the Word also come forward at this time. Holding the lectionary so that all can see, the priest celebrant sends the children forth using his own words or the following:

> *Priest*: **Dear children, Jesus comes near to us and walks with us, though we might not recognize him. However, if we listen attentively, we can hear him speaking to us in the Scriptures. Go now and listen to his voice, and when you come back, we will rejoice with you in his never-failing presence.**

The leader processes out holding the lectionary, and the children follow behind. The parish music minister may have selected a song of dismissal for the assembly to sing while the children leave. A good option is "The Word of God: Children's Dismissal" by M. D. Ridge and Timothy R. Smith (WLP/GIA).

Centering

Continue to sing the song of dismissal that the assembly sang as you left the church. Or sing the refrain from "You Will Show Me the Path of Life" (Haugen), or "Joyous Cup" (Alonso), or have instrumental music playing as the children gather in the space for the Liturgy of the Word.

Place the lectionary on the ambo or lectern. Light the candle placed by the ambo or lectern, and then lead the following prayer:

> **O God,
> may we have new joy as your adopted children during this Easter Time.
> Allow our hearts to be open to your Word so that we may serve
> you completely.
> Through Christ our risen Lord.**

Children: **Amen.**

First Reading

Acts 2:14, 22–33

Responsorial Psalm

Psalm 16:1–2, 5, 7–8, 9–10, 11 (11a) *Sing the same musical setting that is used in your parish's celebration of the liturgy.*

Second Reading

1 Peter 1:17–21

Gospel Acclamation

Sing the Gospel Acclamation used in your parish's celebration of the liturgy.

Gospel Reading

Luke 24:13–35

Homily/Reflection

Alleluia, Jesus Christ is risen! Today, we listen once again to a Gospel about what took place on that first Sunday, that first Easter.

» What happened on that morning at Jesus' tomb?

We listen again to the events of the evening after the women had found the tomb empty in the morning. We hear about a group of disciples who cared deeply about Jesus. They knew the women had discovered the tomb empty but did not yet understand what had happened to Jesus. Jesus' disciples watched their friend whom they loved and hoped in suffer terribly and die. Then things seemed to get worse. Since they did not understand that Jesus had risen, they could only wonder what had happened to Jesus' body. Had someone stolen it, perhaps? When they met a person traveling on the road, they did not recognize that this stranger was the risen Lord. But they recognized that this person knew the Word of God. Their companion helped them to remember the particular ways that God had shown and told that the Messiah would suffer and would enter into glory. He helped them to understand words of the Bible they had heard but not yet understood. The presence of the risen Lord enabled them to know and understand. They felt something as they were walking that they only later realized: they felt their hearts burning.

>> **What might it be like to feel your heart burn? How does it feel to have so much love for your mom or dad or baby brother or sister?** *(Show image of Sacred Heart of Jesus and explain that the burning heart represents Christ's great love for humanity.)*

When they stopped for the night and shared a meal together, this person whom they did not recognize did very particular things that helped the disciples to recognize the resurrected Jesus. He took bread, broke it, blessed it, and shared it. Do these actions sound familiar? We heard these words on Holy Thursday and we hear them at every Mass. These were actions Jesus did when he gave himself in the gift of the Eucharist, the gift of his very self under the form of bread and wine. Once again, the disciples met their Lord in the breaking of the bread, and it was then that they recognized that it was him.

The disciples asked themselves, "Were not our hearts burning?" Even without knowing with their minds or their eyes, they recognized him in their hearts. The feeling was like an inner fire. It is not always clear at first that God is with us, speaking to us. But sometimes, when we take the time to consider our own experiences, we might realize that our own hearts were burning in the presence of the Lord. In order to truly recognize him, perhaps we can do as the disciples did and listen closely to the Word of God. We can be particularly attentive to Jesus' own words. We can gather together and experience the breaking of the bread. Although the Lord is hidden under the signs of the bread and wine, we still recognize him in the Eucharist. We can be with our Lord Jesus.

Profession of Faith

Following the homily or reflection, the prayer leader invites everyone to stand to profess our faith. Together, sing or recite the Apostles' or Nicene Creed. Refer the children to the words of the prayer that you have displayed.

Prayer of the Faithful

Leader: **Christ walks with us every day on our journey as disciples. Our hearts burn within us as we listen to Jesus Christ, who teaches us to remember the needs of others. Please respond, "Risen Lord, hear our prayer."**

May our Church be always open to the Scriptures and break the bread in places where the Lord is rejected, we pray to the Lord: *Risen Lord, hear our prayer.*

May missionaries and all who spread the good news about Jesus throughout the world feel renewed and hopeful, we pray to the Lord: *Risen Lord, hear our prayer.*

May people who suffer in mind, body, or spirit experience divine healing and new strength, we pray to the Lord: *Risen Lord, hear our prayer.*

May all who have been baptized this Easter continue to grow in faith in our risen Christ, we pray to the Lord: *Risen Lord, hear our prayer.*

Invite other intercessions from the children, or add intercessions based on the current needs of the Church, the world, the oppressed or marginalized, and the local community. Conclude each of the children's petitions with **"we pray to the Lord"** and invite the response **"Risen Lord, hear our prayer."**

May God's light shine perpetually on those who have died, we pray to the Lord: *Risen Lord, hear our prayer.*

O Christ Jesus,
hear the children who call to you
and grant us your saving grace.
Who live and reign with God the Father,
in the unity of the Holy Spirit, God, for ever and ever.

Children: **Amen.**

Quietly return with the children to the main assembly. Be mindful of children having difficulty finding their families.

April 30, 2023
Fourth Sunday of Easter
The Voice of the Shepherd

 ## Scripture Background

Connections to Church Teaching and Tradition

- Jesus is the way, the truth, and the life (NDC, 1).
- Jesus is the Good Shepherd (LG, 5, 6; CCC, 754, 764, 2158).

Acts 2:14a, 36–41 Luke has Peter close his Pentecost speech on a climactic note. Overcome, the crowd demands to know, "What are we to do?" This gives Luke the opportunity to introduce some of his favorite themes. "Repent, and be baptized," Peter says. "Be baptized for the forgiveness of your sins, and you will receive the Holy Spirit" (v. 38). This promise is for everyone, even future generations. Luke tells us that more than three thousand people were added to the Church that day. They devoted themselves to the Apostles' teaching, to fellowship, and to the breaking of bread.

Although Luke does not use the shepherd image, we see hints of Jesus as the Good Shepherd. Jesus is obedient to God, faithful as a shepherd, and God has made him Messiah of all nations. Jesus not only keeps his "flock" of believers safe, but he also rescues us from sin. He not only feeds his believers, but he also nurtures us with the gift of the Holy Spirit.

Psalm 23:1–3a, 3b–4, 5, 6 (1) This psalm seems so calm and gentle that it is easy to imagine the psalmist sitting undisturbed in reverent meditation. But if we read between the lines, a different image emerges. The psalmist is running from enemies. He may even have taken refuge in the Temple, where he could have even eaten in front of his adversaries, who would have been, there, legally unable to touch him.

It is no surprise, then, that the psalmist dreams of God as a perfect shepherd. The shepherd had to be strong to defend the flock and powerful enough to provide them with nourishment. With God as his shepherd, the psalmist says, he has everything he needs. He fears no evil, for God leads him to places where he can get food and water in peace. His cup overflows.

Today we celebrate Jesus as the embodiment of the psalmist's hope. We celebrate God's protecting, guiding, and nurturing power. Even when we experience distress or danger, we can still celebrate Jesus, who shepherds us and leads us in "right paths."

1 Peter 2:20b–25 At first, the author's advice seems to invite us to become doormats. He specifically speaks to Christians who are slaves (as many were), saying, "Suffer patiently." He reminds them that Christ did not fight back even when his enemies were killing him. Instead, Jesus endured gracefully, trusting that God would vindicate him in the end. But the author of 1 Peter is not talking about just any suffering; he is talking about unjust suffering, the kind that comes because we have done what is right in the face of evil. When we face that kind of suffering, the best thing to do is be patient and, like Jesus, not return insults but trust God.

In this reading, the Good Shepherd turns out to be a vulnerable lamb who endures all patiently so that evil and violence might be shown for what they really are—sins against God. Through this, 1 Peter assures us, we have been healed. We once strayed like lost sheep, but now we are safe in the care of the "shepherd and guardian of our souls."

John 10:1–10 John 10:1–18 is probably the closest thing we find to a parable in John's Gospel. John's "parable," however, is really an extended metaphor. Indeed, John weaves several metaphors together. His purpose here is to contrast Jesus with others who claim religious authority. The Pharisees are the most obvious target, but John hints at others too, most notably bandits (anti-Roman revolutionaries who were quite popular in Galilee and were often hailed as messiahs). John may even have had in mind certain Church leaders in his own time. These, he says bluntly, are thieves and predators.

While false leaders are only out for their own interests, Jesus looks out for the interests of those who believe in him. Like a good shepherd, he knows each of his flock by name. And like the door of the sheepfold (where sheep were kept safe overnight), Jesus guards his flock and protects them from predators. This reading reminds us that Jesus is not some distant ruler but a nearby shepherd who cares for us deeply enough to give his life for us.

 # Preparation

The shepherd is familiar, loving, providing, and sustaining. The shepherd is the gatekeeper. If we follow the shepherd, we will be on the right path and the shepherd will lead us home. The Fourth Sunday of Easter is often called Good Shepherd Sunday because the Gospel reading invites us to reflect on different aspects of Jesus as the Good Shepherd. In today's Gospel, Jesus promises us an abundance of life. We are called to listen to our Lord, and our ears must be primed for his voice. Rejecting the voices of strangers and false teachers, we focus on the voice of the good, kind shepherd who is Jesus.

Lectionary for Mass #49A

Acts 2:14a, 36–41

Psalm 23:1–3a, 3b–4, 5, 6 (1)

1 Peter 2:20b–25

John 10:1–10

Objectives

- To help children understand that Jesus Christ cares for us as a Good Shepherd.

- To teach them how to listen for Jesus' voice.

Preparation and Materials

- Read the Season Background, the lectionary readings, and the Scripture Background.

- Bookmark the appropriate readings (see page xvi) in the lectionary, children's lectionary, or Bible. Place the book in a convenient location for the leader.

- Write the words of dismissal on a card for the priest celebrant.

- Prepare the words of the song the children will sing as they gather in the space for the Liturgy of the Word.

- Select volunteers (older children or adults) to proclaim the readings.

- Display the responsorial psalm refrain lyrics.

- Display the Apostles' or Nicene Creed.

- Prepare intercessions for the Prayer of the Faithful adapted for the needs of the Church, world, oppressed or marginalized, and local community.

Prayer Leader Reflection Questions

» **Where in your life do you need God's protection and guidance?**

» **In what ways does your parish nurture your faith?**

Procession

Following the Collect of the Mass, the priest celebrant picks up the lectionary and invites those who would like to participate in the Liturgy of the Word with children to come forward and gather in the center aisle. The people who will lead the children out and facilitate the Liturgy of the Word also come forward at this time. Holding the lectionary so that all can see, the priest celebrant sends the children forth using his own words or the following:

> *Priest:* **Dear children, the Lord Jesus knows each one of you and calls you by name. Hear his voice in today's readings and follow him, for though he is the Shepherd, he is as gentle as the sheep. Go in peace.**

The leader processes out holding the lectionary, and the children follow behind. The parish music minister may have selected a song of dismissal for the assembly to sing while the children leave. A good option is "The Word of God: Children's Dismissal" by M. D. Ridge and Timothy R. Smith (WLP/GIA).

Centering

Continue to sing the song of dismissal that the assembly sang as you left the church. Or sing the refrain from "Shepherd Me, O God" (Haugen), or "The Lord Is My Shepherd" (Alstott), or have instrumental music playing as the children gather in the space for the Liturgy of the Word.

Place the lectionary on the ambo or lectern. Light the candle placed by the ambo or lectern, and then lead the following prayer:

> **Living God,**
> **bless us with open minds and hearts to listen to the good news.**
> **Help us rejoice fully throughout Easter Time.**
> **Through Christ our risen Lord.**

> *Children:* **Amen.**

First Reading

Acts 2:14a, 36–41

Responsorial Psalm

Psalm 23:1–3a, 3b–4, 5, 6 (1) *Sing the same musical setting that is used in your parish's celebration of the liturgy.*

Second Reading

1 Peter 2:20b–25

Gospel Acclamation

Sing the Gospel Acclamation used in your parish's celebration of the liturgy.

Gospel Reading

John 10:1–10

Homily/Reflection

» **Do any of you children have pets?**

» **Do you help take care of your pets by feeding them, giving them water, or by keeping their beds clean and washed? Do you brush your pets, or play with them?**

We love our pets and enjoy their company. They are living creatures and because they are in our care, we have to keep them healthy and well. It is our responsibility to take care of everything in creation, including our animals.

Many years ago in Jesus' time, people had sheep. Raising sheep meant that people could have wool and meat. Those who took good care of their sheep were called shepherds. The sheep were not pets, but shepherds appreciated all that the sheep gave them to live. The wool could be used to make cloth and the meat could feed a family. In the villages, the sheep would be kept inside fences for safety reasons, especially at nighttime. The fences kept the sheep away from wolves or thieves. Shepherds were very careful to guard their sheep from any harm.

In today's Gospel, our Good Shepherd, Jesus, loves us very much, and he wants what is best for us. Jesus wants us to be safe; he wants us to be away from anything that might hurt us or hurt our souls. Jesus is like the fence around the sheep—the fence around the sheep that keeps out thieves and wolves. Jesus wants us to stay close to him because he loves us.

In last week's reading the Apostles were with Jesus but didn't recognize him until he broke bread with them. In this reading, Jesus is telling us that we, his sheep, recognize his voice. We are able to hear Jesus and know it is him. Being able to understand Jesus' call is very important. We hear about false teachers or "strangers." These are people who are not really representing Jesus in what they do or say. We do not want to listen to false teachers, we want to listen to Jesus.

When the Gospel of John talks about Jesus as the Good Shepherd, it is a reference to Jesus loving us very much. A good shepherd takes such good care of his sheep that when he speaks and calls to them, they know his voice. Now, we cannot hear Jesus' actual voice with our ears. When we say that we "hear Jesus' voice," that means we hear and understand what Jesus asks of us through the Church's teaching and Scripture. The good shepherd would go so far as to die for his sheep. This is exactly what Jesus did for us. Jesus offered himself as sacrifice so that we would not have to suffer for our sins. Instead of letting us wander off and be hurt by wolves or thieves, Jesus protects us through his sacrifice on the cross and his teaching. Jesus is truly the Good Shepherd!

You are so precious to God that he knows each of you by name. Once you were baptized, you became a child of God. Your parents are raising you to know the voice of Jesus so well that you will always listen to him. You listen to the Word of God each week when we meet for children's Liturgy of the Word. You pray to Jesus each night before you go to bed. You recognize when someone else is acting in a peaceful, Christlike way. So the best part of knowing Jesus as our Good Shepherd is that we don't have to feel scared. We can count on Jesus to be there for us all through our life.

Profession of Faith

Following the homily or reflection, the prayer leader invites everyone to stand to profess our faith. Together, sing or recite the Apostles' or Nicene Creed. Refer the children to the words of the prayer that you have displayed.

Prayer of the Faithful

Leader: **Grateful for our faith, we now bring our prayers to God. Please respond, "Good Shepherd, hear us."**

For the pope and all God's shepherds on earth, that they may faithfully imitate Christ, the Good Shepherd, in accompanying God's people, we pray to the Lord: *Good Shepherd, hear us.*

For those in caring professions, that the Lord's compassion may be visible in them, we pray to the Lord: *Good Shepherd, hear us.*

For those who are ill and suffer, that they may experience God's healing power, we pray to the Lord: *Good Shepherd, hear us.*

For all who have been baptized this Easter, that they may continue to grow in faith in our risen Christ, we pray to the Lord: *Good Shepherd, hear us.*

Invite other intercessions from the children, or add intercessions based on the current needs of the Church, the world, the oppressed or marginalized, and the local community. Conclude each of the children's petitions with **"we pray to the Lord"** and invite the response **"Good Shepherd, hear us."**

For all who have gone before us in faith, that they may enter through Christ into paradise, we pray to the Lord: *Good Shepherd, hear us.*

**Mighty God,
you sent your Son, the Good Shepherd,
who leads us to the still waters and rich pastures of heaven.
Grant what we ask through Christ our Lord.**

Children: **Amen.**

Quietly return with the children to the main assembly. Be mindful of children having difficulty finding their families.

May 7, 2023
Fifth Sunday of Easter

Jesus Is the Way, the Truth, and the Life

 ## Scripture Background

Connections to Church Teaching and Tradition

❋ "Faith . . . means abiding with [Jesus] in the Father who, in him, so loves us that he abides with us" (CCC, 2614).

❋ "The first and last point of reference of this catechesis will always be Jesus Christ himself, who is 'the way, and the truth, and the life'[1]" (CCC, 1698).

❋ "[Christ] tells us who man truly is. . . . He shows us the way, and this way is the truth. He himself is both the way and the truth, and therefore he is also the life which all of us are seeking. He also shows us the way beyond death; only someone able to do this is a true teacher of life" (SS, 6).

Acts 6:1–7 This Sunday's reading from the Acts of the Apostles twice tells us that the number of disciples continued to increase. That increase created the need to appoint new ministers, or deacons. Luke says the Greek-speaking Christians complained that their poor were not being treated as well as those who spoke Aramaic. In response, the Twelve convened a formal assembly and announced that because their first responsibility was to preach, others should serve at the table of the Lord. Among those who were appointed were Stephen, who would become the first martyr, and a Greek-speaking man named Nicholas, who would have been a convert to Judaism before he joined the young Christian community. The task of the seven newly named ministers was to preside at the table and to ensure that all the poor received what they needed.

Psalm 33:1–2, 4–5, 18–19 (22) This hymn is addressed to the faithful, reminding them of the many reasons they have to praise God. Their God is absolutely trustworthy; the signs of God's kindness are everywhere to be seen. Most of all, God never stops watching over them and caring for them.

1 Peter 2:4–9 Peter addresses this letter to people he describes as sojourners: Gentile Christians who already know persecution. Peter encourages them to keep turning to the Lord, and even more than that, to imitate him. Although they are Gentiles, Peter's message is so full of Hebrew images that he seems to be passing the vocation of Israel on to the Christian community. Peter's four descriptions of the diverse community insist on one central reality: they are called not only as individuals but as a people. They are a priesthood, a people of God whose vocation is to spread the Word of God. Like their Master, they will be rejected, but built on him they will also be a spiritual house, a dwelling place of God forever.

John 14:1–12 In this selection from Jesus' last discourse, two disciples ask questions to which they should already know the answers. As a matter of fact, the two questions are simply variations on the same theme. Thomas asks about "the way" (v. 5), and then Philip says, "Master, show us the Father" (John 14:8). Both requests indicate that the disciples do not understand that Jesus is the Way. They do not grasp the fact that to see him is to see the Father.

In typical fashion, John uses uncomprehending characters to allow Jesus to explain something far deeper than they imagined. In the first section of the reading, Jesus explains his departure and the fact that he will return for his own. Then, he reminds them that they know the way to the life he is promising. Thomas disagrees, seemingly asking for a road map for Jesus' upcoming journey. To that, Jesus responds: "I am the way and the truth and the life."

The image of "the way" has a rich scriptural history. The word occurs over 150 times in the psalms, beginning with Psalm 1, which says, "Blessed is the man who does not walk . . . in the way of sinners," (v. 1) and "the LORD knows the way of the just, / but the way of the wicked leads to ruin" (v. 6). Jesus' way is the way of the just, a way of life that the disciples are to imitate.

While imitation characterizes the ordinary relationship between a disciple and a teacher, Jesus' statement has additional implications. In John 8:31–32, Jesus invited his disciples to remain in his word so that they would know the truth that would set them free. As he stood before Pilate, Jesus said, "Everyone who belongs to the truth listens to my voice" (18:37). The truth of which Jesus speaks comes from taking him in, listening, and being freed by him.

---

1 John 14:6.

The prologue to John (1:1–14), describes Jesus as the source of life. In chapter 6, Jesus says "I am the bread of life" (John 6:35), and later on he identifies himself as "the resurrection and the life" (John 11:25). The life he offers is nourishment for the present and an everlasting future.

Jesus' statement "I am the way and the truth and the life" (John 14:6) is a summary of who he is for his disciples: the ones who heard the words and all those who would come after. Jesus is the "way" not simply as an example, but much more because he dwells in the disciples as source of life and truth. Later, in 15:1–10, he will describe that indwelling as akin to a vine and its branches. To accept Jesus as our way, truth, and life means to open ourselves to his dwelling in us. It is a communion that could hardly be more intimate.

Preparation

The letter of Peter offers the image of stone as a way of understanding the identity of Jesus Christ. He is the cornerstone. All else is oriented to him. Although stone is often perceived as hard and cold, the epistle describes Jesus Christ as a living stone. Not everyone who hears the good news of Jesus Christ appreciates it as good, and to those people, Jesus may be a stumbling block. For Christians, living a life of faith involves construction of the self in such a way that we might be temples—places for God to dwell.

Lectionary for Mass #52A

Acts 6:1–7

Psalm 33:1–2, 4–5, 18–19 (22)

1 Peter 2:4–9

John 14:1–12

Objectives

- To explore the image of "stone" as revealing aspects of Jesus Christ's identity.

- To consider how we might invite God to dwell in us.

Preparation and Materials

- Read the Season Background, the lectionary readings, and the Scripture Background.

- Bookmark the appropriate readings (see page xvi) in the lectionary, children's lectionary, or Bible. Place the book in a convenient location for the leader.

- Write the words of dismissal on a card for the priest celebrant.

- Prepare the words of the song the children will sing as they gather in the space for the Liturgy of the Word.

- Select volunteers (older children or adults) to proclaim the readings.

- Display the responsorial psalm refrain lyrics.

- Display the Apostles' or Nicene Creed.

- Prepare intercessions for the Prayer of the Faithful adapted for the needs of the Church, world, oppressed or marginalized, and local community.

Prayer Leader Reflection Questions

>> Jesus assures us, "In my Father's house there are many places." When you think of Jesus preparing a place specifically for you, how does it make you feel?

>> How might you allow yourself to be built into a spiritual house in which God dwells?

Procession

Following the Collect of the Mass, the priest celebrant picks up the lectionary and invites those who would like to participate in the Liturgy of the Word with children to come forward and gather in the center aisle. The people who will lead the children out and facilitate the Liturgy of the Word also come forward at this time. Holding the lectionary so that all can see, the priest celebrant sends the children forth using his own words or the following:

> *Priest*: **Children, we now give you your own time to listen to today's readings, to hear Jesus' promise that he will come and take us to himself and give us a home forever. Go in peace.**

The leader processes out holding the lectionary, and the children follow behind. The parish music minister may have selected a song of dismissal for the assembly to sing while the children leave. A good option is "The Word of God: Children's Dismissal" by M. D. Ridge and Timothy R. Smith (WLP/GIA).

Centering

Continue to sing the song of dismissal that the assembly sang as you left the church. Or sing the refrain from "Let Your Mercy Be on Us" (Haugen), or "Way, Truth, and Life" (Cooney/Daigle), or have instrumental music playing as the children gather in the space for the Liturgy of the Word.

Place the lectionary on the ambo or lectern. Light the candle placed by the ambo or lectern, and then lead the following prayer:

> **Risen Christ,**
> **bless us with open minds and hearts to listen to the good news.**
> **Help us rejoice fully throughout Easter Time.**
> **Who lives and reigns with God the Father**
> **in the unity of the Holy Spirit,**
> **God, for ever and ever.**

> *Children:* **Amen.**

First Reading

Acts 6:1–7

Responsorial Psalm

Psalm 33:1–2, 4–5, 18–19 (22) *Sing the same musical setting that is used in your parish's celebration of the liturgy.*

Second Reading

1 Peter 2:4–9

Gospel Acclamation

Sing the Gospel Acclamation used in your parish's celebration of the liturgy.

Gospel Reading

John 14:1–12

Homily/Reflection

We have been celebrating Easter Time for many weeks now. We have been thinking and talking about Jesus' death and resurrection, and what that means for us as Catholic Christians. This announcement is the very heart of the Christian message. It is so big and such a bold thing to proclaim that its reality changes us.

The letter of Peter in today's second reading gives us the image of a stone. How can a stone help us to think about who Jesus is in our lives?

≫ How would you describe a stone?

We might think of something that is very strong and very hard. Stone lasts a long time. In the time of Jesus, stone was used for making buildings. It was also used to construct the walls that protected big and important cities. We sometimes also think about stones as cold and unmoving; this is how we describe things that are not alive. The letter of Peter describes stone in an unusual way. It says, "Come to him, a *living* stone . . . ." Might we think about Jesus Christ in this way, as someone strong, everlasting, protective, but also one who loves, who moves in us, whose alive-ness is very surprising?

The letter of Peter tells us further that Christ is a particular kind of stone: our cornerstone. Have you ever watched as a house was being built? The most important part of a building is the foundation because if the foundation is not firm, is not whole, the entire structure can fall. When a house is being built, the foundation is the first part that is made. The cornerstone is the very first stone that is laid. All the other stones in the foundation are laid in relationship to that stone so that it determines the position of the whole house.

The letter also says that for some, this stone could make people stumble. At the time of Jesus, most roads would either have been dirt paths or paved with stone. If a big rock was sticking up from the dirt or if one of the paving stones was laid higher than the others, the person traveling along the road could trip and fall on it and experience pain. We could even imagine someone not understanding where the road is and trying to walk through a construction site. The cornerstone would be in the way and could cause someone to fall! The letter warns that Jesus could be a stumbling block; this happens for people who disobey the God's Word of God.

We must be people who obey the Word of God. The most important first step in obeying the Word of God is knowing and keeping close to It. We have to read and study the Bible in order to understand how it helps us to know God and what God is asking us to do. We trust in Jesus Christ as a firm foundation, strong and everlasting. We build up our lives and ourselves in relationship to him, through the choices we make. What we are building is a temple and we know that temples are places where God dwells. If God dwells in us, we show God's love to others and pay particular attention to those who are in need.

>> **In what other ways can we let God dwell in our hearts? to live in us?**

Profession of Faith

Following the homily or reflection, the prayer leader invites everyone to stand to profess our faith. Together, sing or recite the Apostles' or Nicene Creed. Refer the children to the words of the prayer that you have displayed.

Prayer of the Faithful

Leader: **We trust that God hears and answers the prayers of those who turn to him in faith, and so we pray, "Risen Lord, hear us."**

For all Christians to see their lives as valuable and necessary building blocks of the Body of Christ and may remain fitted into the Church, we pray: *Risen Lord, hear us.*

For all people of every language and culture to be treated with respect, we pray: *Risen Lord, hear us.*

For the sick, that they may know the healing power of the risen Christ, we pray: *Risen Lord, hear us.*

For all who have been baptized this Easter, that they may continue to grow in faith in our risen Christ, we pray: *Risen Lord, hear us.*

Invite other intercessions from the children, or add intercessions based on the current needs of the Church, the world, the oppressed or marginalized, and the local community. Conclude each of the children's petitions with **"we pray"** and invite the response *"Risen Lord, hear us."*

For all who have died, that they may behold the face of Christ who is the Way, the Truth, and the Life, we pray: *Risen Lord, hear us.*

**Mighty God,
may the prayers we offer this day
be a sign of our love and fidelity.
Grant what we ask through Christ our Lord.**

Children: **Amen.**

Quietly return with the children to the main assembly. Be mindful of children having difficulty finding their families.

May 14, 2023
Sixth Sunday of Easter
The Presence of God

 ## Scripture Background

Connections to Church Teaching and Tradition

- The Holy Spirit unfolds the divine plan of salvation within the Church, animates the Church, and directs her mission (NDC, 28).

- The Holy Spirit makes the Paschal Mystery present in the human mind (NDC, 28).

- The Holy Spirit animates creation (CCC, 703).

- The Holy Spirit continues God's work in the world (NDC, 92) by awakening faith (CCC, 684), by enabling communion with Christ (CCC, 683), by granting gifts to all (LG, 12; CCC, 2003), by making possible spiritual freedom (CCC, 1742), by allowing and enabling prayer and holiness (CCC, 741, 744, 2652), by having written the Scriptures (CCC, 304), and by revealing God in myriad ways (CCC, 244, 687), primarily but not exclusively through the Church.

- In these ways and in others unique to the Church, the Spirit makes present the mystery of Christ (CCC, 737, 1380–1381).

Acts 8:5–8, 14–17 Luke recounts the way the Gospel, which had been confined to the area around Jerusalem, has now spread to Samaria. At first, Philip's trip to Samaria sounds very much like one of Paul's missionary journeys. However, Philip did not take this journey voluntarily. As we find in the verses preceding this reading, persecution, led by the yet unconverted Saul (Paul), caused all the believers in Jerusalem to be evicted. Most scattered to Judea, but some, like Philip, ended up in Samaria.

Much to everyone's surprise, the persecution did not interfere with the ministry of the Church at all. In fact, the eviction from Jerusalem was a catalyst that propelled the Gospel outward to even more people. Philip may have fled Jerusalem in danger, but he was clearly not defeated. Through the power of the Spirit, he was able to convince multitudes of Samaritans to believe in Jesus. People who might never have heard the Gospel at all were saved in part because of the hostility faced by believers in Jerusalem.

Psalm 66:1–3, 4–5, 6–7, 16, 20 (1) This psalm is rather unusual. The psalmist vacillates between community praise and individual praise, between addressing God and addressing the gathered community, between Exodus images and images from the Exile.

The psalmist's message, though, is crystal clear: no matter what has happened in the life of the people, God has never abandoned or left them. The psalmist praises God, for when Pharaoh's army was about to drive the Israelites into the sea, the waters of the sea parted for them. When God tested the people in the wilderness, God still helped them arrive safely in the Promised Land. Even when the people sinned, even when the psalmist himself sinned, God was always there, ready to forgive.

1 Peter 3:15–18 In this reading, the author of 1 Peter returns to the issue of proper responses to persecution. He has just told us that if we suffer for doing good, we will be blessed. Now he urges us not to fear those who harm us for doing what is right. Instead, he says that we should reverence for Christ. Always be ready to witness to the hope that is in us. Instead of retaliating or lashing out in what may be justifiable anger, 1 Peter counsels us to respond with gentleness. Our behavior, the author says, should be so commendable that those attacking us will be ashamed. This is the model Christ showed us, to "bring you to God."

John 14:15–21 John continues Jesus' response to Philip's request. In last week's reading, Jesus pointed to the unity he shares with the Father and how the Father will be glorified when the disciples also share in that unity. Now Jesus becomes even more direct. He says that if the disciples truly love him, they will keep his commandments, the most important of which he has just given them: "[L]ove one another as I love you" (15:12).

Jesus picks up their unspoken reservations: "How can you expect us mere mortals to love like you do?" Jesus does not expect them to do it by themselves. He will send them the Holy Spirit, through whom Jesus will continue to be with his disciples, guiding them and helping them keep the commandments he has given them.

Again, John weaves the early disciples' concerns about Jesus' departure with his own congregation's sense of Jesus' absence. The promise here is for both groups and for all of us. Even if we have not seen Jesus in person, he neither leaves us desolate nor leaves us to fulfill his commandment to love on our own power. Through the Spirit, Jesus is with all of us more closely than he could ever be in person.

Preparation

As Christians, our hope is in Jesus Christ. Today's second reading tells us that we should be able to give reasons for our hope. Our faith does not compel us to reject our intellect but to use it in our life of faith. We are compelled not only to have reasons but also to share these reasons with others. We can do this through explicit discussion; in order for what we say about our hope in Jesus to be trustworthy, our words and actions should remain consistent with what we profess.

Objectives

- To explore hope in Jesus Christ as consistent with human reason.
- To consider how our words and actions provide credibility for the hope we profess in Jesus Christ.

Preparation and Materials

- Read the Season Background, the lectionary readings, and the Scripture Background.
- Bookmark the appropriate readings (see page xvi) in the lectionary, children's lectionary, or Bible. Place the book in a convenient location for the leader.
- Write the words of dismissal on a card for the priest celebrant.
- Prepare the words of the song the children will sing as they gather in the space for the Liturgy of the Word.
- Select volunteers (older children or adults) to proclaim the readings.
- Display the responsorial psalm refrain lyrics.
- Display the Apostles' or Nicene Creed.
- Prepare intercessions for the Prayer of the Faithful adapted for the needs of the Church, world, oppressed or marginalized, and local community.

Prayer Leader Reflection Questions

>> **What is the relationship between your faith and intellect?**

>> **Do your words and actions affirm your hope in Jesus Christ?**

Lectionary for Mass #55A

Acts 8:5–8, 14–17

Psalm 66:1–3, 4–5, 6–7, 16, 20 (1)

1 Peter 3:15–18

John 14:15–21

Procession

Following the Collect of the Mass, the priest celebrant picks up the lectionary and invites those who would like to participate in the Liturgy of the Word with children to come forward and gather in the center aisle. The people who will lead the children out and facilitate the Liturgy of the Word also come forward at this time. Holding the lectionary so that all can see, the priest celebrant sends the children forth using his own words or the following:

Priest: **Dear children, God performs tremendous deeds, like casting out demons, healing people, and raising Jesus from the dead, but they all have love as their motive. Now, God will speak to you in the Scriptures because he loves you, and soon he will send his Spirit because he loves all of us. Grow in his love and go in peace.**

The leader processes out holding the lectionary, and the children follow behind. The parish music minister may have selected a song of dismissal for the assembly to sing while the children leave. A good option is "The Word of God: Children's Dismissal" by M. D. Ridge and Timothy R. Smith (WLP/GIA).

Centering

Continue to sing the song of dismissal that the assembly sang as you left the church. Or sing the refrain from "Behold, I Make All Things New" (Bell), or have instrumental music playing as the children gather in the space for the Liturgy of the Word.

Place the lectionary on the ambo or lectern. Light the candle placed by the ambo or lectern, and then lead the following prayer:

**Mighty God,
during Easter Time we honor the risen Lord.
Please help us to always keep in mind the great gift
of the resurrection in everything we do.
Allow our hearts to be open to your Word
so that we may serve you completely.
Through Christ our Lord.**

First Reading

Acts 1:1–11

Responsorial Psalm

Psalm 47:2–3, 6–7, 8–9 (6) *Sing the same musical setting that is used in your parish's celebration of the liturgy.*

Second Reading

Ephesians 1:17–23

Gospel Acclamation

Sing the Gospel Acclamation used in your parish's celebration of the liturgy.

Gospel Reading

Matthew 28:16–20

Homily/Reflection

Perhaps some of us know that there are many colors in light. Sometimes we can see the colors separately, like when the sun shines through moisture and a rainbow appears in the sky. When all the colors are together, the light we see is white. In our Church, during this great season of Easter, the color white is prominent in our liturgical environment. We celebrate the fullness of Christ's light.

Jesus Christ is the reason for our hope. Death could not defeat him. When he rose from the dead, he brought with him a light and a life that will never go out. This light and life is not only for himself. He shares this light with us. In baptism, a candle is lit for us and we're invited to receive the light of Christ. We do not have the power to defeat death on our own. We do not have everlasting fullness of life by our own power. We hope that we will share in the fullness of life and light forever.

This light and life is shared from Jesus Christ to us and we are asked to share with others. In today's second reading, we heard that we should always be willing to give an explanation for our hope. We need to be able and willing to talk about Jesus Christ. People may ask us about our hope. Perhaps they see how we live as Catholic Christians. To give reasons, we have to know what they are. We can study and learn about Jesus Christ through the Bible and the teaching of the Church. When the Bible speaks about knowing, though, as we heard in today's Gospel reading, this knowing is a knowing with our head, our heart, and our hands, our bodies. We know someone or something because we are in relationship. We are connected. We are very close. We know Jesus when we are close to him, spending time in prayer, listening to him, being with him. We are close with Jesus in a most special way when we come to the table of the Lord to receive the Eucharist. Loving others with our hearts, our minds, and by our actions brings us close to Jesus. Knowing Jesus allows us to speak clearly about our reasons.

>> Who are the people we can share our faith with?

Those who are already our friends are the easiest people to share what we believe. But what about those we don't know very well? In today's first reading from Acts, we hear about how Phillip explained his hope and gave his reasons for faith in Jesus Christ to people of Samaria. For the Jewish people, Samaritans were outsiders. They worshipped God in a different way and did not come to the temple. They heard Phillip's reasons, though, saw the power of God, and received the good news of Jesus Christ with great joy. The light and the life of the risen Christ spread to them, even though they were different.

We must share the explanation for our hope and give our reasons not only with our words, but also with our actions.

>> What actions will tell others about Jesus?

It is the Holy Spirit who helps us live in the best and most loving way possible. Jesus sent the Holy Spirit as an Advocate. This means a helper. We cannot speak about our reasons perfectly on our own. We do not always make loving choices. Our own power isn't enough. Instead, we can trust in the Holy Spirit who helps us to act with the love of Christ, so that others can share in our hope in the light and life of the risen Christ.

Profession of Faith

Following the homily or reflection, the prayer leader invites everyone to stand to profess our faith. Together, sing or recite the Apostles' or Nicene Creed. Refer the children to the words of the prayer that you have displayed.

Prayer of the Faithful

Leader: **Christ commands us to show our love for him and for the Father by loving one another. By our love, the power of Christ's resurrection is made known to the world. Let us now turn to the Father with our prayers. Please respond, "Risen Lord, hear our prayer."**

That our Holy Father, Pope N., our Bishop, N., and all priests and deacons may have the faith of the Apostles, we pray: *Risen Lord, hear our prayer.*

That world leaders may be inspired by the Holy Spirit with new ways to right injustice and establish peace, we pray: *Risen Lord, hear our prayer.*

That those who are sick, homebound, lonely, or in mourning may be comforted by Christ's unconditional love for them, we pray: *Risen Lord, hear our prayer.*

That all who have been baptized this Easter may continue to grow in faith in our risen Christ, we pray: *Risen Lord, hear our prayer.*

Invite other intercessions from the children, or add intercessions based on the current needs of the Church, the world, the oppressed or marginalized, and the local community. Conclude each of the children's petitions with **"we pray"** and invite the response **"Risen Lord, hear our prayer."**

That those who no longer suffer, our beloved dead, may be welcomed to eternal life, we pray: *Risen Lord, hear our prayer.*

God our Father, send your Spirit of truth into our hearts that we may always reject what is false, live by the commands of Christ, and be true to the love you have shown us. We ask this through Jesus Christ our Lord.

Children: **Amen.**

Quietly return with the children to the main assembly. Be mindful of children having difficulty finding their families.

May 18/May 21, 2023
Solemnity of the Ascension of the Lord
Taken into Heaven

 ## Scripture Background

Connections to Church Teaching and Tradition

- We pause between our celebrations of the Ascension and Pentecost to contemplate our task. The Church's mission is twofold: we are called to continuous conversion, and we are called to bear the Gospel of salvation to all the world (NDC, 10; CCC, 767–769).

- Jesus and the Holy Spirit's mission is accomplished in us (CCC, 737, 778).

- We are to announce, bear witness to, make present, and spread the mystery of the Trinity (CCC, 748–975).

Acts 1:1–14   This is the only place in the entire New Testament that speaks of a forty-day period between the Resurrection and the Ascension. Even the Gospel according to Luke implies that the Ascension took place on Easter evening. This forty-day time of waiting, however, fits perfectly into Luke's purposes in Acts. It gives him a chance to rehabilitate the disciples, most of whom abandoned Jesus at his arrest. More importantly, this transitional period also gives Luke an opportunity to address a major concern in the Church, the delay in the return of Jesus. "Lord, are you at this time going to restore the kingdom to Israel?" The disciples might not have used these exact words, but clearly they were wondering what God would do next and when it would happen. Those were natural questions. Jesus, however, is not concerned with times or places. "Wait for the Spirit," he says. "There is still work to do before God's realm comes in full. The realm will come, but until then I need you to be my witnesses. To do that, you will need the Spirit to help you. So wait until you have been "clothed with power from on high" (Luke 24:49).

Luke's account of the Ascension gives us at least three clues about what is next for us. First and foremost, Jesus wants us to be conscious of the Holy Spirit, who is given at Baptism and Confirmation and is invoked at every Eucharist. Second, he wants us to be his witnesses in the world. And third, he wants to reassure us that he will indeed return when the time is right.

Psalm 47:2–3, 6–7, 8–9 (6)   Ancient Israel often imagined God as a king sitting high on a heavenly throne, looking down on the rulers of the nations. Such images were particularly popular whenever a new king was enthroned. Indeed, Israel may even have held regular festivals celebrating the enthronement of God and his representative on earth, Israel's king. Psalm 47 was composed for just such an occasion. It celebrates God as the ruler of the nations. It calls on the people of the world to acknowledge God's rule and includes a processional liturgy to help them do so (vv. 5–7).

This psalm leaves us no doubt what is next—Christ's enthronement at the right hand of the Father. For much of Christian tradition, the Ascension is Christ's coronation, his ascension to the throne from which he will exercise God's sovereignty over creation. Today we celebrate that rule, and with the psalmist, we sing praises to the Father and to Christ who is highly exalted.

Ephesians 1:17–23   This reading is a prayer of thanksgiving and intercession written in the late first century for the Churches in Asia Minor. Ephesians borrows quite freely from the letter to the Colossians. The first half of the Second Reading is a prayer of intercession, asking God to give them a spirit of wisdom and revelation that helps them know God. It then goes on to ask that they follow Christ's call. This is a wonderful and appropriate prayer for us today as well. The second part of the reading reminds us that God has made Jesus Christ the head of all creation and the source of growth for all parts of the living Body of Christ, his followers.

Matthew 28:16–20   Matthew's account of the Ascension differs markedly from either of Luke's accounts. In Matthew, the Ascension takes place in Galilee, not in Jerusalem. In Matthew, the Ascension takes place shortly after the Resurrection, presumably not long after the disciples arrived in Galilee, according to Jesus' instructions (Matthew 28:7, Mark 16:7). Most remarkable, however, is Matthew's emphasis on the Ascension as the foundational moment for the birth of the Church. Indeed, Matthew is the only New Testament writer to even hint that Jesus consciously intended to found a Church and certainly the only one who recounts that Jesus expressly commanded his disciples to baptize. While Luke leaves the disciples staring into space and not sure what to expect next, Matthew has Jesus leave them with explicit instructions. Their next task is to "Go, therefore, and make disciples" (a deliberate change on Matthew's part from Mark's "proclaim the good news"[16:15] and Luke's "you are witnesses" [24:48]). The disciples are to baptize all nations and teach them to obey "all that [Jesus has] commanded."

 # Preparation

At Christ's ascension, the disciples witnessed Jesus being lifted up in order to enter bodily into heaven. Jesus returned to the Father as he had said he would. He did not have to shed his physical body to do this. This tells us something important about all human bodies—they can be good enough to enter heaven. The epistle describes the "holy ones" or saints who have the inheritance of eternal life. We hope and pray that we can be saints and join Christ in heaven, and in the fullness of time, to do so bodily. The work of saints is to share the good news that others might also become saints and receive this inheritance.

Lectionary for Mass #58A

Acts 1:1–11

Psalm 47:2–3, 6–7, 8–9 (6)

Ephesians 1:17–23

Matthew 28:16–20

Objectives

- To emphasize Jesus' bodily ascension and its significance for the holiness of all bodies.

- To invite the children to consider their part in fulfilling the great commission to "make disciples of all nations."

Preparation and Materials

- Read the Season Background, the lectionary readings, and the Scripture Background.

- Bookmark the appropriate readings (see page xvi) in the lectionary, children's lectionary, or Bible. Place the book in a convenient location for the leader.

- Write the words of dismissal on a card for the priest celebrant.

- Prepare the words of the song the children will sing as they gather in the space for the Liturgy of the Word.

- Select volunteers (older children or adults) to proclaim the readings.

- Display the responsorial psalm refrain lyrics.

- Display the Apostles' or Nicene Creed.

- Prepare intercessions for the Prayer of the Faithful adapted for the needs of the Church, world, oppressed or marginalized, and local community.

Prayer Leader Reflection Questions

>> **How do you carry out Christ's mission to evangelize?**

>> **Do you find it easier to share Jesus' teaching with adults or with children? Why?**

Procession

Following the Collect of the Mass, the priest celebrant picks up the lectionary and invites those who would like to participate in the Liturgy of the Word with children to come forward and gather in the center aisle. The people who will lead the children out and facilitate the Liturgy of the Word also come forward at this time. Holding the lectionary so that all can see, the priest celebrant sends the children forth using his own words or the following:

> *Priest:* **Children, we may be sad to think of Jesus leaving his disciples as he ascended to heaven, but today's readings remind us that he promised to send them the Holy Spirit, and we believe that Jesus is still with us in the Scriptures, in the Eucharist, and in our brothers and sisters. That should make us very glad. Go now and listen to him.**

The leader processes out holding the lectionary, and the children follow behind. The parish music minister may have selected a song of dismissal for the assembly to sing while the children leave. A good option is "The Word of God: Children's Dismissal" by M. D. Ridge and Timothy R. Smith (WLP/GIA).

Centering

Continue to sing the song of dismissal that the assembly sang as you left the church. Or sing "Christ High-Ascended" (T. Dudley-Smith) or the refrain from "God Mounts His Throne" (Haugen), or have instrumental music playing as the children gather in the space for the Liturgy of the Word.

Place the lectionary on the ambo or lectern. Light the candle placed by the ambo or lectern, and then lead the following prayer:

> **Risen Christ,**
> **bless us with open minds and hearts to listen to the good news.**
> **Help us rejoice fully throughout Easter Time.**
> **Who lives and reigns with God the Father**
> **in the unity of the Holy Spirit,**
> **God, for ever and ever.**

Children: **Amen.**

First Reading

Acts 1:1–11

Responsorial Psalm

Psalm 47:2–3, 6–7, 8–9 (6) *Sing the same musical setting that is used in your parish's celebration of the liturgy.*

Second Reading

Ephesians 1:17–23

Gospel Acclamation

Sing the Gospel Acclamation used in your parish's celebration of the liturgy.

Gospel Reading

Matthew 28:16–20

Homily/Reflection

We are gathered today to celebrate a solemnity in the midst of our Easter season. A solemnity is the highest, most important kind of feast—a very special day, almost as special as Easter. *[If the Solemnity of the Ascension of the Lord is celebrated on Thursday and not transferred to the following Sunday, add the following:* This is why we are gathered on a Thursday.*]* Today is the Solemnity of the Ascension of our Lord. Let's say that word together: *ascension.* To ascend means to rise up.

When Jesus was resurrected from the dead, his whole self rose to life, including his physical body. We often think of God as being in the highest heights. On the fortieth day after that first Easter, Jesus ascended back to his Father in heaven. Our faith teaches us that Jesus Christ is fully God and fully human at the same time. Because Jesus Christ is fully God, he had the power to enter heaven. Because Jesus Christ is fully human, his humanity came with him to heaven. That includes everything that it means to be a human being, including having a body. We human beings don't have the ability to enter heaven by our own power. Because Jesus did have that power, though, he paved the way for other human beings, including their bodies, to enter heaven too.

In the letter of Paul to the Ephesians, we hear that this is the inheritance of the "holy ones." The word *saints* is the same as "holy ones." The saints, the holy ones, are those who can enter heaven.

When someone dies, their possessions are passed on to others and we call this "inheritance." Jesus Christ died and rose, and shares his inheritance, his life to the full, with the saints. At our baptism, we are invited to share in this inheritance, to join the other saints in heaven. In a way, we might say that the baptized, even those of us living, are also saints. We have the hope that Jesus Christ who called us by name in baptism will also call us into the fullness of his life in heaven.

Each Sunday when we pray the creed, we announce that we believe in the resurrection of the dead. In the parousia, in the fullness of time when God will be all in all, the bodies of the saints will enter heaven just as Christ himself entered heaven. This tells us something very important about our bodies. Our bodies can get sick or hurt. Sometimes we might use our bodies to hurt other people and other people can hurt our bodies, but we have to take care of and honor our bodies, which are good and beautiful, made by God. Our bodies are capable of inheriting heaven, along with the rest of us.

It is not only our own bodies and our own selves that are made for heaven. Other people are made for heaven as well. When Jesus returned to the Father, he gave his disciples instructions. He said, "Go . . . and make disciples of all nations, baptizing them . . . teaching them . . . ." To be a saint, to be someone who is meant for heaven, to be someone who has been given this inheritance, means that we must share it. We are sent to make more saints, more holy ones, more of those who will share in the hope of heaven.

>> **What are some things you can say or do to help others to have a share in the hope of heaven?**

Profession of Faith

Following the homily or reflection, the prayer leader invites everyone to stand to profess our faith. Together, sing or recite the Apostles' or Nicene Creed. Refer the children to the words of the prayer that you have displayed.

Prayer of the Faithful

Leader: **Before Jesus ascended into heaven, he commissioned his disciples to go out and proclaim the good news to all creation. We pray for the wisdom, the faith, and the love of God to be witnesses in today's unbelieving world to the good news. Please respond, "Risen Lord, hear our prayer."**

May those who have been entrusted with the Word of the Lord proclaim it without hesitation or fear, we pray: *Risen Lord, hear our prayer.*

May we have a greater respect for the gift of human life and oppose all policies and practices that destroy life at every stage, we pray: *Risen Lord, hear our prayer.*

May all who suffer from poverty, injustice, or abuse be healed, and may find love and support in a community of faith, we pray: *Risen Lord, hear our prayer.*

May all who have been baptized this Easter continue to grow in faith in our risen Christ, we pray: *Risen Lord, hear our prayer.*

Invite other intercessions from the children, or add intercessions based on the current needs of the Church, the world, the oppressed or marginalized, and the local community. Conclude each of the children's petitions with **"we pray"** and invite the response **"Risen Lord, hear our prayer."**

May all who have died be welcomed into heaven, we pray: *Risen Lord, hear our prayer.*

Mighty God,
you lifted Jesus Christ up so that we could be lifted up with him.
Accept the prayers of your children through Christ our Lord.

Children: **Amen.**

Quietly return with the children to the main assembly. Be mindful of children having difficulty finding their families.

May 21, 2023
Seventh Sunday of Easter
They Devoted Themselves to Prayer

 ## Scripture Background

Connections to Church Teaching and Tradition

- "While awaiting the Spirit, 'all these with one accord devoted themselves to prayer.'[1] The Spirit who teaches the Church and recalls for her everything that Jesus said[2] was also to form her in the life of prayer" (CCC, 2623).

- "In prayer the Holy Spirit unites us to the person of the only Son, in his glorified humanity, through which and in which our filial prayer unites us in the Church with the Mother of Jesus[3]" (CCC, 2673).

- "Jesus fulfilled the work of the Father completely. . . . Our high priest who prays for us is also the one who prays in us and the God who hears our prayer" (CCC, 2749).

- "In this prayer Jesus reveals and gives to us the 'knowledge,' inseparably one, of the Father and of the Son[4], which is the very mystery of the life of prayer" (CCC, 2751).

- "This is Christian prayer: to be wholly God's, because he is wholly ours" (CCC, 2617).

Acts 1:12–14 After the Ascension on Mount Olivet, the disciples return to Jerusalem and gather in the upper room, the room in which tradition claims Jesus and his disciples celebrated the Last Supper. The upper room is a Sabbath day's journey from Olivet, roughly one kilometer or six tenths of a mile, the distance Jews were permitted to walk on the Sabbath. There, the disciples, minus Judas, gather with some of Jesus' female disciples and Mary. There is no fear or anxiety expressed concerning their state. Rather, all devoted themselves to prayer in preparation for God's promised gift of the Spirit. Luke sees prayer as an essential preparation for the important events that occur in both his account of the Gospel and in the Acts of the Apostles. We, too, are invited to devote ourselves to prayer as a way of continually seeking God's presence and direction in our lives.

Psalm 27:1, 4, 7–8 (13) The psalm expresses strong confidence in God along with a desired longing to seek intimacy with the Lord at all times. The psalmist associates three images with the Lord: light, salvation, and refuge. All three express great confidence in the Lord as one having the power to aid the psalmist in life's distress. As a result of the psalmist's strong confidence in God's gracious presence and power exercised on the psalmist's behalf, the psalmist yearns to seek God's face and dwell with the Lord always. The intimacy, power, and presence of the Lord experienced in the temple is what the psalmist yearns for each and every day. Such yearning for the Lord emboldens the psalmist to call upon the Lord in times of distress, already confident that the Lord will hear and respond. This confidence in and yearning for the Lord should be the prayer stance of all believers.

1 Peter 4:13–16 Suffering again surfaces as an integral component in the life of believers. Fidelity to Jesus' values and lifestyle made his followers' behavior stand out, especially when contrasted with the values and practices of their neighbors. As a result, misunderstanding, rejection, opposition, and persecution surfaced, causing much suffering for Jesus' disciples. The author exhorts them to rejoice because, in their innocent suffering for Christ, they share in Christ's own innocent suffering. Just as God raised up and glorified Christ, so too will we, in the Spirit's power, be raised up and glorified. We are reminded, however, that it is suffering for Christ's sake that brings about ultimate glory in God, and not suffering due to immorality. "But whoever is made to suffer as a Christian, should not be ashamed but glorify God because of the name" (4:16). The name "Christian" might have been used by others as a slur or insult, but disciples should glorify God with it, even in the face of shame or disgrace. Prayer enables us to continually seek the Lord, to endure suffering, and to even rejoice in the face of suffering, assured of God's glory.

John 17:1–11a Chapter 17 of the Gospel of John is an extended prayer of Jesus, culminating his farewell address to his disciples at the Last Supper. Jesus first prays that his mission on earth may be brought to a successful conclusion as his "hour" approaches—John's word for Jesus' Passion, Death, and Resurrection. Jesus' Crucifixion is his ultimate act of glorifying the Father, and by glorifying the Father, the Father will glorify Jesus in return. In the process, all those who have believed in Jesus will benefit from the eternal life that Jesus accomplished in this world.

Jesus' prayer now extends to his disciples, "those whom [God] gave [him] out of the world" (17:6). Everything that Jesus shared with them has its origin in the Father. They have understood all he shared with them and have come to accept it and to believe in Jesus as the one sent

---

1 Acts 1:14.
2 Cf. John 14:26.
3 Cf. Acts 1:14.
4 Cf. John 17:3, 6–10, 25.

by the Father. His prayer is for them and not for the world, understood by John as those who refuse to believe. Since all that Jesus has comes from the Father, and he has glorified the Father by sharing it all with his disciples, both the Father and he are glorified in the disciples as well. By sharing with his disciples the Father's words, and in their understanding of them and their belief in him, both the Father and Jesus are glorified in them. Jesus asserts that he is praying for his disciples, the ones God gave him (17:6), because they will remain in the world to carry on his mission while he returns to the Father. Like Jesus, we too are to call upon the Lord in prayer, seeking to glorify the Lord in all our words and actions.

Preparation

Psalm 27 acclaims God as our "light" and our "salvation." God's glory is described as "shining." Jesus' work of glorifying the Father allows this light to be seen. When we follow the model of Jesus, we reflect God's light.

Lectionary for Mass #59A

Acts 1:12–14

Psalm 27:1, 4, 7–8 (13)

1 Peter 4:13–16

John 17:1–11a

Objectives

- To consider together the significance of God's glory that shines.

- To reflect what we can do and avoid in order to glorify God.

Preparation and Materials

- Read the Season Background, the lectionary readings, and the Scripture Background.

- Bookmark the appropriate readings (see page xvi) in the lectionary, children's lectionary, or Bible. Place the book in a convenient location for the leader.

- Write the words of dismissal on a card for the priest celebrant.

- Prepare the words of the song the children will sing as they gather in the space for the Liturgy of the Word.

- Select volunteers (older children or adults) to proclaim the readings.

- Display the responsorial psalm refrain lyrics.

- Display the Apostles' or Nicene Creed.

- Prepare intercessions for the Prayer of the Faithful adapted for the needs of the Church, world, oppressed or marginalized, and local community.

Prayer Leader Reflection Questions

» **How do you glorify God and reflect God's light in dark places?**

» **What needs to be cleaned or removed in order for you to reflect God's light more fully?**

Liturgy Guide

Procession

Following the Collect of the Mass, the priest celebrant picks up the lectionary and invites those who would like to participate in the Liturgy of the Word with children to come forward and gather in the center aisle. The people who will lead the children out and facilitate the Liturgy of the Word also come forward at this time. Holding the lectionary so that all can see, the priest celebrant sends the children forth using his own words or the following:

> *Priest*: **Dear children, when we pray together, we can take comfort and encouragement from the presence of our brothers and sisters, just as the Apostles and Mary encouraged one another in the upper room. Go now, listen to today's readings and pray together, and when you return, we will continue our prayer with you in joy and gratitude.**

The leader processes out holding the lectionary, and the children follow behind. The parish music minister may have selected a song of dismissal for the assembly to sing while the children leave. A good option is "The Word of God: Children's Dismissal" by M. D. Ridge and Timothy R. Smith (WLP/GIA).

Centering

Continue to sing the song of dismissal that the assembly sang as you left the church. Or sing "Two by Two" (Glover) or have instrumental music playing as the children gather in the space for the Liturgy of the Word.

Place the lectionary on the ambo or lectern. Light the candle placed by the ambo or lectern, and then lead the following prayer:

> **Risen Christ,**
> **bless us with open minds and hearts to listen to the good news.**
> **Help us rejoice fully throughout Easter Time.**
> **Who lives and reigns with God the Father**
> **in the unity of the Holy Spirit,**
> **God, for ever and ever.**

Children: **Amen.**

First Reading

Acts 1:12–14

Responsorial Psalm

Psalm 27:1, 4, 7–8 (13) *Sing the same musical setting that is used in your parish's celebration of the liturgy.*

Second Reading

1 Peter 4:13–16

Gospel Acclamation

Sing the Gospel Acclamation used in your parish's celebration of the liturgy.

Gospel Reading

John 17:1–11a

Homily/Reflection

There are only a few days left until we enter the new season of Ordinary Time. A few days ago, we celebrated the ascension, when Jesus returned to the Father and the disciples saw him lifted up into heaven. We know that this happened so that Christ could be seated at the right hand of the Father in the fullness of his glory. On this Seventh Sunday of Easter, we think together more deeply about the glory of Jesus Christ.

>> **We say this word often, don't we? Can you think of a time when we pray the word *glory* at Mass?**

Most Sundays we say or sing the words "Glory to God in the highest...." *[You might wish to sing the first phrase of the musical setting of the Gloria that your parish uses at Mass. If you are not comfortable singing, consider inviting another adult to sing it with the children. It can be introduced with the words "Let's sing it together."]* Do you remember where these words come from? Many months ago, we heard them when we celebrated Christmas. At the announcement of Christ's birth to the shepherds, the angels sang these words. We heard that the glory of the Lord *shone*.

>> **What are some things that shine?** *[sun, stars, flashlight]*

All these things give light. The word *shine* might make us think of things that we clean and polish and then they are able to reflect light even more. Have you ever looked directly at the sun? Probably, your grown-ups have told you not to do this. The sun is so bright that if we look at it directly, it can damage our eyes. The brightness of the light can hurt us, forcing us to look away, but we need the light of the sun and can appreciate its beauty. The light of the sun helps us to see the beauty of the things that reflect that light. Throughout our history, God gave people ways to experience his bright glory and appreciate the beauty even without seeing it directly.

What can it mean for Jesus to glorify God? In today's Gospel reading, we hear Jesus' words about glory. "Give glory to your son, so that your son may glorify you. . . ." We have said many times that Christ *is* light. The light of Christ comes from God the Father and is the same light. We announce this when we pray the creed at Mass. We describe Jesus Christ as "Light from Light." When Jesus walked and talked on this earth like we do, even after he had risen from the dead, the fullness of his light, the fullness of his glory was still hidden. Jesus' friends who walked and talked with him could be in the presence of God's glory and live. When he ascended to the Father, that light, that glory was no longer hidden but could be seen in fullness in heaven.

We hope and pray that at the end of our life, we will truly be able to be in the presence of the fullness of God's glory and live. As we live our lives now, we can consider what it means for us to glorify God. We remember where the light comes from. It is not from us but from God. We know that in the sacrament of reconciliation, God gets rid of our smudges, our sins, the ways we have separated ourselves from God's light. We can bring ourselves to the table of the Lord so that we can be filled with God's very self, God's own glory.

» How might we reflect God's light to others? What are the things we can do to catch the light of God and direct it to others?

Profession of Faith

Following the homily or reflection, the prayer leader invites everyone to stand to profess our faith. Together, sing or recite the Apostles' or Nicene Creed. Refer the children to the words of the prayer that you have displayed.

Prayer of the Faithful

Leader: **Grateful for our faith, we now bring our prayers to God. Please respond, "Risen Lord, hear our prayer."**

For all men and women discerning their vocation in Christ, that they may have confidence in the God who calls them each as members of his body, we pray: *Risen Lord, hear our prayer.*

For those who govern peoples and nations to pursue justice, we pray: *Risen Lord, hear our prayer.*

For all who suffer for the name of Christ, especially in places where Christianity is persecuted, to remain faithful to his name, we pray: *Risen Lord, hear our prayer.*

For all who have been baptized this Easter, that they may continue to grow in faith in our risen Christ, we pray: *Risen Lord, hear our prayer.*

Invite other intercessions from the children, or add intercessions based on the current needs of the Church, the world, the oppressed or marginalized, and the local community. Conclude each of the children's petitions with **"we pray"** and invite the response **"Risen Lord, hear our prayer."**

For those who have died, may they rejoice in the love of Christ, we pray: *Risen Lord, hear our prayer.*

**Mighty God,
we glorify and praise you!
We trust that you hear the prayers of your children
and ask that you answer them through Christ our Lord.**

Children: **Amen.**

Quietly return with the children to the main assembly. Be mindful of children having difficulty finding their families.

May 28, 2023
Solemnity of Pentecost
Renewed by the Spirit

 ## Scripture Background

Connections to Church Teaching and Tradition

- "When the Father sends his Word, he always sends his Breath. In their joint mission, the Son and the Holy Spirit are distinct but inseparable. To be sure, it is the Christ who is seen, the visible image of the invisible God, but it is the Spirit who reveals him" (CCC, 689).

- "To evangelize is first of all to bear witness, in a simple and direct way, to God revealed by Jesus Christ, in the Holy Spirit, to bear witness that in his Son God has loved the world—that in his Incarnate Word he has given being to all things and has called [all people] to eternal life" (EN, 6).

- "The Church, however, which is so full of youthful vigor and is constantly renewed by the breath of the Holy Spirit, is willing, at all times, to recognize, welcome, and even assimilate anything that redounds to the honor of the human mind and heart, . . . which, from the beginning of time, had been destined by God's Providence to be the cradle of the Church" (PP, 19).

Acts 2:1–11 This reading from Acts is an account of Pentecost. In the Old Testament, Pentecost, the "feast of Weeks," recalled the giving of the Law on Mount Sinai, one of the pilgrim feasts when Jews would come to Jerusalem for the fiftieth day after Passover. The mention of "a noise like a strong driving wind" (2:2) draws our minds to the account of the giving of the Law in Exodus ("there were peals of thunder and lightning . . . and a very loud blast of the shofar" [19:16]). Luke draws a clear line of connection between the Book of Exodus with the experience of Pentecost in the new Christian dispensation.

When the text mentions "they were all filled with the Holy Spirit" (2:4), another resemblance to an earlier section of Luke's account of the Gospel is evoked. At the baptism of Jesus, Luke tells us, "the Holy Spirit descended upon him" (Luke 3:22), and when he returns from the desert temptations, we are told, "Jesus returned to Galilee in the power of the Spirit" (Luke 4:14), where in his hometown Nazareth he reads from the scroll of Isaiah, "The Spirit of the Lord is upon me" (Luke 4:17–18). Acts 2:1–11 asserts that the same Holy Spirit that descended upon Jesus has now come upon his followers who are to be baptized.

Psalm 104:1, 24, 29–30, 31, 34 (see 30) Psalm 104 is a hymn of creation, recounting both the wondrous works of God and the wisdom with which God has ordered the world in harmony and goodness. The opening phrase, "Bless the Lord, O my soul!" (104:1), is a powerful expression of praise. The Hebrew word for soul, *nefesh*, refers to that part of the human person which sustains life and vitality, the life force within an individual. Here the psalmist is calling to his own inner being, that which gives and sustains his life, to lift up praise to God. The opening three stanzas of the responsorial psalm give the psalmist's reasons for giving voice to this praise.

The last stanza twice employs the word spirit, in Hebrew, *ruach*. This word can variously refer to one's breath, the wind, or the spirit. In the Hebrew imagination, both human breath and the wind were mysterious things. In Genesis 1:2, a mighty "wind" swept over the chaotic waters. In Genesis 2:7, the Lord God blew "breath" into a mass of earth and it became a living being, Adam. Likewise in this verse, when God sends forth "spirit," things are created and the face of the earth is renewed. Such images from the Old Testament serve as a prelude to the act of new creation by which Jesus sends his Spirit upon Mary, the Twelve, and those in Jerusalem at the Pentecost.

1 Corinthians 12:3b–7, 12–13 This passage explodes with a message of hope that must be understood on two levels: that of the historical church of St. Paul's day, and that of our own circumstances as Christians today. First, St. Paul saw the factions within the Corinthian community as a threat to their intended unity created by Christ's Resurrection. By their Baptism, the Christians of Corinth had become the Body of Christ, his visible image on earth. While living Jesus' new law of love is a great challenge, Christians are given the profound gift of the Spirit to lead, guide, strengthen, and inspire them. In this Sunday's passage from 1 Corinthians 12, Paul chides these people to live in accord with what they been given: the Spirit. Second, this passage stands as a weighty reminder of both what we have been given, and how we are to use this precious gift within us. Our Baptism, our incorporation into Christ, bestows on us the very gifts of the Spirit which Paul lists in Galatians: love, joy, peace, patience, kindness, generosity, gentleness, self-control (5:22–23). Through these gifts of the Spirit, the mission of Jesus continues to be established in our world today. Could we ever preach this message of St. Paul strongly enough? It is not merely our duty to act in this way; rather, our Baptism marks us in an organic way, showing us our deepest nature in Jesus Christ. We preach it persuasively when we live it!

Sequence: *Veni, Sancte Spiritus*

John 20:19–31   In contrast to St. Luke, the evangelist John describes the coming of the Holy Spirit to the Eleven happening on Easter Sunday evening, not fifty days later. The powerful depiction of the gift of the Spirit is portrayed in relation to forgiveness. After the words of commission ("As the Father has sent me, so I send you" [20:21]), Jesus breathes on them, passing onto them his Spirit. They now possess the Spirit. And what will they do with it? Exactly what the Risen Christ has first done to them: offer them "peace," wholeness by means of forgiveness, and then authorize them to offer that same forgiveness to others. How wounded the Apostles must have been, having betrayed the One who had loved them so completely, even with all their weaknesses. Jesus, risen from the dead, comes among them and with that single word, "peace," he pushes aside their sinfulness and offers what they need most, forgiveness. On that first Easter night, the Risen Christ comes to those who have betrayed him, offering them forgiveness, the fruit of his saving Passion and Death. The Spirit enables us to be instruments of Jesus' own forgiveness and reconciliation.

Preparation

The Solemnity of Pentecost celebrates the gift of the Holy Spirit given to the Church. The Scriptures offer us multiple moments in which the giving of this gift occurred. The Gospel of John describes Jesus breathing on the disciples immediately after the resurrection, while Acts of the Apostles recounts the coming of the Holy Spirit in wind and fire fifty days later. No one image can sufficiently encapsulate the reality of the Spirit's presence. The Spirit is the source of our own unity in diversity.

Lectionary for Mass #63C

Acts 2:1–11

Psalm 104:1, 24, 29–30, 31, 34 (see 30)

1 Corinthians 12:3b–7, 12–13

Sequence: *Veni, Creator Spiritus*

John 20:19–23

Objectives

- To offer the images of fire and wind as images of the Holy Spirit.

- To identify the Holy Spirit as our source of different gifts and talents, and our source of unity.

Preparation and Materials

- Read the Season and Scripture Backgrounds and the lectionary readings.

- Bookmark the appropriate readings (see page xvi) in the lectionary, children's lectionary, or Bible. Place the book in a convenient location for the leader.

- Write the words of dismissal on a card for the priest celebrant.

- Prepare the words of the gathering song the children will sing.

- Select volunteers (older children or adults) to proclaim the readings.

- Display the responsorial psalm refrain lyrics and the Apostles' or Nicene Creed.

- Prepare intercessions for the Prayer of the Faithful adapted for the needs of the Church, world, oppressed or marginalized, and local community.

- Optional: Bring a map of the region surrounding the Mediterranean Sea that includes Asia, Egypt, Libya, Crete, and Saudi Arabia.

Prayer Leader Reflection Questions

>> **What particular gifts do you offer to the Church? How do they contribute to its unity?**

>> **Do you notice the Holy Spirit's power in your ministry with the children? How?**

Procession

Following the Collect of the Mass, the priest celebrant picks up the lectionary and invites those who would like to participate in the Liturgy of the Word with children to come forward and gather in the center aisle. The people who will lead the children out and facilitate the Liturgy of the Word also come forward at this time. Holding the lectionary so that all can see, the priest celebrant sends the children forth using his own words or the following:

> *Priest*: **Children, the Holy Spirit is given to us as a comforter and consoler, as a guide and friend leading us to Jesus and to the Father. The Spirit inspired the Scriptures and will help you to understand them. Go and listen attentively to the Spirit speaking in your hearts.**

The leader processes out holding the lectionary, and the children follow behind. The parish music minister may have selected a song of dismissal for the assembly to sing while the children leave. A good option is "The Word of God: Children's Dismissal" by M. D. Ridge and Timothy R. Smith (WLP/GIA).

Centering

Continue to sing the song of dismissal that the assembly sang as you left the church. Or sing "Spirit Friend" (Glover) or "God of Tempest, God of Whirlwind" (Stuempfle), or have instrumental music playing as the children gather in the space for the Liturgy of the Word.

Place the lectionary on the ambo or lectern. Light the candle placed by the ambo or lectern, and then lead the following prayer:

> **God of Life,**
> **it was your will that the Easter Mystery be experienced over fifty days.**
> **Allow our hearts to be open to your Word**
> **so that we may serve you completely.**
> **Through Christ our Lord.**

> *Children*: **Amen.**

First Reading

Acts 2:1–11

Responsorial Psalm

Psalm 104:1, 24, 29–30, 31, 34 (see 30) *Sing the same musical setting that is used in your parish's celebration of the liturgy.*

Second Reading

1 Corinthians 12:3b–7, 12–13

Gospel Acclamation

Sing the Gospel Acclamation used in your parish's celebration of the liturgy.

Gospel Reading

John 20:19–23

Homily/Reflection

Today, we mark the end of Easter Time. We celebrate a gift that Jesus leaves us, the gift of the Holy Spirit. On this day, the color red is seen all over the church, and perhaps on the altar or on banners and on the chasuble Father wears. Red is the color of fire, and we often think of fire and the Holy Spirit together.

≫ What do you think of when you think of fire? *[Fire warms, gives light, burns, strengthens]*

In the first reading we heard of the tongues of fire that came to rest on the disciples.

≫ The Holy Spirit is also like wind. What does wind do?

Wind can blow hard or as soft as breath. After the resurrection when Jesus appeared to his friends, he told them, "Receive the Holy Spirit." When he did this, he breathed on them. This was his gift, his way of giving the Holy Spirit to the disciples. We need to breathe to live. We can feel someone's breath even when we can't see it. Wind can't be held in your hand, but it can move things. The movement of air is not always soft and gentle like breath, though. Wind can be strong and powerful. Over time, wind can wear down mountains. Wind from tornadoes and hurricanes can leave damaging effects.

On the first Pentecost after Jesus' death and resurrection, the disciples experienced this kind of strong, powerful wind. In the Acts of the Apostles, it was described as sounding like a strong, driving wind. This wind filled the house that they were in. Can you imagine what it would feel like to be inside a house and suddenly this kind of powerful wind is inside with you? The Holy Spirit came to them in fullness in a powerful, maybe even scary, way. Immediately the disciples experienced the effect of the Holy Spirit who is like wind. The disciples were moved to act. They began to speak and told of the mighty acts of God.

The people who heard the disciples speaking about God's acts were different from the disciples. They were from all over the world and spoke many different languages. *[Show map.]* We can recognize some of the places they were from: Asia, Egypt, Libya, Crete, Arabia. Somehow, despite their differences, they could all hear the same message, the good news of Jesus Christ. The Holy Spirit had led the disciples to spread the good news and made it possible to do it in a way that people who were very different could receive the same message. Their differences didn't disappear. But somehow the Spirit enabled the disciples to share the one message of our Lord Jesus Christ by the power of the one Spirit.

Every person is different. The letter to the Corinthians that we heard today reminds us that the different gifts we have, the different ways we have of working and serving others are from God. Even in our differences, we are united. We are together as one. Through the one living Spirit who changes us—sometimes gently and sometimes with great force—the effects can be seen even when the Spirit's action seems hidden.

Profession of Faith

Following the homily or reflection, the prayer leader invites everyone to stand to profess our faith. Together, sing or recite the Apostles' or Nicene Creed. Refer the children to the words of the prayer that you have displayed.

Prayer of the Faithful

Leader: **We gather together this Pentecost trusting the Spirit comes to renew the face of the earth, and we pray, "Holy Spirit, hear our prayer."**

That the movement of the Spirit in the Church may lead us to ever greater unity, we pray to the Lord: *Holy Spirit, hear our prayer.*

That people of every nation and language may be treated with dignity, we pray to the Lord: *Holy Spirit, hear our prayer.*

That those who are ill may experience God's healing Spirit, we pray to the Lord: *Holy Spirit, hear our prayer.*

That all who have been baptized this Easter may continue to grow in faith in our risen Christ, we pray to the Lord: *Holy Spirit, hear our prayer.*

Invite other intercessions from the children, or add intercessions based on the current needs of the Church, the world, the oppressed or marginalized, and the local community. Conclude each of the children's petitions with **"we pray to the Lord"** and invite the response **"Holy Spirit, hear our prayer."**

That those who have died may know God's mercy, we pray to the Lord: *Holy Spirit, hear our prayer .*

O Holy Spirit,
we are from many nations and many languages
but by grace we confess God's name as one.
Accept the prayers of these children.
Through Christ our Lord.

Children: **Amen.**

Quietly return with the children to the main assembly. Be mindful of children having difficulty finding their families.

Season Background for Ordinary Time during Summer

Understanding Ordinary Time during Summer

Ordinary Time begins on Sunday evening right after Evening Prayer of Pentecost. It continues until the Solemnity of Our Lord Jesus Christ, King of the Universe, which will end the current liturgical year. Although it is designated "ordinary," this is an important season. The name simply comes from the Latin root shared with the word *ordinal*, meaning "counted." So, these Sundays are designated by names such as the "Twenty-Third Sunday in Ordinary Time." In this season, the Church gives us an opportunity to reflect on the great feasts we have celebrated during Christmas Time and Easter Time. So much has happened that it almost feels like we need a time of spiritual rest. Ordinary Time provides moments of quiet for us. The first weeks include the Solemnity of the Most Holy Trinity and the Solemnity of the Most Holy Body and Blood of Christ (Corpus Christi). The other days invite us to hear many of the words and works of Jesus and enable us to pattern our lives after his. There is no rush, only bright, warm summer days ahead.

Liturgical Environment

The Church stores its celebratory decorations and now displays the green of Ordinary Time. It is a calming, soothing color that invites us to slow down and notice the outside world turning green and lush. Your prayer environment should include a green cloth and a cross. A green plant on or near the prayer table is another reminder of this season of growth. Invite the children to help care for and water this plant. Just as they care for the living plants, they must remember to care for their spiritual lives during these quiet months.

Overview of the Readings

First Readings   Over the course of the counted Sundays of Ordinary Time in summer, we hear from a variety of Old Testament books. The readings are not in any particular order. This means they do not follow the order of the books in the Old Testament. During this time, we will hear from the major prophets: three from the prophet Isaiah, and one from the prophet Jeremiah. We will also hear from the minor prophet Zechariah, a selection from the Book of Wisdom, and from Exodus. On other Sundays, the first reading will be from the first and second books of Kings.

The first readings of Ordinary Time in Year A include many of the themes of major significance to our faith: humility, the fruitfulness and power of the Word, the freedom to repent from sin, God's mercy, the gifts of wisdom and the everlasting covenant, the awe-inspiring presence of the Lord, God's justice, and Davidic ancestry.

Responsorial Psalms   The responsorial psalm for each Sunday is an integral part of the Liturgy of the Word. The lyrical nature of the psalms lends itself to song. Meant to help everyone in the assembly give voice to their acceptance of the Word of God proclaimed in the first reading, the responsorial psalm is another reading from Scripture, almost always with a short, simple refrain from one of the psalms.

Second Readings   The Second Readings for the two solemnities at the beginning of this period of Ordinary Time are from 2 Corinthians and 1 Corinthians, respectively. Their main themes relate to the nature of the solemnity. The reading from Paul's second letter to the Corinthian community includes an early Trinitarian greeting that we still use in liturgies today. The passage from his first letter to the same community presents the connections between the one bread shared among believers and the one Body that they are. The Second Readings for the counted Sundays of Ordinary Time in summer resume with a semicontinuous reading of Paul's Letter to the Romans, his major theological treatise on faith and justification.

Gospel Readings   After we hear three passages from the Gospel according to John for the two solemnities that occur as Ordinary Time resumes, we hear from the Gospel according to Matthew, which is the lengthiest of the three synoptic Gospels. Matthew understands Jesus as Emmanuel, God-with-us, the one who comes to save. Jesus is the great and humble teacher who forms his disciples in the way of following him. Jesus is also the new Moses who fulfills the prophecies of the Old Testament. Jesus calls his disciples to follow and learn from him, and often uses parables to teach his message. On the Nineteenth Sunday, we hear a well known passage, that of Peter walking on water and becoming afraid. The Gospel readings for the Twentieth and Twenty-First Sundays are accounts of Jesus exorcising a demon from a Canaanite woman's daughter and of Peter's confession of faith. The readings become more and more eschatological with the slow build to the conclusion of the liturgical year. The final judgment and the result of following (or not following) the true King will become clear as the year draws to a close.

June 4, 2023
Solemnity of the Most Holy Trinity

The Mystery of the Triune God

 ## Scripture Background

Connections to Church Teaching and Tradition

⚙ "The mystery of the Most Holy Trinity is the central mystery of Christian faith and life. It is the mystery of God in himself. . . . The whole history of salvation is identical with the history of the way . . . the one true God, Father, Son, and Holy Spirit, reveals himself to men[1]" (CCC, 234).

⚙ "It pleased God, in his goodness and wisdom, to reveal himself and to make known the mystery of his will. His will was that men should have access to the Father, through Christ, the Word made flesh, in the Holy Spirit, and thus become sharers in the divine nature (see DV, 2; cf. Ephesians 1:9; 2:18; 2 Peter 1:4)" (CCC, 51).

⚙ "During the first centuries the Church sought to clarify its Trinitarian faith. . . . This clarification was the work of the early councils, aided by the theological work of the Church Fathers and sustained by the Christian people's sense of the faith" (CCC, 250).

Exodus 34:4b–6, 8–9 Throughout its history, Israel grew in knowledge of God. The God of Abraham, Isaac, and Jacob called Moses and revealed to him the name Yʜwʜ, a mysterious name indicating that no human can comprehend God (Exodus 3:14). All that we can know about God comes from God's interaction with us.

This Sunday we hear that God appeared to Moses and gave him a series of self-descriptions. After the title *Lord*, we hear that God is merciful. The Hebrew word for mercy is related to the word for womb, implying that God has a motherly love for us. That God is gracious signifies God's boundless generosity. That God is slow to anger means that God offers us ample time for repentance. Divine kindness and fidelity assure us that God will never abandon the covenant.

Daniel 3:52, 53, 54, 55, 56 (52b) The canticle we sing this Sunday is a song of victory over persecution. In the third chapter of the Book of Daniel, we hear of Shadrach, Meshach, and Abednego, who were thrown into a fire under the orders of King Nebuchadnezzar because they refused to worship an idol. This is part of the song they sang when the angel of the Lord drove the flames out of the furnace. Its forty-eight verses call on all creation to praise the God of salvation.

2 Corinthians 13:11–13 At the close of his second Letter to the Corinthians, Paul gives instructions and prays what was then an exceptional blessing for the community; today we use it in our Eucharistic celebrations. It is the only explicitly Trinitarian blessing in our Scriptures, and Paul's letter predates Matthew's account of the Gospel, which calls for Baptism in the name of the Father, the Son, and the Spirit.

Paul begins his prayer, by asking that the "grace of the Lord Jesus Christ" will be with the community (2 Corinthians 13:13). In Paul's writing, the Lord's grace is salvation; it includes every type of gift or blessing. Mentioning Christ first indicates that it is through him that we have come to know what we now know about God; most particularly, the revelation of God's great love expressed through Jesus. The third part of the blessing asks for companionship with the Holy Spirit, the experience of knowing God's Spirit in the community. Like his Jewish predecessors, Paul is reflecting knowledge of God rooted in religious experience. Only after much more reflection on that experience will the Church begin to articulate the doctrine of the Triune God.

John 3:16–18 These three verses, like many Gospel citations, could be used to summarize the entire Gospel message. Verse 16 first reminds us of God's love not just for one people or nation but for the whole world. The words "gave his only Son" (v. 16) hearken back to Abraham's willingness to sacrifice his son and God's intervention to save Isaac on the third day (Genesis 22).

Verse 17 recalls God's generous love, insisting that God has no desire to condemn the world. This, too, recalls Jewish tradition expressed in passages like Ezekiel 18:23, where the Lord asks: "Do I find pleasure in the death of the wicked . . . ? Do I not rejoice when they turn from their evil way and live?" It is that same, loving God who sent the Son so that the world might be saved.

Some may read verse 18 as a contradiction to the preceding verses, but the meaning is more subtle than it first appears. Jesus is not demanding belief; he is pointing out that belief is the only path to life. People who do not believe are comparable to people who refuse to appreciate beauty: they are not deprived by another, but they rather deprive themselves of the pleasure beauty can offer. Those who refuse to believe are rejecting salvation.

---

1 GCD, 47.

In the context of the solemnity of the Most Holy Trinity, this passage, like Paul's blessing of the Corinthians, assures us of God's unfailing, immeasurable love for humanity. Our God will stop at nothing to bring us to life. Contemplating all of these readings together, we have a glimpse of God's ongoing self-revelation and the experiences that have brought us to faith in the Triune God.

 # Preparation

The Creed we profess each Sunday at Mass is trinitarian. We announce God as one, and as Father, Son, and Spirit. It is through the works of the persons of the Trinity that we have come to know who these persons are. In a most particular way, Christ's life reveals to us the face of God and the relationship among the persons. The love among them is so abundant that it pours out to us. The Trinity as mystery points us to both God's unknowability and God's infinite knowability.

Lectionary for Mass #164A

Exodus 34:4b–6, 8–9

Daniel 3:52, 53, 54, 55, 56 (52b)

2 Corinthians 13:11–13

John 3:16–18

Objectives

- To invite the children to know God as three persons in one God.

- To help them understand that our way to God and heaven is through Jesus Christ.

Preparation and Materials

- Read the Season Background, the lectionary readings, and the Scripture Background.

- Bookmark the appropriate readings (see page xvii) in the lectionary, children's lectionary, or Bible. Place the book in a convenient location for the leader.

- Write the words of dismissal on a card for the priest celebrant.

- Prepare the words of the song the children will sing as they gather in the space for the Liturgy of the Word.

- Select volunteers (older children or adults) to proclaim the readings.

- Display the responsorial psalm refrain lyrics.

- Display the Apostles' or Nicene Creed.

- Prepare intercessions for the Prayer of the Faithful adapted for the needs of the Church, world, oppressed or marginalized, and local community.

Prayer Leader Reflection Questions

» **How do you know God? What do you do to foster greater intimacy with God in your own life?**

» **As God's abundant love is poured out to you, how are you pouring out love on those around you?**

Procession

Following the Collect of the Mass, the priest celebrant picks up the lectionary and invites those who would like to participate in the Liturgy of the Word with children to come forward and gather in the center aisle. The people who will lead the children out and facilitate the Liturgy of the Word also come forward at this time. Holding the lectionary so that all can see, the priest celebrant sends the children forth using his own words or the following:

Priest: **Dear children, this mystery of the Most Holy Trinity can be summed up in one word: Love—the love between the Father and the Son, and the love the Father has for us in sending his only Son. It's the same love your parents have for you and that we all must have for one another. In that love we send you forth to listen to today's readings.**

The leader processes out holding the lectionary, and the children follow behind. The parish music minister may have selected a song of dismissal for the assembly to sing while the children leave. A good option is "The Word of God: Children's Dismissal" by M. D. Ridge and Timothy R. Smith (WLP/GIA).

Centering

Continue to sing the song of dismissal that the assembly sang as you left the church. Or sing "Most Holy Trinity/Santísima Trinidad" (Florián) or "Praise to the Trinity" (Glover) or have instrumental music playing as the children gather in the space for the Liturgy of the Word.

Place the lectionary on the ambo or lectern. Light the candle placed by the ambo or lectern, and then lead the following prayer:

**Everlasting God,
you are Loving Father,
Holy Redeemer,
Spirit of Life,
Most Blessed Trinity;
be with us always as we listen to your Word.
Through Christ our Lord.**

Children: **Amen.**

First Reading

Exodus 34:4b–6, 8–9

Responsorial Psalm

Daniel 3:52, 53, 54, 55, 56 (52b) *Sing the same musical setting that is used in your parish's celebration of the liturgy.*

Second Reading

2 Corinthians 13:11–13

Gospel Acclamation

Sing the Gospel Acclamation used in your parish's celebration of the liturgy.

Gospel Reading

John 3:16–18

Homily/Reflection

We have spent so many weeks enjoying the great celebration of Easter. On Easter Sunday and throughout Easter Time we remember and celebrate in a deep way that Jesus who died is risen. Alleluia! Today, we are returning to Ordinary Time, to counting time. During Ordinary Time, we see the color green the priest wears.

>> **Where else have you seen the color green here in church?**

Green is the color of growth. We are reminded to continue to grow in faith. Today, we pay special attention to growing in faith, hope, and love of God in God's very self, which we call the Trinity.

At Mass, we profess in the creed that God is one and that God is Father and Son and Holy Spirit. We call this the "mystery of the Trinity." In our faith, a mystery is not a puzzle to be solved or a question that can never be answered. A mystery is something that we can talk about, but that, no matter how much we say and how well we say it, there is always more to say. This is what we mean when we describe God as mystery.

What we do know and believe is that the Trinity is about being in relationship with God—a relationship of love. In today's Gospel, we heard about how much God loves us: "For God so loved the world that he gave his only Son, so that everyone who believes in him might not perish but have eternal life." The whole reading is about God's great love for his human creation. God wants to share heaven, his home, with us. God the Father was willing to send his own son to us to make a way for us to go to heaven. God the Son was willing to do this work for our salvation. Because he loves us, God wants us to know him and love him. He wants us to learn about Jesus, know Jesus, and live out Jesus' teachings. He wants for us to choose Jesus, because belief in Jesus is the path we have to God. God's love for us is so great that nothing will ever stop him from reaching out to the world through his son Jesus.

>> How will you respond to God's call? How will you respond to Jesus?

>> How will you choose to live out the faith into which you are baptized?

Before leaving today, think of one way you will cooperate with Jesus to live out your faith this week. Perhaps think about how you might share with your brother, sister, or friend. Or think about the ways you may help your mom, dad, or grandparents without being reminded. These are just a couple of examples. Let's pause for a moment now to think of one action for this week.

Profession of Faith

Following the homily or reflection, the prayer leader invites everyone to stand to profess our faith. Together, sing or recite the Apostles' or Nicene Creed. Refer the children to the words of the prayer that you have displayed.

Prayer of the Faithful

Leader: **Our God is a God of love, a God of perfect relationship. Through Christ, in the power of the Holy Spirit, we turn to the Father for what we need. Please respond, "Father, Son, and Spirit, hear our prayer."**

For the ministry of the Church around the world, for her strength and endurance, let us pray: *Father, Son, and Spirit, hear our prayer.*

For the world to know and be saved by Jesus Christ, who was sent by the Father in his love for humanity, let us pray: *Father, Son, and Spirit, hear our prayer.*

For those who remain hesitant in faith, that the Spirit of God may move in their hearts and minds, let us pray: *Father, Son, and Spirit, hear our prayer.*

For our families to grow more in the love exemplified by the Most Holy Trinity, let us pray: *Father, Son, and Spirit, hear our prayer.*

Invite other intercessions from the children, or add intercessions based on the current needs of the Church, the world, the oppressed or marginalized, and the local community. Conclude each of the children's petitions with **"let us pray"** and invite the response **"Father, Son, and Spirit, hear our prayer."**

For all who have died, that they may know and live in the full glory of the Trinity, three persons in one God, let us pray:
Father, Son, and Spirit, hear our prayer.

God our Creator,
we thank you for the gift of your only Son,
through whom we may enjoy life forever with you.
Pour out your Spirit upon us,
so that we may grow strong to serve you and others always.
Through Christ our Lord.

Children: **Amen.**

Quietly return with the children to the main assembly. Be mindful of children having difficulty finding their families.

June 11, 2023
Solemnity of the Most Holy Body and Blood of Christ

Our Living Bread

 ## Scripture Background

Connections to Church Teaching and Tradition

- "The *Breaking of Bread* . . . is [the] expression that the first Christians will use to designate their Eucharistic assemblies;[1] by doing so they signified that all who eat the one broken bread, Christ, enter into communion with him and form but one body in him[2]" (CCC, 1329).

- "Those who receive the Eucharist are united more closely to Christ. Through it Christ unites them to all the faithful in one body— the Church. Communion renews, strengthens, and deepens this incorporation into the Church, already achieved by Baptism" (CCC, 1396).

- "'The Eucharist is our daily bread. . . . Its effect is then understood as unity, so that, gathered into his Body . . . we may become what we receive'[3]" (CCC, 2837).

Deuteronomy 8:2–3, 14b–16a   Deuteronomy presents Moses' farewell discourse to the people as they are about to enter the Promised Land. In this passage, Moses counsels the people to remember the mighty deeds that God has done on their behalf during their desert sojourn. God promised to be with the people and was faithful to that promise by providing everything they needed. The testing in the desert was God's way of seeing how faithful the people were to their part of the covenant promises. Hunger was one of the desert afflictions that God satisfied by miraculously providing manna. This was God's way of stressing trust and dependence upon the one who satisfies all hungers. Moses repeats his advice that they are not to forget that in their nothingness, God provides for all their needs. Like them, we must seek God rather than material wealth, trusting that God will provide everything we need.

Psalm 147:12–13, 14–15, 19–20 (12)   Psalm 147 personifies Jerusalem as a mother gathering her children to herself. All are summoned to praise the Lord in thanksgiving for his Word, which brings life and abundance. God's Word has blessed Jerusalem, strengthened her gates and walls, granted peace, and brought fertility to the fields. God has done this for no other nation. Only Israel has been so blessed, and thus Israel is summoned to praise the Lord. The psalm stresses that God's Word brings forth all blessings. God, who gives totally and completely to satisfy all hungers, is the source of these blessings. God's Word is a dynamic reality that goes forth from God throughout the earth, accomplishing all that God commands. For this reason, all of Israel is called to praise the Lord, as we are, for the rich blessings in our lives.

1 Corinthians 10:16–17   In his first Letter to the Corinthians, Paul shares a significant aspect of his teaching, which concerns Christ and the community as the Body of Christ. Jumping off his cultural experience of the bonding that comes from breaking bread and sharing wine at table, Paul stresses that our share in Christ's Body and Blood intimately bonds us to Christ. Our sharing bonds us to the sacrifice of Christ's Body and Blood, which he willingly shed for all. Our communal sharing also bonds us to one another as the Body of Christ, a community that willingly commits itself to a life of sacrifice for the sake of others, in imitation of Christ. Sharing at the Lord's table leads to a transformation of the participants into Christ, both individually and communally.

Sequence: *Lauda Sion*   This Sunday, the Church sings one of the four sequences—ancient, poetic songs that precede the singing of the Gospel Acclamation. The sequence for the Most Holy Body and Blood of Christ, *Lauda Sion*, is ascribed to St. Thomas Aquinas, who is thought to have written it at the request of Pope Urban IV. The sixth stanza of the sequence reminds us of the history of the Eucharistic feast.

John 6:51–58   The context for these verses on Jesus as "the living bread that came down from heaven" (John 6:51) is the Eucharistic celebration of the early Christian communities. The Eucharist of the early communities was always aligned with the total saving event of Christ, who gave his Body and shed his Blood for our sakes. John connects the two realities when he has Jesus state that "the bread that I will give is my flesh for the life of the world" (John 6:51).

---

1   Cf. Acts 2:42, 46; 20:7, 11.

2   Cf. 1 Corinthians 10:16–17.

3   St. Augustine, Sermo 57.7: PL 38, 389.

For John, God the Father, the source of all life, shares with Jesus the fullness of that life. Jesus, the Living Bread that came down from heaven, gives of his life for all. The phrase "flesh and blood" expresses the fullness of the life of Jesus. Those who believe, who accept and partake of the whole Jesus, the Living Bread, will live forever.

God's gift to Israel of the manna and of the law as true nourishment is now fulfilled in Jesus, the Living Bread. Those who eat of that flesh and drink of that blood abide with Jesus, and he abides with them. The manna is given new meaning in the life, Death, and Resurrection of Jesus. Jesus, the manna of God, feeds us eternally with his very self.

Preparation

We celebrate the Eucharist in a special way on Corpus Christi, the Solemnity of the Most Holy Body and Blood of Christ. Jesus Christ has given us the gift of his very self under the form of bread and wine. This gift was prefigured by the gift of manna, the bread from heaven, to the people of Israel. Our experiences of earthly meals, our own hunger and satisfaction, our enjoyment of the food we eat all help us to know the meaning of the spiritual meal we share. When we come together for Mass, we savor and are nourished by God's presence.

Lectionary for Mass #167A

Deuteronomy 8:2–3, 14b–16a

Psalm 147:12–13, 14–15, 19–20 (12)

1 Corinthians 10:16–17

Sequence: Lauda Sion

John 6:51–58

Objectives

- To consider together the Eucharist as nourishment that we savor.

- To define the word *manna* for the children.

Preparation and Materials

- Read the Season Background, the lectionary readings, and the Scripture Background.

- Bookmark the appropriate readings (see page xvii) in the lectionary, children's lectionary, or Bible. Place the book in a convenient location for the leader.

- Write the words of dismissal on a card for the priest celebrant.

- Prepare the words of the song the children will sing as they gather in the space for the Liturgy of the Word.

- Select volunteers (older children or adults) to proclaim the readings.

- Display the responsorial psalm refrain lyrics.

- Display the Apostles' or Nicene Creed.

- Prepare intercessions for the Prayer of the Faithful adapted for the needs of the Church, world, oppressed or marginalized, and local community.

Prayer Leader Reflection Questions

>> **How do you prepare yourself to receive Christ in the Eucharist each week?**

>> **How can you help very young children have reverence for Christ in the Eucharist?**

Procession

Following the Collect of the Mass, the priest celebrant picks up the lectionary and invites those who would like to participate in the Liturgy of the Word with children to come forward and gather in the center aisle. The people who will lead the children out and facilitate the Liturgy of the Word also come forward at this time. Holding the lectionary so that all can see, the priest celebrant sends the children forth using his own words or the following:

> *Priest*: **Dear children, Christ's love for us is so great that he gave us himself in the Eucharist. How might we express our love for one another? Who are the people in our lives who act out of love for us? What are some other signs that God gives us his love for us? As you listen to today's readings, consider these questions and all the wonderful things God has done for us. Go in peace.**

The leader processes out holding the lectionary, and the children follow behind. The parish music minister may have selected a song of dismissal for the assembly to sing while the children leave. A good option is "The Word of God: Children's Dismissal" by M. D. Ridge and Timothy R. Smith (WLP/GIA).

Centering

Continue to sing the song of dismissal that the assembly sang as you left the church. Or sing "Table of Plenty" (Schutte), or the refrain from "Taste and See" (Moore or Hurd), or have instrumental music playing as the children gather in the space for the Liturgy of the Word.

Place the lectionary on the ambo or lectern. Light the candle placed by the ambo or lectern, and then lead the following prayer:

> **Holy God,**
> **feed us with your Sacred Scripture**
> **so that we may be prepared to receive the Body and Blood of Christ.**
> **We ask this through Christ our Lord.**

> *Children:* **Amen.**

First Reading

Deuteronomy 8:2–3, 14b–16a

Responsorial Psalm

Psalm 147:12–13, 14–15, 19–20 (12) *Sing the same musical setting that is used in your parish's celebration of the liturgy.*

Second Reading

1 Corinthians 10:16–17

Gospel Acclamation

Sing the Gospel Acclamation used in your parish's celebration of the liturgy.

Gospel Reading

John 6:51–58

Homily/Reflection

Our Sunday celebration today has a special name: Solemnity of the Most Holy Body and Blood of Christ. For many years, much of the Church prayed in a language called Latin to celebrate Mass. In Latin, the words for *"Body of Christ"* are Corpus Christi. You might sometimes hear people call this day Corpus Christi Sunday. On Corpus Christi Sunday, we think and talk and pray about the beautiful gift of Christ Jesus present with us in the Eucharist.

» As human beings, we have to eat, don't we? What are some of your favorite foods?

Our bodies need the food we eat at meals to have energy, to grow, and to heal when we are sick or injured. Food is also meant to be enjoyed, just like you enjoy the foods you named. We can savor together great feasts on special days of celebration.

When we don't have enough to eat and we are hungry, we can feel it in our bodies. The lack of nourishment affects everything we do. In today's first reading, the Israelites who had been led by Moses out of Egypt knew what it was like to be hungry. Before they reached the promised land, they spent a long time in the desert, where food was hard to find. They would not have been able to get enough on their own. But God provided a miracle for them. God sent a food called "manna," which is bread from heaven. It appeared on the ground when the people awoke in the morning, and they could gather it up to eat. But the manna only lasted for the day. The people couldn't save any for the next day. They had to trust that God would continue to provide nourishment for them every day.

When Jesus said that he is "the living bread that came down from heaven" (John 6:51), he was referring to God providing for the people by sending him. Our souls also need energy, growth, and healing. Jesus offers all of this to us. He is our spiritual nourishment. We can also savor Jesus as our true food when we come to the table of the Lord. God provided physical nourishment by manna, and he provides spiritual nourishment by sending Jesus to us.

Sometimes we use the expression "You are what you eat." We hear in the second reading, "The bread that we break, is it not a participation in the body of Christ?" (1 Corinthians 10:16b). Just as our body builds itself from the nourishment we receive in our meals, our whole self, including our spirits, are built up by the spiritual nourishment we receive in the Eucharist, the body of Christ. If we truly become what we receive, we have to act like it. We have to show the love of Christ to all our sisters and brothers in Christ, as a part of the one Church, the one family of God. Our love has to be so great that it spills out to the whole world so that all people can be nourished by and enjoy Christ's presence.

>> **We, too, can bring new life to the world when we show love. What are some ways we can do this?**

Profession of Faith

Following the homily or reflection, the prayer leader invites everyone to stand to profess our faith. Together, sing or recite the Apostles' or Nicene Creed. Refer the children to the words of the prayer that you have displayed.

Prayer of the Faithful

Leader: **Our souls are nourished by the Eucharist we receive. We trust that our loving God will hear us as we pray to him for our other needs. Please respond, "Lord, hear our prayer."**

That the Church, the Body of Christ, become for others the very bread of life that we eat, we pray: *Lord, hear our prayer.*

That those who hunger for peace, justice, and more of a share in the world's abundant resources may be satisfied, we pray: *Lord, hear our prayer.*

That those who have little or no food to eat find generous-hearted people willing to share their resources, we pray: *Lord, hear our prayer.*

That this community of faith may be a shining example of outreach and support for those who hunger and need help, we pray: *Lord, hear our prayer.*

Invite other intercessions from the children, or add intercessions based on the current needs of the Church, the world, the oppressed or marginalized, and the local community. Conclude each of the children's petitions with **"we pray"** and invite the response **"Lord, hear our prayer."**

That all who have died may enjoy the heavenly banquet together with Jesus Christ, we pray: *Lord, hear our prayer.*

O Jesus,
in the Eucharist, we remember how you died and rose.
The mystery of your Body and Blood, present to us, is wonderful.
Accept the prayers of the children.
Who lives and reigns with God the Father,
in the unity of the Holy Spirit, God, for ever and ever.

Children: **Amen.**

Quietly return with the children to the main assembly. Be mindful of children having difficulty finding their families.

June 18, 2023
Eleventh Sunday in Ordinary Time

A Holy Nation

 Scripture Background

Connections to Church Teaching and Tradition

- The Church has a mission, and we must do our best to fulfill it: we must work for the salvation of all (AG, 1, 2, 5, 7–9, 15; GS, 40–43; CCC, 849–856).

- A most important aspect of our mission is the reconciliation of the world with God and healing rifts among people (LG, 8, 11, 22, 40; CCC, 1427–1449).

- Everyone is called to enter the kingdom of heaven, even the poor and the lowly (CCC, 543–544), so Jesus enlisted the help of others for his ministry (CCC, 858).

Exodus 19:2–6a God calls Moses and the Israelites to Mount Sinai, the mountain where God was first revealed to Moses in the burning bush (3:1, there called "Horeb"). On the mountain, Moses was reminded that God brought them out of slavery in Egypt. On Sinai, God entered a covenant with the people, a special relationship by which they became God's people. God previously made covenants with the human race through Noah (Genesis 9:9) and to Abraham and his descendants (Genesis 15:18).

In the covenant with Abraham, God unilaterally promised him posterity and the possession of the land. On Sinai, God goes further by making demands of the people. If the people obey God's voice and keep the covenant, they would be God's "special possession" (Exodus 19:5b). When Moses summons the people and tells them the words God pronounced, Israel replies, "Everything the LORD has said, we will do" (v. 8a; the details of the covenant and the Ten Commandments are enumerated in chapter 20). The people are told to prepare themselves for God's revelation. A dense cloud, thunder and lightning, smoke, fire, and an earthquake (a theophany, or divine manifestation in nature) herald God's presence. These awesome forces emphasized the sacredness of the moment. God's people were not only chosen, but they were also formed by God to be "a kingdom of priests, a holy nation" (v. 6a).

Psalm 100:1–2, 3, 5 (3c) Psalm 100 is among the shortest in the psalter. The people probably sang it while they made solemn entrance through the gates of the Jerusalem Temple and into the courts to offer up sacrifice to God. The people are invited to serve God "with gladness" (v. 2a) and rejoice in God's presence. The psalmist reminds the people that they are not only God's creatures, but they are also God's Chosen People, the flock that God shepherds. The worshipers are exhorted to come before God with thanksgiving and praise for God's goodness and care. God's love is eternal; God's faithfulness is without end.

Romans 5:6–11 Paul writes to the Roman Christian community, explaining that Jesus Christ dying for the human race was proof of God's love. Paul says it would be hard enough to convince someone to die for a just person or for some great principle. It might be possible for them to have such great love for their friends that they would lay down their lives for them. But Jesus Christ died for humanity when they were still sinners and in a state of alienation from God. Through Jesus, the status of sinners was changed, and they were put into a right relationship with God. This change of status is called justification, the saving process by which people are made right with God through Christ's Death on the Cross. The saving process goes on through sanctification; that is, through God's grace whereby sinful men and women are made God's holy people. Jesus did not come to change God's wrathful attitude toward the human race; he came to show what was always there, that through God's love, people have received reconciliation and salvation.

Matthew 9:36—10:8 When Jesus healed a possessed mute (9:32–33), the last miracle in a series of them in Matthew's Gospel (chapters 8–9), the people were in awe at this unprecedented event. Everywhere Jesus went, in the towns, villages, and synagogues, the good news of the Kingdom was ushered in through Jesus' words and works. Many responded to these miracles with faith, but some refused to believe in him. The religious leaders, who should have welcomed the appearance of God's reign, rejected Jesus' works, claiming they came from the evil one. Jesus was moved with compassion because the people were like "sheep without a shepherd" (9:36). The Greek word Matthew uses for "compassion," *splagchnizomai*, is formed from the word that means "the bowels." It describes the depths of human feeling. The people longed for God, and the religious leaders had nothing to offer them. Jesus asks his disciples to pray that the "master of the harvest" (v. 38) would send out more laborers to care for God's people. The divine shepherd and harvest master needed human cooperation. Jesus chose twelve ordinary men to be his Apostles. The word *apostle* literally means one who is "sent out" (10:5). Those Jesus called to share his authority and mission had no wealth, no special education, no social standing. Yet Jesus sent them forth to announce God's reign to the "lost sheep of the house of Israel" (v. 6). The miracles that accompanied their proclamation were signs of God's presence in them. The gift that they received was to be shared freely with others.

 # Preparation

God established a covenant with the people of Israel and offered special love and care that was made manifest in their deliverance from Egypt. The people were invited to lovingly respond to the covenantal relationship through fidelity and obedience to God. We can respond to God's love in a similar way. Despite our failings, however, the Father sent the Son to save us. This good news of God's love is given to us, and we are invited to share it with others through our words and actions.

Lectionary for Mass #91A

Exodus 19:2–6a

Psalm 100:1–2, 3, 5 (3c)

Romans 5:6–11

Matthew 9:36—10:8

Objectives

- To announce God's special love and care for the people of Israel that is also shared with us.

- To invite the children into the mission of the whole people of God to spread the good news of God's love through words and actions.

Preparation and Materials

- Read the Season Background, the lectionary readings, and the Scripture Background.

- Bookmark the appropriate readings (see page xvii) in the lectionary, children's lectionary, or Bible. Place the book in a convenient location for the leader.

- Write the words of dismissal on a card for the priest celebrant.

- Prepare the words of the song the children will sing as they gather in the space for the Liturgy of the Word.

- Select volunteers (older children or adults) to proclaim the readings.

- Display the responsorial psalm refrain lyrics.

- Display the Apostles' or Nicene Creed.

- Prepare intercessions for the Prayer of the Faithful adapted for the needs of the Church, world, oppressed or marginalized, and local community.

Prayer Leader Reflection Questions

» **When have you experienced God's love and care in your own life?**

» **How are you living out God's call to mission? How are you spreading the good news through your words and actions?**

Procession

Following the Collect of the Mass, the priest celebrant picks up the lectionary and invites those who would like to participate in the Liturgy of the Word with children to come forward and gather in the center aisle. The people who will lead the children out and facilitate the Liturgy of the Word also come forward at this time. Holding the lectionary so that all can see, the priest celebrant sends the children forth using his own words or the following:

> *Priest*: **Jesus taught us to listen for his voice so we may know God better and live as he wants us to live. We send you with your leader(s) to listen carefully to God's Word. Pay attention to what God is saying to you today. May the Holy Spirit help you understand and live this good news. Go now in peace.**

The leader processes out holding the lectionary, and the children follow behind. The parish music minister may have selected a song of dismissal for the assembly to sing while the children leave. A good option is "The Word of God: Children's Dismissal" by M. D. Ridge and Timothy R. Smith (WLP/GIA).

Centering

Continue to sing the song of dismissal that the assembly sang as you left the church. Or have instrumental music playing as the children gather in the space for the Liturgy of the Word.

Place the lectionary on the ambo or lectern. Light the candle placed by the ambo or lectern, and then lead the following prayer:

> **Loving God,**
> **we praise you and thank you for this time together.**
> **Help us hear your Word so our hearts may be changed by it.**
> **Through Christ our Lord.**

> *Children:* **Amen.**

First Reading

Exodus 19:2–6a

Responsorial Psalm

Psalm 100:1–2, 3, 5 (3c) *Sing the same musical setting that is used in your parish's celebration of the liturgy.*

Second Reading

Romans 5:6–11

Gospel Acclamation

Sing the Gospel Acclamation used in your parish's celebration of the liturgy.

Gospel Reading

Matthew 9:36—10:8

Homily/Reflection

Today is the Eleventh Sunday in Ordinary Time. In church, we see the color green in what Father is wearing. We see the color green in the living and growing things like the plants and flowers that decorate our worship space.

» Do you remember what the color green signifies?

During Ordinary Time, we count the Sundays in order as we move forward in our year. Little by little, we grow closer to God. We are growing in our faith.

In today's first reading from Exodus, we heard God telling the people of Israel, "You will be my treasure" (Exodus 19:5).

» What do you think of when you hear the word *treasure*?

Treasures are what we consider most precious or valuable. God had already shown amazing love and care for the people leading them out of slavery to freedom. In the second reading, St. Paul tells us how far this love of God reaches. It was not only for the people who had been taken out of Egypt thousands of years ago. It was not only for the people who live in the region of Israel. God's love extends through time and space to us today.

When we are so loved and given such great gifts, there might be something we want to do in return. We might want to say thank you and that we love you too. God told the people of Israel how to do this. God told them how to show that they belong to God. Obeying God was how they could say thank you and that they loved God. The people could show in that way that they were God's treasure.

» In what other ways might we show God that we love him and thank him?

In baptism, we are called by name to be a part of the Church, the people of God. We are together as one with all other people who have been called God's treasure. We are also called by name to do a job. We call this our "mission." In the Gospel, we hear Jesus giving his disciples a job. He sent them out to cure people of what made them sick in body and spirit, to help them to know God's love and care. We have this same call today. All of us have the job of going out to the whole world and helping others to know that they are God's treasures as well. We can let them know without words that God loved them so much that Jesus Christ was sent for them, even though they haven't always obeyed. We can show them what it looks like to obey God's Word. We can treat them like treasures, showing them the love that God has for every one of us.

» What are some ways we can spread the good news of God's love?

Profession of Faith

Following the homily or reflection, the prayer leader invites everyone to stand to profess our faith. Together, sing or recite the Apostles' or Nicene Creed. Refer the children to the words of the prayer that you have displayed.

Prayer of the Faithful

Leader: **With humble hearts, we bring our needs to you, heavenly Father, trusting that you are listening. Please respond, "Lord, hear our prayer."**

May the Church always be on mission, spreading Christ's message by word and deed, we pray to the Lord: *Lord, hear our prayer.*

May all nations work together to promote the responsible use of creation, by showing reverence to God's work, and ensuring the existence of natural resources for generations to come, we pray to the Lord: *Lord, hear our prayer.*

May all those suffering mentally, physically, or spiritually find healing in God, we pray to the Lord: *Lord, hear our prayer.*

May we all recognize our need for God as we grow in faith and allow him to help us each day and follow as he leads us to new and fuller life, we pray to the Lord: *Lord, hear our prayer.*

Invite other intercessions from the children, or add intercessions based on the current needs of the Church, the world, the oppressed or marginalized, and the local community. Conclude each of the children's petitions with **"we pray to the Lord"** and invite the response **"Lord, hear our prayer."**

May all who have died live as God's treasured possessions forever, we pray to the Lord: *Lord, hear our prayer.*

God our Father,
your love for us is unconditional and eternal.
May we always know that love
and walk in the light of your presence.
Accept the prayers of your children.
Through Christ our Lord.

Children: **Amen.**

Quietly return with the children to the main assembly. Be mindful of children having difficulty finding their families.

June 25, 2023
Twelfth Sunday in Ordinary Time
Do Not Be Afraid

 ## Scripture Background

Connections to Church Teaching and Tradition

- God alone rescues us (CCC, 169).

- The prophets heard God's call to repentance and faithfulness. They prepared for the intervention of God in human history (CCC, 2584).

- The Church is the instrument of God's works, an assistant in God's work of salvation (CCC, 737, 778).

- The Church's deepest vocation is to live as communion. The Church is a community (LG, 51; CCC, 959), even a family.

Jeremiah 20:10–13 Jeremiah, one of the four major prophets in the Old Testament, was chosen by God when he was very young, and he served faithfully for five decades. When Jeremiah received his call, Judah was under Assyrian domination; the people had fallen into the worship of pagan gods; the Temple was in disrepair; the Law of Moses was disregarded. Jeremiah's prophetic call came in the year 626 BC, on the eve of the religious reform of King Josiah. Unfortunately, Josiah died in a military campaign in 609 BC, and the reforms were never fully realized. During the last half of Jeremiah's career, the Assyrian empire collapsed and Babylon became the supreme power, which eventually led to the destruction of Jerusalem and the Exile of God's people in 587 BC. Chapter 20 of Jeremiah contains his confessions, his inner struggle with his vocation, and his complaints for the persecution that he suffered on behalf of God. Despite his lamentation, he ends with praise: "Sing to the LORD; praise the LORD! For he has delivered the life of the needy from the hands of evildoers" (v. 13).

Psalm 69:8–10, 14, 17, 33–35 (14c) Psalm 69 is a lament. The psalmist was faithful to God, and ardent zeal for the Temple of God had consumed him. Nevertheless, the psalmist suffered shame and dishonor. He became a "stranger" to his own "kindred," and an alien to his "mother's children" (v. 8). The scorn of those who insulted God fell on him. Brokenhearted and in despair, he "looked for compassion, but there was none; / for comforters, but found none" (v. 20). Although the psalmist expresses intense misery, he ends on a note of hope, a declaration of praise and confidence in God's ability to save: "For the LORD hears the poor, / and his own who are in bonds he spurns not" (v. 33).

Romans 5:12–15 The Easter Proclamation (Exsultet) proclaims Adam's sin as a "happy fault" that led to the redemption of the human race in Jesus Christ, which far outweighed what was lost in the fall. Paul explained that through Adam's sin, all people were alienated from God. Yet, by the righteousness of Jesus Christ, all were restored to a right relationship with God. For just as in Adam all die, so also all shall live in Christ. To understand Paul's thought, it is necessary to recognize the Jewish self-understanding of the time. The Jewish people did not think of themselves as individuals, but as part of a family, a clan, or a nation. Because of human solidarity, all people actually sinned in Adam. Adam's sin was not one person's sin but the sin of all. Thus, through one person, Adam, death entered the world. Likewise, through one person, Jesus Christ, all have a share in his resurrection of the dead. Paul emphasized that this gift of eternal life is a free gift that sinful humanity did not deserve. Through God's mercy, the free gift of righteousness was given "in the grace of the one man, Jesus Christ" (v. 15).

Matthew 10:26–33 Jesus came as the full revelation of God to the world, but many were obstinate and refused to believe the truth of his words. Despite the darkness of unbelief, light came through the proclamation of Jesus' faithful Apostles. Jesus warned them, however, that just as they shared his mission of proclaiming God's reign, they would also share in his Passion. Students were not above their teachers, and slaves could not outrank their masters (v. 24). Jesus' disciples would be despised by their fellow Jews and rejected by members of their own families. When they were brought to trial for their faith, they should not be concerned about how they would defend them selves. The Holy Spirit would inspire them to be faithful witnesses (v. 19). Fear of persecution and death should not deter them from boldly speaking the message they received.

They should not fear those who could kill them; a greater peril would be to lose their immortal souls. The one they should fear is the evil one who could lead them to eternal destruction.

Jesus encouraged his followers by reminding them of their worth before God. If God cared for the tiny sparrows that were sold in the Temple for sacrifice, how much more valued were God's children? Despite the coming darkness and opposition, the Twelve must be fearless in proclaiming the light and truth of the Gospel. If they are faithful in their task, Jesus would defend them on the Day of Judgment.

 # Preparation

Fear is a human response meant to protect us and keep us safe. The early Christians, and indeed Christians today, face fear when living the Gospel message, but Jesus reassures us that God's love and concern for us is so encompassing that every hair on our heads is known to him. Through God's love, we can stand firm and not be afraid, knowing that those who could hurt the body cannot hurt the soul.

Lectionary for Mass #94A

Jeremiah 20:10–13

Psalm 69:8–10, 14, 17, 33–35 (14c)

Romans 5:12–15

Matthew 10:26–33

Objectives

- To explain to children that God loves and cares for each individual person.

- To help them understand that God's love gives us courage and that we can place our hope and trust in him.

Preparation and Materials

- Read the Season Background, the lectionary readings, and the Scripture Background.

- Bookmark the appropriate readings (see page xvii) in the lectionary, children's lectionary, or Bible. Place the book in a convenient location for the leader.

- Write the words of dismissal on a card for the priest celebrant.

- Prepare the words of the song the children will sing as they gather in the space for the Liturgy of the Word.

- Select volunteers (older children or adults) to proclaim the readings.

- Display the responsorial psalm refrain lyrics.

- Display the Apostles' or Nicene Creed.

- Prepare intercessions for the Prayer of the Faithful adapted for the needs of the Church, world, oppressed or marginalized, and local community.

Prayer Leader Reflection Questions

>> Have you ever been persecuted for your commitment to announce the good news of God? How did your faith and trust in God help you?

>> What fears might young children face? How might you help them face those fears?

Procession

Following the Collect of the Mass, the priest celebrant picks up the lectionary and invites those who would like to participate in the Liturgy of the Word with children to come forward and gather in the center aisle. The people who will lead the children out and facilitate the Liturgy of the Word also come forward at this time. Holding the lectionary so that all can see, the priest celebrant sends the children forth using his own words or the following:

> *Priest*: **Dear children, today Jesus tells us to fear no one. When we are in danger or feeling lost or are suffering, he is with us to protect us and save us. So be confident and courageous. Go now and listen to Jesus, who loves you very much.**

The leader processes out holding the lectionary, and the children follow behind. The parish music minister may have selected a song of dismissal for the assembly to sing while the children leave. A good option is "The Word of God: Children's Dismissal" by M. D. Ridge and Timothy R. Smith (WLP/GIA).

Centering

Continue to sing the song of dismissal that the assembly sang as you left the church. Or sing the refrains from "Be Not Afraid" (Dufford), or "Christ Be Our Light" (Farrell), or have instrumental music playing as the children gather in the space for the Liturgy of the Word.

Place the lectionary on the ambo or lectern. Light the candle placed by the ambo or lectern, and then lead the following prayer:

> **O God,**
> **help us open our hearts to listen to the wisdom of your Word**
> **and help us remember that wisdom in our everyday lives.**
> **We ask this through Christ our Lord.**

> *Children:* **Amen.**

First Reading

Jeremiah 20:10–13

Responsorial Psalm

Psalm 69:8–10, 14, 17, 33–35 (14c) *Sing the same musical setting that is used in your parish's celebration of the liturgy.*

Second Reading

Romans 5:12–15

Gospel Acclamation

Sing the Gospel Acclamation used in your parish's celebration of the liturgy.

Gospel Reading

Matthew 10:26–33

Homily/Reflection

>> **Have you ever been afraid?**

>> **What have you been scared of?**

All people are scared of something at one time or another, even grownups sometimes feel afraid!

>> **What does it feel like when you are scared?**
> *(Your heart might beat very fast; you might feel sick or dizzy; tummy ache; crying.)*

Being afraid is normal. Even Jesus' disciples sometimes felt afraid too. Do you remember how they all locked themselves in a room after the crucifixion? They were afraid then. Do you remember how St. Peter denied Jesus three times just before the crucifixion? He denied knowing Jesus because he was afraid of what people would do to him if he admitted to knowing him.

Remember they lived in a land that was occupied by Rome. Violence and persecution were a part of the people's everyday lives, so people felt scared all the time. In today's Gospel, Jesus is reminding the Apostles that they should not fear any person. Jesus meant that their souls had nothing to fear from those who might hurt their bodies. This was an important message for the Apostles to hear. Think about how much the disciples were suffering because of their belief in Jesus. Jesus explained to the Apostles that they were all very precious to God—so precious, that God knew how many hairs were upon their heads. God watches over us so lovingly and with such care.

>> **So do you think the Apostles felt less scared after Jesus reassured them? Do you think they felt some peace of mind?**

God knows everything about us and loves us very much. If anything were to happen to one of God's children, he would know about it and take care of that person. Jesus didn't want fear of persecution to stop the disciples from spreading his message. He wanted the disciples to be brave and ready to face the possibility of persecution. He wanted them to understand that no matter what happened, God would be with them, and that saving souls was more important than being persecuted.

God is also with each of us, caring for us, and loving us. Like the disciples, he wants for us to be brave in the face of any troubles or worries. Our mission is to live out Christ's message and to share that message with everyone. Sometimes we might be afraid of doing the right and good thing. Jesus assures us that when we are scared of what others might say or do, we should still stand strong in living out the Gospel. So, if we ever feel worried about something, we can place our trust in God. When we pray, we can give our fears and worries to God and ask God to take care of it for us. Sometimes things are very hard to understand, and we may see people having problems that seem too big to fix, all we can do is trust that God always wants to bring light to darkness. God always wants goodness to win. God always wants us to feel loved, even in hard times. So, when we offer our fears and worries to God, that also helps us grow in faith, because we learn to depend upon God, and because God is big enough to handle it all.

Before you leave today, think about a time you may have felt scared about doing something that is right and good. Think about how God loves and cares for you, and how he wants us to learn to be fearless in living out Jesus' good news.

Profession of Faith

Following the homily or reflection, the prayer leader invites everyone to stand to profess our faith. Together, sing or recite the Apostles' or Nicene Creed. Refer the children to the words of the prayer that you have displayed.

Prayer of the Faithful

Leader: **Jesus reassures us and tells us not to be afraid. So with courage and confidence we now turn to God with our prayers, for ourselves and for our world. Please respond, "Merciful Lord, hear our prayer."**

For Church leaders who are called to guide us and help us grow in faith, we pray: *Merciful Lord, hear our prayer.*

For peace in the world, especially in the places where there is war, we pray: *Merciful Lord, hear our prayer.*

For those paralyzed by fear, who are sick, isolated, oppressed, in mourning, and wounded, that they may be reassured of God's love and supported by the community, we pray: *Merciful Lord, hear our prayer.*

For our own parish community, that we may share God's love with others by our words and actions, we pray: *Merciful Lord, hear our prayer.*

Invite other intercessions from the children, or add intercessions based on the current needs of the Church, the world, the oppressed or marginalized, and the local community. Conclude each of the children's petitions with **"we pray"** and invite the response **"Merciful Lord, hear our prayer."**

For those who have died, that they may be made new to live in the presence of our heavenly Father, we pray: *Merciful Lord, hear our prayer.*

Heavenly Father, hear your children gathered here to praise and thank you. Grant our prayers through Christ our Lord.

Children: **Amen.**

Quietly return with the children to the main assembly. Be mindful of children having difficulty finding their families.

July 2, 2023
Thirteenth Sunday in Ordinary Time

Give without Expectation

 ## Scripture Background

Connections to Church Teaching and Tradition

- Christian charity should be genuine, and hospitality should be practiced (CCC, 1971). God rewards those who are patient in need and constant in prayer.

- Through Baptism, we enter the life, Death, and Resurrection of Jesus (CCC, 1213).

- Jesus calls us to conversion through Baptism. Through God's mercy and love, we continue the process of conversion (CCC, 1427–1428).

2 Kings 4:8–11, 14–16a   The books of 1 and 2 Kings span the four-hundred-year history of Israel, from the royal dynasty of David's son Solomon to the division of the united kingdom and the destruction of the Temple in 587 BC. It chronicles the reigns of incompetent and ruthless kings whose policies led to the Exile, and the religious reforms of good kings, Hezekiah and Josiah. The author's purpose was not so much to write a history as to explain why things happened as they did. The author wanted to instill faith in those who saw the last king in David's line defeated and deported to Babylon. The books of Kings report the prophetic careers of Elijah and his disciple, Elisha, who continued the work of the great prophet by proclaiming God's faithfulness to the covenant. Elisha's encounter with the Shunammite is the story of a prominent woman who was interested in promoting the work of God, as shown in the hospitality she provided for the prophet without expecting anything in return. In due time, the woman was rewarded for her service. She conceived and bore a son as Elisha promised.

Psalm 89:2–3, 16–17, 18–19 (2a)   Psalm 89 includes prayers for the king because it is through him that the people of God are blessed. The opening line announces the theme of God's faithfulness over time. Terms like *forever* and *all generations* convey the lasting depth of the covenant and reflect God's continual promise to David's house. Seen in light of a possible military loss, it is certain that, despite defeat, God's love for David does not change. This Sunday, we sing praise and proclaim the faithfulness of God for the entire world to know.

Romans 6:3–4, 8–11   In his letter to Roman Christians, Paul carried on an argument against an imaginary opponent. He wanted to help them know that God forgave sins, but he also wanted to know something more important. In Baptism, all sins are remitted because God cannot punish sins committed before a person is born. Paul went on to explain what happens in Baptism. The person is "dead to sin and living for God in Christ Jesus" (v. 11). In the early Church, Christian converts often came from pagan roots. They had to make a decision that meant leaving their former lives behind and beginning life all over again. When they were immersed in the baptismal font, the water closed over them, and it was like being buried. When they emerged from the water, it was like rising from the grave. They were not only united with Christ's Death, but also his Resurrection. The Church expresses this new life in Christ as sanctifying grace. Through Baptism, Christians are joined to Christ, and the life of God is infused in them, a gift that they must continue to live by faith.

Matthew 10:37–42   As opposition to Jesus' message grew, he exhorted his disciples to have courage under persecution. Jesus knew that not everyone would accept the Gospel his followers proclaimed. Even members of their families might be their adversaries. In Jesus' time, one of the beliefs concerning the "day of the LORD," when God would break into history through the coming of the Messiah, was that a division would occur among families. Jesus preached a message of total renunciation. His disciples must be willing to sacrifice everything for the sake of the Kingdom. Nothing or no one must deter them from their dedication to Christ and his mission. To encounter Jesus demands a choice: to accept him or to reject him. Those who deny Jesus to save their earthly lives risk losing eternal salvation. Those who choose this difficult path can be sure that they will share Jesus' destiny of persecution and suffering. Those who wish to follow in Jesus' footsteps must be willing to put the Gospel before all else, even their own lives. Whoever refuses to "take up his cross" and follow him was "not worthy" of being his disciples (v. 38). Like the prophets of old, they must be prepared to suffer for speaking God's Word. Jesus' disciples were Christian "prophets" who spoke God's saving message of the New Covenant. Whoever offered them hospitality received Jesus himself and God who sent him. They will be rewarded for their kindness to God's messengers.

Preparation

In providing for the feeding and housing of Elisha, the woman of Shunem showed great hospitality toward the prophet. Elisha expressed gratitude through the gift of the announcement of a child to be born to the woman. This gift was generous and unexpected. We can show hospitality toward others, even perform small acts of generosity. For the gifts that we have been given, we can express gratitude to the givers, and to the ultimate Giver who is God.

Lectionary for Mass #97A

2 Kings 4:8–11, 14–16a

Psalm 89:2–3, 16–17, 18–19 (2a)

Romans 6:3–4, 8–9

Matthew 10:37–42

Objectives

- To offer the woman of Shunem and Elisha as models for our own moral life.

- To affirm prophets as those who listen for God's voice and then speak.

Preparation and Materials

- Read the Season Background, the lectionary readings, and the Scripture Background.

- Bookmark the appropriate readings (see page xvii) in the lectionary, children's lectionary, or Bible. Place the book in a convenient location for the leader.

- Write the words of dismissal on a card for the priest celebrant.

- Prepare the words of the song the children will sing as they gather in the space for the Liturgy of the Word.

- Select volunteers (older children or adults) to proclaim the readings.

- Display the responsorial psalm refrain lyrics.

- Display the Apostles' or Nicene Creed.

- Prepare intercessions for the Prayer of the Faithful adapted for the needs of the Church, world, oppressed or marginalized, and local community.

Prayer Leader Reflection Questions

» **How do you offer hospitality?**

» **How do you express gratitude?**

Procession

Following the Collect of the Mass, the priest celebrant picks up the lectionary and invites those who would like to participate in the Liturgy of the Word with children to come forward and gather in the center aisle. The people who will lead the children out and facilitate the Liturgy of the Word also come forward at this time. Holding the lectionary so that all can see, the priest celebrant sends the children forth using his own words or the following:

> *Priest*: **Dear children, listen to what the Shunammite woman did for the prophet Elisha in today's first reading, how she was kind to him. We are reminded in the Gospel that whoever receives a prophet receives Jesus. The kindness we show to each other, we show to God. Remember this as you go about your week at home and at school. Go in peace.**

The leader processes out holding the lectionary, and the children follow behind. The parish music minister may have selected a song of dismissal for the assembly to sing while the children leave. A good option is "The Word of God: Children's Dismissal" by M. D. Ridge and Timothy R. Smith (WLP/GIA).

Centering

Continue to sing the song of dismissal that the assembly sang as you left the church. Or sing the refrain from "Only This I Want" (Schutte) or have instrumental music playing as the children gather in the space for the Liturgy of the Word.

Place the lectionary on the ambo or lectern. Light the candle placed by the ambo or lectern, and then lead the following prayer:

> **O God,**
> **help us open our hearts to listen to the wisdom of your Word**
> **and help us remember that wisdom in our everyday lives.**
> **Through Christ our Lord.**

Children: **Amen.**

First Reading

2 Kings 4:8–11, 14–16a

Responsorial Psalm

Psalm 89:2–3, 16–17, 18–19 (2a) *Sing the same musical setting that is used in your parish's celebration of the liturgy.*

Second Reading

Romans 6:3–4, 8–9

Gospel Acclamation

Sing the Gospel Acclamation used in your parish's celebration of the liturgy.

Gospel Reading

Matthew 10:37–42

Homily/Reflection

Over these weeks, we have been growing together as we move forward in time, counting each week and each Sunday. We are moving toward the end of Ordinary Time in our liturgical year, but we are also moving toward the parousia, the time when God will be "all in all" (1 Corinthians 15:28). During this period of growth in our faith, we may ask ourselves, "As Christians, how should we live?" We can consider together what kind of choices we should make or not make, and why.

» How should we treat other people?

Sometimes, the way we know how we should act is by looking at the example of someone else who acted in the right way. In the first reading, the woman of Shunem treated the prophet Elisha in an admirable way. We may remember that a prophet is one who listens for God's voice and then speaks. Elisha was a prophet who traveled around the land of Israel doing his work. The woman of Shunem knew that this work was important and wanted to help Elisha. She opened her home to him, so he had a place to rest and food to eat. She even asked her husband to build a room in their house so that when he came to their city, he would be comfortable. She took care of Elisha.

Elisha also acted considerately. He recognized that the woman of Shunem was kind to him. Elisha wanted to say thank you. He asked what she needed and learned that she had no children. Elisha listened for God's voice and spoke of a baby that she would have soon. This was very surprising to her; maybe she might not have imagined such a wonderful gift was possible. She received a gift that was more than what she needed and more than what she asked for. We hear echoes of this care in Jesus' words from the Gospel today. Jesus told his friends how important it is to take care of other people. He spoke of giving a cup of cold water to someone who shares the good news as being a kind and important thing to do.

>> **How can we be like the woman of Shunem, who was generous and hospitable?**

>> **How can we be like Elisha, who wanted to show his gratitude?**

Like the woman of Shunem, we can look around us and see people who need help. We can choose to do something about their need. Like the prophet Elisha, we can pay attention to when people take care of us and when they go out of their way for us. We can look for ways to say thank you. Our thanks can be more than just words. We can find ways to say thank you in a thoughtful and considerate way. Maybe we can provide more than just what they need.

We can be like Elisha in another way. We can listen for God's voice with our whole selves. Really listening for God might mean spending time in quiet. Perhaps, like Elisha, God might give us words to speak to others. We might also have words to speak back to God. We know that all good gifts come from God and so we might want to say thank you in prayer. We might want to think about what we might give to God to show how grateful we are. When we have discovered what we know God wants from us, perhaps our love, our care, our work, can be offered back to God.

Profession of Faith

Following the homily or reflection, the prayer leader invites everyone to stand to profess our faith. Together, sing or recite the Apostles' or Nicene Creed. Refer the children to the words of the prayer that you have displayed.

Prayer of the Faithful

Leader: **With confidence in the love of God, we turn to our Lord with our prayers. Please respond, "Lord, hear us."**

That all the faithful in the Body of Christ may bring hope and new life to our world, let us pray: *Lord, hear us.*

That communities may work together to end violence and so bring lasting peace for their children, let us pray: *Lord, hear us.*

That all who minister in soup kitchens and social service agencies may give witness to Christ with all they meet, let us pray: *Lord, hear us.*

That we may offer our thanks to God for all the gifts we have received, and that we may hear the voices of the prophets in our midst, let us pray: *Lord, hear us.*

Invite other intercessions from the children, or add intercessions based on the current needs of the Church, the world, the oppressed or marginalized, and the local community. Conclude each of the children's petitions with **"let us pray"** and invite the response **"Lord, hear us."**

That those who have died may know eternal light, rest, and peace, let us pray: *Lord, hear us.*

O God,
you have revealed your love for us
in the death and resurrection of Jesus your Son.
Increase our love for one another
and help us to be hospitable and generous.
Through Christ our Lord.

Children: **Amen.**

Quietly return with the children to the main assembly. Be mindful of children having difficulty finding their families.

July 9, 2023
Fourteenth Sunday in Ordinary Time
Jesus Reveals the Mysteries of God's Kingdom

 ## Scripture Background

Connections to Church Teaching and Tradition

- "Jesus confesses the Father, acknowledges, and blesses him because he has hidden the mysteries of the Kingdom from those who think themselves learned and has revealed them to infants, the poor of the Beatitudes[1]" (CCC, 2603).

- "From the beginning, Jesus associated his disciples with his own life, revealed the mystery of the Kingdom to them, and gave them a share in his mission, joy, and sufferings[2]" (CCC, 787).

- "In preaching the gospel to the nations they will proclaim with confidence the mystery of Christ whose legates they are" (AG, 24).

Zechariah 9:9–10   Zechariah encourages Jerusalem to rejoice as he pronounces the coming of a future king who will be humble in appearance and demeanor. Instead of parading on a war horse, the king will ride an ass to demonstrate his humble reliance on God as the source of the king's victory and rule. In establishing his peaceful kingdom, the king will banish all instruments of war—namely the chariot, the war horse, and the bow. Relying on God's power and help, the king will proclaim peace to all the nations, thus becoming the source of God's peace and blessing for all people.

All four evangelists use this passage as the backdrop to Jesus' entrance into Jerusalem on Palm Sunday. Jesus' disciples linked Zechariah's vision of a humble king establishing peace for all to their understanding of Jesus' mission and ministry. For his followers, Jesus is the humble king who is the source of God's wisdom, blessings, and peace for all.

Psalm 145:1–2, 8–9, 10–11, 13–14 (see 1)   The psalmist affirms his desire to praise God's name always and everywhere. The desire stems from the psalmist's experience of God, the Lord and king, as gracious and merciful, slow to anger, of great kindness, and always good and compassionate toward all. This creedal affirmation by Israel grounds the Jewish Scriptures' understanding of God and is the basis for Jewish worship and praise.

God's love and fidelity lasts forever, is never revoked, and is all-inclusive. The repeated use of the word *all* stresses this point emphatically. God clearly manifests his love, power, and justice in his care and concern for all who are falling or bowed down. Such works are a clear manifestation of God's Kingdom and might. The all-powerful God loves and cares for all, most especially the weak and powerless. Let all praise forever the name of our king and God.

Romans 8:9, 11–13   Paul offers all humanity the choice of two ways or paths of living, that of the flesh or that of the spirit. Both stem from the choice we make to live either closed to God (the flesh) or open and attuned to God (the spirit). In Christ, all have been given the Spirit of God, who raised Jesus from the dead. The Spirit is always life-giving, bringing new meaning, significance, and life out of meaninglessness and death.

If we choose to cooperate with the Spirit and attune ourselves to God's ways and wisdom, then we, too, will always be with God, no matter what happens to us, including death. If, however, we choose not to cooperate with the Spirit of God, then we close ourselves off from God and life. Paul presents two paths in our relationship with God. What we choose will determine whether our lives will end in death or in life forever with God.

Matthew 11:25–30   In this passage, Matthew recounts Jesus' various affirmations about himself, both in his relationship to God and to his followers. The passage centers on what wisdom is and where it can be found. Matthew contrasts the wisdom found among the "wise and learned," symbolized by the scribes and Pharisees, with the wisdom that Jesus reveals to his followers, the "little ones." Jesus begins by praising God for revealing the mysteries of the Kingdom to the "little ones," and not to the wise and learned who think they know and therefore are not open to other sources of wisdom. Jesus is the source of God's wisdom because of the special relationship that Jesus has with the Father. That special relationship enables Jesus to know the Father, and in return, the fullness of God is revealed in Jesus. Anyone who is open to the person and wisdom that Jesus shares will also come to know God.

---

1   Cf. Matthew 11:25–27 and Luke 10:21–23.
2   Cf. Mark 1:16–20; 3:13–19; Matthew 13:10–17; Luke 10:17–20; 22:28–30.

The last few verses are unique to the Gospel according to Matthew, which addresses issues important to his community. The invitation to come to know Jesus, the wisdom of God, is universal, offered to all who are willing to learn from him and follow through on the demands of discipleship. The *yoke* of discipleship calls one to live in humility and meekness, attuned to God and concerned for the other. Such a lifestyle is in contrast to the Pharisaic *yoke* that shackled and burdened people with many regulations but not much wisdom.

Jesus, the Wisdom of God, offers all, not just Jews, a yoke that is free, liberating, easy, restful, and ultimately life-giving. Humility, openness, and a willingness to enter into relationship with God in and through the person of Jesus is the key to knowing the mysteries of God's Kingdom.

Preparation

In today's Gospel, we hear Jesus promising that if we come to him, he will give us rest. This is a comforting image, especially in the summer, when most of the children are enjoying a break from studies. The summer season is a time of rest and a time to grow in faith. We do this by participating in the work that is to be done in God's kingdom. As Christians we are not exempted from the labor of fulfilling the law. In Christ, however, this labor is easy because we are yoked to him. We do the labor together. He can bear much more than us and does so on our behalf out of love. His yoke is easy, and his burden is light.

Lectionary for Mass #100A

Zechariah 9:9–10

Psalm 145:1–2, 8–9, 10–11, 13–14 (see 1)

Romans 8:9, 11–13

Matthew 11:25–30

Objectives

- To define the words *burden* and *yoke* in the context of the Gospel passage.

- To invite the children to embrace the yoke of Christ and what that means in Christian discipleship.

Preparation and Materials

- Read the Season Background, the lectionary readings, and the Scripture Background.

- Bookmark the appropriate readings (see page xvii) in the lectionary, children's lectionary, or Bible. Place the book in a convenient location for the leader.

- Write the words of dismissal on a card for the priest celebrant.

- Prepare the words of the song the children will sing as they gather in the space for the Liturgy of the Word.

- Select volunteers (older children or adults) to proclaim the readings.

- Display the responsorial psalm refrain lyrics.

- Display the Apostles' or Nicene Creed.

- Prepare intercessions for the Prayer of the Faithful adapted for the needs of the Church, world, oppressed or marginalized, and local community.

- Optional: have available an image of two oxen yoked together pulling a plow.

Prayer Leader Reflection Questions

» What does the work of discipleship look like in your life?

» How might you encourage the children to continue to grow in discipleship, even when these summer months are a time of rest?

Procession

Following the Collect of the Mass, the priest celebrant picks up the lectionary and invites those who would like to participate in the Liturgy of the Word with children to come forward and gather in the center aisle. The people who will lead the children out and facilitate the Liturgy of the Word also come forward at this time. Holding the lectionary so that all can see, the priest celebrant sends the children forth using his own words or the following:

Priest: **Beloved children, we send you now to listen carefully to the Word of God. Think about how you can be more like Jesus. May you open your hearts wide to the truth of the Scriptures. Go in peace.**

The leader processes out holding the lectionary, and the children follow behind. The parish music minister may have selected a song of dismissal for the assembly to sing while the children leave. A good option is "The Word of God: Children's Dismissal" by M. D. Ridge and Timothy R. Smith (WLP/GIA).

Centering

Continue to sing the song of dismissal that the assembly sang as you left the church. Or sing "Psalm 145: I Will Praise Your Name" (Roberts), or the refrain from "Good News" (Glover), or have instrumental music playing as the children gather in the space for the Liturgy of the Word.

Place the lectionary on the ambo or lectern. Light the candle placed by the ambo or lectern, and then lead the following prayer:

**Loving God,
help us to remember and understand the good news.
Increase our faith and help us to bear the yoke of discipleship with joy.
Through Christ our Lord.**

Children: **Amen.**

First Reading

Zechariah 9:9–10

Responsorial Psalm

Psalm 145:1–2, 8–9, 10–11, 13–14 (see 1) *Sing the same musical setting that is used in your parish's celebration of the liturgy.*

Second Reading

Romans 8:9, 11–13

Gospel Acclamation

Sing the Gospel Acclamation used in your parish's celebration of the liturgy.

Gospel Reading

Matthew 11:25–30

Homily/Reflection

During Ordinary Time, we think about growing. We consider this time in the Church year as an opportunity to grow in faith.

≫ What are some living things that grow and are green?

We are like plants in a farmer's field that get bigger and bigger. We hope and pray that we can bear fruit and one day we can be a part of the great harvest in the fullness of the kingdom of God.

Jesus' words today are about a farmer's field and about the work of plowing it. Before a farmer puts seeds in the ground, the soil has to be made ready. It gets turned over and the rich soil from underneath is brought to the top so that newly planted seeds have enough nourishment to grow. This is called plowing. Sometimes farmers grow seeds in big fields, and they need help to do this work. These days, tractors often pull the plow, the tool that turns the soil. Plows are heavy! In Jesus' time, though, there were no tractors. A plow would have been pulled by animals such as oxen. Jesus said, "Come to me, all you who labor and are burdened" (Matthew 11:28). A burden is something heavy that is carried by a person or an animal. Carrying a burden is sometimes an important part of how work gets done. In order to do the work of plowing the field, the oxen have to pull the heavy burden of the plow.

Jesus told those with burdens that he would give them rest. We might imagine that giving rest would mean taking the work away, but he said something more that lets us know that he meant something different. Jesus went on to say, " Take my yoke upon you and learn from me . . ." (Mathew 11:29). In order to pull the plow, oxen often wear something called a yoke. *[Show image of yoked oxen pulling a plow.]* In Jesus' time, the yoke would have been made of a wooden beam and put on the oxen's shoulders. There might have been two oxen in a yoke, and each would have a collar that would keep the yoke in place on the ox's shoulders. Each side of the wood would be attached to the plow that was pulled as the oxen moved forward.

Taking on a yoke might not sound pleasant, but Jesus assures us that "my yoke is easy, and my burden is light" (Matthew 11:30). An easy yoke would be one that is gentle; our Lord loves us and doesn't wish to harm us. To say that his burden is light means that he doesn't expect the impossible from his people—he meets all of us with tremendous mercy, love, care, and understanding. Just as oxen often are yoked together, we are not alone in this work. The disciples of Jesus Christ are joined together in one community. We can help one another to do the work of loving even when it doesn't seem easy. We can encourage one another and pray for one another. As disciples, we are yoked to someone else, someone much more powerful than other disciples. We are yoked to Jesus Christ.

It is summertime so normally this is a time to rest and take things easy, but discipleship doesn't take a vacation. We are called to be good disciples every day for the rest of our lives. We can always do small things. St. Thérèse of Lisieux is a beautiful example of how to show Jesus' kindness and love to others. She was humble in her actions. She concentrated on doing small things for others, but having great love while offering those small prayers and kindnesses. She even made sure she quietly did kind things for those who were not her friends or family. Take a few moments to think about how you can live your life the way St. Thérèse did, just by doing small things with great love.

Profession of Faith

Following the homily or reflection, the prayer leader invites everyone to stand to profess our faith. Together, sing or recite the Apostles' or Nicene Creed. Refer the children to the words of the prayer that you have displayed.

Prayer of the Faithful

Leader: **We pray for the needs of the world as well as our own. Please respond, "Lord, hear our prayer."**

May the Church always remain yoked to Christ, we pray:
Lord, hear our prayer.

May leaders of nations recognize the great responsibility of protecting and cherishing the gift of life, we pray: *Lord, hear our prayer.*

May the neglected, the housebound, the sick and those who are terminally ill know the Lord's comfort and support, we pray:
Lord, hear our prayer.

May all who work be compensated fairly for their effort and time, we pray: *Lord, hear our prayer.*

Invite other intercessions from the children, or add intercessions based on the current needs of the Church, the world, the oppressed or marginalized, and the local community. Conclude each of the children's petitions with **"we pray"** and invite the response **"Lord, hear our prayer."**

May those who have died rest in peace through God's mercy, we pray:
Lord, hear our prayer.

**O God our Father,
we place our prayers before you,
trusting in your goodness and mercy.
Help us grow closer to you every day and to show us how to be better disciples.
Through Christ our Lord.**

Children: **Amen.**

Quietly return with the children to the main assembly. Be mindful of children having difficulty finding their families.

July 16, 2023
Fifteenth Sunday in Ordinary Time
Fertile Ground for God's Word

 Scripture Background

Connections to Church Teaching and Tradition

❀ "The Decalogue, the Sermon on the Mount, and the apostolic catechesis describe for us the paths that lead to the Kingdom of heaven. Sustained by the grace of the Holy Spirit, we tread them, step by step, by everyday acts. By the working of the Word of Christ, we slowly bear fruit in the Church to the glory of God[1]" (CCC, 1724).

❀ "Modern civilization itself, though not of its very nature but because it is too engrossed in the concerns of this world, can often make it harder to approach God" (GS, 19).

Isaiah 55:10–11 Isaiah provides an extended metaphor for the Word of God. Comparing the Word of God to the rain and snow, Isaiah indicates several correlations that enable us to understand the richness of God's Word. Rain and snow are sent by God to accomplish their purpose on earth. They provide water to the ground, making it fertile and providing food for all his creatures. Once they have accomplished their purpose, the rain and snow return to God, having fully nourished and cared for God's creation. So, too, is God's Word. It originates from God, sent to accomplish the task of attuning all to God's wishes, desires, and intentions. God ensures that it will accomplish its purpose. God's Word brings fertility, meaning, and significance to all of life. God assures us that when we attune ourselves to his Word, the Word will nourish and satisfy all our hungers.

Psalm 65:10, 11, 12–13, 14 (Luke 8:8) While the refrain picks up the theme of the Gospel parable of the sower, the psalm itself focuses on God's rich blessing, especially during harvest time. God's blessing upon an abundant harvest is the possible backdrop to this hymn of praise and thanksgiving to God.

Picking up on the fertility of the ground brought about by the rain and snow from the first reading, the psalm praises and thanks God for his blessing to the people exemplified by an abundant harvest. The rains that God sends provide the necessary conditions that enrich the earth for continued fertility and new life. As all creation cooperates with God, not only are humans sustained, but there also is an abundance of flocks and food to sustain all creation. The only response from humans and the rest of creation is to "shout and sing for joy" (v. 14).

Romans 8:18–23 Paul addresses the suffering that we experience in life, placing it within the context of future hope manifested in the Risen Lord. Paul uses Genesis as a backdrop to explain that humans suffer as a result of their refusal to attune themselves to God. In refusing to attend to God, humans not only made things more difficult for themselves, but they also brought all of creation down with them.

All nonhuman creation is unwillingly subject to futility and frustration. Because of human sin, creation cannot accomplish the purpose for which it was created—to be the means through which humans glorify and give praise to God. According to Paul, God sent Jesus to redeem and save us and all of creation. In the Risen Lord, we have the assurance of salvation and redemption. This hope, however, is still in its seedling stage. The time is coming when that hope will fully bloom. All of creation awaits this moment. Paul places the world's present sufferings in this context, as a clear indication that the long-awaited redemption is close at hand. We, along with all of creation, groan as in labor pains for the fulfillment of God's saving action, already made real in the Risen Lord.

Matthew 13:1–23 or 13:1–9 Matthew 13 is a series of seven parables on the Kingdom of Heaven, situated at the center of the Gospel. The parable of the sower, which begins this chapter, is not so much focused on the sower or the seed but rather on different kinds of soil and their receptivity. Matthew is addressing a key concern of his Christian-Jewish community—namely, why some Jews accepted Jesus and other Jews rejected him and his message of the Kingdom. The parable is an attempt to explore this mystery.

---

1 Cf. the parable of the sower: Matthew 13:3–23.

In the parable, Jesus explains that some are influenced by the evil one, while others are shallow; some are too concerned with worldly affairs, while others seek riches. Those who are open and attuned to Jesus' message grow in rich soil that produces abundant fruit.

The mystery concerning acceptance or rejection of Jesus' message centers on our willingness to open ourselves to how God is present and acting in the world. It means developing ears that listen attentively and a mind that discerns thoughtfully. With God's help, this kind of soil will produce abundant fruit.

 # Preparation

Jesus often used parables to communicate what he intended, and he made clear that this was not incidental, but integral to his approach. The practice of considering the meanings of the parable engage the listener to perceive deeper truth in much the same way that the kingdom of God, while hidden, is the deeper truth. In what is often referred to as the parable of the sower, Jesus invited his listeners to consider how to receive the Word of God well. Preparation of the heart can foster growth and the bearing of fruit.

Lectionary for Mass #103A

Isaiah 55:10–11

Psalm 65:10, 11, 12–13, 14 (Luke 8:8)

Romans 8:18–23

Matthew 13:1–9 or 13:1–23

Objectives

- To offer parables as a paradigm for arriving at truth about the mysteries of the kingdom of God.

- To invite the children to prepare themselves to receive the Word of God fruitfully.

Preparation and Materials

- Read the Season Background, the lectionary readings, and the Scripture Background.

- Bookmark the appropriate readings (see page xvii) in the lectionary, children's lectionary, or Bible. Place the book in a convenient location for the leader.

- Write the words of dismissal on a card for the priest celebrant.

- Prepare the words of the song the children will sing as they gather in the space for the Liturgy of the Word.

- Select volunteers (older children or adults) to proclaim the readings.

- Display the responsorial psalm refrain lyrics.

- Display the Apostles' or Nicene Creed.

- Prepare intercessions for the Prayer of the Faithful adapted for the needs of the Church, world, oppressed or marginalized, and local community.

- Note: The homily/reflection draws from content in the longer Gospel reading, but it is recommended to proclaim the shorter version in order to explore the meaning of the parable without first having it fully explained.

Prayer Leader Reflection Questions

» **Do you take time to read God's Word? How might you nurture your spiritual life more by reflecting on the Scriptures and applying the Living Word to your own life?**

» **How does the liturgical environment for children's Liturgy of the Word help to nurture the faith of children at your parish? How might you instill in the children that it is just as important to nourish their spiritual lives as their physical bodies?**

Procession

Following the Collect of the Mass, the priest celebrant picks up the lectionary and invites those who would like to participate in the Liturgy of the Word with children to come forward and gather in the center aisle. The people who will lead the children out and facilitate the Liturgy of the Word also come forward at this time. Holding the lectionary so that all can see, the priest celebrant sends the children forth using his own words or the following:

> *Priest*: **Dear children, seeds start small and grow into flowers and plants and trees. Jesus' words are seeds that, as you grow, will grow within you, give you life, and make you strong in spirit. Go now and listen to these words of him who loves you very much.**

The leader processes out holding the lectionary, and the children follow behind. The parish music minister may have selected a song of dismissal for the assembly to sing while the children leave. A good option is "The Word of God: Children's Dismissal" by M. D. Ridge and Timothy R. Smith (WLP/GIA).

Centering

Continue to sing the song of dismissal that the assembly sang as you left the church. Or sing "Praise to You, O Christ, Our Savior" (Farrell) or the refrain from "All Grownups, All Children" (Shelley), or have instrumental music playing as the children gather in the space for the Liturgy of the Word.

Place the lectionary on the ambo or lectern. Light the candle placed by the ambo or lectern, and then lead the following prayer:

> **O God,**
> **help us open our hearts to listen to the wisdom of your Word**
> **and help us remember that wisdom in our everyday lives.**
> **Through Christ our Lord.**

> *Children:* **Amen.**

First Reading

Isaiah 55:10–11

Responsorial Psalm

Psalm 65:10, 11, 12–13, 14 (Luke 8:8) *Sing the same musical setting that is used in your parish's celebration of the liturgy.*

Second Reading

Romans 8:18–23

Gospel Acclamation

Sing the Gospel Acclamation used in your parish's celebration of the liturgy.

Gospel Reading

Matthew 13:1–9 or 13:1–23

Homily/Reflection

Jesus offered a parable about growth that comes from the earth and bears fruit. A *parable* is a story with more than one meaning.

» Why did Jesus speak in parables?

This is a question Jesus' own disciples asked him. Jesus' favorite thing to talk about was the kingdom of God, and he used parables to help his listeners understand what it is like. He used ordinary, everyday things or situations that his listeners would have been familiar with to make comparisons to God's kingdom.

» Which of you helps grow flowers or vegetables at home? Can you describe what happens after seeds are planted and how long they grow?

Seeds that were planted in the ground in the spring sprout up and reach toward the sun, growing throughout this time, summer. Flowers bloom and fruits and vegetables grow. The fruit of the plants are ready to be harvested and enjoyed in autumn.

» What could the parable of the sower and the way the seeds fell have meant?

Jesus was speaking about seed being put into the ground in different kinds of soil, but there is a deeper meaning that Jesus wanted his listeners to understand. In today's first reading, Isaiah spoke about growth that comes from the earth and it bears fruit. He explained that he was comparing this kind of growth to the effect of God's Word in the world. When Jesus spoke about the growth of seeds, he was also speaking about God's Word.

>> **If the seed is God's Word, what could the soil be? What happens to God's Word? How is it spread?**

One way it is shared is when it is read out loud at Mass, or here, during liturgy of the Word with children.

>> **Where does God's Word go?**

It goes into our ears. We hear the Word of God. So, perhaps, *we* are the soil.

Some seed fell on a path and birds came and ate it up: The seed did not really go into the soil, only on it, and then it was gone. When we are not listening at all, the Word of God has no effect on us. It doesn't change us. Some seed fell on rocky ground: It had some growth but not enough depth, and it withered in the sun without the moisture and nutrients from deep roots. Perhaps we listen to the Word of God for a time but fall away when discipleship becomes difficult. Some seed fell in good rich soil and produced a huge amount of fruit. This is the type of soil we want to be! We want the Word of God to grow in us richly and have a lot of fruit.

>> **How can we make our soil ready for this kind of growth? What can we do?**

We want to keep our ears really open to the Word of God so that it goes deep within us. Spending time studying the Word of God and listening to the words of wise teachers and preachers can help us understand more fully. Maybe some things are keeping the Word of God from really growing in us. Some of those things might be sins. We can confess our sins and ask for forgiveness in the sacrament of reconciliation. We know that in the Eucharist, we are fed the good rich food of Christ's Body and Blood. This can nourish us well.

Profession of Faith

Following the homily or reflection, the prayer leader invites everyone to stand to profess our faith. Together, sing or recite the Apostles' or Nicene Creed. Refer the children to the words of the prayer that you have displayed.

Prayer of the Faithful

Leader: **Trusting in the power of God's Word to change our lives and to change our world, we place all our needs before God. Please respond, "Lord, graciously hear us."**

For all preachers, teachers, and catechists, that they may help to sow seeds of faith in the hearts of all their hearers, we pray: *Lord, graciously hear us.*

For those in authority around the world to act with integrity, relieve poverty, and bring an end to injustice, we pray: *Lord, graciously hear us.*

For those who feel worthless, that they may know that they are chosen and loved by God, we pray: *Lord, graciously hear us.*

For all farmers and those who make a living from the fruits of creation, we pray: *Lord, graciously hear us.*

Invite other intercessions from the children, or add intercessions based on the current needs of the Church, the world, the oppressed or marginalized, and the local community. Conclude each of the children's petitions with **"we pray"** and invite the response **"Lord, graciously hear us."**

For all who have died, that they may live in God's light forever, we pray: *Lord, graciously hear us.*

God our Father, open our hearts to your grace that we may always know and do your will. We ask this through Christ our Lord.

Children: **Amen.**

Quietly return with the children to the main assembly. Be mindful of children having difficulty finding their families.

July 23, 2023
Sixteenth Sunday in Ordinary Time
The Lord Is Our Strength

 ## Scripture Background

Connections to Church Teaching and Tradition

❋ "Only faith can embrace the mysterious ways of God's almighty power. This faith glories in its weaknesses in order to draw to itself Christ's power[1]" (CCC, 273).

❋ "God is the *Father* Almighty, whose fatherhood and power shed light on one another: God reveals his fatherly omnipotence by the way he takes care of our needs; by the filial adoption that he gives us . . . finally by his infinite mercy, for he displays his power at its height by freely forgiving sins" (CCC, 270).

❋ "The Christian . . . should strive by works of mercy and charity, as well as by prayer and the various practices of penance, to put off completely the 'old man' and to put on the 'new man'[2]" (CCC, 1473).

Wisdom 12:13, 16–19 Wisdom, a late Old Testament book composed in Greek, is accepted by Catholics as inspired but is not included in either Jewish or Protestant canons. In addressing God, this passage focuses on God's supreme might and power over all things. The community asserts that "mastery over all things" enables God to be "lenient to all" (v. 16). As "master of might," God judges "with clemency, and with much lenience" (v. 18). God's power on behalf of the people has been clearly manifested in Israel's past. God's liberating power exercised on behalf of poor and oppressed slaves is the ground for hope in a God believed to hold supreme power over all. By modeling how power is to be exercised, God teaches people "that those who are just must be kind" (v. 19). God is our strength and hope because we know that whenever God's might is at work, it is always exercised with kindness, leniency, and forgiveness. Whenever we experience God's gracious and merciful touch, we experience the manner in which true power is to be exercised.

Psalm 86:5–6, 9–10, 15–16 (5a) This lament psalm manifests great trust and confidence in God who is always "good and forgiving" toward all (v. 5). Such trust is engendered through God's "kindness to all who call upon [him]" (v. 5). *Kindness* is a translation of the Hebrew word *hesed*, meaning faithful, enduring covenant love. The psalmist's confidence in God's goodness and mercy comes out of God's covenant love relationship. This covenant relationship enables the psalmist to ask God to "hearken . . . and attend to the sound of [the psalmist's] pleading" (v. 6). Because God has done great deeds on behalf of the people, not only do the people trust in God's help, but all the nations come to acknowledge and praise him. The last stanza is a traditional summary credo associated with the people's experience of God at the Exodus. Affirming key covenant attributes, the credo identifies God as "merciful and gracious, / slow to anger, abounding in kindness and fidelity" (v. 15). This strong affirmation of God's goodness and mercy propels the psalmist to ask God for mercy and for strength whenever weakness tends to overwhelm. God is our true source of strength, always ready to reach out, reconcile, and forgive.

Romans 8:26–27 Continuing the theme of Psalm 86, Paul asserts that, as human beings, we are weak and fallible, resulting in our inability to pray "as we ought" (v. 26). We are prone to distraction, clouded motivations, desires and needs that pull us in various directions, and other human weaknesses. Being linked to Christ through our baptismal call, however, we are gifted with the Spirit who intercedes for us "with inexpressible groanings" (v. 26). God's Spirit comes to our aid by identifying with our weakness and helping us express to God what we often find inexpressible.

God, intimately knowing us as "the one who searches hearts" (v. 27), also intimately knows the Spirit's intention and purpose. The Spirit helps us get in touch with his will, interceding for us even when we do not know what or how to ask. God's gracious love and mercy toward us gifts us from within with God's very presence and strength, helping and guiding us to draw more closely to God and to align ourselves with God's will. God's gracious and healing touch is ours, and we experience it every time we reach out to God in prayer.

Matthew 13:24–43 or 13:24–30 Three parables are presented in this passage, highlighting the parable of the weeds and the wheat that begins and ends this selection. The parable

1 Cf. 2 Corinthians 12:9; Philippians 4:13.

2 Ephesians 4:22, 24.

zeroes in on the master as God. Because we are created with freedom, some will choose God and some will not. How does God deal with this reality?

Matthew's Jesus stresses that God is just and allows the wicked to live along with the good till the time of final judgment, when justice will reign. But from the psalm we learn that those exercising justice must also be kind. Therefore, God allows the wicked time to repent and turn back. Knowing our weakness, God give us time to reach out in freedom and experience his gracious kindness and healing touch. From the Romans passage, we know that God gives us the Spirit, who aids us in our weakness, especially when we are challenged to conform ourselves to God's will. Ultimately, for Matthew, God is good and merciful, giving us the time we need to repent and turn back. In our weakness, God is our strength and our help.

 # Preparation

St. Paul's letter to the Romans offers us insight into the work of the Holy Spirit. Although we may be weak, the Spirit can be strong on our behalf. This is true in a particular way in prayer. Even when we can't pray, the Spirit prays for us and asks for what we need. The Spirit's communication is mysterious and ineffable, but it is for our benefit. The Spirit knows both our own needs and God's will even better than we do.

Lectionary for Mass #106A

Wisdom 12:13, 16–19

Psalm 86:5–6, 9–10, 15–16 (5a)

Romans 8:26–27

Matthew 13:24–43 or Matthew 13:24–30

Objective

- To announce the Holy Spirit as enabling and supporting our life of faith, especially our prayer.

Preparation and Materials

- Read the Season Background, the lectionary readings, and the Scripture Background.

- Bookmark the appropriate readings (see page xvii) in the lectionary, children's lectionary, or Bible. Place the book in a convenient location for the leader.

- Write the words of dismissal on a card for the priest celebrant.

- Prepare the words of the song the children will sing as they gather in the space for the Liturgy of the Word.

- Select volunteers (older children or adults) to proclaim the readings.

- Display the responsorial psalm refrain lyrics.

- Display the Apostles' or Nicene Creed.

- Prepare intercessions for the Prayer of the Faithful adapted for the needs of the Church, world, oppressed or marginalized, and local community.

Prayer Leader Reflection Questions

>> **How do you allow the Holy Spirit to guide your prayer?**

>> **How do you make difficult choices? Do you rely on the Holy Spirit to help you?**

| Procession | Following the Collect of the Mass, the priest celebrant picks up the lectionary and invites those who would like to participate in the Liturgy of the Word with children to come forward and gather in the center aisle. The people who will lead the children out and facilitate the Liturgy of the Word also come forward at this time. Holding the lectionary so that all can see, the priest celebrant sends the children forth using his own words or the following: |

> *Priest*: **Dear children, Jesus calls us and gives us strength to follow him, and when we fail, he has mercy on us and lifts us up. We send you forth to listen to him and learn from him for he will never leave your side. When you come back to us, we will continue our celebration with joy. Go in peace.**

The leader processes out holding the lectionary, and the children follow behind. The parish music minister may have selected a song of dismissal for the assembly to sing while the children leave. A good option is "The Word of God: Children's Dismissal" by M. D. Ridge and Timothy R. Smith (WLP/GIA).

| Centering | Continue to sing the song of dismissal that the assembly sang as you left the church. Or sing "Psalm 145: I Will Praise Your Name Forever" (Roberts), or the refrain from "Love One Another" (Glover), or have instrumental music playing as the children gather in the space for the Liturgy of the Word. |

Place the lectionary on the ambo or lectern. Light the candle placed by the ambo or lectern, and then lead the following prayer:

> **O heavenly Father,**
> **allow our hearts to be open to your Word**
> **so that we may serve you completely.**
> **We ask this through Christ our Lord.**

Children: **Amen.**

| First Reading | Wisdom 12:13, 16–19 |

| Responsorial Psalm | Psalm 86:5–6, 9–10, 15–16 (5a) *Sing the same musical setting that is used in your parish's celebration of the liturgy.* |

| Second Reading | Romans 8:26–27 |

| Gospel Acclamation | *Sing the Gospel Acclamation used in your parish's celebration of the liturgy.* |

| **Gospel Reading** | Matthew 13:24–43 or Matthew 13:24–30 |

| Homily/Reflection | The liturgical season of Ordinary Time began just after the Solemnity of Pentecost. At Pentecost, we remembered and celebrated the gift of the Holy Spirit given to the Church. Just as we are in a period of growing toward God, we are also in a period of growing toward God in our time in history. Two thousand years ago, the gift of the Holy Spirit was given to the Church in a most particular way and that gift, the presence of the Spirit, continues to be a gift we can enjoy now. |

» Who is the Holy Spirit?

We can see the Spirit working in our own lives. In the Scriptures, we listen to how the Spirit worked in the lives of the first disciples. The Church also remembers the lives of the people of God who came after them and before us, and who could speak about the work of the Spirit. Some of those people are called Doctors of the Church. They are special teachers who have helped us to speak about God in ways we know are trustworthy.

One particular person who helps us to understand the Holy Spirit working in the world is St. Paul. Paul didn't know Jesus before he died, but he was someone special to whom Jesus showed himself after his resurrection. Paul wrote about the work of the Holy Spirit in his letter to the Romans, the second reading. Paul understood that we are not perfect. We don't always have the strength we need to follow God's will completely. We need help. It is the Holy Spirit who helps us. This is true for our prayer life, just as it is for other ways we live as Christians. We might describe prayer as a conversation with God. A true conversation involves listening as well as talking. It is not always easy to quiet our bodies and our minds and our hearts so that they are not louder than what God is speaking to us. It is the Spirit who gives us the ability to really listen. When we can't do it on our own, the Spirit's power can do it for us.

We do not always know what to say in return. What are the right words to use to communicate with the Mighty One who is from all time and has all power? How beautiful that God who is so great wants to know what we have to say because of love! The Spirit can give us the words to do this. The Spirit even prays *for us.* The Spirit can do this without words. Paul calls this "inexpressible groanings" (Romans 8:26). Paul also says that, as "holy ones," as those who hope to join the other saints in heaven, the Spirit asks for things we need on our behalf. How great a gift that the Holy Spirit comes to us and helps us in this way! Let's take a moment to let the Spirit help us to pray. *[Allow the children some time for silence in prayer.]*

Profession of Faith

Following the homily or reflection, the prayer leader invites everyone to stand to profess our faith. Together, sing or recite the Apostles' or Nicene Creed. Refer the children to the words of the prayer that you have displayed.

Prayer of the Faithful

Leader: **The Spirit helps us choose words to pray properly. Open to the Spirit's help, we bring our petitions to God. Please respond, "Holy Spirit, pray for us."**

That Christians everywhere may fulfill the call to transform the world with the light of the Gospel and build a world that shows mercy and protects the vulnerable, let us pray: *Holy Spirit, pray for us.*

That civil authorities may always treat people fairly, especially those who are considered to be on the margins of society, let us pray: *Holy Spirit, pray for us.*

That those who struggle to make good choices may guided by the Holy Spirit, let us pray: *Holy Spirit, pray for us.*

That children and families who spend time this summer in relaxation and recreation may be kept safe, let us pray: *Holy Spirit, pray for us.*

Invite other intercessions from the children, or add intercessions based on the current needs of the Church, the world, the oppressed or marginalized, and the local community. Conclude each of the children's petitions with **"let us pray"** and invite the response **"Holy Spirit, pray for us."**

That those who have died may be gathered in like wheat to the great harvest of heaven, let us pray: *Holy Spirit, pray for us.*

O Holy Spirit,
move us to continue the work of Jesus.
Hear our prayers in accord with the grace
that Father and Son give
through you, the Spirit of love.

Children: **Amen.**

Quietly return with the children to the main assembly. Be mindful of children having difficulty finding their families.

July 30, 2023
Seventeenth Sunday in Ordinary Time
An Understanding Heart

 ## Scripture Background

1 Kings 3:5, 7–12   Solomon's reputation for wisdom has its source in this text. In the context of a dream, God invites Solomon, David's son and designated successor, to ask for anything and God would grant it. God's generous offer manifests God's graciousness toward the king and the people. Solomon asks for "an understanding heart to judge [God's] people and to distinguish right from wrong" (v. 9). Since reason and intellect were seen as residing in the heart in his time, Solomon asks God for a pastoral and discerning mind. His request is based on an awareness of his own inexperience, as well as the vast size of the people he is to govern.

Since Solomon has chosen well, showing concern only for God and the people, God showers Solomon not only with great wisdom but with all other good gifts besides. In biblical wisdom tradition, seeking wisdom is life's best calling, bringing with it all other goods. Such seeking aligns us with God's purposes and desires.

Psalm 119:57, 72, 76–77, 127–128, 129–130 (97a)   Psalm 119, the longest psalm, is an acrostic wisdom psalm extolling the benefits of knowing God's law and relishing its delights. God's law brings with it wisdom, light, happiness, joy, peace, and direction on living rightly. God's law is not perceived as oppressive legalism, but as the gracious path that God provides. The refrain sums up well the attitude that wisdom tradition attributes to the law, "Lord, I love your commands" (v. 97a).

God's law or wisdom is more precious to the psalmist than all the world's riches. The law has its source in God's enduring covenant love, which brings comfort and delight. Love of the law and attentiveness to its demands provide sure guidance for moving forward on true paths and away from falsehood. The Lord's decrees are wonderful, shedding "light, / giving understanding to the simple" (v. 130). If one desires to gain an understanding heart, attentiveness to God's law is the surest path to gaining wisdom and establishing right relationship with all.

Romans 8:28–30   These beloved verses surface theological themes often misinterpreted and misused by Christians. With complete trust in God's gracious love, Paul affirms that "all things work for good for those who love God" (v. 28). Paul is not saying that those who love God will never have a hard time in life. Rather, Paul insists that no matter what happens in life, even in life's worst difficulties and challenges, God's love is always there, transforming times of trouble into events that are ultimately life giving.

For Paul, God's loving plan for creation existed from the beginning. God activated that plan by means of covenant love relationship and by ultimately sending Christ, the "firstborn among many brothers and sisters" (v. 29). In Christ, God's fullest outflow of love is realized as God calls all humanity to be conformed to Christ's image. This does not mean that all have to become Christian, but rather that all are to conform to the values and lifestyle that Christ modeled and manifested. In so doing, all are "justified," or saved, and at the end time, all will be "glorified" (v. 30). For Paul, God's loving plan for all humanity has been operative from the beginning to the end of time.

Matthew 13:44–52 or 13:44–46   In this text, two of the three parables concerning the Kingdom of Heaven are similar while the third recalls the parable of the wheat and weeds from last Sunday. The parables of finding treasure buried in a field and a merchant seeking and finding a pearl of great price underscore the great value of being part of God's Kingdom. One is

Connections to Church Teaching and Tradition

- "God has not willed to reserve to himself all exercise of power. He entrusts to every creature the functions it is capable of performing, according to the capacities of its own nature. This mode of governance ought to be followed in social life. The way God acts in governing the world, which bears witness to such great regard for human freedom, should inspire the wisdom of those who govern human communities" (CCC, 1884).

- "Human society can be neither well-ordered nor prosperous without the presence of those who, invested with legal authority, preserve its institutions and do all that is necessary to sponsor actively the interests of its members" (PT, 46).

willing to sacrifice all for its sake. As we learn from Solomon and Psalm 119, gaining this wisdom is more valuable than riches.

The parable of the net catching various fish that have to be sorted once brought on board describes the diversity of God's Kingdom, along with its mixture of both good and bad. The end time judgment will sort through the differences. In the meantime, all are called and given time to conform themselves to the image of Christ, as Paul asserts in the Second Reading. The passage ends with the disciples' claim that they have understood all that Jesus has instructed them about the Kingdom of Heaven. Jesus, praising their response, confirms their role as scribes or teachers in the Kingdom of Heaven. Jesus' teaching, which they are to carry on, is a deeper reflection on and a newer understanding of the wisdom that they have inherited. Both new and old are to be used in carrying on Jesus' mission and ministry.

 # Preparation

During Jesus' preaching ministry, he offered many parables of the kingdom of God, some of which are only a sentence or two long. This is true of the parable of the merchant and the pearl and the parable of the hidden treasure. Although short, they highlight great truths of the kingdom of God. It is hidden but if we search, we may find it. When we do, it will bring great joy. Its worth is incomparable to anything else we have.

Lectionary for Mass #109A

1 Kings 3:5, 7–12

Psalm 119:57, 72, 76–77, 127–128, 129–130 (97a)

Romans 8:28–30

Matthew 13:44–52 or Matthew 13:44–46

Objective

- To explore with the children the parable approach as a means to understand the hiddenness of the kingdom of God.

Preparation and Materials

- Read the Season Background, the lectionary readings, and the Scripture Background.

- Bookmark the appropriate readings (see page xvii) in the lectionary, children's lectionary, or Bible. Place the book in a convenient location for the leader.

- Write the words of dismissal on a card for the priest celebrant.

- Prepare the words of the song the children will sing as they gather in the space for the Liturgy of the Word.

- Select volunteers (older children or adults) to proclaim the readings.

- Display the responsorial psalm refrain lyrics.

- Display the Apostles' or Nicene Creed.

- Prepare intercessions for the Prayer of the Faithful adapted for the needs of the Church, world, oppressed or marginalized, and local community.

Prayer Leader Reflection Questions

>> **What values do you hold dear?**

>> **How do you make God's kingdom your priority? How does it give you joy?**

Procession

Following the Collect of the Mass, the priest celebrant picks up the lectionary and invites those who would like to participate in the Liturgy of the Word with children to come forward and gather in the center aisle. The people who will lead the children out and facilitate the Liturgy of the Word also come forward at this time. Holding the lectionary so that all can see, the priest celebrant sends the children forth using his own words or the following:

> *Priest:* **Children, Jesus taught us to listen for his voice so we may know God better and live as he wants us to live. We send you with your leader(s) to listen carefully to God's Word. Pay attention to what God is saying to you today. May the Holy Spirit help you understand and live this good news. Go now in peace.**

The leader processes out holding the lectionary, and the children follow behind. The parish music minister may have selected a song of dismissal for the assembly to sing while the children leave. A good option is "The Word of God: Children's Dismissal" by M. D. Ridge and Timothy R. Smith (WLP/GIA).

Centering

Continue to sing the song of dismissal that the assembly sang as you left the church. Or sing "Psalm 138: In the Sight of the Angels" (Joncas), or the refrain from "We Walk by Faith" (Haugen), or have instrumental music playing as the children gather in the space for the Liturgy of the Word.

Place the lectionary on the ambo or lectern. Light the candle placed by the ambo or lectern, and then lead the following prayer:

> **O God,**
> **help us open our hearts to listen to the wisdom of your Word**
> **and help us remember that wisdom in our everyday lives.**
> **Through Christ our Lord.**

> *Children:* **Amen.**

First Reading

1 Kings 3:5, 7–12

Responsorial Psalm

Psalm 119:57, 72, 76–77, 127–128, 129–130 (97a) *Sing the same musical setting that is used in your parish's celebration of the liturgy.*

Second Reading

Romans 8:28–30

Gospel Acclamation

Sing the Gospel Acclamation used in your parish's celebration of the liturgy.

Gospel Reading

Matthew 13:44–52 or Matthew 13:44–46

Homily/Reflection

During this period of Ordinary Time, when the church is decorated in green, we spend time growing in our knowledge and love of the kingdom of God. This was Jesus' favorite subject to talk about when he walked and talked with his friends on earth like you and I do now.

❯❯ What is a kingdom? What is a king?

A kingdom is a place where a king is in charge for his whole life. When we imagine a kingdom, we might think of a crown or a castle. Is the kingdom of God like that? How will we find it and how will we know we have found it? These are questions we might ask ourselves and they are questions that Jesus wanted his friends to consider as he shared his parables.

❯❯ What is a parable?

We might remember that a parable is a story with more than one meaning. The first meaning is about the things of this world. They are often things from everyday life in the time of Jesus, but there is more meaning besides the things of this world. The parables that we hear today tell us more about what the kingdom of God is like. They don't say everything there is to say about the kingdom of God, but they help us to understand something true. They also help us to look beyond the things of this world to find deeper meaning.

One parable we heard today was about a merchant. A merchant is someone who buys and sells things. This particular merchant was interested in pearls. Perhaps you have seen a pearl before. Pearls are round like a bead and can be strung together to form a necklace. They are white and shiny and reflect light. This merchant was searching for beautiful pearls, perhaps to buy and sell. He found one beautiful pearl. It was so special that he knew it could not be bought or sold. When he found that one precious pearl, he recognized its value and did whatever he needed to do to have it.

>> **In order to find the kingdom of God, do we need to be looking for it like the merchant who was searching for and found the precious pearl?**

Another parable we heard was about a man who found a treasure in a field. He was so joyful when he found this treasure! He knew how valuable it was, so he sold everything he had to buy the field that held the treasure.

>> **When we find the kingdom of God, I wonder if the joy we feel helps us to recognize it. Will the joy be so great that we want the kingdom of God more than anything else?**

Jesus offered many parables about the kingdom of God. These are only two of them that touch on how valuable God's kingdom is. There is always more to say about God's kingdom. Listening deeply to each parable helps us to be able to do that for ourselves.

Profession of Faith

Following the homily or reflection, the prayer leader invites everyone to stand to profess our faith. Together, sing or recite the Apostles' or Nicene Creed. Refer the children to the words of the prayer that you have displayed.

Prayer of the Faithful

Leader: **We are called to wisely search for the kingdom in our midst and to cherish it as a great treasure. Please respond, "Lord, hear us."**

May all Church leaders guide us in right relationship with God, we pray to the Lord: *Lord, hear us.*

May we actively preserve the beauty and diversity of our world and remember our own responsibilities to care for God's creation, we pray to the Lord: *Lord, hear us.*

May we selflessly break the bread of abundance with the hungry, we pray to the Lord: *Lord, hear us.*

May all young people's minds and hearts be filled with wisdom and self-understanding so that they may recognize their gifts and use them in the service of God and neighbor, we pray to the Lord: *Lord, hear us.*

Invite other intercessions from the children, or add intercessions based on the current needs of the Church, the world, the oppressed or marginalized, and the local community. Conclude each of the children's petitions with **"we pray to the Lord"** and invite the response **"Lord, hear us."**

May those who have died live forever in the joy of the kingdom of God, we pray to the Lord: *Lord, hear us.*

**Creator God,
you sent Jesus to show us how to live a life of faith.
Guide us, we pray, by the Holy Spirit,
who lives and reigns with you and your Son,
God, for ever and ever.**

Children: **Amen.**

Quietly return with the children to the main assembly. Be mindful of children having difficulty finding their families.

August 6, 2023
Feast of the Transfiguration of the Lord
Power Made Known

 ## Scripture Background

Connections to Church Teaching and Tradition

- In the Transfiguration Jesus' real nature is revealed to his followers and to us (CCC, 464–469, 480–482).

- Face-to-face with the mystery of Christ's dual nature, the apostles respond in wonder (CCC, 554–556, 568).

- The Transfiguration is a preview of God's glory, visible only with the eyes of faith (CCC, 2809).

Daniel 7:9–10, 13–14 At about the time that Daniel was written, the Jewish people lived under the rule of Antiochus Epiphanes. Antiochus wanted to impose Greek culture and religion on his Jewish subjects. The dreams and visions described in chapters 7–12 are addressed to persecuted people, particularly those persecuted by Antiochus. In the verses that precede the reading, four mythical beasts emerge from an abyss. These beasts can be identified as empires that ruled over the people of Israel: Assyria, Babylon, Persia, and Greece. These beasts terrorize and destroy people (7:5). Amid this destruction comes an "Ancient One" (v. 9), taking his throne of fiery flames. God appears and judges the beasts, in particular a beast's horn that represented Antiochus. The horn is destroyed (v. 11), and on the horizon a new vision arises. A being in human form appears before the Ancient One and receives authority over the world for eternity (vv. 13–14). For the people undergoing persecution, this vision promises that God, not human rulers, reigns over the world and throughout history.

The Book of Daniel promises that faith will triumph: the good and righteous will be saved and the wicked destroyed. Later Christians interpreted the one given authority to be Jesus Christ, whose power comes from God and whose rule is eternal.

Psalm 97:1–2, 5–6, 9 (1a, 9a) Psalm 97 celebrates the reign of God over Israel. The people experience God as a mysterious force, like "clouds and darkness" (v. 2). God's reign is founded on justice (v. 2), and God's power is overwhelming. The highest points on earth dissolve in the presence of the mighty one (v. 5). The psalm proclaims that no god is greater than the God of Israel (v. 9).

2 Peter 1:16–19 The early Christians, who once believed that Christ would return momentarily, became confused as the years progressed. Some people began to teach that belief in Christ's return was one of several clever "myths" (v. 16). In the Second Letter of Peter, someone writing in his name addressed these false teachers.

The passage defends belief in Christ's return with an appeal to the Apostles' experience of the Transfiguration. According to the author, the experience of Jesus' transformation and the words spoken from heaven revealed him to be the one from God. The Transfiguration is like a window offering a view into the reality to come. Present time is compared to darkness, but Christ's reappearance will mark the dawn of a new day. Until then, believers must stand firm in their faith founded on the Apostles' witness.

Matthew 17:1–9 The Transfiguration is a mysterious event that revealed Jesus' divine nature and the glory that would be his after the Resurrection and exaltation into heaven. Peter, James, and John, the same disciples who accompany Jesus to the garden at Gethsemane, are led to a mountain to see Jesus transform into a being of light. Two great leaders, Elijah and Moses, also appear. Moses and Elijah both experienced the glory of the Lord on a high mountain: Moses received the Law (Exodus 19–34) and Elijah heard the voice of God (1 Kings 19:8–14). They may represent the law and the prophets that Jesus has fulfilled.

In all three Gospel accounts, the Transfiguration immediately follows Jesus telling his followers that discipleship involves denying oneself and taking up the cross (Mark 8:34–38). The Gospels teach that if the disciples persevere through suffering and trial, they will also share a glorious encounter with God.

Sometimes God comes to us with light and glory, but God usually comes to us at the deepest levels of our ordinary experiences: in the beauty of a flower, in the love of a child, in a creative project. The memory of these meetings with God provides strength in the deep valleys of life and gives us hope that one day we will reach the final mountain we call heaven.

Preparation

The second letter of Peter affirms our faith in Jesus Christ's glory. Jesus' status as the Father's beloved Son is supported by good evidence. It is not invented by humans who crafted their own story. Eyewitnesses Peter, James, and John saw the fullness of Christ's glory at the transfiguration and testified to its truth. They heard the voice of God proclaiming Christ's identity. They recognized Moses and Elijah who accompanied him. We who have received this testimony can trust in its authenticity and await our own encounter with the fullness of Christ's glory in the parousia.

Lectionary for Mass #614

Daniel 7:9–10, 13–14

Psalm 97:1–2, 5–6, 9 (1a, 9a)

2 Peter 1:16–19

Matthew 17:1–9

Objectives

- To consider how the glory of Jesus Christ that was revealed to Peter, James, and John at the transfiguration is that same glory that will be revealed to all in the parousia.

- To propose the reliability of the Bible as evidence for the truth of our faith.

Preparation and Materials

- Read the Season Background, the lectionary readings, and the Scripture Background.

- Bookmark the appropriate readings (see page xvii) in the lectionary, children's lectionary, or Bible. Place the book in a convenient location for the leader.

- Write the words of dismissal on a card for the priest celebrant.

- Prepare the words of the song the children will sing as they gather in the space for the Liturgy of the Word.

- Select volunteers (older children or adults) to proclaim the readings.

- Display the responsorial psalm refrain lyrics.

- Display the Apostles' or Nicene Creed.

- Prepare intercessions for the Prayer of the Faithful adapted for the needs of the Church, world, oppressed or marginalized, and local community.

Prayer Leader Reflection Questions

» Whose testimony has influenced you in your faith in Jesus Christ? Who has shared their own experiences of Jesus Christ in their life in a way that has helped you to deepen your own relationship with God?

» How might you transfigure your personal and family life and the life of your community?

Procession

Following the Collect of the Mass, the priest celebrant picks up the lectionary and invites those who would like to participate in the Liturgy of the Word with children to come forward and gather in the center aisle. The people who will lead the children out and facilitate the Liturgy of the Word also come forward at this time. Holding the lectionary so that all can see, the priest celebrant sends the children forth using his own words or the following:

> *Priest:* **Dear children, go together to listen to God's holy Word. Listen closely to what God may have to say to you today. May you learn and grow in love for God so that you may live in the Holy Spirit, and share the good news of Jesus Christ, this day, and every day. Go in peace.**

The leader processes out holding the lectionary, and the children follow behind. The parish music minister may have selected a song of dismissal for the assembly to sing while the children leave. A good option is "The Word of God: Children's Dismissal" by M. D. Ridge and Timothy R. Smith (WLP/GIA).

Centering

Continue to sing the song of dismissal that the assembly sang as you left the church. Or have instrumental music playing as the children gather in the space for the Liturgy of the Word.

Place the lectionary on the ambo or lectern. Light the candle placed by the ambo or lectern, and then lead the following prayer:

> **Lord Jesus,**
> **thank you for the Word that helps us to understand the Father's will better.**
> **May your Spirit enlighten our actions**
> **and grant us the strength to practice that which your Word has revealed to us.**
> **Who live and reign with God the Father, in the unity of the Holy Spirit, God, for ever and ever.**

> *Children:* **Amen.**

First Reading

Daniel 7:9–10, 13–14

Responsorial Psalm

Psalm 97:1–2, 5–6, 9 (1a, 9a) *Sing the same musical setting that is used in your parish's celebration of the liturgy.*

Second Reading

2 Peter 1:16–19

Gospel Acclamation

Sing the Gospel Acclamation used in your parish's celebration of the liturgy.

Gospel Reading

Matthew 17:1–9

Homily/Reflection

Today we are celebrating the Feast of the Transfiguration of the Lord. Christ's transfiguration is so special that we remember it on its own special day. The word *transfiguration* means "to change appearance." We hear in the Gospel how Jesus was changed in front of his friends Peter, James, and John.

» Do you remember what happened to Jesus?

Jesus had led his friends up a mountain, a high place on earth that reaches up to the highest heavens. It was there that his friends heard the voice of God the Father calling Jesus his beloved Son. Jesus' face shone and his friends could see the fullness of his glory. With their own ears and their own eyes, they could recognize who Jesus truly is. I wonder what it might have been like for Jesus' friends to see his glory with their eyes and hear God's words about him with their ears. There were only three people there: Peter, James, and John. Only a few people had the opportunity to witness this beautiful truth, to see Jesus as he truly is. How do we know then that this happened? Because Peter, James and John shared the good news of this event. They told people about it and they shared the news in a way that could be trusted. We call this "testimony." This testimony continued to be shared generation after generation throughout the years until this news reached us today.

Peter, James, and John also told of another event of the good news of Jesus Christ, but one that has not happened yet. We call this day the parousia. The parousia is the time at the end of history when God will be "all in all" (1 Corinthians 15:28). God's glory will shine so brightly that there will be no more need for the sun or the moon because the light of God will be enough. Jesus Christ will come again, and his power will not be hidden. In the parousia, we will not have to wonder any longer about what it was like to see Jesus' glory. We will be able to see it with our own eyes. We will hear the voice of the Father with our own ears.

Until the parousia comes, the fullness of Jesus' glory is still hidden, but we can recognize it anyway. It is the Holy Spirit who helps us to know God's presence in our lives and we can ask for help in prayer. We can listen more deeply and closely to the testimony of Peter, James, and John and all the eyewitnesses whose testimony is contained in the Bible. There are many wise people in our lives who have learned how to see God's glory in their own lives: people like parents, godparents, priests, and teachers.

>> Who has helped you to know God?

Following their example and asking for their aid can help us to recognize God's glory. We can come together around the table of the Lord and receive the glory of the Lord in our very selves when we receive the Body and Blood of Christ in the Eucharist.

Profession of Faith

Following the homily or reflection, the prayer leader invites everyone to stand to profess our faith. Together, sing or recite the Apostles' or Nicene Creed. Refer the children to the words of the prayer that you have displayed.

Prayer of the Faithful

Leader: **United in faith, let us bring our prayers before our loving God. Please respond, "God, in your mercy, hear our prayer."**

For the Church, that her testimony may always be trustworthy, we pray to the Lord: *God, in your mercy, hear our prayer.*

For judges, lawyers, news reporters, and all whose work depends on the testimony of eyewitnesses, that they may always seek the truth, we pray to the Lord: *God, in your mercy, hear our prayer.*

For all who doubt their worth or have lost hope, that the glory of the transfiguration may free them from despair and open a new vision for what God can do for them, we pray to the Lord: *God, in your mercy, hear our prayer.*

For all who go about their daily routines this week, that may they see God's glory in work colleagues, in neighbors and friends, and in those we fear or find hard to get along with, we pray to the Lord: *God, in your mercy, hear our prayer.*

Invite other intercessions from the children, or add intercessions based on the current needs of the Church, the world, the oppressed or marginalized, and the local community. Conclude each of the children's petitions with **"we pray to the Lord"** and invite the response **"God, in your mercy, hear our prayer."**

For all who have died, may God's love transform them to the fullness of life, we pray to the Lord: *God, in your mercy, hear our prayer.*

**O heavenly Father,
you are our Creator and guide.
You make us new and keep us safe.
Accept the prayers of your children.
Through Jesus Christ our Lord.**

Children: **Amen.**

Quietly return with the children to the main assembly. Be mindful of children having difficulty finding their families.

August 13, 2023
Nineteenth Sunday in Ordinary Time
"Take Courage, It Is I"

 ## Scripture Background

Connections to Church Teaching and Tradition

❋ "In their 'one to one' encounters with God, the prophets draw light and strength for their mission. Their prayer is not flight from this unfaithful world, but rather attentiveness to the Word of God. At times their prayer is an argument or a complaint, but it is always an intercession that awaits and prepares for the intervention of the Savior God, the Lord of history[1]" (CCC, 2584).

❋ "Filial trust is put to the test when we feel that our prayer is not always heard. The Gospel invites us to ask ourselves about the conformity of our prayer to the desire of the Spirit" (CCC, 2756).

❋ "Certain constant characteristics appear throughout the Psalms . . . the distraught situation of the believer who, in his preferential love for the Lord, is exposed to a host of enemies and temptations, but who waits upon what the faithful God will do, in the certitude of his love and in submission to his will" (CCC, 2589).

1 Kings 19:9a, 11–13a   Fleeing Jezebel's death threats for having slaughtered all of the Baal prophets, Elijah travels for forty days to Horeb, God's mountain. Horeb, also known as Mount Sinai, is where Moses encountered the Lord during his forty-day stay. Elijah is distressed because of the people's infidelity to God's covenant and to the threats on his life. In his distress, Elijah doubts his prophetic vocation and is tempted to give up. His forty-day journey to Horeb is God's way of reassuring Elijah that the Lord is still with him.

Arriving at Horeb, Elijah waits patiently for an experience of the Lord's presence. Like Moses on Mount Sinai, Elijah experiences a strong mighty wind, an earthquake, and fire; God was not in any of these. Not experiencing God in these usual patterns, Elijah comes to know God's presence in a tiny whispering sound. Out of reverence he hides his face in his cloak and goes out to encounter the Lord. In our distress, the Lord reaches out to comfort and strengthen us. But, like Elijah, we must attune ourselves to God's presence, often in ways we least expect.

Psalm 85:9, 10, 11–12, 13–14 (8)   Psalm 85 is a lament psalm in which the Israelite community seeks to experience once again God's covenant love, peace, and salvation. In the midst of distress, the community trusts in the Lord, asking that covenant love, truth, justice, peace, and God's saving ways be made evident. The psalm is an anticipatory prayer waiting upon the Lord to respond. They trust that God will respond because they are God's people, loyal to the covenant, and because they have awe and reverence for the Lord. Love, truth, justice, and peace manifest different qualities of the covenant relationship. The last stanza envisions a triumphal procession occurring as the Lord responds to the people's request for help and salvation. Justice shall walk before the Lord as a procession unfolds God's actualizing presence and qualities among the people. With the Lord in our midst, there is nothing to fear.

Romans 9:1–5   Paul expresses "great sorrow and constant anguish" (v. 2) over other fellow Jews who have not accepted Jesus as God's Messiah. Like Moses before him, Paul was willing to sacrifice everything for his people. He would give anything, even forfeit his own connection to Christ, if they could experience God's presence and saving power that is his in Christ Jesus. Despite God's many blessings on his people, they have not come to recognize Christ Jesus as Messiah.

Paul stresses that the people have been gifted with a unique name, Israelites, and are specially favored by God. God's glory has been manifested to them and their special relationship to God has been cemented in loving covenant bonds. God gave them the Law, the path to life, guided them in worship, and always proved faithful to covenant promises. From the beginning God presented them with models of faith in the patriarchs and now, "from them according to the flesh, is the Christ" (v. 5). Paul knows that the Lord is uniquely present with us in Christ. While in distress, he waits in hope for the time when all will be one in Christ.

Matthew 14:22–33   Jesus' prayer on the mountain, which he prayed after having dismissed the crowd he had just fed by multiplying loaves and fish, connects the Elijah reading to the Gospel. When Jesus walks on water, he demonstrates his divine power. Water, while necessary for life, also exhibits powerful destructive forces, which led to its association with chaos, disorder, and evil. In the creation narrative, God's Word subordinates the watery chaos, bringing order, light, and life to the world. By walking on water, Jesus manifests similar divine attributes, showing his disciples that he is the source of order, life, and light in their chaotic world.

---

1   Cf. Amos 7:2, 5; Isaiah 6:5, 8, 11; Jeremiah 1:6; 15:15–18; 20:7–18.

The storm-tossed boat is symbolic of the struggle that disciples have in carrying out Jesus' mission. Approaching them on water, he soothes their fears with divine assertions and calms the storm. Jesus shows himself to be their source of strength and courage amidst life's chaos. Peter asserts faith in Jesus when at Jesus' command he ventures into the water. But doubt overtakes him and, as he begins to sink, Jesus reaches out to save him. As Jesus comes into the boat, the wind dies down as the rest of the disciples acknowledge their belief in him as the Son of God. Discipleship demands acknowledging God as our source of courage, and recognizing the Lord's presence whenever doubt and chaos overwhelm us.

Preparation

The miracle stories of the Gospel put Jesus' power on display. Jesus, who is fully human, is also the Lord of all creation who has the power to suspend the laws of nature. The disciples were in a boat tossed by the waves and were unable to make progress forward in a headwind. The same Lord Jesus who has the power to walk on water used that power to draw nearer to his friends. Peter's faith in Jesus' power was great enough to trust that Jesus could enable him to walk on water also. When Peter doubted and cried out, Jesus reached out and caught him. In our own spiritual lives, we may experience storms and gales; we know that no forces prevail against the power of God who reaches out and saves us. Jesus invites us to take courage and remember that God is with us, even in times of doubt or trouble. God's presence is all around us, and how happy are we who notice God's presence working in our lives.

Lectionary for Mass #115A

1 Kings 19:9a, 11–13a

Psalm 85:9, 10, 11–12, 13–14 (8)

Romans 9:1–5

Matthew 14:22–33

Objectives

- To invite the children to have courage in times of trouble and have faith that God is with us.

- To help children to pay attention for God's presence.

Preparation and Materials

- Read the Season Background, the lectionary readings, and the Scripture Background.

- Bookmark the appropriate readings (see page xvii) in the lectionary, children's lectionary, or Bible. Place the book in a convenient location for the leader.

- Write the words of dismissal on a card for the priest celebrant.

- Prepare the words of the song the children will sing as they gather in the space for the Liturgy of the Word.

- Select volunteers (older children or adults) to proclaim the readings.

- Display the responsorial psalm refrain lyrics.

- Display the Apostles' or Nicene Creed.

- Prepare intercessions for the Prayer of the Faithful adapted for the needs of the Church, world, oppressed or marginalized, and local community.

Prayer Leader Reflection Questions

>> **When have you experienced "storms" and "rough winds" in your own spiritual life? How much do you trust God in times of difficulty?**

>> **How can you help raise the children's awareness of God's presence in their midst?**

Procession

Following the Collect of the Mass, the priest celebrant picks up the lectionary and invites those who would like to participate in the Liturgy of the Word with children to come forward and gather in the center aisle. The people who will lead the children out and facilitate the Liturgy of the Word also come forward at this time. Holding the lectionary so that all can see, the priest celebrant sends the children forth using his own words or the following:

> *Priest:* **Dear children, God is majestic and powerful, but he also speaks to us in intimate, personal ways, such as the gentle whispering that Elijah heard or in the hand Jesus reached out to Peter to save him from drowning. Listen today to him speaking in the Scriptures, and listen always to how God speaks to you in your heart. Go in peace.**

The leader processes out holding the lectionary, and the children follow behind. The parish music minister may have selected a song of dismissal for the assembly to sing while the children leave. A good option is "The Word of God: Children's Dismissal" by M. D. Ridge and Timothy R. Smith (WLP/GIA).

Centering

Continue to sing the song of dismissal that the assembly sang as you left the church. Or sing "How Firm a Foundation" (various publishers) or the refrain from "Here I Am, Lord" (Schutte), or have instrumental music playing as the children gather in the space for the Liturgy of the Word.

Place the lectionary on the ambo or lectern. Light the candle placed by the ambo or lectern, and then lead the following prayer:

> **Mighty God,**
> **allow our hearts to be open to your Word**
> **so that we may serve you completely.**
> **We ask this through Christ our Lord.**

> *Children:* **Amen.**

First Reading

1 Kings 19:9a, 11–13a

Responsorial Psalm

Psalm 85:9, 10, 11–12, 13–14 (8) *Sing the same musical setting that is used in your parish's celebration of the liturgy.*

Second Reading

Romans 9:1–5

Gospel Acclamation

Sing the Gospel Acclamation used in your parish's celebration of the liturgy.

Gospel Reading

Matthew 14:22–33

Homily/Reflection

≫ Have you ever played with a toy boat in the bath or in a swimming pool?

You might have pushed the boat forward and seen how it could glide quickly through the water. Maybe you made big splashes and watched the boat rock on the waves. Perhaps you noticed that the boat was constantly moving even if the water seemed very still. If we travel on a boat, we can feel that motion with our bodies. We can notice how the boat is never quite still, especially when the waves in the water are big. During the time when Jesus walked and talked on this earth like you and I do now, Jesus spent much of his time in Galilee, where there was a large lake called the Sea of Galilee. People used boats to travel around the sea. Fishing was a way for people to get food and work.

In today's Gospel reading, we hear of the boat that the disciples were traveling on being tossed on the waves. Then they saw Jesus walking on the choppy waves. It was shocking to them to see Jesus using his power this way. They thought they were seeing a ghost, a spirit with no body. They were terrified. Jesus saw this and reassured them. He told them that it was really him and to have courage. Peter did just that. He said something brave. He told Jesus, "Lord, if it is you, command me to come to you on the water" (Matthew 14:28). Jesus said, "Come." Peter did come toward Jesus, and he too was walking on the water. He was doing this not by his own power, but by Jesus' power. When he became frightened by the wind, he began to sink. He cried out to Jesus to help him. Jesus reached out and caught him. Jesus said, "Take courage!" Jesus wanted Peter to know that Jesus will always be there for him, even in scary or troubled times.

God will always listen to us when we call, but sometimes people wonder where God is, and whether God is listening to our prayers.

≫ Do you ever feel like that?

Because we can't see God, it's not easy to know that God is active and present within us, that God is working in our lives. We can see each other here, we can hear each other, and when you say something, I can say something back to you. It is easy to feel each other's presence.

≫ Is it easy to feel God's presence?

In today's first reading, we heard the author tell us that God can sometimes be found in "a tiny whispering sound." So sometimes, we will need to quiet ourselves to notice God. This is especially important during those times when we feel scared or uncertain. There might be times when we feel like we are on a boat being tossed around. We might feel like there are things we can't control that are making us nervous, scared, even terrified. At other times, we might be frustrated at not getting where we want to go and having forces pushing us in the wrong direction. When our life feels like rough seas, we can be brave like Peter. We can trust that God can help us to do surprising things. We know that even if we feel like we are sinking, Jesus comes to us. We trust that he will answer our call. He will reach out and he will catch us in his loving arms.

Profession of Faith

Following the homily or reflection, the prayer leader invites everyone to stand to profess our faith. Together, sing or recite the Apostles' or Nicene Creed. Refer the children to the words of the prayer that you have displayed.

Prayer of the Faithful

Leader: **God's help is near for those who believe, so we present our petitions with confidence. Please respond, "Lord, hear us."**

That in times of need we the Church may trust in the Lord to save us, we pray: *Lord, hear us.*

That those who serve in public office may promote true justice and peace, we pray: *Lord, hear us.*

That all whose faith is tested may rely on the guidance of the Holy Spirit, we pray: *Lord, hear us.*

That those who earn a living by fishing the seas and who are, at times, put in situations of great danger may be protected by God, we pray: *Lord, hear us.*

Invite other intercessions from the children, or add intercessions based on the current needs of the Church, the world, the oppressed or marginalized, and the local community. Conclude each of the children's petitions with **"we pray"** and invite the response **"Lord, hear us."**

That all those who have died may be caught up in the arms of the Lord, we pray: *Lord, hear us.*

**Lord Jesus Christ,
you commanded St. Peter to come to you on the water.
You did not let him falter but caught him and renewed his faith.
Catch us when our faith is tested,
for you live and reign with the Father and the Holy Spirit,
God, for ever and ever.**

Children: **Amen.**

Quietly return with the children to the main assembly. Be mindful of children having difficulty finding their families.

August 15, 2023
Solemnity of the Assumption of the Blessed Virgin Mary

Rejoice in the Lord

 ## Scripture Background

Connections to Church Teaching and Tradition

* "The Assumption of the Blessed Virgin is a singular participation in her Son's Resurrection and an anticipation of the resurrection of other Christians" (CCC, 966).

* "The Virgin Mary . . . is acknowledged and honored as truly the Mother of God and of the Redeemer. . . . But, being of the race of Adam, she is at the same time also united to all those who are to be saved. . . . Therefore she is hailed as a preeminent and as a wholly unique member of the church, and as its exemplar and outstanding model in faith and charity" (LG, 53).

Revelation 11:19a; 12:1–6a, 10ab This end-time vision of God's anointed initiating an era that will result in the defeat of evil powers is filled with apocalyptic and mythological images. The vision begins with the heavenly temple opened for all to see the ark of the covenant. Both temple and ark are images indicating God's presence among the people. The vision switches to a pregnant "woman clothed with the sun" (12:1) who is laboring to give birth. A destructive dragon, symbolic of evil, stands ready to devour the pregnant woman's child. The woman gives birth to a son, "destined to rule all nations with an iron rod" (12:5). Through God's intervention, both mother and child are rescued from the dragon, while a voice loudly proclaims that "now have salvation and power come / . . . the Kingdom of God / and the authority of his Anointed One" (12:10).

The woman is often interpreted as God's people, Israel, and by extension both Mary and the Church. The dragon represents all evil powers out to destroy God's anointed. God's intention both now and at the end-time is that Christ, God's anointed, reigns among us with salvation and power, destroying evil and establishing God's eternal Kingdom of peace. Today we celebrate Mary, the first among us to experience fully the effects of God's saving actions, which are intended for all humanity.

Psalm 45:10, 11, 12, 16 (10bc) This psalm is a wedding song celebrating a royal marriage, possibly that of King Ahab and Jezebel, who was a princess of Tyre and Sidon as referenced in verse 13. The refrain and first verse chosen for this feast focus on the honor rendered to the king by having such a beautiful and richly adorned queen stand at his right hand. The other verses chosen speak directly to the queen, advising her to forget her people and give all her attention to the king, who is now her lord. The last verse recounts the bridal procession of queen and maids entering the king's palace "with gladness and joy" (45:16).

The Solemnity of the Assumption celebrates Mary being welcomed, body and soul, into God's royal abode. Standing at God's right hand, she is crowned Queen of Heaven. The psalm's wedding song images speak to this event in Mary's life, which is nowhere in Scripture but has been traditionally held by Catholic Christians. With Mary, we honor and sing praises to God who, through Christ Jesus, has enabled both Mary and us to be so richly blessed.

1 Corinthians 15:20–27 Paul sings God's praises for having raised Christ from the dead, "the firstfruits of those who have fallen asleep" (15:20). Since death entered through humanity's (Adam's) sinfulness, so too in Christ, a human like us, all humanity "shall . . . be brought to life" (v. 22). Paul articulates an apocalyptic process and time frame for these events. Upon Christ's return, all who belong to Christ will rise. Next comes the end of time, in which Christ will defeat all forces contrary to God. Death is the "last enemy to be destroyed" (v. 26), at which time Christ will hand over all to the Father who commissioned him for this purpose.

With Mary's Assumption, we sing praises to God for bringing Mary to life and allowing her full entrance into the heavenly Kingdom. We, too, live in hope that through Christ's defeat of death, we will be brought to life and join Mary and all the saints in God's heavenly Kingdom to sing God's praises forever.

Luke 1:39–56 Two women form the frame in this Lucan painting. Elizabeth, the barren one, and Mary, the virgin, are both pregnant. Together they honor one another, as they sing praises to God's mercy and care for all the people. John, Elizabeth's child, begins his ministry of preparing the Messiah's path by jumping for joy in his mother's womb, at the recognition of the child in Mary's womb. Elizabeth honors and praises Mary for God's gift to her, for believing God's Word, and for being willing to cooperate with God's merciful plan of salvation.

Mary honors Elizabeth with her visit and her assistance during her pregnancy while she praises God's greatness in the Magnificat. Her song of praise is an affirmation of God's ways in contrast to human patterns of thinking and acting. The song speaks of God's graciousness in reversing expectations by choosing the lowly, the hungry, and the poor as vehicles through whom God's work of salvation is accomplished. In and through Mary, God's lowly handmaid, salvation has come. With Mary, all we can do is rejoice and sing God's praises for the Almighty has done great things for all of us.

Preparation

Celebrating the Solemnity of the Assumption helps us to celebrate the dignity of all human life, but especially the life of Mary, the Mother of God. Mary's role in the Church is significant as she brought Jesus to us with her life. Taken up to heaven, she continues by her constant intercession to bring us the gifts of salvation. Children will find Mary a comfortable, relatable figure.

Lectionary #622

Revelation 11:19a;
   12:1–6a, 10ab

Psalm 45:10, 11, 12,
   16 (10bc)

1 Corinthians 15:20–27

Luke 1:39–56

Objectives

- To celebrate Mary, the Mother of God, and her dignity as a woman, loved by the Trinity.

- To celebrate the dignity of all women.

Preparation and Materials

- Read the Season Background, the Lectionary readings, and the Scripture Background.

- Bookmark the appropriate readings (see page xvii) in the Lectionary, children's Lectionary, or Bible. Place the book in a convenient location for the leader.

- Write the words of dismissal on a card for the priest celebrant.

- Prepare the words of the song the children will sing as they gather in the space for Liturgy of the Word.

- Select volunteers (older children or adults) to proclaim the readings.

- Display the responsorial psalm refrain lyrics.

- Display the Apostles' or Nicene Creed.

- Prepare intercessions for the Prayer of the Faithful adapted for the needs of the Church, world, oppressed or marginalized, and local community.

Prayer Leader Reflection Questions

» **Mary was a woman full of joy. How can you help the children to experience joy in the Liturgy of the Word this week?**

Procession

Following the Collect of the Mass, the priest celebrant picks up the Lectionary and invites those who would like to participate in the Liturgy of the Word with children to come forward and gather in the center aisle. The people who will lead the children out and facilitate the Liturgy of the Word also come forward at this time. Holding the Lectionary so that all can see, the priest celebrant sends the children forth using his own words or the following:

> **Priest: Dear children, go together to listen to God's holy Word. Listen closely to what God may have to say to you today. May you learn and grow in love for God so that you may live in the Holy Spirit, and share the Good News of Jesus Christ, this day, and every day. Go in peace.**

The leader processes out holding the Lectionary and the children follow behind. The parish music minister may have selected a song of dismissal for the assembly to sing while the children leave. A good option is "The Word of God: Children's Dismissal" by M. D. Ridge and Timothy R. Smith (WLP/GIA).

Centering

Continue to sing the song of dismissal that the assembly sang as you left the church. Or sing "Hail Mary: Gentle Woman" (Landry), or "I Say 'Yes,' My Lord"/ "Digo 'Sí,' Señor" (Peña), or have instrumental music playing as the children gather in the space for the Liturgy of the Word.

Place the Lectionary on the ambo or lectern. Light the candle placed by the ambo or lectern and then lead the following prayer:

> **God our Father,**
> **through the intercession of the Blessed Virgin Mary,**
> **nourish our faith with your truth.**
> **We ask this through Christ, your Son, who lives and reigns with you in the unity of the Holy Spirit, God, for ever and ever.**

Children: **Amen.**

First Reading

Revelation 11:19a; 12:1–6a, 10ab

Responsorial Psalm

Psalm 45:10, 11, 12, 16 (10bc) *Sing the same musical setting that is used in your parish's celebration of the liturgy.*

Second Reading

1 Corinthians 15:20–27

Gospel Acclamation

Sing the Gospel Acclamation used in your parish's celebration of the liturgy.

Gospel Reading

Luke 1:39–56

Homily/Reflection

Today we celebrate the Assumption of Mary, the Mother of God. After she died, she joined her son Jesus in heaven. Sometimes when I pray with children and they share the prayers they have in their hearts, they pray for their grandparents who have died. One child prayed about her grandma, "So that she has a good time in heaven!" Isn't that a wonderful prayer? Today we celebrate that Mary, the Mother of God, is up in heaven having a good time. And we know that she is!

Mary was a very special woman, because she said yes to God. She didn't understand everything that God was asking her to do, but she trusted in God to have it all come out right in the end. Her life shows us that women all over the world are called to bring forth life in special ways. Mary was Jesus' mother; she helped to bring him into the world. Some women become mothers, and some women bring forth life through their prayers or through their work. God has given every person dignity, women *and* men. All of us have special gifts that God wants us to share with the world.

We recognize Mary as our mother in heaven, too, because of all of the wonderful ways she helps us to get closer to God.

≫ Can anyone here tell me any of the prayers of Mary?

Some of the popular ones are the Hail Mary, the Magnificat, and the Rosary. When we pray these prayers, we remember the role that Mary had in salvation history. We honor her for her love and obedience to God.

We are all children of God. We know that each and every one of us has dignity in the eyes of God. Dignity means being special, precious, and valuable in the eyes of God for just being yourself.

So, today as we celebrate Mary, let us celebrate the dignity of all women, and the dignity of all men, and the dignity of all children. We are all one family in the house of God.

Profession of Faith

Following the homily or reflection, the prayer leader invites everyone to stand to profess our faith. Together, sing or recite the Apostles' or Nicene Creed. Refer the children to the words of the prayer that you have displayed.

Prayer of the Faithful

Leader: **United in faith, let us bring our prayers before our loving God. Please respond, "Lord, hear our prayer."**

For the Church around the world, that we may all look to our Blessed Mother as an example of faith and obedience, we pray: *Lord, hear our prayer.*

For those who are elected to positions of public responsibility, that they may show compassion and justice to the weakest of our society, we pray: *Lord, hear our prayer.*

For the poor, that they may be granted the dignity they deserve, and that we may never turn from them in their need, we pray: *Lord, hear our prayer.*

For all families, that they may live and grow in love and forgiveness, we pray: *Lord, hear our prayer.*

Invite other intercessions from the children, or add intercessions based on the current needs of the Church, the world, the oppressed or marginalized, and the local community. Conclude each of the children's petitions with, "**we pray,**" and invite the response, "**Lord, hear our prayer.**"

For all those who have died, that they may live with God forever, we pray: *Lord, hear our prayer.*

**Everlasting God,
hear our prayers and petitions, fill our lives with light and love,
be with us always as we live in the grace of your most Holy Trinity.
Through Christ our Lord.**

Children: **Amen.**

Quietly return with the children to the main assembly. Be mindful of children having difficulty finding their families.

August 20, 2023
Twentieth Sunday in Ordinary Time

God's Mercy Is for All Peoples

 ## Scripture Background

Connections to Church Teaching and Tradition

- "The gathering together of the People of God began at the moment when sin destroyed the communion of men with God, and that of men among themselves. The gathering together of the Church is, as it were, God's reaction to the chaos provoked by sin. This reunification is achieved secretly in the heart of all peoples[1]" (CCC, 761).

- "Jesus is as saddened by the 'lack of faith' of his own neighbors and the 'little faith' of his own disciples[2] as he is struck with admiration at the great faith of the Roman centurion and the Canaanite woman[3]" (CCC, 2610).

Isaiah 56:1, 6–7 Isaiah 56—66, the third and last part of the prophetic book, addresses the Jewish community that has returned from the Babylonian exile. The community continues to restore the land and rebuild the Temple. Building on the work the author wrote during the exile, this part of the Book of Isaiah begins with a stress on observing and doing what is right and just. Ethical living is what God requires for salvation to be revealed.

The question of acceptance or inclusion of foreigners was a major concern for the returned exiles. Some counseled exclusion and purity of race and worship. Others, like Isaiah, understood God to be accepting and inclusive. If foreigners enter into relationship with the Lord, keeping the Sabbath holy and holding to the covenant promises, then the Lord invites them to the holy mountain, the Temple, and the house of prayer. Their offerings and prayers will be acceptable to the Lord, for the Lord's house is "a house of prayer for all peoples" (v. 7). God and salvation are accessible to all.

Psalm 67:2–3, 5, 6, 8 (4) Psalm 67 is a prayer of blessing to God, asking not only the Jewish community, but all nations to offer praise for God's blessings. The community asks God's face to shine upon them so that they and all the nations will come to know and bless the Lord. As God's benefits and salvation are made manifest to the Jewish people, the community prays and hopes that through them the nations will know that God guides, rules, and blesses all.

The Jewish community has consistently understood itself not only as God's Chosen People but also as a light to the nations. Their enduring hope was that, through their covenant relationship with God and fidelity to God's ways, they would become the vehicles of God's blessings upon all people. Through their faithful living, other nations would be attracted to the Lord and live according to his ways, standing in awe and giving praise to him. They would become light to the world, as we are called to be today.

Romans 11:13–15, 29–32 In this passage, Paul continues to grapple with the question of why most of his people have rejected the Gospel. Addressing Gentiles in Rome who have accepted the Gospel, Paul hopes that the blessings they have received by accepting the Gospel will make his people jealous and move them toward accepting the Gospel as well. In the divine plan, Paul optimistically understands the Jewish rejection of the Gospel as the means through which the Gentiles have been reconciled to God. If rejection brings about such good results, Paul imagines that Jewish acceptance will activate the life that is ours eternally from God.

Paul stresses that the Gentiles who were distant from God have been reconciled to God because of the rejection of the Gospel by the Jews. Now, the Jews have distanced themselves from God by not accepting the Gospel. Paul's hope is that, seeing the mercy extended by God to the Gentiles, Jews will also accept the Gospel and be reconciled to God in Christ. Human disobedience and rejection of God are used by God as a means of displaying love and mercy to all. No group can claim to have cornered God's love and mercy. Being open to all people so they can know God through us is a challenge that we all face in our daily interactions with people of diverse backgrounds.

Matthew 15:21–28 Jesus' healing of the Canaanite woman's daughter tormented by a demon brings to the surface many issues concerning relationships between Jews and Gentiles. The consequences of breaking boundaries seem to enlighten all to the nature of God and the ministry of Jesus. Jesus crosses into Gentile territory (Tyre and Sidon) and a woman from a

1 Acts 10:35; cf. LG, 9, 13, 16.
2 Cf. Mark 6:6; Matthew 8:26.
3 Cf. Matthew 8:10; 15:28.

nation (Canaan) historically despised by Jews approaches him on behalf of her sick daughter. Both actions would have been seen as culturally negative. Yet, through the dialogue and interaction that ensues, both parties, along with the disciples and Matthew's community, learn an important lesson. Jesus displays the typical Jewish mindset that his ministry and God's salvation are exclusively for the Jews, referring to her as a dog, the common slur of Jews toward Gentiles. This closed mindset does not deter a mother's love, as the mother reminds Jesus that even the dogs are fed scraps from the children's table. Her faith overwhelms Jesus, who directly heals her daughter. Thus, we learn that Jews and Gentiles alike are part of God's family.

Preparation

The end of the Book of Isaiah first addressed people who had returned from exile and who wrestled with an important question: who can rightly worship their God? God's answer made clear that those who love the Lord and obey the commandments can serve God even if they are foreigners. Paul affirmed to the first Christians that salvation in Jesus Christ is available to Gentiles, the Jewish word for non-Jews, but also for the "nations" or the "peoples." God's love for us is universal and available to all.

Lectionary for Mass #118A

Isaiah 56:1, 6–7

Psalm 67:2–3, 5, 6, 8 (4)

Romans 11:13–15, 29–32

Matthew 15:21–28

Objectives

- To announce that the good news of God's love and his healing mercy is for all people.

- To explain that God created all people; we are all brothers and sisters who share a common humanity.

Preparation and Materials

- Read the Season Background, the lectionary readings, and the Scripture Background.

- Bookmark the appropriate readings (see page xvii) in the lectionary, children's lectionary, or Bible. Place the book in a convenient location for the leader.

- Write the words of dismissal on a card for the priest celebrant.

- Prepare the words of the song the children will sing as they gather in the space for the Liturgy of the Word.

- Select volunteers (older children or adults) to proclaim the readings.

- Display the responsorial psalm refrain lyrics.

- Display the Apostles' or Nicene Creed.

- Prepare intercessions for the Prayer of the Faithful adapted for the needs of the Church, world, oppressed or marginalized, and local community.

Prayer Leader Reflection Questions

» **How can you help the children to see past their differences and discover unity in Christ?**

» **How do you live as a part of the Body of Christ, which is composed of peoples of different cultures?**

Procession

Following the Collect of the Mass, the priest celebrant picks up the lectionary and invites those who would like to participate in the Liturgy of the Word with children to come forward and gather in the center aisle. The people who will lead the children out and facilitate the Liturgy of the Word also come forward at this time. Holding the lectionary so that all can see, the priest celebrant sends the children forth using his own words or the following:

> *Priest:* **Dear children, today's readings remind us that God's love is for all people. Just as God chose us to be members of his Church, we need to welcome all who come to us, no matter how different from us they might seem to be, for everyone is a child of God. Go now and listen to the Word of God our Father.**

The leader processes out holding the lectionary, and the children follow behind. The parish music minister may have selected a song of dismissal for the assembly to sing while the children leave. A good option is "The Word of God: Children's Dismissal" by M. D. Ridge and Timothy R. Smith (WLP/GIA).

Centering

Continue to sing the song of dismissal that the assembly sang as you left the church. Or sing "Psalm 63: In the Morning I Will Sing" (Haugen), or the refrain from "All Are Welcome" (Haugen), or have instrumental music playing as the children gather in the space for the Liturgy of the Word.

Place the lectionary on the ambo or lectern. Light the candle placed by the ambo or lectern, and then lead the following prayer:

> **God our Father,**
> **open our hearts to your holy Word and help us to follow Jesus Christ,**
> **your Son, who lives and reigns with you in the unity of the Holy Spirit,**
> **God, for ever and ever.**

> *Children:* **Amen.**

First Reading

Isaiah 56:1, 6–7

Responsorial Psalm

Psalm 67:2–3, 5, 6, 8 (4) *Sing the same musical setting that is used in your parish's celebration of the liturgy.*

Second Reading

Romans 11:13–15, 29–32

Gospel Acclamation

Sing the Gospel Acclamation used in your parish's celebration of the liturgy.

Gospel Reading

Matthew 15:21–28

Homily/Reflection

As we gather together today, we know that we are in Ordinary Time. We can look around and see the color green that reminds us of this season in the Church year.

» Where do you notice the color green here in church?

We can see it on the chasuble of the priest, the special garment he wears. We might see it in the plants and flowers that adorn our worship space. Green can make us think of green grass and the green leaves of plants and trees. Many plants are very green when they are most full of life and perhaps getting ready to bear fruit. We want to be like those plants. We want to grow to the fullness of life in God and bear the fruit of that life for others.

» Who are the others? Who might we bear fruit for?

Today's readings help us think about the question of who can belong to the kingdom of God. In the time of Isaiah, the Jewish people worshipped God in a special way in the temple in Jerusalem. The temple was on a mountain, up in a high place. We speak of God as in the highest heights and sometimes high places make us feel like we are reaching up to God. The temple in Jerusalem was the place where the Jewish people felt closest to God. The temple had a place called the Holy of Holies, where the tablets containing the gift of the Law were kept. Only the high priest could go in the Holy of Holies, but other people who loved God could come to the outer court of the temple to worship. Isaiah was a prophet who listened for God's voice and Isaiah heard God say, "I will bring [all people] to my holy mountain and make them joyful in my house of prayer" (Isaiah 56:7).

The people of Israel have a word that you may have heard before: *Gentiles*. The word *Gentile* refers to people who are not Jewish. It can also mean "nations" and "peoples." Nations are countries. Peoples are communities that have shared characteristics, like language and traditions. Another word might be *cultures*. When God said that foreigners could join themselves to the Lord, this told the listeners something very important about who God loves. God loves the Jewish people and God loves the Gentiles, the people of all nations, the people of all cultures. It doesn't matter what language we speak or what country we come from. God loves us all.

We want to love like God loves. God is full of mercy. To have mercy means to have compassion and understanding for someone no matter what. When Jesus walked the earth, he had an attitude of mercy with everyone he met. Mercy is being kind to someone even when they don't necessarily deserve it. When someone is merciful, they recognize the dignity of all people, even people who are different from us, people who are foreigners, or who are not a part of our group. Even when people are not a part of our group—because maybe they live in a different city or country, or because they look different, or go to a different church, or practice a different religion—they still deserve mercy because God made all of us. We are all a part of God's family, and we share a common humanity. We are sisters and brothers in the human family. When we look at it that way, we see many more things in common with each other that help us to love one another in the way that Jesus taught us.

Profession of Faith	Following the homily or reflection, the prayer leader invites everyone to stand to profess our faith. Together, sing or recite the Apostles' or Nicene Creed. Refer the children to the words of the prayer that you have displayed.
Prayer of the Faithful	*Leader:* **The Lord is our King of Peace, Prince of Justice. Let us now pray for all our needs. Please respond, "Merciful Lord, hear us."**

May the Church boldly profess Jesus as Lord and help others to come to know him, we pray: *Merciful Lord, hear us.*

May nations of the world live together in peace, we pray: *Merciful Lord, hear us.*

May those who are ill be comforted in their time of trial, we pray: *Merciful Lord, hear us.*

May all who have helped us strengthen our faith—parents, teachers, and those who give witness by their life—continue to be examples of Christian discipleship to all who encounter them, we pray: *Merciful Lord, hear us.*

Invite other intercessions from the children, or add intercessions based on the current needs of the Church, the world, the oppressed or marginalized, and the local community. Conclude each of the children's petitions with **"we pray"** and invite the response **"Merciful Lord, hear us."**

May those who have died know God's love in heaven, we pray: *Merciful Lord, hear us.*

**O God,
you bring those who are faithful to you to be together as one.
Hear our prayers and petitions.
Fill our lives with light and love,
and be with us always.
Through Christ our Lord.**

Children: **Amen.**

Quietly return with the children to the main assembly. Be mindful of children having difficulty finding their families.

August 27, 2023
Twenty-First Sunday in Ordinary Time
"Who Do You Say That I Am?"

 ## Scripture Background

Connections to Church Teaching and Tradition

- Christ is the head of the Church, and the Church participates in Jesus' kingly office (CCC, 908–913).

- Animated by the Holy Spirit, the Church continues to do Christ's work in the world (CCC, 542–546, 567).

- Catholics honor the authority of the pope and other bishops as being in direct line from the authority given by Jesus to Peter and the other Apostles (CCC, 851, 862).

- God continues to gift the Church by calling leaders to guide the people (CCC, 863).

Isaiah 22:19–23 Isaiah the prophet addresses oracles to various nations, announcing their impending doom (chapters 3–23). Chapter 22 is an oracle against Jerusalem, the City of David. Isaiah makes the point that Jerusalem, too, was subject to God's judgment. This oracle may have been delivered when Sennacherib, the king of Assyria, launched a siege against Jerusalem. Although Jerusalem was miraculously spared, the people refused to acknowledge that their sins brought destruction near. Shebna, the steward or overseer of the house of Hezekiah, appears to have been the leader of the party that favored an alliance with Egypt against Assyria, rather than trusting in God. Shebna is the only individual against whom the prophet issued an oracle of doom. Isaiah's wrath was aroused by the wanton luxury of Shebna, especially the lavish tomb he built for himself, which the prophet predicted he would never occupy. Because of his pride, Shebna was ejected from his office and Eliakim (Hebrew: "God raises up") was given supervision over the house of David. The *key* was a symbol of power for Israel: "I will place on his shoulder the key of the house of David; he shall open, and no one shall shut; he shall shut, and no one shall open" (v. 22). Fixed in a secure place, Eliakim too would fall when he failed to put his trust in God.

Psalm 138:1–3, 6, 8 (8bc) Psalm 138 is a heartfelt prayer of thanksgiving offered by a petitioner in the Temple. Clearly, there were times when the psalmist was in danger, but he had confidence that God would rescue him. The psalmist is moved to sing of God's "steadfast kindness" and "truth" (v. 2b): "When I called, you answered me" (v. 3a). The psalmist is not saved because of his virtues but because of God's fidelity. He trusts in God's continual help and prays that others might experience God's love and thereby be stirred to offer God praise.

Romans 11:33–36 Paul battled with a heartbreaking problem of his own people's rejection of Jesus Christ. He examined the question with every resource he possessed. A certain paradox existed: God gave Paul a great mind, and it was his duty to use that mind. But sometimes his human limitations were reached. The mystery of salvation could not be understood solely by the mind but by a heart that loved God. Paul says that there was nothing more to be said: "For who has known the mind of the Lord / or who has been his counselor?" (v. 34). Paul's theology now turns to poetry; his seeking of the mind turns to the adoration of the heart. Paul declares that all things came from God, that all things have their being through God, and that all things end in God. Having done his best, Paul was content to accept the divine mystery of redemption.

Matthew 16:13–20 Jesus took his disciples to the area of Caesarea Philippi in northern Israel near Baniyas, where the Cave of Pan (identified with the Roman god of fields and forests, flocks and shepherds) stood. There may also have been a temple in this area built by Herod to honor the Emperor Augustus. In this pagan territory, Jesus asks his disciples, "Who do people say that the Son of Man is?" (v. 13b). Peter confesses his belief in Jesus as God's Son, the "Christ" (v. 16; the "anointed one"). Jesus declares that Peter is "blessed" for announcing this revelation from God. Jesus, in turn, affirms Peter's identity and mission as the foundation, the "rock," of his Church. The Aramaic word for "rock" (*kepha*) was transliterated into Greek as "Cephas," the name Paul used for Peter in his writings (see 1 Corinthians 1:12). Matthew used the Greek masculine word *petros* (for the feminine *petra*), thus "Peter" in English. Because of Peter's new position among the Twelve, Jesus confers supreme authority on him, promising divine assistance to guide the Church. Peter received "the keys of the kingdom of heaven" (Matthew 16:19).

These powers to "bind" and "loose"—that is, the power to absolve or not to absolve a person from sin—are given to the Church through Peter and his successors. The rock of Peter's faith would enable him to follow Jesus right up to his own death as a martyr.

 # Preparation

God announced to Isaiah that the scribe Eliakim would be tasked with a particular authority and power to work according to God's plan. Eliakim would bear the key of the house of David on his shoulder. The Gospel of Matthew recounts another mention of keys: those to the kingdom of God. Jesus Christ invited the apostles to share his own power and authority in binding and loosing. While children are too young to be invited to possess the apostolic power of binding and loosing, they are nonetheless entrusted to participate in the mission of Christ. All the baptized, no matter their age, are invited by God to participate in the work of God's plan.

Lectionary for Mass #121A

Isaiah 22:19–23

Psalm 138:1–2, 2–3, 6, 8 (8bc)

Romans 11:33–36

Matthew 16:13–20

Objectives

- To explore the image of key as corresponding to power over access and participation in work.
- To announce that we are invited to be co-laborers in the work of God.

Preparation and Materials

- Read the Season Background, the lectionary readings, and the Scripture Background.
- Bookmark the appropriate readings (see page xvii) in the lectionary, children's lectionary, or Bible. Place the book in a convenient location for the leader.
- Write the words of dismissal on a card for the priest celebrant.
- Prepare the words of the song the children will sing as they gather in the space for the Liturgy of the Word.
- Select volunteers (older children or adults) to proclaim the readings.
- Display the responsorial psalm refrain lyrics.
- Display the Apostles' or Nicene Creed.
- Prepare intercessions for the Prayer of the Faithful adapted for the needs of the Church, world, oppressed or marginalized, and local community.
- Optional: Bring a padlock and key to show children.

Prayer Leader Reflection Questions

» **Who do you say that Jesus is when you speak of him to others?**

» **How do you work together with God in the unfolding of God's plan?**

Procession

Following the Collect of the Mass, the priest celebrant picks up the lectionary and invites those who would like to participate in the Liturgy of the Word with children to come forward and gather in the center aisle. The people who will lead the children out and facilitate the Liturgy of the Word also come forward at this time. Holding the lectionary so that all can see, the priest celebrant sends the children forth using his own words or the following:

> *Priest*: **Dear children, the Father revealed to Peter that Jesus was the Messiah, and Jesus chose him as the foundation of his Church. God gives each one of us a special gift, a calling, and an important role to play in the Church. Remember this as you listen to today's readings—each one of you is unique and chosen by the God who loves you very much. Go in peace.**

The leader processes out holding the lectionary, and the children follow behind. The parish music minister may have selected a song of dismissal for the assembly to sing while the children leave. A good option is "The Word of God: Children's Dismissal" by M. D. Ridge and Timothy R. Smith (WLP/GIA).

Centering

Continue to sing the song of dismissal that the assembly sang as you left the church. Or sing the refrain from "Jesus in the Morning" (Jesus in the Morning) or have instrumental music playing as the children gather in the space for the Liturgy of the Word.

Place the lectionary on the ambo or lectern. Light the candle placed by the ambo or lectern, and then lead the following prayer:

> **God our Father,**
> **open our hearts to your holy Word and help us to follow Jesus Christ,**
> **your Son, who lives and reigns with you in the unity of the Holy Spirit,**
> **God, for ever and ever.**

> *Children:* **Amen.**

First Reading

Isaiah 22:19–23

Responsorial Psalm

Psalm 138:1–2, 2–3, 6, 8 (8bc) *Sing the same musical setting that is used in your parish's celebration of the liturgy.*

Second Reading

Romans 11:33–36

Gospel Acclamation

Sing the Gospel Acclamation used in your parish's celebration of the liturgy.

Gospel Reading

Matthew 16:13–20

Homily/Reflection

During Ordinary Time, we count our weeks as we continue our growth in faith and move closer to God. As we come near to the harvest of the autumn, we also hope and pray that we are bearing the fruit of God's life inside us and that we can be a part of the great harvest of the parousia when God will be "all in all" (1 Corinthians 15:28).

>> *[Show padlock and key.]* **What is this object? How does it open and secured?**

A key is a tool that can open and close a padlock like this. Without a lock, a key doesn't really have a use on its own. Without a key, a lock cannot do its work. Someone who holds a key decides who gets to be inside and who gets to be outside, or who has access to something or does not have access. They might choose to open the door for one person or close it for someone else.

The prophet Isaiah spoke of someone who had a key. God had said, "I will place the key of the House of David on [Eliakim's] shoulder; when he opens, no one shall shut, what he shuts, no one shall open" (Isaiah 22:22). Eliakim was a scribe. In the time of Isaiah, a scribe would have been an important person whose job involved reading and writing and keeping records. During this time, there were no computers and printers to make books, so some scribes even had the job of copying the words of the Bible. Many people could hear the Word of God and his message would never be lost or forgotten. Isaiah listened for God's voice and then spoke. He told others what he had heard.

The house of David wasn't a house like one we might live in. The house of David was the household, the family of King David. The king during this time, King Hezekiah, was a descendant of King David, who the greatest king of the Jewish people. The house of David meant the king. God was giving Eliakim power like a key opens a lock, and the key had the power of the king.

We know that God is all-powerful and that God has had a plan since before the beginning of time to bring us and all of creation close together with God. God invited Eliakim to be a part of the plan, to share in the work of its unfolding. Although we are not all given power like a king, God wants us to be a part of the plan like Eliakim. God asks us to share in the work, the work of evangelization. Being a follower of Jesus comes with a lot of responsibility. Did you know that being a disciple means sharing the good news about Jesus with others? That is called evangelization. When we tell the good news about who Jesus is to us, we help other people come close to Jesus. One way we can do that is to describe for others who Jesus is for us.

>> **In today's Gospel, when Jesus asked the disciples, "Who do you say that I am?" how did Peter answer?**

Peter said, "You are the Christ, the Son of the living God."

>> **What other names do we have for Jesus?** *The Good Shepherd, Savior, Prince of Peace, Emmanuel, Holy Lord, Light of the World, Living Water, Living Bread come down from heaven, our brother, our friend, Jesus of Nazareth.*

>> **What are some other ways you will share what you know about Jesus with others?**

Profession of Faith

Following the homily or reflection, the prayer leader invites everyone to stand to profess our faith. Together, sing or recite the Apostles' or Nicene Creed. Refer the children to the words of the prayer that you have displayed.

Prayer of the Faithful

Leader: **As disciples of the Lord, we are summoned to identify him as our redeemer, as "Christ, the Son of the living God." In Christ's name, we ask our heavenly Father to listen to our needs. Please respond, "Heavenly Father, hear our prayer."**

That the Catholic Church may bear witness to the Gospel values of faith, hope, and love, we pray: *Heavenly Father, hear our prayer.*

That those responsible for governing peoples be men and women of justice and peace, we pray: *Heavenly Father, hear our prayer.*

That the weak, sick, or impoverished, and those lacking in resources may build up strength by the Lord, we pray: *Heavenly Father, hear our prayer.*

That all who are beginning a new academic year—students, teachers, parents, and administrators—may learn together as they grow in wisdom and love, we pray: *Heavenly Father, hear our prayer.*

Invite other intercessions from the children, or add intercessions based on the current needs of the Church, the world, the oppressed or marginalized, and the local community. Conclude each of the children's petitions with **"we pray"** and invite the response **"Heavenly Father, hear our prayer."**

That the faithful departed may be quickly purified to sing the praises of the Lord in the presence of the angels, we pray: *Heavenly Father, hear our prayer.*

O God our Father, we offer you these prayers asking that you grant them if it is your will. Through Christ our Lord.

Children: **Amen.**

Quietly return with the children to the main assembly. Be mindful of children having difficulty finding their families.